LIMITING NUCLEAR PROLIFERATION

LIMITING NUCLEAR PROLIFERATION

Edited by
JED C. SNYDER
and
SAMUEL F. WELLS, JR.

Foreword by
JAMES R. SCHLESINGER

BALLINGER PUBLISHING COMPANY
A Subsidiary of Harper & Row, Publishers, Inc.
Cambridge, Massachusetts

International Standard Book Number: 0-88730-042-1

Library of Congress Catalog Card Number: 85-3967

Printed in the United States of America

Library of Congress Cataloging in Publication Data
Main entry under title:

Limiting nuclear proliferation.

Includes index.
1. Nuclear nonproliferation.   I. Snyder, Jed C.
II. Wells, Samuel F.
JX1974.73.L56   1985   327.1'74   85-3967
ISBN 0-88730-042-1

CONTENTS

LIST OF TABLES

FOREWORD

James R. Schlesinger

It is now almost forty years since a distinguished American scientist posed the rhetorical question: "What happens when *Swaziland* gets the bomb?" That disturbing phrase captures quite effectively the issue of nuclear proliferation. At the same time it also embodies one approach to the problem—through its implicit apprehension and its telescoping of time. By contrast, since nuclear spread has occurred far more slowly than predicted and since many nations more advanced than Swaziland have deliberately chosen not to acquire nuclear weapons, others have come to believe that the problem is secondary. Indeed, hand-wringing and complacency together have largely dominated public discussion of the issue.

Wise policymakers recognize that the appropriate response lies somewhere in between. They can afford neither to despair nor to neglect. The potential spread of nuclear weapons remains one of the most important of our foreign policy problems. Yet it is a long-range problem. And the fate of long-range problems is that high rates of discount tend to be applied. Immediate policy objectives in dealing with potential proliferators all too frequently dominate the more important, though more distant, goal.

The structure of the problem is very much what it was when I led a RAND Project on nuclear proliferation some two decades ago. There is, of course, the same hand-wringing and the same complacency. We should take considerable comfort in that the world has done far better than the alarmists then suggested. The acquisition of nuclear capabilities by additional nations has been far, far slower than was then anticipated, and *none* of the detonations of weapons in anger that were predicted have actually taken place. On the other hand, time does cause erosion. Policymakers should not expect perfection in terms of precluding further nuclear spread. It is sound policy to offer steady and persistent resistance to further nuclear proliferation, yet at the same time to recognize that there will be a slow, hopefully a very slow, retreat, as additional nations succumb to temptation.

If there is stability in the substance, there has been fluctuation in both the policy and the attention toward the issue. France and China among the nuclear weapons states professed for some time to be unconcerned about the problem of nuclear spread. But even here in the United States the policy has been erratic. In the Kennedy, Johnson, Ford, and Carter administrations, concern has been high and remedies have been vigorously (sometimes desperately) pursued. By contrast, at least in the initial years of both the Nixon and Reagan administrations there was a professed indifference to the problem and some individuals argued that weapons acquisition by America's friends would be beneficial. With time those attitudes changed, and in both the Nixon and Reagan administrations the U.S. stake in resisting the spread of nuclear weapons came to be better understood. But such fluctuations in interest precluded the consistency in policy that the issue demands.

Policy must not only be consistent; it must be realistic. To assume that all states that might acquire nuclear weapons can be handled in a uniform way has been one of the illusions afflicting policy prescriptions. States vary widely in their capabilities and motivations, and effective policy must take these differences into account. One category of states, mostly the advanced industrial nations, already has the capability to produce nuclear weapons. In such cases one must political incentives to avoid further spread. If one attempts to withhold technology, as in the case of France during the Kennedy years, one may simply whet the appetite. Nations in this category must be assured that their security will be better protected *without* the acquisition of nuclear weapons. For other states, those industrially less-advanced, a strategy of technology denial continues to be effective. But that is a demanding strategy since all states have a legitimate interest in peaceful technology—and what must be done is to deny only those technologies specifically related to weapons development. With the passage of time a strategy of technology denial becomes somewhat less effective, as the current listing of the threshold states will make clear. Consequently in dealing with these states and others one must gradually increase the emphasis on the political incentives to avoid proliferation. American pressure on Pakistan in this connection has been widely reported in recent years. It comes later, and may be less successful, than earlier American pressures directed toward such countries as South Korea and Taiwan.

In monitoring the difficult boundary between legitimate peaceful exploitation and avoidance of weapons diversion, some mention must be made of the International Atomic Energy Agency. The IAEA maintains a system of safeguards, which is less than perfect but which, nonetheless, remains an outstanding technical and political accomplishment. The IAEA, perhaps uniquely, possesses the right of on-site inspection in sovereign states. If the IAEA did not already exist, it could not be created today. It is a product of political evolution that cannot be separated from its historic roots.

Regrettably, support for the IAEA has weakened in the United States, reflecting both the widespread disenchantment with the United Nations and the continuing controversy over Israel within the IAEA ever since the Israeli attack on the Osirak reactor. That is shortsighted. The general American disaffection with U.N. agencies is basically irrelevant in the case of the IAEA. As Israel's neighbors such as Egypt acquire nuclear reactors, the Israelis above all will want an effective system of safeguards. For the United States, the International Atomic Energy Agency will continue to be an indispensable element in any national strategy for resisting the further spread of nuclear weapons.

Limiting Nuclear Proliferation brings the subject up-to-date. The essays focus on the threshold states and on those instruments that might constrain nuclear spread. The authors rightly point to the long-term importance of the problem of nuclear proliferation. They rightly stress the need for joint action by the United States and other supplier nations, if we are to restrict the spread of nuclear weapons. Finally, they rightly conclude that these policies must be more carefully coordinated and more consistently and vigorously pursued than they have been in the past.

ACKNOWLEDGMENTS

The production of a volume by numerous specialists presents a series of editorial and administrative problems whose resolution requires the cooperation and coordination of many individuals. In completing this volume we have been fortunate to be supported by extraordinary talent ranging from the special group that helped us design the series to the authors whose work appears in the volume and the staff who checked facts, edited text, and keyboarded the manuscript.

The publication of this book represents the culmination of over two years of planning and work. The concept for the series was developed by Samuel Wells with the assistance of Myra Struck McKitrick. The detailed planning was done by a small group at the Center including the two editors of the volume, Warren Donnelly of the Congressional Research Service, and two Wilson fellows, Arnold Kramish and Peter Clausen. The volume was developed in a series of nine research seminars held at the Woodrow Wilson International Center for Scholars in Washington, D.C. from December 1982 through December 1983. Each seminar session was structured around commissioned papers, the final versions of which comprise this volume. The authors of these papers were all distinguished government officials, scholars, and analysts, only some of whom are represented in this volume. The inevitable space constraints imposed by publication prevented us from including all of the series' papers in this volume, but we would like to acknowledge the valuable assistance of all of the authors and commentators in providing ideas that are reflected here. We would also like to express appreciation to the roughly seventy specialists on nuclear issues who convened for each of these sessions from the academic, governmental, and journalistic communities to assess the new challenges that nuclear technology and the politics of proliferation provide for the international community in the coming decades.

The fundamental motor of any sustained research project of this sort is the generosity of those who finance the work. The International Security Studies Program was especially fortunate in having for this project the enthusiastic support of the Robert Wood Johnson, Jr. Charitable Trust. We are grateful to all of the directors of this trust and especially to Mr. Seymour Klein, a firm friend and supporter of our program's research efforts for a number of years. We hope that this volume will justify the sustained interest that the Johnson Trust has demonstrated in international security generally and issues of nuclear proliferation in particular.

Within our own program staff we are especially grateful for the services of Carol Evans, who functioned as manuscript editor and supervised all phases of our editorial process. Her editing skill, energy, and good-humored dedication produced a volume which does not reflect many of the stylistic shortcomings of multiple author books. In her editorial efforts she was ably assisted by Eric Nenon and Lee Frazier.

We are also most appreciative to Suzanne Stewart for typing and proofreading the manuscript in several variations and providing invaluable support in the checking of changes in the production of the final manuscript. Various other important elements of assistance to this volume were provided by Jane Mutnick of our program staff, Eloise Doane of the Center's wordprocessing facility, and William Dunn, the Center's Assistant Director for Administration.

A final word of thanks is in order for our publisher. Throughout our editing process Carol Franco, President of Ballinger Publishing Company, has shown genuine enthusiasm for this project and support of our desire to make this a timely and high-quality product. We also appreciate the care and efficiency showed by David Barber of Ballinger who coordinated the editorial process.

The editors are extremely pleased to have this volume appear, but we recognize that the responsibility for any errors rests with us.

INTRODUCTION

Jed C. Snyder and
Samuel F. Wells, Jr.

More than three decades ago, President Dwight Eisenhower stood before the United Nations General Assembly to announce the creation of a U.S. program designed to harness the destructive potential of nuclear weapons for peaceful purposes. The Atoms for Peace plan unveiled in December 1953 was not the first American effort at sounding the alarm about nuclear proliferation. The Acheson-Lilienthal Report and the Baruch Plan had been introduced in 1946 one year after the first atomic test by the United States at Alamogordo, New Mexico and three years before the second nuclear power—the Soviet Union—exploded its first nuclear device in August 1949. By the time Eisenhower proposed Atoms for Peace and the International Atomic Energy Agency (IAEA), Britain had detonated its first device in October 1952. Two more nations joined the club of declared nuclear weapons states—France in 1960 and the People's Republic of China in 1964. A sixth, India, exploded a "peaceful" nuclear device in 1974, but it is not a declared nuclear weapons power and does not appear to have a program to field such weapons. In addition there are another four states (Iraq, Israel, Pakistan, and South Africa) with research programs sufficiently advanced to allow them to join the nuclear weapons fraternity by 1990 if they choose to do so.

While optimists have reason to remind us that earlier dire predictions of "many" nuclear powers by 1970 were exaggerated, it is safe to say that we are approaching a plateau similar to that reached in 1974 with the Indian explosion. Expectations of growth in the number of nuclear weapons states appear justified. A widely respected study estimated in 1979 that by 1985 "about forty countries will have enough fissile material to make three bombs or more; almost as many are likely to have enough fissile material for from thirty to sixty weapons or more."[1] Increasingly the scientific and engineering obstacles that once represented almost impenetrable barriers to reaching a nuclear weapons capability are being eroded. At the same time a number of negative factors are contributing to the slow but steady corrosion of the international nuclear nonproliferation regime. Among these factors are the irresponsible behavior of some nuclear suppliers, the search by developing nations for instruments of international prestige, the dangerous desire by a few leaders to possess the ultimate blackmail weapon, and the lack of sufficiently stringent inspection and safeguard mechanisms.

As this book illustrates, the basic elements of a nation's decision to develop a nuclear weapon (technical, economic, and political) have changed appreciably since the dawning of the atomic age in 1945. With maturing weapons technologies, the range of choice, particularly for developing countries, has expanded. Regional rivalries have created security dilemmas for smaller states, which may increasingly view nuclear weapons—absent other alternatives—as the only hedge against the fear of long-term conventional conflicts with neighboring or competing states. Yet it is also true that other states have refrained from pursuing the nuclear weapons option for diverse reasons including high development costs, internal political opposition, and the conclusion that a nuclear capability might decrease the nation's security.

The overwhelming majority of nuclear specialists concur that, while we may be able to delay the expansion of the nuclear community by retarding the progress of certain countries toward the construction and detonation of a nuclear device, its growth is ultimately inevitable. The opportunities for reducing incentives that propel nuclear proliferation have become increasingly difficult to identify as the potential economic and military rewards that may attend the development of a nuclear capability (peaceful and military) appear more attractive and, on occasion, imperative. Finally, while in 1953 one might have expected the goal of halting the growth in the number of nuclear weapons states to be universally applauded, such is not the case today. A school of thought has developed among academic researchers, represented by Shai Feldman's contribution to this volume, which questions this maxim and suggests that in some circumstances a gradual increase in the number of nuclear weapons states may actually enhance global stability.[2]

The editors and most of the contributors to this volume agree that nuclear proliferation should receive increased attention as a policy goal of the United States and of all nations concerned with nuclear programs, whether civilian or military. Since 1950 the United States has devoted considerable national attention and resources to conflicts in the developing world. To underscore the importance of nonproliferation to this country, one need only imagine the implications for the respective regions of a nuclear weapons capability in Pakistan, South Africa, or Libya. Making the problem even more critical is the fact that in most developed countries military staffs and war colleges spend very little time planning about how to deal with additional nuclear states, and among academic and government researchers only a handful of specialists concentrate on proliferation issues.

The analyses in this book also indicate that the United States cannot prevent the spread of nuclear weapons by itself. Successful nonproliferation policy requires the cooperation of all the nuclear exporting powers and the weapons states. In addition, it needs the support of as many of the nonnuclear weapons states as possible in creating a climate of opinion against the further spread of nuclear weapons. A widely supported and highly effective International Atomic Energy Agency is also an absolute requirement. Finally, it is important to note that nonproliferation policy is one of the few areas where the Soviet Union and the United States have had common interests over a number of years and where their policies have run in generally parallel directions.

The United States has found it extremely difficult to develop an effective nuclear export policy. This is partly attributable to differences among political groups over the importance of nonproliferation compared with nuclear exports to the developing world, and these differences are exaggerated by the natural rivalry between the executive and legislative branches of government. Further complicating the development of coherent policy is the fact that some technologies have a dual-use capability for both nuclear energy and nuclear weapons programs. The congressional debates over nuclear export policy have vividly displayed the different goals and assumptions of the contending groups. Here the choice has often been between legislation based on the principle of technology denial with the goal of retarding the progress of obvious weapons programs and laws that allow the transfer of certain sensitive technologies combined with conventional military and economic assistance in an effort to persuade states that their security interests do not require nuclear weapons. But a vexing complication developed when it became clear that certain states, whose activities were decidedly suspicious, could not be said with absolute confidence to be engaged in nuclear weapons research.

The health of the nonproliferation regime has become a central point of controversy among academics and practitioners alike. Shortly after the Nuclear Non-Proliferation Treaty (NPT) was opened for signature in 1968, a debate ensued over the nature of future improvements to the regime. Although a total of 127 nations signed the accord (124 nonweapons states and 3 nuclear weapons states), there was immediate concern over the behavior of nonsignatories, which included the nuclear powers of France and the People's Republic of China (PRC) as well as a number of states suspected of having covertly developed or designed weapons programs. These threshold states became the focus of concern. Most signatories appear to have accepted the permanent abstention of France and the PRC, although both nations have recently accepted safeguards on most of their own sensitive nuclear exports.

Prescriptions offered to improve the regime frequently seemed designed to repair perceived inadequacies of current U.S. policy. The 1973–74 embargo of oil by the Organization of Petroleum Exporting Countries (OPEC) provided immediate economic motives for near-term proliferators to pursue more vigorously the development of nuclear power reactors for generating electricity, and the 1974 Indian nuclear test gave an example for others to follow. In response, the mid–1970s saw a strengthened emphasis in Congress and the Ford administration on supplier controls and a concern over the reprocessing of spent fuel to produce plutonium. The Symington (1976) and Glenn (1977) amendments to the Foreign Assistance Act stated an implicit congressional policy of discouraging the supply of enrichment and reprocessing technologies through the threat of cutting off certain items of economic and security assistance. Modified in later years to deter India and Pakistan from obtaining and detonating a nuclear weapon, these amendments remain the principal elements of U.S. law that use sanctions in economic and security assistance as an element of nonproliferation policy.

The most intense debate on proliferation issues began in 1977 with the administration of Jimmy Carter. Emphasis shifted from President Ford's concern over reprocessing to a broader examination of the nuclear fuel cycle, principally through an elaborate and comprehensive multinational investigation by the International Fuel Cycle Evaluation (INFCE) which was actually intended as a complement to President Ford's Reprocessing Evaluation Program. As Joseph Nye (who directed President Carter's nonproliferation policy as an advisor to the Under Secretary of State) notes, while "the net effect of these findings was to reduce the pressures for the widespread reprocessing of plutonium" in fact, INFCE "laid the foundation for a cautious introduction of plutonium use."[3]

Congressional concern during the Carter years focused on the need for supplier constraints. The Nuclear Non-Proliferation Act of 1978 sought to establish conditions for a country to be eligible to receive U.S. nuclear assistance or hardware. Prospective recipients would be required to refrain from constructing a nuclear explosive device and enriching, reprocessing, or re-exporting U.S.-supplied nuclear fuel without prior U.S. approval. This unilateral act required the administration to renegotiate all nuclear cooperation agreements with foreign countries and made further cooperation contingent on their acceptance of full-scope safeguards, i.e., adoption of IAEA safeguards for all nuclear equipment regardless of source or date of acquisition. The legislation provided for automatic termination of assistance if these conditions were violated. The act does allow the president to waive the sanctions under specific national security conditions subject to congressional override.

The sanction provisions of the Non-Proliferation Act and the Symington amendment came under attack due principally to the failure of these measures to halt Pakistan's acquisition of reprocessing and enrichment technology after U.S. military and economic assistance to President Zia's government was suspended informally in 1977 and formally in 1979. In 1981 the Reagan administration won a waiver of these restrictions and negotiated a six-year $3.2 billion military and economic assistance agreement with Pakistan in an effort to offer a positive inducement rather than exert a negative pressure as the Carter administration had unsuccessfully attempted. Evidence continues to mount that Pakistan is proceeding steadily toward development of a nuclear weapons capability, and in June 1984 U.S. agents arrested a Pakistani citizen attempting to smuggle out of the country fifty timing devices, known as krytrons, whose main function is to trigger nuclear weapons. In the face of these determined efforts, the Reagan administration has abandoned its attempts to prevent progress on nuclear weapons development and has taken its stand on the position that any Pakistani nuclear test will lead to the termination of U.S. military and economic assistance.[4] From these events it is clear that the U.S.-imposed sanctions proved fruitless in influencing Pakistan's behavior. Before joining the Reagan administration, Lewis Dunn argued that "a sanctions strategy needs to contain a mix of automatic and optimal measures" and that "nuclear weapons activities short of open testing also might trigger a broad range of sanctions."[5] The best available evidence indicates that total reliance upon either strict constructionist models of sanctions or inducement policies is likely to fail as a strategy designed to deter the nuclear choice, particularly if such a policy is applied late in the day.

Another weakness of the nonproliferation regime lies in the significant range of differences between the United States and the European nuclear suppliers about the threat of further proliferation and the value of sanctions and embargoes in dealing with such risks. For most European leaders, proliferation is not a major problem. In France, for example, there was virtually no public opposition when the government refused to sign the Non-Proliferation Treaty and when it made secret but widely known contracts to sell nuclear reactors to Iraq. As we are writing, there is renewed discussion in the press of a possible French sale of two nuclear power reactors to Israel. In the mid–1970s France and Germany sold unsafeguarded reactors and reprocessing plants to problem states, and more recently corporations in Belgium, Switzerland, and Italy have collaborated in selling supplementary technologies that can contribute to bomb development. Any improved nonproliferation regime must work toward minimizing these differences of perspective and policy among the nuclear suppliers.

There are signs of a firmer nonproliferation commitment developing among many of the nuclear suppliers. In January 1976 a group of suppliers adopted a set of rules for international nuclear sales. These regulations, widely known as the London Supplier Guidelines, require that recipients of nuclear equipment, materials, or technology must pledge not to use them to make nuclear explosives, accept IAEA safeguards on the transferred items, agree not to re-export to third parties unless they accept the same terms, and provide adequate security to prevent theft or sabotage. These guidelines have been adopted by seventeen nations including the United States, Great Britain, France, West Germany, Canada, the Soviet Union, Belgium, Italy, and Switzerland. France has also set stiff terms for rebuilding the Osirak reactor complex destroyed by the Israelis and refused to bid on the Pakistani reactor project. The People's Republic of China has recently declared that it will in the future follow the London Supplier Guidelines in its nuclear exports.[6]

An even more serious threat to the nonproliferation regime is the resentment of most nonnuclear states to the constraints placed upon them. Most states in the developing world feel that the nonproliferation regime is a conspiracy of the nuclear powers to prevent their full economic and political development. They feel that the regime codifies in international law the segregation of the "haves" from the "have-nots." These states want compensation for pledging not to develop nuclear weapons, and they believe that they have not received it in the past. The Non-Proliferation Treaty contained two basic pledges to the non-nuclear states that many claim have not been honored.

First, many of the treaty's signatories complain that nuclear technology has not been transferred as freely as intended in Article IV of the treaty that recognizes the "inalienable right of all the parties to the Treaty to develop research, production and use of nuclear energy for peaceful purposes without discrimination."[7] A number of parties to the treaty, for example, note that certain provisions of the London Supplier Guidelines and the 1978 U.S. Non-Proliferation Act are inconsistent with Article IV of the NPT, since they restrict the transfer of sensitive nuclear technology beyond that which the NPT intended.

A second violation leveled at the regime is that the superpowers have not engaged in serious arms control negotiations as called for in Article VI of the NPT. Although there is some value in continued pressure on the superpowers to come to an arms control accord from states critical of the nonproliferation regime, there is surely no evidence to suggest that if Washington and Moscow reached a strategic arms control agreement tomorrow, the objections of the signatories and nonsignatories alike would disappear. The argument that "vertical proliferation" (the growth of the superpower nuclear stockpiles) has a direct effect on the rate of "horizontal proliferation" is contrived and unproven and assumes a link between the behavior of the superpowers and other states which in the case of arms control does not exist. There is no evidence to suggest, for example, that during the periods subsequent to the signing of major U.S.-Soviet arms control agreements (e.g., the Partial Nuclear Test Ban, SALT I, the ABM Treaty) other states either abandoned or slowed their efforts to gain nuclear weapons. Progress in arms limitation between the superpowers will not likely alter the policy choices of a threshold nuclear state, whose motives are primarily determined by internal and regional factors.

Advocates of a stronger nonproliferation regime have criticized the international IAEA safeguard provisions that are designed to verify that nuclear materials are being utilized solely for peaceful applications. The safeguard guidelines, found in what is commonly referred to as the "Blue Book" (INFCIRC/153), apply to all nonnuclear weapons states party to the NPT.[8]

The safeguard system is essentially a mechanism that allows periodic inspection of nuclear facilities by IAEA inspectors who protect against the diversions of nuclear material from peaceful nuclear activities, deterring such diversions by the risk of early detection. There is, however, no effective mechanism for enforcement. Should an IAEA inspector discover activities that suggest diversion, the IAEA is authorized to seek to resolve the issue with the state concerned. Should that prove fruitless, the only recourse is submission of a noncompliance report to the IAEA Board of Governors and to the General Assembly and Security Council of the United Nations. The IAEA Board may elect to suspend technical assistance to the state involved or call on other member states to do so or seek to suspend that state from IAEA membership. To date, the IAEA has never filed a report of noncompliance or sought to expel a member state for noncompliance with safeguard provisions.

There are significant constraints to the effectiveness of IAEA safeguards. As a 1984 General Accounting Office report on safeguards notes:

> IAEA inspectors do not have unlimited access during their inspections, and IAEA safeguards are not designed or intended to search for undeclared or clandestine facilities. IAEA officials state that the Agency is *not* a police force, but rather a monitoring group responsible for sounding an alarm.[9]

A number of incidents have raised questions about the efficacy of IAEA safeguards, the most recent one being the June 1981 Israeli air attack on the Osirak reactor near Baghdad, Iraq. The Israeli government destroyed a facility it was convinced represented a key element in a nuclear weapons program. Privately some IAEA officials and other nonproliferation specialists agree with Israeli leaders on Iraqi motives, yet IAEA inspections of this safeguarded research reactor complex had disclosed no violations. This incident reignited a debate over the IAEA's ability to detect diversions in a timely manner, and it also raised ominous questions about "vigilante nonproliferation." The Iraqi nuclear program is discussed in Chapter 1.

In addition to the Osirak case, the IAEA did become concerned over activities at the Pakistani KANUPP reactor. For the first time since its creation in 1956, the agency announced that it was unable to assure its members of its ability to account adequately for all nuclear material at the KANUPP facility. The IAEA did not seek to apply sanctions to Pakistan in response to this report, and as one knowledgeable U.S. official asserts, "No one who knows the facts has ever claimed there was a diversion at KANUPP. There were poor safeguards, and after threats the Pakistanis substantially improved the safeguards."

Although one cannot expect the IAEA system of safeguards to operate in a leak-proof manner, there is clearly room for improvement. One must acknowledge that this system of safeguards represents the only international mechanism which conducts on-site inspections of international treaty obligations by third parties. And as a recent National Academy of Sciences publication concluded, "it is extremely unlikely that a system anywhere near as effective as the existing one would be accepted internationally if it had to be negotiated from scratch at the present time."[10] But there still remains good reason to question the deterrent effect in critical cases of the safeguards as they are now operating.

Decisions to pursue a nuclear weapons program are made in the context of national security interests and comparative policy choices. The evidence suggests that cooperation and co-optation are the best ways to prevent further proliferation. Superpower policies clearly help to influence the environment in which nonnuclear states make their security decisions. Security assistance, confidence-building measures, and security guarantees can be extremely useful when put in the appropriate combinations and political context to make them credible. It has become equally obvious that the sanctions and export controls as frequently dictated by legislation in the United States have had a very limited effect in preventing proliferation.

* * * * *

Many of the themes presented here are dealt with in detail in the chapters that follow. The reader will quickly discern that this book represents a rich collection of views, both in terms of professional experience and political perspective. It was our deliberate intention to produce a study that did not simply replicate an already voluminous literature. We were sensitive to the need for a book that emphasized the changing nature of the nuclear proliferation threat and the need to address an old problem in a rigorous analytical framework which encouraged innovative, if often provocative, analyses.

The papers in this book were originally commissioned for the 1982–83 International Security Studies Program "Core Seminar" on Nuclear Proliferation at the Woodrow Wilson International Center for Scholars in Washington, D.C. In the course of their drafting and revision, the papers were thoroughly reviewed and critiqued by those who attended the seminar meetings, including a number of senior specialists in the academic, congressional, journalistic, intelligence, and policy arenas.

The book is divided into three sections. Section I, "The Nuclear Threshold States: Selected Cases," examines the nuclear programs of seven states—Iraq, Israel, India, Pakistan, Argentina, Brazil, and South Africa. The states in this group represent the greatest challenge for nonproliferation. They are at quite different stages of nuclear development with India and Israel probably only a step away from becoming overt nuclear weapons states and, at the other end of the spectrum, Brazil showing revived interest in weapons development but being some years away from this goal. Taken individually and as a group, the countries analyzed in this section reflect a unique set of political, economic, and military motivations which provide a broad perspective on the range of challenges to international security and stability. In order to concentrate on the most pressing aspects of the problem, we chose not to investigate countries such as Taiwan, South Korea, Iran, and Libya, which represent proliferation threats of a less immediate and quite different nature.

Section II, "The Nonproliferation Regime," includes two chapters that examine the nonproliferation and nuclear export policies of the United States and the Soviet Union in comparative perspective. The final section of the book, Section III, "Management Strategies and Policy Alternatives," exemplifies the editors' intent to provide a variety of analytical and policy viewpoints. In many ways, this section includes the most original contributions in the volume as the authors attempt to frame the policy alternatives in ways that suggest new approaches to the problem. Some of these analyses and proposals conflict with others, and the editors do not necessarily share all the views expressed in the volume. We do strongly believe that each of these perspectives deserves careful consideration. In the same vein, the contributors do not necessarily share the editors' views as expressed in the Introduction and Conclusion. To provide a sense of the scope of the volume, we have briefly summarized the main arguments of each chapter in the remaining pages of the Introduction.

PART I: "THE NUCLEAR THRESHOLD STATES: SELECTED CASES"

Jed Snyder's chapter on the Iraqi nuclear program presents a detailed analysis of how President Saddam Hussein created and directed an ambitious nuclear research effort whose ultimate goal was almost certainly the construction of a nuclear explosive device. Snyder documents how through the acquisition of raw materials and technical assistance from several critical suppliers—several of whom depended upon Iraq for a significant percentage of their petroleum supplies—Iraq was able to train the scientists, build the facilities, and accumulate the fissile material for a potentially dangerous nuclear capability.

The progress of the Iraqi nuclear program—halted (perhaps temporarily) by the June 1981 Israeli air attack which destroyed the Osirak reactor—is examined in light of Baghdad's acceptance of IAEA safeguards and its signature of the Non-Proliferation Treaty. Operating within the constraints established by international convention, Iraq had taken significant steps toward a nuclear weapons capability which would further threaten the stability of one of the world's most troubled regions. These events highlight a central concern of the book—the responsibility of nuclear suppliers for the creation and maintenance of an *effective* nonproliferation regime.

The second chapter in this section by George Quester illustrates how Israel has pursued a policy of nuclear deterrence that is almost entirely dependent upon public uncertainty. Because the cloak of official secrecy has so effectively shrouded the activities of Israel's nuclear scientists, it is impossible to discuss with any precision the dangers posed by this probable "bomb in the basement." Nevertheless, it is almost universally assumed by specialists that Israel possesses nuclear weapons. Added to the suspicions about Israel's nuclear capability are the "cloak and dagger" stories of Israel's covert attempts to acquire the ingredients of a weapons program. These uncertainties have some influence on Israel's relations with its regional adversaries. Yet it is unclear whether Israel's suspected nuclear capability would be regarded as stabilizing or destabilizing in the event that another Middle East war proceeded to the point where Jerusalem's options were so narrowed as to force a test of whether Israel possessed the ultimate weapon.

In Chapter 3, Richard Cronin presents an analysis of the Indo-Pakistani rivalry in which the acquisition of a nuclear weapon by a neighboring state appears to be the primary foreign policy concern in both New Delhi and Islamabad, although the interests of the two states are not identical. India's nuclear reactor program seems to have flowed initially from a critical requirement for electric power generation, while Pakistan's effort appears to be driven primarily by a weapons desire. A long-term adversarial relationship exacerbates the problems of an uneven race in which India exploded a nuclear device more than a decade ago and Pakistan is trying to catch up. Territorial claims and superpower involvement in the nuclear programs of both countries are among the variables that create a complicated security dilemma in South Asia. The United States has been heavily involved in this dilemma as Washington has sought to reduce the nuclear incentives of both states through a combination of sanctions and inducements, principally by offering conventional weapon systems to Pakistan and threatening India with the termination of peaceful nuclear assistance which jeopardized the operation of at least one reactor. In addition, India and Pakistan have become the focal points of recent debates in the U.S. Congress over amendments to the 1978 Nuclear Non-Proliferation Act. The author concludes that the likelihood of a nuclear-armed India and Pakistan "in the 1990s if not before" is high.

Despite repeated insistence that its nuclear intentions are peaceful, in Chapter 4 Daniel Poneman finds Argentina's nuclear program to be "riven by apparent contradictions."

Argentina is nearly totally dependent upon technology and economic assistance from the advanced industrial states, yet its policy of actively seeking the security benefits of nuclear technology steers it toward a more independent stance. It has striven to create an independent nuclear fuel cycle including enriching its own uranium fuel utilizing gaseous diffusion technology, and reprocessing plutonium from indigenous spent fuel. It has rejected the NPT and signed but not ratified the Treaty of Tlatelolco (which establishes a nuclear-weapon-free zone in most of Latin America). Argentina's quest for independence does not appear to have significantly retarded its progress in nuclear power generation, as it has in other countries that have sought fuel cycle autonomy.

Prominent among Argentinian nuclear interests is the prestige (particularly within states in the developing world) that would accompany a successful nuclear weapons program. The security motivations are multiple but include concern over "lost territories" and a rivalry with the neighboring state of Brazil. Argentina has rejected international efforts at curbing proliferation, labeling them as "discriminatory" in favor of those states already possessing nuclear weapons and therefore seeking to deny the developing world a potentially critical economic tool. This argument, offered by many parties and nonsignatories of the treaty, has become the standard around which much of the developing world has congregated.

In Chapter 5, David Myers describes the Brazilian nuclear program as a captive—perhaps to a greater extent than the other threshold states—of a fierce rivalry with Argentina. Like a number of other threshold states, Brazil inaugurated its nuclear program with a U.S.-supplied research reactor transferred under the Atoms for Peace program in the 1950s with a commitment to abide by international controls. Brazil soon discovered that its desire for nuclear independence, reflected by its refusal to sign the NPT, would dictate a route which guaranteed a break with United States policy. The break occurred in 1975 when the Brazilian government signed an agreement with the Federal Republic of Germany which offered the transfer of a complete nuclear fuel cycle—fuel enrichment (using the West German Becker jet-nozzle technology), fuel fabrication, and spent-fuel reprocessing. Currently, none of Brazil's nuclear research efforts is covered by international safeguards. Like Argentina's, Brazil's nuclear research is heavily influenced by the military, whose interests dominate the decisionmaking. Ironically, Brazil and Argentina have entered into reciprocal nuclear assistance agreements from which both countries have benefited. This cooperation stopped abruptly after the April 1982 Argentine invasion of the Falkland Islands.

In the final chapter of this section on threshold states, Robert Jaster traces the peculiar combination of political, economic, and military incentives that have propelled South Africa's nuclear research. Much like the Israeli program, Pretoria's nuclear efforts are protected by strict official secrecy, although unexplained events like the September 1979 "flash" over the South Atlantic have caused public alarm within the scientific community and reinforced the suspicions of many that South Africa has indeed developed a nuclear weapon. While the evidence is not conclusive, Jaster argues that "for several years South Africa has had the capability to design, produce and deliver a low-yield nuclear weapon" and "may already have tested" such a device.

The South African case presents an almost unique example of U.S.-Soviet nonproliferation cooperation. The Soviet government first sounded the alarm to the United States in 1977 that the Pretoria government was preparing to test a nuclear device. That warning accelerated U.S. satellite reconnaissance efforts. The Jaster chapter includes a detailed look at how South African nuclear policy is but one component of the pariah state's "Total National Strategy," which includes the delicate management of repressive internal policies.

PART II: "THE NONPROLIFERATION REGIME"

In Chapter 7, Peter Clausen analyzes U.S. nonproliferation policy from its genesis in the Atoms for Peace proposal in 1953 to future prospects for American influence through nuclear export policy. He contests the view that the 1950s and 1960s represented a "golden age" when the U.S. was able to serve as both international broker and constable in forging a consensus against the proliferation of nuclear weapons. Despite some progress on retarding the spread of nuclear weapons, he argues that "important states remained outside the consensus" and "agreement was often reached by papering over differences and deferring difficult issues." Clausen is less critical of U.S. non-proliferation policy in the late 1970s, which was dominated by President Carter's attempt to gain leverage over supply through INFCE. Clausen, who served in the Carter administration as a nonproliferation specialist in the Department of Energy, acknowledges that this reliance on supply leverage proved to be controversial because it challenged the "plutonium economy" which was an increasingly attractive route for many of our European allies. In many ways, the Carter years represented a watershed when a number of extremely complicated technical and political issues converged to challenge the survival of the nonproliferation regime.

The Reagan administration's nuclear export and nonproliferation policy, Clausen contends, essentially rejected the Carter emphasis on supply leverage for a more pragmatic focus on the security dimension. This departure was based in part on the view that a threshold state might be dissuaded from developing nuclear weapons if alternate economic and military paths were offered. In addition, "the Reagan administration was less ambivalent than its predecessor about nuclear power development and more energetic (though not more successful) in promoting American nuclear exports." While the willingness to use plutonium as a reactor fuel was an important shift, the Reagan approach, Clausen concludes, was not a "radical departure" from previous U.S. policy. In looking to the future, Clausen contends that the continuation of today's buyer's market in nuclear technology will increase the challenges to the nonproliferation regime.

In Chapter 8, William Potter provides an analytical treatment of Soviet nuclear export policy. Prior to 1954, Soviet leaders were primarily concerned with matching American capabilities and viewed efforts at nuclear arms limitation as attempts to keep Russia in a permanently inferior status. Responding to the Eisenhower Atoms for Peace initiative, Moscow showed interest in international civilian nuclear energy and began its first transfers of nuclear technology abroad to the East European satellites and the PRC. But when the Peking government announced in 1958 that it would develop its own nuclear weapons, the Soviets suspended nuclear assistance and reevaluated their nonproliferation policy.

By 1959 Moscow initiated a policy of controlling the transfer of nuclear technology in order to avert the alarming prospect that other Soviet nuclear clients, particularly the East Europeans, might seek to emulate the PRC. This more cautious Soviet policy coincided with the initiation of bilateral nuclear arms control discussions with the United States, beginning with the Nuclear Test Ban Treaty of 1963, which included Great Britain as a signatory. The early part of this period also saw Soviet-American cooperation in encouraging states to sign the NPT, which was opened for signature in 1968.

After examining possible lapses from earlier caution in recent export decisions concerning Argentina, Cuba, India, and Libya, Potter concludes that Soviet nuclear export policy has compiled "a mixed but generally positive" record. He suggests that, while Moscow has often criticized Western nonproliferation policy as the captive of economic interests rather than a serious reflection of concern over the spread of nuclear weapons, the expanded Soviet role in the nuclear export market may expose Moscow to the same economic pressures.

PART III: "MANAGEMENT STRATEGIES AND POLICY ALTERNATIVES"

Concerned over the dangers posed by plutonium, Victor Gilinsky, who recently completed two terms as a Commissioner of the Nuclear Regulatory Commission, combines historical and current analysis to assess the prospects for continued utilization of this fuel. He probes the three primary elements of the non-proliferation regime (IAEA safeguards, the NPT, and supplier guidelines) to examine the role of plutonium in U.S. non-proliferation policy. Discussing the early period of nuclear power development, Gilinsky laments that "we apparently had no sense of the strength of our position in guiding the long-term development of commercial nuclear power." Even in the mid–1950s, it was clear that the dangers posed by plutonium formed "the root of the security problem" posed by nuclear commerce. From the initial development of nuclear power, the United States recognized that plutonium was only one of two fuels suitable for a nuclear explosive and distinguished between reprocessing (by which plutonium is produced) and uranium enrichment (by which bomb-grade U^{235} is produced). But Washington was slow to recognize that the plutonium produced by power reactors could be used to build weapons, he contends, and when it did so, European suppliers continued to provide unsafeguarded technologies to threshold states.

Gilinsky's perspective on the value of supplier controls to limit access to plutonium contrasts sharply with that provided by Peter Clausen. The Carter administration's erratic and ineffective nonproliferation policy, Gilinsky argues, sharply reduced the potential force and effectiveness of the London Supplier Guidelines and the Ford administration's decision to cease the commercial use of plutonium. The United States, Gilinsky concludes, should improve and exploit the potentially effective synergism between supplier controls and safeguards in constructing a more effective nonproliferation regime which would limit the use of plutonium.

In Chapter 10, Lewis Dunn describes the nonproliferation policy of the Reagan administration, in which he has served as a senior official in the Department of State and currently in the Arms Control and Disarmament Agency. He provides a moderately optimistic assessment of the health of the nonproliferation regime, and acknowledging that the United States can no longer "unilaterally define the rules of the nuclear game," he argues that a strong and confident America can play a leading role in preventing further proliferation as long as it deals with the world as it is and wins the cooperation of the other industrial states for its policies. He rejects the "more may be better" view of proliferation management (a variant of which is provided by Shai Feldman in this volume), arguing against the thesis that adding to the list of nuclear weapons states might actually promote stability by increasing concern over nuclear destruction and therefore encouraging caution. He contends that "the spread of nuclear weapons to conflict-prone regions, rather than encouraging the peaceful settlement of traditional disputes, is far more likely to enhance the longstanding suspicions and tensions among rivals." The danger of preemption must always be guarded against.

Dunn calls for a nonproliferation "defense in depth," which rejects narrower prescriptions that cater only to one symptom of the problem. He contends that the two major barriers to a state's development of a weapons capability are the acquisition of fissile material and the design and construction of an explosive device, and he shows how the current U.S. administration has moved to make these obstacles more difficult to cross. Looking toward the 1985 NPT Review Conference, Dunn describes the current U.S. consultations with both Western and Eastern states designed to strengthen adherence to the treaty and improve the system of IAEA safeguards.

Shai Feldman provides the most provocative contribution to this volume. Convinced that nuclear proliferation (defined as "activities aimed at developing nuclear weapons") is "a process continuously taking place," his major concern is diminishing the threat of regional nuclear war precipitated by regional rivalries. While he does not share Dunn's view of the dangers inherent in the acquisition of nuclear weapons by additional states, he declares categorically that he does not endorse policies which create "a world of many additional nuclear states. . . ." Instead, he advocates a policy of "proliferation management" made more plausible, he argues, by the relatively slow rate of horizontal proliferation to date.

In his effort to reduce the risks of the continuing and inevitable process of proliferation, Feldman argues that an overt nuclear posture (i.e., a declared capability) is less dangerous than a covert posture (i.e., a "bomb in the basement") and that "the superpowers should make covert or ambiguous nuclear postures overt." The key issue for the United States and the Soviet Union, according to Feldman, is whether they should assist "primitive" nuclear weapon states in order to "expedite a transition from primitive to secure second-strike nuclear forces." He argues that they should and that making a primitive force "safer and more sophisticated will enhance stability." The superpowers must assume the burden for global nonproliferation policy, Feldman concludes, because they will ultimately have to determine "whether measures for proliferation management should be taken even at the expense of non-proliferation goals."

In the final chapter of the book, Lawrence Scheinman analyzes what elements should constitute a comprehensive nonproliferation policy and how such an approach could increase the visibility of nonproliferation concerns in U.S. foreign policy generally. He recognizes the international consensus that the differential status between "haves" and "have-nots" should not allow the former to discriminate against the latter's interests. This is particularly true of the way in which the superpowers pursue bilateral arms control negotiations, and he argues that the failure of weapons states "to make sincere and demonstrable efforts toward nuclear arms control involving a reduction of nuclear arsenals..." will negatively affect NPT adherence.

Through an examination of four definitions of comprehensiveness, Scheinman fashions a broad, integrated nonproliferation strategy including the need for a consensus among supplier countries on how to react to indicators that a recipient state has violated or may be about to violate the peaceful intent of the nonproliferation regime. In the final analysis, a commitment among all nuclear suppliers that such activities cannot be ignored is central to any reasonable approach to a comprehensive strategy. Scheinman concludes by advancing a series of policy initiatives that could broaden and strengthen the nonproliferation regime.

In addressing the problem of nuclear proliferation, this volume presents an unusually broad range of analytical perspective, particularly relating to assessments of past U.S. policy and future policy prescriptions. While the contributors share common ground on a number of issues (including the dangers presented by current trends and the potential U.S. role in curbing horizontal proliferation), differences exist among them, especially on policy choices for the future. In addition, the editors wish to emphasize to the reader that their opinions (as expressed in the Introduction and the Conclusion) should not be regarded as reflecting those of the authors. All of us, authors and editors alike, strongly support the need for a renewed dialogue on nuclear proliferation which encompasses the entire spectrum of opinion. We hope that you will find this book a contribution to such a dialogue.

NOTES

1. Albert Wohlstetter, *et al., Swords From Plowshares* (Chicago: University of Chicago Press, 1979), p. 126.

2. The acknowledged leader of this school (which includes the author of chapter 11, Shai Feldman) is Kenneth Waltz. See Kenneth N. Waltz, *The Spread of Nuclear Weapons: More May Be Better*, Adelphi Papers, no. 171 (London: International Institute for Strategic Studies, Autumn 1981).

3. Joseph Nye, "Sustaining Non-Proliferation in the 1980's," *Survival* 23, no. 3 (May/June 1981): 102.

4. For a detailed account of Pakistani nuclear developments since 1974, see Leonard S. Spector, *Nuclear Proliferation Today* (Cambridge: Ballinger Publishing Co., 1984), pp. 78–110; and Seymour M. Hersh's account of the attempt to smuggle fifty krytrons out of the United States to Pakistan in *The New York Times*, February 25, 1985.

5. Lewis A. Dunn, *Controlling the Bomb: Nuclear Proliferation in the 1980s*, (New Haven: Yale University Press, 1982), pp. 117–118.

6. Spector, *Nuclear Proliferation Today*, pp. 317–324, 446–451.

7. See the text of the Nuclear Non-Proliferation Treaty (NPT) in *Arms Control and Disarmament Agreements: Texts and Histories of Negotiations* (1982 edition), Washington, D.C.: U.S. Arms Control and Disarmament Agency (ACDA, 1982), pp. 82–98.

8. For a brief early history of the safeguards issue, see Arnold Kramish, *The Watched and the Unwatched: Inspection in the Non-Proliferation Treaty*, Adelphi Papers, no. 36 (London: International Institute for Strategic Studies, June 1967).

9. *New and Better Equipment Being Made Available For International Nuclear Safeguards*, General Accounting Office Report to the Chairman, Subcommittee on Energy, Research and Protection, Committee on Science and Technology, House of Representatives, GAO/NSIAD-84-46, June 14, 1984, p. 4.

10. "Non Proliferation of Nuclear Weapons" in *Nuclear Arms Control: Background and Issues* (Washington, D.C.: National Academy Press, 1985), p. 252.

LIMITING NUCLEAR PROLIFERATION

THE NUCLEAR THRESHOLD STATES: SELECTED CASES

1 IRAQ

Jed C. Snyder

The Iraqi nuclear program presents an instructive case study for nonproliferation specialists for several reasons. First, it shows what a country with no indigenous technological capability can achieve. Iraq lacks the sophisticated infrastructure to support the scientific effort required for a nuclear weapons program, and it has no pool of trained scientists and engineers who might form the nucleus of any national effort. Also, the critical technologies associated with a nuclear weapons program, including chemical engineering, nuclear engineering, metallurgy, and electronics, are poorly developed or nonexistent in Iraq.

Second, the Iraqi nuclear effort illustrates the extent to which oil may provide political leverage. Saddam Hussein, the president of Iraq and chairman of the all-powerful Revolutionary Command Council (RCC), has been able to utilize Iraq's enormous oil revenues to: (1) finance an expensive and ambitious nuclear research program; and (2) pressure European states (who have been dependent upon Iraqi crude) into providing the sophisticated training, material, and personnel for Iraq's nuclear effort. As will be explored later, Iraq's principal nuclear benefactors were all critically dependent upon Baghdad for the majority of their petroleum needs.

Third, despite signing the 1968 Treaty on the Non-Proliferation of Nuclear Weapons (NPT) and acceptance of full-scope safeguards as prescribed and monitored by the International Atomic Energy Agency (IAEA), Iraq had nearly reached the point where it had (prior to the July 1981 bombing of its Osirak reactor) both the accumulated fissile material and technical support to explode a small nuclear device at least as powerful as that which devastated Hiroshima and Nagasaki. The Iraqis demonstrated that while operating within IAEA constraints, a nation can (without violating these agreements) acquire the fissile material and technical training necessary for a nuclear weapons program. Although Hussein had begun to acquire a nuclear infrastructure, the Iraqi scientists were still some distance from assembling a device. The nuclear engineering skills required to assemble a bomb are considerable, and the Iraqi scientists needed time to master them.

This chapter will trace the development of the Iraqi nuclear program from its genesis, including a detailed discussion of the French and Italian assistance efforts. There is also an analysis of the alternative proliferation paths and technological choices open to the Iraqi government and a discussion of the Israeli decision to attack the Tuwaitha nuclear facility near Baghdad.

BUILDING A NUCLEAR PROGRAM

Early Soviet Support

Iraq's interest in nuclear energy can be retraced to 1959 when, in discussions with the Soviet Union, an agreement was reached to provide Iraq with its first nuclear research reactor to be located at the Tuwaitha Atomic Center near Baghdad. The center had been built with Western funds[1] when Iraq was a member of the Baghdad Pact.[2] The Soviet-supplied reactor was delivered only after Iraq withdrew from the pact.

The Soviet reactor, an IRT–2000, was a small research model, with a rated capacity of only two megawatts thermal [mw(th)]. The reactor began operating in 1968; its output was later upgraded to 5mw(th) in 1978. In addition, the Soviet Union constructed a small radioisotope laboratory. The Soviet-supplied reactor was neither sufficient for Iraq's timetable nor its nuclear appetite, although by 1978 the Soviet Union had begun to provide Iraq with 80 percent enriched uranium fuel[3] (the original fuel was less than 10 percent enriched).[4] At that time, the IRT–2000 had been used primarily for medical and other civilian research applications on a very small scale.[5] Although there has been widespread speculation that the Iraqis approached Moscow for an additional reactor and were refused, there is no confirmation of this exchange in the open literature. This reactor and its associated laboratory facilities represented the beginning and the end of Soviet nuclear assistance to Baghdad.

Historically Moscow has been quite cautious and strict in its nuclear assistance efforts, generally insisting that nuclear client states follow the letter of the law in operating Soviet-sponsored facilities. The Soviet Union is, in fact, much more cautious with such investments than are Western governments, probably as a result of lessons learned in the 1950s from Soviet assistance to China's nuclear program. (Chinese scientists were provided nuclear engineering technology that greatly accelerated Peking's development of nuclear weapons.)

The French Connection

The key to Iraq's acquisition of nuclear research facilities was Baghdad's enormous annual revenues from the export of oil (with proven reserves estimated as the sixth largest in the world)[6] and President Saddam Hussein's ability to use these revenues to finance the most ambitious nuclear research program in the Arab world. Revenues obtained from Iraqi oil exports raised the Iraqi gross national product from $2.5 billion in 1967 to $16 billion in 1976.[7]

Realizing that the French nuclear industry was advanced and seeking clients, Hussein approached the French government initially to solicit a general nuclear cooperation accord. This agreement was signed during French premier Jacques Chirac's trip to Baghdad in 1974.[8] In their book, *The Islamic Bomb*, Steve Weissman and Herbert Krosney report that the French were quite enthusiastic about a potential sale to Iraq, and according to a French official who traveled to Baghdad with

Chirac, were "determined to keep an inside track on the contracts."[9] The Iraqis were being courted by other suppliers, including the Canadians, who may have offered the CANDU (Canadian-Deuterium-Uranium) natural uranium reactor.[10]

The Iraqis' first choice was a French 500mw natural uranium-fueled gas-graphite power reactor, utilized by the French primarily as a source of plutonium for the *Force de frappe*,[11] as well as for the generation of electric power. The production of gas-graphite power reactors had been phased out by the French in the early 1970s, as they turned to more efficient power-generating models like the pressurized water and boiling water reactors. The Iraqi request for a gas-graphite facility apparently raised French suspicions about the nature of Baghdad's nuclear research effort. If the Iraqis were seriously interested in power generation or civilian research, the gas-graphite reactor was inappropriate. If, however, Hussein coveted a source of plutonium for a nuclear weapons program, the graphite reactor was a good choice.

There is substantial disagreement as to how the French responded to the Iraqi gas-graphite request. Weissman and Krosney maintain that French premier Chirac initially agreed to the gas-graphite sale.[12] Whether Chirac understood the capabilities of the reactor (as compared to other reactors) is unclear, although it seems doubtful that he would not have been briefed on the range of reactor characteristics, including the relative proliferation risks of all French-built models. In any event, Chirac was accompanied on his trip to Baghdad by nuclear experts who would certainly be able to describe the proliferation dangers of a gas-graphite reactor. Yves Girard, then an advisor on nuclear affairs to the French Atomic Energy Commission (CEA), accompanied Chirac and was also well-informed on this issue. One proliferation specialist argues that the French rejected the Iraqi request out-of-hand, sensing an ulterior Iraqi motive.[13]

Weissman and Krosney describe how a combination of bureaucratic and economic considerations converged to produce a fierce debate within the French government as to whether the gas-graphite reactor should be sold to the Iraqis or whether an alternative would be offered. An additional factor in the debate was that the French atomic construction company, Framatome, had ceased building gas-graphite power reactors. Dr. Bertram Goldschmidt of the CEA, emphasizing the industrial difficulties with the Iraqi request, concludes that the gas-graphite reactor was disapproved for "reasons that had nothing to do with nuclear proliferation."[14]

The French offered the Iraqis a version of an alternative reactor that had been operating at the French nuclear center at Saclay and that was originally developed to study new fuel elements. The reactor was named Osiris after the ancient Egyptian god of the dead. In an attempt to blend the name Osiris with the recipient country, the French labeled the Iraqi model "Osirak." Hussein, however, wanted the reactor identified with the 1968 coup which brought the Ba'th party to power in Iraq and chose the name "Tammuz" after the month in the Arabic calendar that coincided with the coup. As the Tuwaitha facility included two reactors, the Iraqis refer to them as Tammuz I and Tammuz II.[15]

Several alternative reactors may have been considered. The Israeli government's official report, arguing its rationale for the 1981 Osirak bombing, states that after the French rejected the gas-graphite request, they offered the Iraqis either of two power reactor models, a pressurized water reactor or a boiling water reactor[16]—both of which were more suitable for an embryonic power generation program. The Iraqi interest in the gas-graphite model and subsequent rejection of alternatives strongly suggest that Baghdad was interested in acquiring a reactor that would yield a significant amount of plutonium, rather than one that optimized power generating capability or civilian research. This factor must have been obvious to the French.

Paris finally offered the Iraqis the Osiris-type model, which in its original design was rated as a 70mw(th) research reactor built to test the influence of radiation on power reactor construction materials and fuel elements, and in particular how materials react to very high bombardments of neutrons or neutron flux. This materials-testing reactor also had the capability of producing significant amounts of plutonium, if the reactor were modified. Despite many inaccurate reports to the contrary, Osirak was not designed for the optimal production of large amounts of plutonium. Had the Iraqis wanted to maximize plutonium production, a heavy water-moderated, natural uranium-fueled reactor like the Canadian Nuclear Reactor Experimental (NRX) design provided to India and Taiwan would have been the better investment.

Osirak would clearly have given the Iraqis more than enough plutonium for a clandestine bomb program, but the choice of this reactor suggests the Iraqi purchase was driven more by Hussein's emulation of the French (and, particularly, former French president Giscard d'Estaing) than by prudent investment planning.[17] This view is also consistent with the hypothesis that Hussein was considering the future of Iraq's nuclear program—possibly yielding a significant amount of bomb-grade plutonium over a long period during which Iraqi scientists would receive training critical to the project's success. Since the Tuwaitha research center was Iraq's primary scientific facility, it represented Hussein's only opportunity to develop a cadre of indigenously trained engineers and nuclear physicists. Contracting for the sale of a facility, which would raise proliferation concerns, might jeopardize that training effort. The Osirak reactor, while potentially quite useful as an instrument of proliferation, would less alarm the IAEA than other reactors labeled by the nonproliferation community as overtly hazardous (e.g., the French-supplied Israeli reactor at Dimona).

The Iraqis agreed to the Osirak sale and also signed a contract providing Baghdad with a smaller 800kw critical assembly modeled on the French Isis reactor (the sister model of the larger Osiris reactor). The Iraqis named this reactor Tammuz II.

Tammuz I, or Osirak, is a light water, swimming pool reactor fueled by highly enriched uranium (93 percent) whose output is rated at 70mw(th).[18] The core load of reactor fuel is about 15kg of uranium–235. In order to operate the reactor continuously for one year, five to six core loads of fuel would be required.[19] The French initially agreed to supply Iraq with 70kg of highly enriched uranium fuel, sufficient to operate the reactor for one year. Subsequently the French indicated that the fuel would not be provided in a single shipment, but only as the reactor required fresh fuel. Limiting each fuel shipment to that which was immediately required to operate the reactor would help reduce the opportunity for diversion of the fuel for military purposes. To run the reactor continuously and engage in clandestine bomb-related projects would be difficult with only 15kg of uranium fuel. The French decision confirms Paris' early suspicions of Saddam Hussein's authentic research agenda, despite official statements to the contrary.

Osiris was designed primarily for nations engaged in the indigenous production of nuclear power reactors. Iraq has no such program; Osirak does not generate electric power. With its large oil reserves, Iraq has no great economic or energy incentive to establish a nuclear power generating capacity. In addition, power reactors are generally fueled by low-enriched uranium, which is not suitable for nuclear explosive devices or bombs. Although the Iraqis continued to claim interest in a civilian power generating capability, had they been truly interested in developing that potential, they would have looked more seriously at commercially proven power reactor designs, which burn slightly enriched uranium and produce relatively small amounts of plutonium. In the Iraqi case there is no evidence to suggest such an effort; quite the contrary.

Osirak is a much more powerful reactor than the Iraqis needed for simple research purposes. Sources at Techicatome, one of the partners in the French consortium that contracted to build Osirak, confirmed that although Tammuz I had a rated capacity of 70mw(th), its "nominal operating capacity" was actually 40mw(th).[20] The question over whether Osirak operated at 40 or 70mw raises several larger issues, including one that is still debated today—was Osirak an exact copy of the French Osiris reactor, which had been modified to operate at 70mw?

The Iraqis wanted to upgrade the reactor to 70mw(th) and asked the French to supply the additional necessary cooling systems. That modification would allow the production of more plutonium in a clandestine "blanket"[21] or within the fuel itself, as there is a proportional relationship between the power rating of the reactor and the amount of plutonium produced. It should be noted, however, that such a power upgrade could have legitimate peaceful research applications as well. A higher power rating would allow scientists to test the thermal and mechanical properties of reactor materials in an environment that more closely duplicated conditions of an operating nuclear reactor. Considering the embryonic state of the Iraqi nuclear research effort, however, such experimentation would not occur until later in the project. Therefore, the only plausible explanation for the Iraqi power upgrade request is the consequent increase in plutonium production capability. The deputy director general of the IAEA, Hans Gruemm, has estimated that a uranium blanket at Osirak could yield enough plutonium for one to two bombs per year.[22]

There was general agreement within the U.S. government that absent any power generating program, a nuclear weapons capability was a probable goal of the Iraqi program.[23] Although key members of Congress had been briefed on the Tuwaitha atomic project, U.S. legislators did not concentrate on the issue until March 1981, when California senator Alan Cranston announced that U.S. government officials had reported that Iraq was engaged in a "Manhattan Project–type approach," which would yield a nuclear weapon.[24] Cranston also alleged that Iraq was then at a critical juncture in its mastery of the fuel cycle. Some officials have offered privately that Cranston's revelations were somewhat exaggerated and possibly Israeli-inspired. Nevertheless, he helped to focus congressional concern on the weapons potential of the Iraqi nuclear effort. His more recent statements concerning the direction of Pakistan's nuclear program have had even more dramatic results.[25]

The Search for a Reprocessing Plant

Having obtained a powerful research reactor fueled by highly enriched uranium, Hussein searched for laboratory facilities to enhance the research component of the project, particularly to enable Iraq to reprocess spent fuel.[26] In the hope of diversifying his sources, Hussein approached the Italians in 1975 for reprocessing equipment. Italy had signed the NPT, and although its nuclear program was still developing, it had launched a fuel-reprocessing program as early as 1969.[27]

Reactor Technologies and the Iraqi Choice

To understand the problem of plutonium proliferation (the major concern associated with the Iraqi nuclear program), it is necessary to describe briefly the alternative paths of proliferation that exist in a civilian reactor program.

Currently nuclear power generation programs can be divided into two broad categories based on reactor technologies: heavy water reactors (HWR) fueled by natural uranium (manufactured by Canada, West Germany, and India) and light water reactors (LWR) fueled by enriched uranium (originally developed by the United States and manufactured by France, West Germany, Japan, the Soviet Union, and Sweden). Both reactors use a once-through fuel cycle that includes four major steps: uranium enrichment (for the LWR), fuel fabrication, irradiation in the reactor, and spent-fuel storage. Weapons-grade material (from which fission explosives can be made without isotope enrichment) does not exist except in the spent fuel, where plutonium produced in the reactor is mixed with highly radioactive fission waste products and large amounts of uranium–238.[28] To obtain bomb-grade plutonium, the irradiated uranium must be reprocessed. This process involves removing the spent fuel from the reactor vessel, chopping it up, and dissolving the pieces in an acid bath. Once dissolved, the plutonium is chemically separated from the uranium and fission wastes. Although the primary purpose for which Tammuz I was designed is the irradiation of large and bulky testing materials, it may also be used for irradiating either natural or depleted uranium to produce plutonium. A significant plutonium yield would require reprocessing laboratory facilities at the reactor site, which the Iraqis were not able to build themselves.

One virtue of the Osirak reactor is the ease with which it can be modified for a range of procedures. As noted earlier, Hussein's scientists had already requested one modification—additional cooling systems. Furthermore, the Iraqis reportedly requested a second modification that (like the first modification) would have affected the rate of plutonium production. Hussein asked that a heavy water (i.e., Deuterium D_2O) tank, modelled after similar installations at French facilities, be installed in Tammuz I. This request was fulfilled and the tank was installed, allowing rather sophisticated neutron-beam experimentation. Richard Wilson, chairman of the physics department at Harvard University, visited the Tammuz site at the invitation of the Iraqi foreign ministry. He reports that there is some mystery surrounding the neutron-beam experimentation and that he was unable to determine the application of such experiments to the Iraqi research effort.[29] Such experiments, however, would be a critical component of a weapons research effort.

Oil Pressure and the Italian Connection

Although several countries could furnish Iraq with the plutonium separation facilities it sought, only a couple showed a willingness to provide them. That cooperative attitude was influenced considerably by dependence on Iraqi oil. Hussein was in a position to exploit Iraq's very large oil revenues and its position as a critical supplier to Europe to drive his negotiations. Both France and Italy imported a significant percentage of their petroleum supplies from Iraq.[30]

As Table 1–1 shows, in September 1973 (prior to the oil embargo by OPEC) Iraq supplied 15 percent of French OPEC imports. In 1979 (three years after the French-Iraqi nuclear assistance agreement was signed) that dependency increased to 21 percent. Although the French contract remains secret, there has been much speculation that Saddam Hussein offered a continued (and possibly enhanced) oil export relationship with the French in return for the sale of Tammuz I and II.[31]

The Italian case (as illustrated in Table 1–2) is a more extreme example of growing dependency during the Iraqi contract period. Italian imports of Iraqi crude as a percentage of total OPEC imports increased to 24 percent in 1979 from a 1973 preembargo level of 17 percent.

The value of the oil lever for Iraq has since been reduced to almost zero primarily as a result of the continuing Iran-Iraq war. Repeated attacks on Persian Gulf oil terminals, storage facilities, and en-route tankers have severely curtailed Iraqi exports. Subsequent developments have exacerbated the situation, including the closure by Syria of an Iraqi-Syrian pipeline in April 1982, which carried 700,000 barrels of oil per day.[32] Iraqi president Saddam Hussein has attempted to minimize the war's damage to Iraq's export capacity by planning to build new pipelines through Saudi Arabia and to the Gulf of Aqaba and by

Table 1–1.   French Imports of Iraqi Crude Oil (thousands of barrels/day).

	Imports from Iraq	Total OPEC Imports	As Percentage of Total OPEC Imports
1973[a]	375	2,555	15.0
1978	411	2,091	20.0
1979	489	2,271	21.0
1981	46	1,492	3.0
1982	29	1,141	2.5
1983	39	892	4.4

a. Pre-oil crisis level.
Source: *International Energy Statistical Review*, Central Intelligence Agency, DI IESR 83–005 (May 31, 1983): 6; DI IESR 84–005 (May 29, 1984): 7.

expanding an existing Turkish pipeline. Hussein's insistence, however, for guarantees against potential sabotage attacks has stalled progress.[33] The Iran-Iraq war has reduced the availability of Iraqi petroleum to the point where in 1983 French imports of Iraqi crude represented only 4.4 percent of total OPEC sources. The war with Iran has dramatically reduced Iraqi crude oil production capacity. Prewar production was 2.5 million barrels per day (mbd), whereas in 1984 production was only 1.2 mbd. As a result, crude oil exports have declined signif-

Table 1–2.   Italian Imports of Iraqi Crude Oil (thousands of barrels/day).

	Imports from Iraq	Total OPEC Imports	As Percentage of Total OPEC Imports
1973[a]	383	2,273	17.0
1978	379	1,839	21.0
1979	447	1,885	24.0
1981	156	1,079	14.0
1982	114	1,263	9.0
1983	94	1,072	8.8

a. Pre-oil crisis level.
Source: *International Energy Statistical Review*, Central Intelligence Agency, DI IESR 83–005 (May 31, 1983): 7; DI IESR 84–005 (May 29, 1984): 7.

icantly. Prior to September 1980 Iraq exported 2.3 mbd. In 1984 the total daily crude exports totalled only 950,000 barrels, a decrease of more than 41 percent.[34]

The Italian situation is similar to France in one respect and quite different in another. Italian imports have been significantly reduced, but as Table 1–2 shows, Italy still depended in 1983 on Iraq for nearly 9 percent of its imports. Although the Iran-Iraq war is the major reason for overall reduction in OPEC dependency, the European powers have, for the most part, reduced domestic consumption as a component of a larger Western strategy to reduce crude imports.

The Italian Laboratories

It is unclear whether Hussein approached the French for separation facilities before asking the Italians, although the *Frankfurter Allgemeine* reported a French refusal to provide a "hot cell" (for the reprocessing of plutonium) to the Iraqis, resulting in Iraq's approach to the Italians.[35] There is no available data detailing the full scope of the French contract so it is not possible to confirm whether the French did provide Iraq with supporting facilities. Richard Wilson, however, describes the existence of "a separate large building with machine shops" near the reactor building,[36] which to the author's knowledge (confirmed by discussions with U.S. government officials) was never inspected by the IAEA.

The Italians offered to sell a radiochemistry laboratory that included three interconnecting lead-shielded "hot cells" for the handling of highly radioactive material, ideal for the separation of plutonium by dissolving irradiated uranium dioxide present in the Osirak spent fuel. In 1976 the Italian Nuclear Agency— Comitato Nazionale per l'Energia Nucleare—signed a ten-year agreement with Iraq to assist Baghdad's nuclear research effort. The Italians also agreed to sell the Fuel Fabrication Laboratory (FFL) used to manufacture material for fuel rods, vital to the operation of a nuclear power reactor. Since Iraq had no power reactor requiring these rods, the most plausible use for the FFL is the manufacture of uranium dioxide pellets to be irradiated in the Osirak reactor, after which plutonium would be obtained via a reprocessing procedure.[37] Had the Iraqis been interested in experimenting with reactor fuel they could easily have obtained prefabricated fuel pellets for this purpose. Absent this requirement, the production of plutonium is a quite reasonable assumption. The five laboratories supplied by the Italians would allow the Iraqis to proceed toward the manufacture of bomb-grade material through four steps: (1) acquiring natural uranium; (2) fabrication of fuel pellets; (3) irradiation of the pellets to produce plutonium; and (4) reprocessing of the plutonium in a "hot cell." A waste treatment laboratory was also provided.

There is disagreement concerning the quantity of plutonium that could be produced in the three "hot cells." French nuclear engineers argue that the maximum would be 300 to 500 grams per year,[38] far less than the amount required for a nuclear weapon. The Israelis believed the amount was much greater, perhaps 6 to 10 kilograms per year.[39] Although an accurate assessment would depend on specific data concerning the operation of Tammuz I, the French figure is considered reasonable but low, while the Israeli estimate is the maximum, assuming the most efficient and competent operation by technicians who clearly had not reached that state of sophistication and experience.[40]

The U.S. Department of State became concerned over the sale of "hot cells" and asked the Italians to explain the agreement. Officials in Rome assured the State Department that Iraq intended to use the facility for medical and industrial purposes, although the Italian government also acknowledged the theoretical possibility of bomb production.[41]

The Italian agreement was secret until Richard Burt, then national security affairs correspondent for *The New York Times*, reported it in March 1980. Most damaging politically for the Italians was Burt's revelation that Rome had agreed to "provide nuclear assistance in exchange for long-term access to Iraqi oil."[42] In addition, Burt reported that U.S. intelligence agencies calculated that the "hot cells" would allow Iraq to produce enough plutonium for one bomb per year, or five to ten kilograms.[43] This estimate agreed with the Israeli figure but was substantially larger than the French calculation.

Not contained in Burt's article was a description of an Italian contract to sell Iraq four naval combat vessels, all of which were subject to U.S. approval, as the frigates contained engine components built by a U.S. company, General Electric. The United States finally approved the license for part of the sale, but the Italians were concerned that approval for the full sale might be delayed pending Rome's final determination on whether to transfer sensitive nuclear technology to Iraq.[44] The Italian government, responding to an avalanche of criticism, revealed that it had consulted with the U.S. government during the early stages of the "hot cell" talks and that Washington had raised no objections.[45] One U.S. official revealed that several other West European nations had been competing with Italy for the naval contract, but the Italian "hot cell" agreement eliminated any serious competition for the frigate contract.[46]

Holding the French to the Bargain

When the French government agreed in 1976 to sell the Tammuz I and II nuclear reactors to Iraq, they also agreed (as mentioned earlier) to supply 93 percent enriched U^{235} fuel to operate it. Prime Minister Chirac later fell from power and the French reassessed their nuclear export policies toward Iraq and Pakistan, both of whom were strongly suspected of having plans to produce atomic weapons. Paris suspended an agreement to supply Pakistan with a reprocessing plant at Chasma, and French president d'Estaing had reservations about Iraqi intentions, causing him to question the wisdom of providing highly enriched uranium for Tammuz I.

There was considerable debate within the French government over whether or not to honor the contract with Iraq. The French foreign ministry—the Quai d'Orsay—suggested an alternative reactor fuel that, because it is only slightly enriched, would not be suitable for a uranium-based nuclear bomb. This "caramel" fuel would be enriched to only 6.8 percent, well below the threshold for bomb-grade material.[47] Burning "caramel" in a reactor does produce plutonium, however. The issue of which fuel to supply precipitated another bureaucratic struggle within the French government. The Quai d'Orsay felt the transfer of "caramel" fuel would signal a new French concern over proliferation risks, while CEA argued that the original contract should be honored.

A compromise was reached whereby the highly enriched uranium would be shipped, but only in quantities immediately necessary for the reactor's operation. The French decision was announced at the final meeting of the International Nuclear Fuel Cycle Evaluation in Vienna in February 1980. Bryon de l'Estaing, the director of international relations at the CEA, announced that in the future French policy would limit fuel sales to low-enriched uranium only.[48]

Shopping for Uranium

Assuming Iraq was interested in utilizing Tammuz I for clandestine construction of a plutonium-based nuclear weapon,[49] large amounts of natural uranium would be required to blanket the reactor. The Iraqis began to search for potential suppliers of natural uranium, and as before, targeted states whose dependence on Iraqi crude increased the likelihood of a favorable response. Brazil was an ideal candidate, dependent on Iraq for nearly 45 percent of its oil supplies. Brazil's known natural uranium reserves were high and had increased dramatically in 1979 after a major new find in Ceara.[50] After eight months of negotiation, Brazil signed a nuclear cooperation agreement with Iraq that included the supply of natural and slightly enriched uranium. In addition, both sides agreed to inform the IAEA of negotiations over safeguards.[51]

The Brazilians had to be cautious about the language in this agreement, particularly in light of their $16 billion nuclear contract with West Germany, signed in 1975. This agreement with West Germany forbade the transfer of sensitive nuclear technology to a third country. The foreign ministry in Bonn determined, however, that items in the Iraqi agreement were outside the definition of sensitive.[52] The natural uranium that Brazil provided Iraq amounted to only a small percentage of the uranium the latter acquired from Portugal and Niger, which totalled over 250 tons.[53] The troubling aspect of the Iraqi-Brazilian agreement was the potential for clandestine transfer of sensitive technology.

In early 1980 West German officials became alarmed over reports that ten tons of uranium had been sold by the West German conglomerate Nukem to Italy, which then sold the fuel to Iraq. The West Germans were concerned that other European Atomic Energy Community (EURATOM) nations might interpret nuclear export restrictions less strictly than they did, contributing to the leakage of sensitive material and technology to potential proliferating states. The transfer of this uranium was part of the Italian "hot cell" agreement, and under great criticism and pressure, EURATOM officials could only point to Iraq's signature on the 1968 NPT as evidence of Baghdad's benign intentions.[54] The transfer included four tons of natural uranium and six tons of depleted fuel. The agreement was not secret, although the Italians did not publicize it. This uranium, like that supplied to Iraq by Brazil, Portugal, and Niger, could easily be irradiated in the Tammuz I reactor after which plutonium could be extracted in the "hot cells." The West Germans felt that the Italian government should have notified Bonn prior to the transfer, when (Bonn claimed) the German government would have taken a careful look at the application.[55] The U.S. government also indicated its concern over Italy's agreements with Iraq, suggesting Washington might refuse to grant nuclear export licenses to Italy and possibly to EURATOM.[56] Iraq's accumulation of massive amounts of natural uranium is one of the most compelling and unimpeachable pieces of evidence that suggest Hussein was seeking a nuclear weapons capability. Since Tammuz could not operate on natural uranium fuel, a clandestine bomb program is the only plausible explanation for this stockpiling.

The most disturbing and convincing indication of a nuclear weapons program was Iraq's foiled attempt to obtain uranium-metal fuel pins under a contract arranged by Nukem. A large amount of depleted uranium fuel was to be sent from West Germany to Canada, where it was to be fabricated into metal billets.[57] From there the billets would be manufactured into pins that could fuel the early models of Canadian reactors but could not be inserted into the Osirak reactor, which used uranium plates.[58] These metal pins could serve only one function—the production of plutonium. Uranium metal is, in fact, the "material of choice" in any reprocessing effort as opposed to uranium oxide, the most common form of uranium reactor fuel. The transfer was stopped after the U.S. Nuclear Regulatory Commission (NRC) was informed of the uranium's ultimate destination.[59] Had there been no U.S. corporate involvement in the attempted transfer, the NRC would not have been alerted, and the Iraqis would probably have obtained the pins, accelerating any reprocessing effort.[a]

BEGIN'S PREEMPTIVE STRIKE: THE OSIRAK ATTACK

On the afternoon of June 7, 1981, two formations of U.S.-built aircraft left Etzion Airbase near Eilat, Israel, for a preemptive strike on the Osirak nuclear reactor. Eight F–16 Falcon aircraft escorted by six F–15 Eagles dropped a total of sixteen 2,000–lb iron bombs on the reactor facility. According to one account, the pilots had been training for this mission since October 1980.[60] This was the first of several sabotage operations directed against the Iraqi nuclear program.

La Seyne-Sur-Mer

The first of several incidents involving the sabotage of potential Iraqi nuclear weapons production occurred in the early morning of April 6, 1979, in the French Mediterranean town of La Seyne-Sur-Mer, near the port city of Toulon, where the bulk of the French Mediterranean fleet is harbored. Shortly after 3:00 a.m. several blasts rang out at the assembly hangar of the French engineering firm Constructions Navales et Industrielles de la Méditerranée (CNIM), where construction had just been completed on two nuclear reactor cores for the Tammuz I and II

a. This episode illustrates one major difficulty in dealing with large and often dangerous transfers of reactor fuel to a potential proliferator: How to respond to suspicious and potentially dangerous proliferation behavior by an NPT signatory? Had the West Germans objected to the sale, the Iraqis could quite rightfully have complained about discrimination and abrogated their adherence to the treaty, possibly encouraging other potentially troublesome states to do the same. It is unlikely that countries such as India, Brazil, and Pakistan would accept full-scope safeguards, if such "discrimination" had occurred. Such quiet transfers as the Italian case, however, also undermine the basis for the NPT, which can function only if its signatories refrain from agreements that subvert the intent of the nonproliferation regime.

facilities. Five explosive charges were set off, damaging both cores and other nuclear-related equipment destined for West Germany and Belgium. In a telephone call to the Paris newspaper *Le Monde*, a French ecological group claimed responsibility, citing the Three Mile Island incident as the event that provoked the bombing.[61]

By all accounts, there was very little security at the CNIM plant, with no obvious protective structures surrounding it.[62] The French authorities refused to speculate publicly as to who was responsible for the blast, although privately they suggested Israeli complicity.[63] Both the Tammuz I and II reactor cores were severely damaged, delaying their delivery for six months.

The Meridien Murder

In June 1980 Dr. Yahya el-Meshad, an Egyptian scientist with a Ph.D. in electrical engineering and trained in the Soviet Union on the IRT-2000, was found murdered in the Meridien Hotel in Paris. Meshad had been a professor of nuclear engineering at the University of Alexandria in Egypt. He had also worked for the Egyptian Atomic Energy Commission from 1961 to 1968 and was recruited by the Iraqis in 1975 to assist them with the Tammuz project. Meshad's skills were widely known in the Arab world. Libya's leader, Colonel Muammar el Qaddafi, had approached Meshad to assist in Libya's nuclear effort, but Meshad found the Iraqi offer more attractive.[64]

Apparently Meshad functioned as an intermediary between Baghdad and Paris in the negotiation of shipments of highly enriched uranium fuel for the Tammuz reactor.[65] Meshad's murderers were never apprehended. Suspicion of Israeli involvement in the murder grew, although the method employed to kill Meshad was generally considered to be unprofessional and not typical of that used by the Mossad.

The Iranian Attack

On September 30, 1980, less than two weeks after the start of the Iran-Iraq war, the Tuwaitha Atomic Center was bombed by

Iranian aircraft, causing minor damage to the facility. At the time of the attack the Tammuz I reactor was still under construction and was thought to be roughly three months from completion.[66] Despite earlier sensational reports in the press that Israeli pilots had carried out the attack, further investigation confirmed that the Iranian air force had been responsible for the bombing. In addition, several reports suggested that the Iranian pilots did not realize they were attacking a nuclear facility and that the attack was not planned in advance.[67]

Shortly after the attack, the French government announced it would not suspend shipments of the highly enriched uranium to Osirak, that it was not concerned about the proliferation risks of the Iraqi program, and that the Iraqis "have the right to civilian nuclear technology."[68] At the same time, the Iraqis informed the IAEA that they were temporarily suspending the agency's inspection schedule for the Tuwaitha facility due to "current war conditions." Both the French and the IAEA were alarmed by this action since earlier reports had indicated no damage to the reactor itself. Interviews with French technicians assigned to Tuwaitha revealed that twenty-six pounds of highly enriched uranium fuel (which had been powering the smaller reactor Tammuz II) had been removed from the core and were being stored in an underground canal.[69] Of some concern was confirmation that the French technicians were no longer supervising the operations at the Tuwaitha center, since nearly all of them had been repatriated shortly after the Iranian attack. Some volunteers remained, but it was unclear whether they were actually onsite continuously.[70]

Operation Babylon

These three incidents fueled discussion and speculation about the progress of the Iraqi program and Israeli concerns. Shortly after the Meshad murder, Israeli nuclear scientist Professor Yuval Ne'eman warned in an interview with *The Jerusalem Post* that Iraq had only to decide on "which sort of bomb they [would] prefer," and that the ingredients had been acquired.[71] Ne'eman also announced that Iraq could have a bomb assembled within one year.[72] Although evidence linking the Israelis to the three incidents has never materialized, Israeli complicity is strongly suspected. For example, two days before the Iranian attack on the Tuwaitha facility, the chief of Israeli military intelligence, General Yehoshua Saguy, wondered aloud on Israeli television why the Iranians had not yet destroyed the Osirak reactor.[73]

At this time, the Israeli government began to publicize its fears of the Iraqi nuclear program. In late July 1980 Israeli foreign minister Yitzhak Shamir summoned a high-ranking French official to his office to express officially Israel's "profound concern" over the Osirak reactor. France denied that any real danger of nuclear proliferation existed at Osirak and later replied that "Iraq, like any other country, has the right to the peaceful uses of nuclear energy and [France] does not see any reason for this right to be refused."[74] Two days later an editorial in *Le Monde* suggested that French access to Iraqi oil was driving Paris' effort to assist the Baghdad nuclear program. Responding to Washington's criticism of the French assistance effort, the editorial also suggested that the U.S. agreement to assist the Pakistani nuclear program was more dangerous than the French contracts with Iraq.[75]

Although the Iraqis had erected limited defenses around the complex (after the Iranian attack), they proved ineffective in defending the reactor from the Israeli strike. Iraqi anti-aircraft fire proved useless, and the French Crotale and Roland ground-to-air missile batteries were not even fired. "Operation Babylon" appeared to be a complete success.

After the attack the Israeli government declared that under no circumstances would it "allow the enemy to develop weapons of mass destruction against our nation; we will defend Israel's citizens with all the means at our disposal."[76] This statement and others have been interpreted as a new "doctrine" and a component of Israel's strategy of deterrence. This was elaborated upon by Israeli defense minister Ariel Sharon in December 1981, six months after the Osirak attack: "Israel cannot afford the introduction of the nuclear weapon. For us, it is not a question of a balance of terror but a question of survival. We shall therefore have to prevent such a threat at its inception."[77]

The implication is that Israel will oppose with force any nuclear weapons program in the Middle East in an effort to maintain its predominant position. Whether this policy is to be extended to the less radical Arab states, which might already have a peaceful nuclear program (e.g., Egypt), is uncertain. Clearly it applies to hostile states such as Libya, Iraq, Syria, and Iran. One analyst has suggested that Israeli prime minister Menachem Begin was limiting the application of the policy to only the more "fanatical" states.[78] In essence, the Israeli government considered the Osirak bombing "a legitimate act of self defense, based on the principles of international law." The official Israeli government report on the Osirak attack listed three major reasons for the decision to bomb the reactor:

- Imminent realization of Iraq's plans to acquire a military nuclear capability.
- Iraq's declared maintenance of a state of war with Israel and its persistent denial of Israel's right to exist.
- The failure of Israel's diplomatic efforts to prevent the extension of foreign assistance to Iraq in the implementation of its nuclear program.[79]

The government report also cited Article 51 of the United Nations Charter which grants each member state the "inherent right of individual or collective self-defense in the event of an armed attack."[80] The Israeli government clearly saw its act as safeguarding nonproliferation. In an official statement, Tel Aviv presented a detailed analysis of the flaws present in the current nonproliferation regime, concluding that:

> ... the act of subscribing to the NPT, or unilateral adherence to full-scope safeguards, cannot in itself be considered a guarantee against the proliferation of nuclear weapons in the Middle East, since the area is characterized by the repeated violation of international obligations in this field. *Restrictions of a technical or institutional nature alone can hardly protect the area from nuclear proliferation*[81] [emphasis added].

Finally Israel used the Osirak bombing to advocate (as it had previously) agreement to a nuclear-weapon-free zone in the Middle East, modelled on the Treaty of Tlatelolco, which had established a free zone in Latin America.[82]

The Iraqi reaction to the Israeli bombing was prompt and outspoken. The senior foreign affairs officer in the Ba'th government stated that the attack was "tangible and blatant evidence that the Zionist entity is nothing more than a racist, aggressive and expansionist entity hostile to all the values of freedom, justice, and right. . . ."[83] The officer also alluded to Israel's possession of nuclear weapons and questioned why Iraq was not allowed "to possess peaceful technological and scientific means."[84]

Condemnation of the Israeli attack was virtually universal. After negotiations between the United States, Iraq, and other parties, the United Nations passed Resolution 487, condemning the Israeli attack as a violation of the UN Charter but refraining from imposing sanctions against Israel. The IAEA also adopted a resolution that included a suspension of any further technical assistance to the Israeli nuclear program.[85]

Many questions have been raised concerning the timing of the Israeli attack. Tel Aviv expressed concern that the Osirak reactor would become operational within a short period of time, possibly as soon as early July 1981.[86] Several factors contributed to the timing of the attack. Most prominent among these was the French announcement, less than a week before the attack, that President François Mitterrand had assured the Iraqis that the French government would provide the enriched uranium fuel necessary for the operation of Tammuz I.[87] In addition, just two weeks prior to the attack, several scientists at the French National Center for Scientific Research released a report that concluded that "the high flux Osirak reactor, capable of significant and efficient radiation levels, is well-suited for producing plutonium with a potential for the production of explosives."[88]

At the time of the raid there was a great deal of speculation that Prime Minister Begin had chosen early June for the attack in order to maximize the domestic political benefit. Preelection polls in Israel were forecasting a defeat for Begin's Likud party, which would have resulted in the prime minister's downfall. According to this hypothesis, Begin could have reached two conclusions: (1) If the Likud party lost a majority in the Israeli Knesset and Begin was forced to step down as prime minister, his probable successor was Shimon Peres, leader of the Labor

Party (who directed Israel's nuclear research program in the 1950s); or (2) the only way Begin could increase his standing in the polls would be to assert Israeli military power, providing yet another demonstration that Likud leadership would continue to guarantee Israel's security.

Begin had reason to doubt Peres's response to the Osirak threat should Peres become prime minister. In December 1980 Begin briefed Peres on the Iraqi nuclear program and on the Israeli contingency plan to bomb the Tuwaitha facility. In May 1980 Peres urged Begin to "refrain from taking any action," suggesting that an air strike would further isolate Israel from the moderate states in the Middle East and from the United States as well.[89] In addition, Peres and the Israeli Labor Party had close ties with the French Socialist Party, whose leader, François Mitterrand, had just been elected president.

Peres had reason to believe that Mitterrand's nuclear export policy would differ from that of his predecessor, Giscard d'Estaing. In addition, Mitterrand's statements during the election campaign and in the past had indicated a greater sympathy for Israel's security concerns than d'Estaing had exhibited. There is some evidence to support the hypothesis that Mitterrand's administration would alter French nuclear export policy. Weissman and Krosney have argued that the French president was in fact about to review a policy paper recommending a revision of France's nuclear agreement with Iraq. Mitterrand was expected to adopt the recommendations closing loopholes that had increased the potential for diversion of nuclear materials at Osirak.[90]

Radioactive Fallout

The Israeli government decided on the June attack date primarily because of its assessment that Osirak would shortly become operational or "hot." An attack after the reactor was operational would, according to this assessment, endanger the civilian population of Baghdad, exposing it to radioactivity released as a result of damage to the reactor vessel. The Israelis estimated that "the destruction of the Iraqi reactor even a short time following its start-up would have resulted in extremely high population exposures, and because no proper emergency organization exists for such cases, in potential loss of life, especially in the areas adjacent to the reactor."[91]

This assessment has been questioned and generally repudiated. For example, a study was commissioned by the Brookhaven National Laboratory on the effect of a nuclear accident at its reactor. The maximum fission product would be about the same for both reactors, so the comparison is instructive. In a memorandum W. A. Higgenbotham noted that the greatest danger from a rupture of the reactor vessel would be the release of iodine isotopes. The memo concluded that perhaps as much as 50 percent of the iodine might escape into the atmosphere and that the radiation might result in "serious, though not lethal doses to people in the immediate vicinity. The exposure in Baghdad, 19 miles away, would be comparable to the natural annual exposure or less."[92] The U.S. Department of Energy (DOE) corroborated this assessment and similarly concluded that "it is most likely that there would have been no adverse health effects at all in Baghdad and under no circumstances would such an attack have resulted in any prompt fatalities or even radiation sickness."[93] The DOE study assumed (in a worst case scenario) that Osirak had been operating long enough for the reactor to have consumed 30 percent of the fuel, which would have coincided with the highest possible fission-product inventory. Using a similar data base, the Congressional Research Service agreed with this analysis.[94]

Immediately after the bombing there was speculation as to the degree of possible damage to a reinforced structure like Osirak from conventional rather than nuclear munitions. Assuming pinpoint accuracy, the 2,000–lb ordinance used by the Israelis could have severely damaged (and in fact did damage) the reactor. These iron bombs were able to pierce up to eleven feet of concrete and up to fifteen inches of steel.[95]

The Secret Chamber

Of particular concern to Israeli intelligence officials was the installation of a small chamber directly below the reactor. Israeli prime minister Begin dramatically revealed the existence of this "secret" chamber located (according to him) forty meters below the reactor vessel. In fact, the chamber, reportedly destroyed in the Israeli raid, was located only four meters below the reactor (Begin later admitted to his mistake) and was designed to test the effect of radiation on a range of materials. Theoretically it would be possible to use this neutron-guide chamber to bombard U^{238} with a beam of neutrons, producing plutonium. The process, however, is extremely slow and not useful for any significant plutonium production.[96] This same chamber also exists at the French Osiris reactor at Saclay.

Begin's dramatic announcement was entirely inaccurate and very irritating to the French. In an interview with *The Washington Post*, President Mitterrand complained, arguing that Begin had made "an error in technical judgment" as well as a political error in publicly discussing the chamber without consulting the French beforehand.[97]

Rebuilding Osirak

The destruction of Osirak has obviously suspended any progress on the Iraqi nuclear program and its quest for a bomb. However, that suspension is in all probability temporary. The embarrassment caused by the successful attack was borne personally by Iraqi president Saddam Hussein and will probably stimulate an accelerated effort by Iraqi scientists to construct a new reactor and arrange for fuel. Funding the rebuilding of Tammuz I should not be difficult for Iraq. The Saudi Arabian government has announced its offer to finance the project, having discussed it with the French only a week after the attack.[98] The French government reportedly will supply the Iraqis with enriched fuel for the reactor, although Foreign Minister Claude Cheysson had announced that there would be a "doubling and quadrupling" of safeguards on any assistance effort.[99] In addition, U.S. government officials have said privately that the French are insisting on low-enriched uranium fuel, consistent with their announced policy. Recent reports indicate, however, that negotiations for rebuilding the facility are deadlocked and currently suspended. According to the author's discussions in the summer of 1984 with U.S. officials, there has been no new construction at the Tuwaitha facility, and the Iraqis are not currently pressing for the rebuilding of Osirak.

French concerns about a renewed military program at Osirak were heightened when Hussein called upon "all nations to help the Arabs acquire the atom bomb in order to deter Israel from using its nuclear weapons against the Arab nations."[100] In an interview with *The Washington Post*, President Mitterrand stated quite clearly that had he been prime minister when the secret French-Iraq agreement was negotiated, he "would have refused to sign the contract," or that he "at least would have called for additional guarantees concerning the nuclear policy of the country in question."[101]

The IAEA shared the French concerns. The agency's director general at the time, Sigvard Eklund, announced shortly after the Israeli bombing that additional safeguard measures had been planned for Osirak since October 1980, but were postponed due to the Iran-Iraq war. These measures were to have included biweekly inspections of Osirak and a "tamper-proof" automatic camera to record any changes in the reactor core.[102] It is not clear how safeguards will be altered if and when Osirak is rebuilt.

CONCLUSIONS

As this chapter has documented, there is a wealth of evidence to support a conclusion that the Iraqi nuclear research center at Tuwaitha was engaged in a clandestine effort to acquire the capability for bomb production. The following facts should be considered:

1. The Osirak reactor was modified at the request of Iraq to facilitate the production of a greater amount of plutonium;
2. The "hot cells" and other laboratories allowed reprocessing and fuel fabrication for which there was no civilian research requirement;
3. Iraq obtained large amounts of natural uranium which were unsuitable for operation of the Osirak reactor (as it ran only on highly enriched uranium fuel), but would provide the raw material for a reactor "blanket," thereby

allowing the production of plutonium. There is no other explanation for stockpiling such large amounts of natural uranium; and

4. Iraq had attempted covertly to secure uranium-metal fuel pins useful to the Iraqis only in plutonium production.

In all four of the above cases there was no plausible reason for Iraq to proceed along this course, unless a clandestine nuclear weapons program was proceeding.

As noted earlier, some of the evidence presented is ambiguous. It is unclear, for example, why the Iraqis purchased the Osirak reactor when other models would have been more suitable for a bomb project. The choice of Osirak, however, may reveal Hussein's ultimate intent. Extensive discussions with individuals having access to critical data suggest that President Hussein had two parallel goals: (1) to train a cadre of Iraqi scientists and engineers in the disciplines related to nuclear power; and (2) a clandestine effort to accumulate the raw materials required for nuclear weapons over a sufficiently long period of time so as not to alarm the international community or the IAEA. Hussein used Iraq's signature of the NPT to reduce proliferation concerns over the Tammuz nuclear research effort. This ruse allowed Iraq to pursue a nuclear weapon while publicly adhering to restrictions embodied in the agreements themselves. Had Iraq not been a signatory to the NPT, demands to investigate the nature of the Iraqi nuclear program would have been much greater—as was demonstrated by IAEA reluctance to launch an investigation into the Iraqi program even after the Israeli attack. Further, IAEA officials admit privately that monitoring practices at Osirak were less than airtight.[103]

The ambiguous nature of some evidence (particularly the choice of reactor) does not suggest a benign intent so much as it strongly implies a sophisticated and calculated program of deception and leverage to obtain covertly what could not be obtained openly. Finally, the difficulty in theorizing about Iraqi intentions is both a function of the very secretive nature of the Tuwaitha research program and the internal decisionmaking processes of the Iraqi leadership.[104]

The Responsibility of Nuclear Suppliers

French and Italian nuclear export policy toward Iraq was cavalier and remarkably irresponsible. The French government, while initially under extreme pressure to provide nuclear technology to Saddam Hussein, or face the possibility of an oil supply crisis, was careless in the extreme during its negotiations with Iraq. The administration of Giscard d'Estaing had some latitude in its early discussions with Hussein and could have presented alternatives to Osirak that would have provided Baghdad with a sophisticated research reactor without the attendant proliferation risks. The French had successfully dissuaded Iraq from the original demand of a gas-graphite reactor, and there is every reason to believe they might have been able to persuade Baghdad to consider a research model designed primarily for an embryonic nuclear program like Hussein's.

In fact, there is some evidence to suggest that the Iraqis were initially quite dependent on French counsel in the planning of their nuclear project. The Iraqi quest for a nuclear weapon was likely directed by individuals whose long-term goal was clear (the acquisition of a nuclear weapon), but who initially lacked any "strategic plan" in the pursuit of that goal. Sophistication about nuclear energy was so sparse that early choices of reactor models, for example, were born of a simplistic perception—that one could easily obtain the necessary military technology and hardware required for a weapons program on the market. At a later stage it became apparent that a permanent and indigenous scientific infrastructure would be required to maintain a nuclear research program and to apply this technical expertise to a wide range of other scientific pursuits. American officials have reported privately that while the Iraqi scientists were quite capable physicists, the lack of trained engineers and maintenance technicians retarded progress at Tuwaitha to the point where French technicians found they were engaged in daily routine tasks simply to ensure that construction of the reactor proceeded on schedule.[105] At this point the French government realized that any nuclear assistance effort would be a long-term commitment until a self-sustaining infrastructure was created. As a result, the French would have been able to manage the Iraqi program during a period when Hussein was just beginning to formulate a long-term prospectus.

Of importance to remember is that while Hussein held the levers of economic pressure, the French were one of the few potential suppliers of the reactor technology attractive to Iraq. That potential lever was not used by d'Estaing. Perhaps the most puzzling aspect of the French-Iraqi contract is the agreement to supply Osirak with highly enriched uranium fuel. The French did not actually deliver the fuel until after the Iran-Iraq war began. Although Paris was heavily dependent on Iraqi crude during the period of the contract, the Iran-Iraq war had severely reduced Iraqi exports to Western Europe, and particularly to the French, who were forced to replace Iraq as a primary source of crude. Thus, a threat from Baghdad to curtail oil exports was less credible; the leverage was greatly diluted. In addition, the war with Iran was invariably a great drain on the Iraqi treasury, and in fact the French oil market was even more valuable to Baghdad than in the past.[106]

The war had altered the political-military situation for the French. Had Paris insisted in the fall of 1980 (when the first order of highly enriched uranium fuel was shipped to Iraq) on supplying only "caramel" fuel for Osirak, the Iraqis would have been in a more vulnerable situation and might have been forced to accept this fuel as a substitute. Although burning "caramel" produces larger amounts of plutonium than highly enriched uranium fuel, reprocessing the spent fuel to obtain the plutonium is extremely difficult. In sum, the French government missed (or ignored) a significant opportunity to reduce the proliferation risks of Osirak, focusing instead on the large financial benefit to accrue from the lucrative fuel supply contract.

The current French president, François Mitterrand, has publicly stated his intention to limit fuel transfers to the Iraqis to only a low-enriched variant. He has also assured the IAEA that any agreement to rebuild Osirak would be accompanied by the most stringent safeguard provisions. [107] The French are clearly embarrassed by their role in the Iraqi nuclear program, and Mitterrand has indicated that French priorities will change. [108] However, the question of fuel supply probably will trigger another great bureaucratic debate within the French government. Some informed observers of the French nuclear energy bureaucracy have suggested privately that the Israeli raid has had very little effect on the direction of French nuclear export policy, and that officials at the French Atomic Energy Agency will continue to dominate the bureaucratic process, advocating policies that, from a proliferation standpoint, are irresponsible. Foreign Minister Dumas will have to convince Mitterrand that French foreign policy has been damaged by the Iraqi assistance effort, and that a new direction in nuclear export policy is in the interest of both France and the international nonproliferation regime.

The Italian agreement with Iraq is particularly troubling. Without the Italian-supplied "hot cells," Iraqi scientists would have been unable to reprocess spent fuel from the French reactor, and thus much of the proliferation concern surrounding Osirak would never have materialized. Apparently the major incentive and catalyst for the Italian agreement was a very lucrative contract to build four combat vessels for the Iraqi navy. In addition, U.S. officials have privately confirmed that the Italian government continues to abide by its original nuclear assistance agreement with Iraq, suggesting that the infamous "hot cells" (which were not damaged in the Israeli raid) may be operating.

One unanswered question is the extent to which the French and Italian governments were informed about each other's role in the Osirak project. Evidence offered privately by U.S. government officials, who had monitored the Iraqi nuclear program, suggests that Hussein was careful to compartmentalize the Italian and French efforts, restricting the movement of French technicians to French-sponsored facilities and limiting the movement of Italian technicians to the laboratories only.[109] The reason for such restrictions is obvious—to separate the two nationalities and to prevent their scientists and technicians from exchanging intelligence data. Nevertheless, the United States was aware of both contracts, and under the rubric of the London Suppliers Club, it had expressed concern to both the Italian and French governments about the Iraqi nuclear program.[110]

The French and Italian nuclear energy officials were clearly aware of Iraq's intention to utilize the two nuclear assistance agreements to obtain a nuclear weapon. Additionally evidence of a covert weapons program would unlikely have been withheld from the highest levels of the French and Italian governments. While several aspects of the Italian and French assistance efforts are troubling, the most dangerous is the failure to distinguish between strictly civilian nuclear research efforts and those that had an obvious military emphasis. Unless supplier states discriminate in their nuclear assistance efforts, there is no reasonable hope that ambitions like those of Hussein's will be dashed. Nuclear suppliers are the key to slowing the spread of military-nuclear technologies to the nonweapons states. Without their cooperation, the NPT and IAEA become worthless as effective retardants against nuclear proliferation.

Political-Military Implications of the Israeli Raid

The June 7, 1981, Israeli bombing of Osirak resolved the most immediate issue of whether Iraq would be allowed to proceed with its research effort to produce a nuclear explosive device. The raid devastated Baghdad's nuclear program, postponing any resumption of work at the Tuwaitha facility for at least several years. Such an unprecedented event inevitably raises a series of policy questions as well as moral issues. Prominent among these questions is whether the Israeli raid will be viewed as a precedent, encouraging other states (whose neighbors may be engaged in worrisome nuclear research) to emulate Israel and launch military initiatives against the nuclear facilities of their adversaries. The Indo-Pakistani relationship leaps to mind, for example.[111]

Israel's status as the preeminent military power in the Middle East virtually guaranteed no military response from either Iraq or its allies. Several factors would have contributed to this assessment, including Iraq's most immediate preoccupation—the war with Iran. That conflict is severely draining the Iraqi economy as oil revenues are small due to several incapacitating attacks on Iraqi refineries, pipelines, and tankers leaving Iraqi ports.

The only other state capable of launching an effective military reprisal against Israel is Egypt, which felt bound by its peace agreement with Israel and its participation in the ongoing dialogue of the Middle East peace process. In addition, former Egyptian president Anwar el-Sadat had publicly criticized President Hussein's anti-Israeli diatribes, and may not have been upset by the destruction of a nuclear energy installation built by a prominent Arab rejectionist leader, who (along with Libya's Qaddafi) led the criticism of Sadat's moderate policy toward Israel. Sadat's criticism of the Israeli raid was mild in comparison to that uttered by other states, including Saudi Arabia and Syria.

Saddam Hussein linked his desire for nuclear weapons with his condemnation of "the followers of Zionism." There is a history of Hussein's violent opposition, characterized by public statements that are among the most hostile uttered by an Arab leader, to the existence of Israel as a sovereign state. In August 1980, for example, during a debate over whether Arab nations should consider an economic boycott of any nation that continues to maintain an embassy in Jerusalem, Hussein offered his solution: "Some people may ask if this decision is the best that can be taken. *No, a better decision would be to destroy Tel Aviv with bombs"*[112] [emphasis added]. Such a declaratory policy that explicitly threatens the security of a regional state should dictate extreme caution on the part of nuclear supplier states. In that light, reports that Hussein has "acknowledged Israel's security concerns"[113] should be read with some skepticism.

An estimate of the effect of the Israeli raid on the Middle Eastern military balance is difficult to reach. Certainly another nuclear weapon state in the region would have altered the security calculations of states in the area and of the superpowers as well. One cannot ignore an Iraqi nuclear weapons capability in virtually any security assessment made of the region. Such a capability would also affect (and probably enhance) Hussein's standing in the Arab rejectionist community, and would exacerbate the longstanding rivalry between the Syrian Ba'th wing and the Baghdad Ba'th party. A nuclear-armed Iraq would probably complicate U.S. efforts in sponsoring a resolution of the Arab-Israeli dispute. Certainly Iraq would have to be taken seriously as a participant in an Arab-Israeli dialogue, which, to date, has not been the case. Armed with a nuclear weapon, Iraq might devote more attention to its quest for leadership of a Pan-

Arab movement. That quest would certainly affect the Arab-Israeli dialogue. There is a relationship between the heat generated by Arab rivalries in the region and resolution of the Arab-Israeli dispute. Some analysts have even suggested that resolution of the latter would refocus attention on the former.[114]

The Iraqi nuclear program has initiated a healthy reexamination of the process by which the international community monitors nuclear proliferation. It has also dramatically illustrated the extent to which that community is at the mercy of the political and economic exigencies of its members. Lessons will only be learned if the Iraqi effort results in altering the rules that govern the behavior of nuclear supplier and client states.

NOTES

1. Congressional Research Service, *Analysis of Six Issues About Nuclear Capabilities of India, Iran, Libya, and Pakistan* (Washington, D.C.: Government Printing Office, January 1982), p. 46.

2. The Baghdad Pact was a mutual assistance agreement signed in 1955 by Great Britain, Iran, Iraq, Pakistan, and Turkey. It was designed to protect Western security interests, particularly those of Turkey, against the Soviet Union. The Eisenhower administration favored the negotiation of separate alliances with Iran, Pakistan, and Turkey—the so-called northern tier—and thus never joined the Baghdad Pact. See John L. Gaddis, *Strategies of Containment: A Critical Appraisal of Postwar American National Security Policy* (Oxford: Oxford University Press, 1982), p. 152n.

3. Bruce Schechter, "Could Iraq Have Built the Bomb," *Discover* (August 1981): 61.

4. In its natural state, uranium contains only a small percentage of the isotope U^{235} which most easily undergoes fission (i.e., splitting of an atomic nucleus with a consequent release of a large amount of energy). As a result, uranium must be "enriched" to increase the level of U^{235} to the point where it is suitable for nuclear weapons.

The modification of the IRT–2000 and the replacement of 10 percent enriched fuel with 80 percent enriched material make it less difficult to use either the fuel directly for a nuclear weapon or to obtain plutonium from the spent fuel. It should be noted that the IRT–2000 has been operating with 80 percent enriched uranium for over six years, thus raising the possibility that by 1988 enough plutonium will have been accumulated for a small nuclear weapon. Additionally, because the reactor operates at such a low power level (5mw), inspections by the IAEA are infrequent, resulting in little available data concerning the reactor's operating history and increasing opportunities for clandestine activities.

5. The low power rating of the IRT–2000 greatly reduces immediate proliferation concerns.

6. Iraq's proven oil reserves are estimated at 41 billion barrels. Saudi Arabia's reserves—162 billion barrels—are the world's largest. See *Oil and Gas Journal* (December 27, 1982): 78–79.

7. See testimony by Joseph J. Malone in *The Israeli Air Strike*, Hearings before Committee on Foreign Relations, U.S. Senate, 97th Congress (Washington, D.C.: Government Printing Office, 1981), p. 263.

8. Shai Feldman, "The Bombing of Osirak—Revisited," *International Security* 7, no. 2 (Fall 1982): 131.

9. Quoted in Steve Weissman and Herbert Krosney, *The Islamic Bomb* (New York: New York Times Books, 1981), p. 91.

10. Author's interview with U.S. government officials.

11. Feldman, "The Bombing of Osirak," p. 115.

12. Weissman and Krosney, *The Islamic Bomb*, p. 92.

13. Feldman, "The Bombing of Osirak," p. 115.

14. Weissman and Krosney, *The Islamic Bomb*, p. 92.

15. The French refer publicly to the reactors as Osirak, while the Iraqis use the Arabic name Tammuz. Tammuz is the more "official" of the two.

16. See *The Iraqi Nuclear Threat—Why Israel Had to Act*, Government of Israel (Jerusalem: 1981), p. 9.

17. Saddam Hussein traveled to Saclay to tour the French nuclear center, where he viewed the Osiris and Isis reactors (the models for Tammuz I and II). The Osiris-Isis pairing is one of the few examples of a tandem nuclear reactor program. As originally conceived, Isis was a prototype of the larger Osiris reactor. As the French nuclear research effort grew, however, Isis was used as a test facility where experiments would be carried out at much lower power levels (800kw vs. 70mw in Osiris) before equipment was installed in the large reactor. The Iraqis operated Tammuz II in the same way the French used Isis—as a

testing facility for their scientists and to conduct experiments on reactor materials prior to installation in Tammuz I.

18. There is some debate over the actual operating level of Osirak. This debate, which bears significantly on the proliferation risks associated with the reactor, is explained in later sections.

19. Warren H. Donnelly, "Fact Sheet on the Iraqi Nuclear Research Reactor Bombed by Israel on June 7, 1981," Congressional Research Service, Library of Congress (1981), p. 1.

20. *Nucleonics Week* 22, no. 25 (June 25, 1981): 1.

21. One method of clandestine plutonium production is to construct a ring or "blanket" of uranium oxide around the reactor core. Large amounts of plutonium are produced, but the operation generates a great deal of heat, requiring additional cooling mechanisms. The Iraqi request for additional cooling systems at Osirak could be related to their intention to blanket the reactor core.

22. Hans Gruemm, "Safeguards and Tammuz: Setting the Record Straight," *IAEA Bulletin* 23, no. 4 (1981): 12.

23. The author, during his time in government, recalls that there was general interagency consensus on this question, although considerable debate occurred over interpretation of the evidence.

24. *Congressional Record*, 97th Cong., 1st Sess., March 17, 1981, p. S2236.

25. See "Cranston Says Pakistan Can Make A-Bomb," *The New York Times*, June 21, 1984, p. A–14.

26. Reprocessing is the separation (by various means) of potentially useful plutonium and unburned uranium fuel elements from other nonusable components of spent fuel. Arguments against reprocessing focus on the proliferation dangers and the improvident character of the process itself, given the depressed prices and ample supply of uranium. There is no commercial incentive to utilize plutonium so long as supplies of U^{235} are available at reasonable cost. See "Fuel Reprocessing and Spent Fuel Management," in *Nuclear Proliferation Factbook*, Prepared for the Committee on Foreign Relations, U.S. Senate (Washington, D.C.: Government Printing Office, 1980), p. 206.

27. Simon Rippon, "Reprocessing—What Went Wrong?" *Nuclear Engineering International* 21, no. 23 (February 1976): 21–27.

28. Ted Greenwood, Harold A. Feiveson, and Theodore Taylor, *Nuclear Proliferation* (New York: Council on Foreign Relations, 1976), p. 87.

29. Richard Wilson, "A Visit to the Bombed Nuclear Reactor at Tuwaitha, Iraq," *Nature* (March 31, 1983). Wilson does not argue, however, that his inability to identify a civilian use for neutron-beam experimentation suggests a nuclear weapons potential.

30. *International Energy Statistical Review,* Central Intelligence Agency (November 30, 1982).

31. This was the conclusion of the U.S. intelligence community.

32. *Middle East Economic Digest* 26 (December 17, 1982).

33. "Iraqi Pipeline Talks Head for Impasse," *Middle East Economic Digest* (July 20, 1984): 4.

34. See *International Energy Statistical Review,* Central Intelligence Agency, IESR 84–007 (July 31, 1984): 1–3.

35. *Worldwide Report: Nuclear Development and Proliferation,* Foreign Broadcast Information Service, October 20, 1980, p. 3.

36. During a recent discussion between the author and a senior French official, the French government unequivocally denied that it had provided Iraq with any reprocessing facilities.

37. Feldman, "The Bombing of Osirak," p. 118.

38. Weissman and Krosney, *The Islamic Bomb,* p. 101.

39. *The Iraqi Nuclear Threat,* p. 51.

40. Extensive discussions with individuals knowledgeable about the level of training at Osirak and the reactor's capacity revealed a nearly unanimous view that the Israeli estimate of plutonium production at Osirak was excessive and that a more realistic figure would be half that amount.

41. Thomas O'Toole, "Iraq Will Get Nuclear Laboratories," *The Washington Post,* March 19, 1980, p. A –26.

42. Richard Burt, "U.S. Says Italy Sells Iraq Atomic Bomb Technology," *The New York Times,* March 18, 1980, p. 1.

43. Ibid.

44. "Italy Supplying N–Technology to Iraq," *The Washington Post,* March 18, 1980, p. A–6.

45. "Italy Says It Consulted with U.S. on Nuclear Sale to Iraq," *The New York Times,* March 20, 1980, p. A–4.

46. Ibid.

47. Milton Benjamin, "France Plans to Sell Iraq Weapons-Grade Plutonium," *The Washington Post,* February 28, 1980, p. A–29.

48. Ibid.

49. Interviews with nonproliferation specialists and physicists confirm that a plutonium path was the only plausible proliferation route for Iraq since a uranium-based weapon could only be

obtained by directly diverting the reactor fuel, thus sacrificing the operation of the reactor itself. This would presumably result in inquiries by the French government and the IAEA. If those inquiries resulted in a determination that a clandestine bomb was being pursued at Osirak, the French would cease shipment of the highly enriched uranium fuel, and the Iraqis would realize only one or two bombs. A plutonium route, however, would theoretically allow the Iraqis to run the reactor while producing plutonium simultaneously.

50. "Brazil, Iraq Ink Pact for Nuclear Use," *Journal of Commerce* (January 9, 1980): 32.
51. Ibid.
52. Ibid.
53. *The Israeli Air Strike*, Hearings before the Committee on Foreign Relations, U.S. Senate, 97th Congress (Washington, D.C.: Government Printing Office, 1981), p. 263.
54. For an excellent and technically sophisticated treatment of the military applications of civilian nuclear energy programs and a discussion of the effectiveness of the nonproliferation regime on limiting such applications, see Albert Wohlstetter et al., *Swords from Plowshares* (Chicago: University of Chicago Press, 1979).
55. *Nuclear Fuel* 5, no. 10 (May 12, 1980): 2.
56. *Nucleonics Week* 22, no. 7 (February 19, 1981): 1.
57. *The Energy Daily* 8, no. 188 (October 2, 1980): 1–2.
58. Author's interviews with U.S. government officials.
59. *The Energy Daily*, p. 2.
60. Amos Perlmutter et al., *Two Minutes Over Baghdad* (London: Vallentine, Mitchell & Co., Ltd., 1982), p. 130.
61. Ronald Koven, "Saboteurs Bomb French Plant Constructing 2 Reactors for Iraq," *The Washington Post*, April 7, 1979, pp. A–1, A–7.
62. Weissman and Krosney, *The Islamic Bomb*, p. 232.
63. Flora Lewis, "France Imposes Blackout on News of its Inquiry into Blast at A–Plant," *The New York Times*, April 11, 1979, p. 14.
64. William Dowell, "Iraqi-French Nuclear Deal Worries Israel," *The Christian Science Monitor*, July 31, 1980, p. 10.
65. Weissman and Krosney, *The Islamic Bomb*, p. 240.
66. *Nucleonics Week* 21, no. 41 (October 9, 1980).
67. Felix Kessler, "Iraq to Keep Getting French Atomic Fuel Despite Iran's Attack on Nuclear Facility," *The Wall Street Journal*, October 17, 1980, p. 35.

68. Ibid.
69. Ronald Koven, "Baghdad Blocks Inspection of its Nuclear Reactors," *The Washington Post*, November 7, 1980, pp. A–1, A–25.
70. Ibid.
71. *The Jerusalem Post*, July 17, 1980.
72. Ibid.
73. *Science* 210, no. 31 (October 1980): 507.
74. Foreign Broadcast Information Service (FBIS), *Western Europe*, July 31, 1980, p. K–1.
75. Ibid., p. K–2.
76. *Ha'aretz* (Israel), reported in FBIS, *Middle East and North Africa*, June 9, 1981.
77. FBIS, *Middle East and North Africa*, December 18, 1981, p. I–17.
78. Amos Perlmutter, "The Israeli Raid on Iraq: A New Proliferation Landscape," *Strategic Review* (Winter 1982): 35.
79. *The Iraqi Nuclear Threat*, p. 37.
80. Article 51 is often cited by Israeli officials to justify military actions.
81. *The Iraqi Nuclear Threat*, p. 44.
82. Ibid., p. 45.
83. FBIS, *Middle East and North Africa*, June 11, 1981, p. E–4.
84. Ibid.
85. "Military Action on Iraqi Nuclear Research Center and its Implications for the Agency," *IAEA General Conference*, 25th Regular Session, p. 2.
86. Thomas O'Toole, "Plant Was To Be Ready Within Month," *The Washington Post*, July 9, 1981, p. A–12.
87. Ibid.
88. *The Israeli Air Strike*, p. 81.
89. *Ha'aretz* (Israel) in FBIS, *Middle East and North Africa*, June 9, 1981.
90. Mitterrand's statements during the election campaign and after the Osirak bombing suggested his concern for poorly drafted contracts that allowed potentially dangerous clandestine activities by nuclear recipient states.
91. *The Iraqi Nuclear Threat*, p. 44.
92. "Radioactive Fallout from Sabotage of OSIRAK," *Brookhaven National Laboratory Memorandum*, June 25, 1981, p. 1.
93. M. H. Dickerson et al., "Estimating the Maximum Credible Radiological Consequences of an Attack on the Iraqi Research Reactor," U.S. Department of Energy paper, p. 1.

94. Warren Donnelly, "Possible Contamination of Baghdad from Bombing of the Osiraq Reactor," *Congressional Research Service*, June 18, 1981, p. 5.

95. Bennett Ramberg, *Destruction of Nuclear Energy Facilities in War* (Boston: D.C. Heath, 1980), p. 66.

96. *Nucleonics Week* 22, no. 25 (June 25, 1981): 1.

97. Interview with François Mitterrand by the *The Washington Post* as reported in *Le Monde*, June 19, 1981, p. 3.

98. "Iraq Favoring Saudi Funding for Atom Plant," *The Wall Street Journal*, July 17, 1981, p. 18.

99. *Nucleonics Week* 22, no. 26 (July 2, 1981): 1.

100. "Iraq Favoring Saudi Funding for Atom Plant," p. 18.

101. Interview with François Mitterrand by the *The Washington Post*, op. cit., p. 3.

102. *World Business Weekly* (August 3, 1981): 19.

103. Author's discussion with IAEA officials.

104. I am grateful to Christine Helms of the Brookings Institution for an illuminating description of the Iraqi Ba'th bureaucracy. Also see the comprehensive study by Helms, *Iraq: Eastern Flank of the Arab World* (Washington, D.C.: The Brookings Institution, 1984).

105. Author's interviews with U.S. government officials. The French and Israelis differ in their assessment of the level of sophistication of Iraqi scientists and technicians: The French have said privately that the Osirak scientists lacked the technical competence to produce a nuclear weapon before 1985, while the Israelis felt production was imminent.

106. For a discussion of the economic aspects of the Iran-Iraq war, see Bijan Mossavar-Rahmani, "Economic Implications for Iran and Iraq," in *The Iran-Iraq War: Implications for Third Parties* (Tel Aviv: Jaffee Center for Strategic Studies of Tel Aviv University, 1984).

107. Author's discussion with IAEA officials.

108. The French government has assured State Department officials that President Mitterrand is seriously committed to a more responsible nuclear export policy than that followed by his predecessors.

109. Author's interviews with U.S. government officials.

110. Ibid.

111. Pakastani officials have offered privately that concern over an Indian nuclear weapons capability continues to be the dominating factor in assessing future relations with New Delhi.

112. FBIS, *Middle East and North Africa*, August 20, 1980.

113. See the report of a discussion between Saddam Hussein and U.S. congressman Stephen Solarz in Maamoun Youssef, "Iraqi President Acknowledges Israeli Need for 'State of Security'," *The Washington Post,* January 3, 1983, p. A –21.

114. See, for example, Henry S. Rowen and Richard Brody, "The Middle East: Regional Instabilities," in Joseph A. Yager, ed., *Nuclear Proliferation and U.S. Foreign Policy* (Washington, D.C.: The Brookings Institution, 1980), p. 193.

2 ISRAEL

George H. Quester

When Israel, some twenty-five years ago, was first suspected of seeking nuclear weapons, there was little evidence of Arab willingness to coexist with the Zionist state. Amid periodic references to pushing Israel "into the sea," and the subsequent Palestine Liberation Organization Covenant calling for a unified secular Palestinian state, Israelis could understandably conclude that their Arab neighbors intended to duplicate the ouster of the crusaders seven centuries earlier. A state whose very existence is threatened is then inevitably suspected of wanting nuclear weapons, for the threat posed by such weapons serves status quo powers much more than it serves the forces of irredentism.

Much has transpired in the Middle East during the last two decades. Israeli conventional military victories brought control of the West Bank, for a time the Sinai Desert, and more recently, a portion of southern Lebanon. Arab rhetoric has also changed in light of demonstrated Israeli military strength (and in light of rumors and assumptions regarding Israeli nuclear options). Still, some outsiders continue to conclude, as many Israelis continue to argue, that the Arabs would eliminate Israel tomorrow if there were an opportunity to do so.

43

RUMORS OF ISRAELI ACTIVITIES

One can produce nuclear weapons either with plutonium or with enriched uranium, and Israel is rumored to have pursued both avenues to the atomic bomb. As early as 1960 Israel reportedly had begun work on an unsafeguarded reactor at Dimona. First described by the Israeli government as a "textile plant," the reactor was supplied secretly by the French government and apparently became operational in 1963.

The Dimona reactor had an initial thermal capacity of approximately twenty-six megawatts (mw), which could generate eight to ten kilograms of plutonium annually, an amount required for the production of one atomic bomb. Claims have been advanced that Dimona's capacity was expanded in the 1970s to approximately 70mw, which if true would have increased the plutonium flow enough to produce three atomic bombs each year. Thus, for decades the Dimona reactor has been considered the world's largest unsafeguarded facility (outside the admitted nuclear weapons states), capable of producing fissionable materials for an atomic bomb. Even at a rate of one bomb per year, Israel could stockpile as many as twenty "bombs in the basement." Another reactor capable of producing plutonium exists in Israel, but this facility, at Nahal-Soreq, supplied openly by the United States, has been under International Atomic Energy Agency (IAEA) safeguards throughout its years of operation, and has not been the object of any serious weapons speculation.[1]

Additionally rumors have circulated about Israeli research work on bomb design, including computer programming intended to simulate the achievement of critical mass for a nuclear explosion. Thirty-nine years after the world's first nuclear detonation at Alamogordo, there is now little need for an actual test-detonation of a nuclear device to ensure that it would work in a real war. (Even the first such weapon used in combat—the uranium bomb dropped on Hiroshima—had never been "tested," since the test explosion at Alamogordo was of a plutonium device, a design substantially different from that of the uranium bomb.)

The necessary delivery systems are already at hand for combat use of nuclear warheads in the Middle East, so this factor does not offer any assurances against proliferation. The jet airliners and transports of the various countries in the region could be used to carry nuclear weapons. More directly and importantly, these weapons could be deployed by the advanced fighter-bombers possessed by all the air forces in the area. Cities—the most salient targets in the Middle East—are generally close to the bases from which an adversary would strike. Also within Israeli reach are foreign warships in the Mediterranean Sea and in the Persian Gulf, as well as the cities of the southern Soviet Union. Thus, there are no inherent or insurmountable obstacles to Israel's possession, or use, of nuclear weapons.

Almost all of these rumors and reports are more interesting than reliable. A clear example is the *Time* magazine report of April 1976 indicating that American reconnaissance planes had seen Israeli nuclear warheads being moved from their bunkers to air fields during the darker days of the 1973 Middle East war.[2] Since it is difficult to envisage what would make any nuclear warheads, of either plutonium or enriched uranium, so visible from the air or from space, the entire report loses credibility.

Similarly spectacular "cloak and dagger" stories tell of Israeli exploits in the stealing, or clandestine purchase, of fissionable materials. They also allude to Israeli secret service interference with Arab efforts to obtain similar materials. Some of these reports turn out to be quite factual—a prime example was the Israeli air force attack on the Iraqi reactor at Tuwaitha—but others remain speculative.

The Purpose of Rumors

While these rumors can never be validated, one can establish that the source of such rumors has in a number of instances been the Israeli government itself, or at least sources known to be agents of Israel. A most brazen example came in 1969 when Israeli agents in the United States openly inquired whether the F–4's they were purchasing could be fitted with bomb racks suitable for nuclear weapons. This request was certain to be denied, but was also sure to be leaked to reporters in Washington and around the world.[3] Paradoxically another major source citing a possible Israeli stockpile of nuclear weapons has been the Arab governments.

By what logic could it be in the interests of two such total adversaries to circulate the same reports and rumors about nuclear weapons? If such reports serve the national interests of one side, should they not be seen as undermining the interests of the other side? The Arabs circulate such reports presumably hoping that there will be international political and moral reaction against further nuclear proliferation. They advance an accusation for which Americans and Europeans might condemn the Israelis if the reports were proven true. When Israeli agents attempt to circulate similar reports, their actions presumably reflect the Israeli government's belief that such rumors (as long as they are not confirmed) will not bring such condemnation as to outweigh intimidation of the Arab states.

When the rumors of bomb projects begin to attract too much attention, the Israelis then elect to mute them with various forms of governmental denial. After a time, some Arabs must feel that these rumors are not bringing condemnation of Israel; rather, they are reinforcing deterrence, and psychologically undermining the Arab cause. Consequently Arab leaders will dispute the validity of these rumors, seeking to shift the subject of discussion to the failings of Israel, or to the prospect of future conventional conflicts.

RUMORS OF ARAB NUCLEAR ACTIVITIES

Recently one has heard rumors about nuclear weapons capabilities for a number of pro-Arab states. The Libyan regime of Colonel Muammar el-Qaddafi reportedly requested assistance for nuclear weapons projects from France, China, and India. There is further speculation regarding Libyan assistance to Pakistani nuclear projects—both in terms of money and the movement of uranium from Niger, with the implication that Pakistan might willingly share any resulting "Islamic bomb" with its Libyan benefactor.[4] Concerns have also been raised about the intentions of Iraq, which has invested in the Osirak nuclear reactor purchased from France, and in "hot cells" purchased from Italy—facilities that would expedite the production of nuclear weapons.[5]

Both Libya and Iraq are signatories of the Treaty on the Non-Proliferation of Nuclear Weapons (NPT), and thus are required to place their peaceful nuclear facilities under the IAEA safeguards. Israel, which destroyed the Iraqi reactor despite the fact that the reactor was under IAEA safeguards, contended that Iraq had means of deceiving and bypassing IAEA inspectors and that the Baghdad regime intended to use the facility for nuclear weapons purposes.

Iraq and Libya are thus the two principal sources of concern about nuclear proliferation in the Arab world. Earlier, when Egypt showed interest in nuclear reactors, similar objections were voiced, but such projects have languished and Egyptian moderation toward Israel has lessened tensions. Nonetheless, the possibility remains that any Pakistani nuclear weapon, once developed, might be deployed on behalf of the Arab states confronting Israel, just as Pakistani fighter pilots and military officers have reportedly been deployed in the past.

ISRAELI DENIAL OF ASSURANCES TO NEIGHBORS

The official Israeli declaratory posture on possible nuclear weapons projects, at least since 1964, has been standardized: "Israel will not be the first country to introduce nuclear weapons into the Middle East."[6] Since the United States was already the first by the presence of its Sixth Fleet in the Mediterranean, with the Soviet Union's Fifth Eskadra a likely second, the Israeli statement is far less forthcoming and reassuring than it sounds; the statement seems intended to soothe the feelings of friends, while keeping alive the deterring anxieties of enemies. Implicit in the formulation is the threat that Israel would not allow much time to elapse, after Arab acquisition of nuclear weapons, before it would elect to be identified as "the second" (Israel might very well have bombs ready for assembly in some basement or bunker). The ambiguity of the Israeli position was voiced by Yigal Allon in 1964 when he was quoted as saying,

"Israel would not be the first to introduce nuclear weapons into the Middle East, but it would not be the second either."[7]

Other Israeli leaks have converged along the same lines, always covered by official Israeli government statements that all speculation about Israeli nuclear weapons was idle, yet reinforcing the impression that most of the preparatory work for any weapons acquisition had already been accomplished.

Israel has rejected the imposition of IAEA safeguards on its facility at Dimona, advancing various arguments about the unreliability of such safeguards, or presumed bias on the part of IAEA inspectors. Israel has not signed the NPT and has given no indication that it would like to do so.

Until 1975 Israel basically demanded conventional arms control and disarmament as a prerequisite for any nuclear disarmament discussions. This posture made perfect sense since the conventional warfare possibility was the Arabs' one hope of bringing Israel to terms, while the nuclear possibility was Israel's strong suit. Since 1975 this precondition has been dropped, but the Israeli endorsement of a nuclear-weapon-free zone is now premised on at least two other conditions rendering Arab acceptance of such a zone difficult: first, that the agreement be negotiated directly by the parties affected; and second, that it include Pakistan and India.

The Israeli government thus managed to slide into a position of endorsing, rather than scoffing at, the idea of a nuclear-weapon-free zone including Israel and its neighbors. The change in position may have been intended to defuse international criticism of the Israeli refusal to accept IAEA inspection. Couched on the model of the Tlatelolco Latin American nuclear-weapon-free zone (i.e., negotiated for the region by the parties within the region), the new Israeli position presupposes direct negotiations with the Arabs, thus requiring some degree of Arab recognition.

Various Arab governments have called for the submission of Israeli facilities to IAEA safeguards, and more recently have asked for the establishment of a safeguarded nuclear-weapon-free zone in the Middle East. But such Arab proposals suggest that this zone be legislated and inaugurated by the UN General Assembly, or by some other organ of the United Nations, thereby avoiding prior Arab-Israeli negotiations that might acknowledge the legitimacy of Israel's status quo. Any such recognition, according to Arab spokesmen, must be withheld as a bargaining chip, and the Arab Palestinians might wish to hold it back forever, on the grounds that the Israelis are not morally entitled to such recognition.

After two decades of unsafeguarded operation of the Israeli reactor at Dimona, not to mention the other possibilities of an Israeli clandestine acquisition of fissionable material, Arab interest in an imposition of IAEA safeguards may seem a little paradoxical. While the safeguards of the Vienna agency might ensure that no further bomb material is produced, it would be a far larger, probably unattainable, task for the agency to assure the Arabs and the world that no bomb materials had been squirreled away, that is, that Israel had no "bombs in the basement." The effectiveness and relevance of IAEA inspection might be severely challenged if Israel did adhere to NPT safeguards, or to some Middle East regional nuclear-weapon-free zone. The current IAEA safeguards on the U.S.-supplied Israeli research reactor at Nahal Soreq are not being questioned, but the Arabs obviously fear that Israeli bombs have been produced elsewhere, since safeguards are not "full-scope" for Israel.

Yet Arab attitudes, seemingly bizarre on technological considerations, are not so unrealistic politically. If and when Israel submits to safeguards, it will dim the impression that it is coveting a nuclear weapons stockpile. Over time, Israeli submission to safeguards could lead to demands for a fuller accounting of the fissionable plutonium that might have been produced. Even if such demands were not raised, or were not met, a commitment to pledges comparable to those of the NPT would steer the internal Israeli debate away from a reliance on nuclear weapons options.

Another prominent issue regarding Middle East nuclear developments is the extent of American surveillance that has been accepted by the Israelis. No formal safeguards, American or IAEA, have ever been accepted for Dimona. Yet the United States apparently applied strong pressure on Israel in the 1960s to tolerate some *de facto* American inspection, with the result that two "visits" a year by American government nuclear specialists were accepted.[8] Since these operations were labeled "visits" rather than "inspections," Israeli feelings may have been assuaged, and the U.S. government may have been reassured that no bombs were in production. (As an ironic footnote, no true "visits" were thereafter tolerated, even if they simply entailed a walk around the Dimona facility, since further "visits" might then have been construed in the Israeli Knesset as an increase in the intensity of inspection.)

Given American pressure, and given Israeli strategic needs, it is therefore possible that this arrangement left the United States fully assured against Israeli "bombs in a basement," but assured in a form that was not convincing to the Arab powers—the best of all worlds from an Israeli standpoint. Analysts need to know more about the effectiveness of such American visits and how often and for how long they were conducted. If a similar compromise is still in effect as the *quid pro quo* for major U.S. economic and conventional military assistance, the agreement by its very nature would have to remain hidden from the outside world. Once again speculation thus replaces factual knowledge about Israeli nuclear weapons potential.

The Arab victory in denying Israeli credentials at the general conference of the IAEA in September 1982 raises some interesting questions about Arab strategy and political assumptions. Perhaps the Arabs deliberately chose the IAEA, rather than the United Nations Educational, Scientific, and Cultural Organization (UNESCO) or the International Telecommunications Union (ITU), to force the issue, precisely because they sensed that the United States and some of its Western allies had a vested interest in keeping the Vienna agency going, specifically for its contribution to halting nuclear proliferation. Expecting that the United States would not risk the demise of the IAEA or reduce its participation in the agency in protest over an insult to Israel, the Arabs presumably pushed the issue to embarrass Washington in its relations with the Israeli government. Thus, the U.S. suspension of its IAEA participation for five months (until February of 1983) must have come as a surprise, particularly the upset this caused for the general antiproliferation effort around the globe.

Do the Arab nations then desire a demise of the IAEA, if this might be the result of such a crisis following an American withdrawal? In attempting to keep the Middle East conflict non-nuclear, many Arab states do not want the IAEA to collapse.

Despite their demand for the expulsion of Israel from the agency, they have over the same years demanded the extension of IAEA safeguards to all Israeli nuclear facilities, most especially to the worrisome Dimona reactor. Perhaps Iraq and Libya might desire a weakening of the IAEA, for they have had to submit to IAEA safeguards, and may regard this intervention as a nuisance or worse. But the Arab neighbors of these two regimes surely do not look forward to any termination of international safeguards.[9]

Of course, some Arabs may have given up on the relevance of safeguards to their problem. But such a resignation to a more explicit Israeli nuclear weapons status has surely not gripped the Arab states yet, or has at least not gripped them equally.

ISRAELI POLICY CHOICES AND POLICY PAYOFFS

Israel's own public discussion of the nuclear weapons issue has grown in magnitude over the past decade. Earlier the Israeli press and public accepted a self-imposed censorship: One did not speculate about possibilities, but patriotically accepted official Israeli government dismissals as if these statements were straightforward responses to all the nuances of the question. Israeli newspapers would occasionally carry press speculation about rumors of Israeli bomb projects, but these reports rarely led to any public discussion, even among Israeli academics interested in arms policy.

Such self-restraint inevitably wore out. The years of Prime Minister Menachem Begin opened up deeper rifts in Israeli public opinion than had surfaced earlier. The opening to Egyptian president Anwar el-Sadat, the strident nationalism of Begin's Likud party, the foreign accusations of secret nuclear activity, and the costs of the Lebanon invasion made Israeli foreign policy discussion more tumultuous and interesting. During the late 1970s, before and after Osirak, fuller exploration of the nuclear issue was initiated. Some commentators advocated an open Israeli acquisition of nuclear weapons. Others vigorously opposed the acquisition, while a few demanded Israeli submission to a ban on nuclear weapons, accompanied by IAEA safeguards. Yet, according to recent Israeli public opinion polls, the average Israeli apparently concludes that Israel has nuclear weapons, or will soon get them, and is supportive of the idea.

One very important and interesting area of open analysis centers on whether an Israeli acquisition of nuclear warheads would be consistent with Israeli moderation in foreign policy, and perhaps with Arab accommodation. The straightforward "dove/hawk" dichotomy over the issue of nuclear weapons exists in Israel like anywhere else. However, the more thoughtful "dove" might see advantages in nuclear weaponry rather than conventional arms, while the more thoughtful "hawk" might see symmetrical advantages to staying away from any such reliance on the nuclear side.[10]

The standard Israeli justification for occupying such ethnically Arab territories as the West Bank is that a conventional defense of Israel will be impossible without the buffer such territories provide. An explicit Israeli acquisition of nuclear weapons, in some "dovish" Israelis' view, might make such buffers less necessary, and thus eliminate the excuse for territorial expansion which Begin and his supporters have desired.

Arab critics of Israeli policy often like to tie all their indictments together into a continuous whole, and thus sometimes claim that Israeli nuclear weapons have been used for expansion. Yet the opposite linkage is at least as likely to apply, as expansionists may see territory as a preferable alternative to nuclear weapons, or see an absence of nuclear weapons as an excuse for expansion.

If the Israeli military performance against the Syrians and the PLO in Lebanon in 1982 holds any lessons for the nuclear proliferation issue, the lessons have to be mixed. As the most advanced in Soviet tanks were destroyed by Israeli anti-tank weapons, and as the latest in Soviet-supplied anti-aircraft missiles proved ineffective against Israeli fighter-bombers, the immediate lesson was that the Arabs did not have a significant advantage in conventional warfare, and that Israel would have had less reason than ever to brandish "bombs in a basement."[11] Holding a buffer in southern Lebanon, and the possibility of a negotiated settlement with the new Lebanese government (by which Lebanon would opt out of war), Israel might have been expected to relax.

Yet the casualties imposed on the Arab civilian population in Lebanon, capped by the final massacre of Palestinian refugees by a Lebanese Christian militia, turned world opinion against Israel, and in particular against the government of Prime Minister Begin. Feeling more than ever like a "pariah," in danger of expulsion from the United Nations, the Israelis might have felt the need to count on nuclear weapons as their ultimate "ace in the hole"—their ultimate reminder to the world that Israel cannot be ignored or forgotten as a nation, cannot be pushed into the sea, or made into a nonnation by international parliamentary fiat.

Have the rumors and possibilities of Israeli nuclear weapons as yet had any impact? It is just as difficult to prove such impact as it is to prove that Israel has such weapons, but some indications of the impact do exist.

Exactly why President Sadat elected to go to Jerusalem to begin normalization of relations with Israel will never be known. Concern for the economic burdens of constant military preparation, or other forms of weariness with the struggle, must have played a role. Defenders of Sadat's approach argue that his initiatives served to liberate the West Bank, or more of Palestine from Israeli rule, by forcing Israel to make concessions, and by turning world opinion against Israel as the Arabs show themselves to be more moderate. Yet another explanation of Sadat's policy could easily be traced to the persistent rumors of Israeli nuclear weapons, as the Egyptians realize that a conventional-war defeat of Israel would lead to nuclear retaliation against Cairo, Alexandria, and the Aswan Dam.

Those skeptical of the impact of potential Israeli nuclear deterrents can point to the Egyptian and Syrian decisions to attack Israel in the 1973 Yom Kippur war. If the threat of Israeli nuclear retaliation is so awesome (given that rumors of Israeli bomb projects had been in circulation already for more than a decade), how could Sadat have dared to send his troops across the Suez Canal?

The evidence suggests, however, that the Egyptian offensive was planned from the outset to achieve very limited territorial advances, and the Syrian offensive apparently was not more ambitious than this either. Such Arab moderation can be explained partly by the need for the security blanket of surface-to-air missiles that effectively reduced the impact of Israeli tactical air power.[12] However, another reason for this restraint and moderation would be fully consistent with a respect for Israeli nuclear deterrence.[13]

One can attempt to wrest territory away from a nuclear power as long as one does not threaten the internal territories and very existence of that power. If Arab tank columns had ever posed a direct threat to Israel's center, rather than merely reclaiming Egyptian territories east of the Suez Canal, then more serious Israeli responses would have had to be feared.

THE INVOLVEMENT OF THE OUTSIDE WORLD

Rumors of Israel's nuclear weapons potential have often cited alleged accomplices. If materials were stolen from the United States or Western Europe, these democratic regimes, long sympathetic to Israel, naturally are suspected of acquiescing to such thefts.[14] Impossible to prove or disprove, charges have come from Arab sources and from the Soviet Union and Eastern Europe. On balance, these allegations are far more likely to be false than true, for the societies involved are too open to permit a lengthy cover-up of such complicity—complicity contradicting U.S. and other attempts to prevent nuclear proliferation.

Additional rumors have linked Israel with states that similarly face military threats from neighbors, and similarly are ostracized by such international bodies as the UN General Assembly. Because of its possession of natural uranium deposits, and its advanced scientific competence in the nuclear field, South Africa has been accused several times of conspiracy with Israel. In return for South African nuclear technology assistance, Israel perhaps has offered conventional military aid (or even nuclear engineering assistance in a pooling effort).[15] Some other nuclear partners may include Taiwan, South Korea, Brazil, and Argentina.

The United States is clearly opposed to the further spread of nuclear weapons, even if the emphasis of American governments has vacillated. The Reagan administration's approach, for example, is certainly more low-key and subtle than that of the Carter administration. Nonetheless, the United States also opposes any threats to the national existence of Israel. Americans desire peace in the Middle East, but not a peace achieved simply by removing the Israeli thorn from the Arab side.

Indeed, some U.S. policymakers and analysts might quietly welcome the rumors of Israeli nuclear weapons, as long as they are not confirmed by any detonations (test detonations or use in combat), or by any official pronouncements claiming such weapons. Such "quasi-proliferation" has curiously less of a "domino" impact than would a more explicit acquisition of nuclear arms. If the rumors and possibilities of Israeli nuclear weapons played any role in encouraging former President Sadat to visit Israel, or in pressuring other Arab states to coexist with Israel, Americans will quietly applaud this strategic gimmick that forced the Arabs to confront a different reality.

While the American attitude toward Israeli nuclear armaments is somewhat ambivalent, the Soviet attitude is more pronounced. If ever Israel should be confronted with a kind of desperate Massada situation, in which Israel lashed out at Arab cities as a last-gasp act of revenge, it is not beyond the imagination, or the technological possibility, that Israel might attack Soviet targets to spread the revenge where it was due.

Soviet warships in the Mediterranean Sea or cities in the southern Soviet Union might be Israeli targets. There are scenarios for one-way missions, stretching to the limits the range and carrying capacity of U.S.-supplied fighter-bombers. Whether or not the Israelis would ever launch F–4's with nuclear warheads on a kamikaze strike at Odessa, the accusation has been made that the Israeli government has floated such ideas, for whatever deterrent and warning effect this would have on the USSR. Soviet officials have never publicly endorsed the elimination of Israel as espoused by the PLO. Having voted for the United Nations partition plan of 1948 (the plan that would have left Jerusalem under international control, and Arabs with more land than they were to hold at the end of the fighting in 1949), the Soviet Union still remains committed to this partition, rather than to the Palestinian Arab dream of a "unified secular" (i.e., non-Israeli) Palestine. Moscow's moderation is reinforced by a recognition that any war in the region could become a nuclear war, and that any such war could later engulf the superpowers.

Americans, similarly, cannot with any equanimity shrug off Israeli nuclear threats to Soviet cities, because of humane considerations or because the safety of American cities against a Soviet intercontinental missile attack depends on the safety of the Soviet cities. American concern about continued war in the Middle East and its global repercussions is an important ingredient for general U.S. opposition to nuclear proliferation, in the Middle East, or South Asia, or South America, or anywhere else.

If Israel were to detonate a nuclear warhead, or were publicly to proclaim that it had such warheads, the world—which at the moment still treats the rumors of Israeli "bombs in a basement" as only interesting speculation—would regard proliferation as having occurred. Israel may have done more in the nuclear weapons field thus far than has India, but the Indian detonation of a "peaceful nuclear explosive" in 1974 had a larger impact in alarming the world about further nuclear proliferation.

Factors as psychological and illogical as these can thus make a great deal of difference in politics. The United States will still have accomplished something quite significant for arms control if it achieves nothing more than holding Israel where it has been on the nuclear front—holding Israel indeed where it has been for the past twenty years.

NOTES

1. For some much earlier discussions of Israeli nuclear weapons capability see John W. Finney, "U.S. Hears Israel Moves Toward A-Bomb Potential," *The New York Times*, December 19, 1960, p. A–1; Dana Adams Schmidt, "Israel Assures U.S. On Reactor," *The New York Times*, December 22, 1960, p. A–5; C. L. Sulzberger, "The Little Old Man in the Desert," *The New York Times*, November 16, 1963, p. A–26; George H. Quester, "Israel and the Nuclear Non-Proliferation Treaty," *Bulletin of the Atomic Scientists* 25, no. 6 (June 1969): 7–9, 44–45; Fuad (Paul) Jabber, *Israel and Nuclear Weapons* (London: Chatto and Windus, 1971); Hedrick Smith, "U.S. Assumes the Israelis Have A-Bomb or Its Parts," *The New York Times*, July 18, 1970, p. A–1; William Beecher, "Israel Believed Producing Missile of

Atom Capability," *The New York Times*, October 5, 1971, p. A–1; Avigdor Hasselkorn, "Israel: From an Option to a Bomb in a Basement?" in R. M. Lawrence and J. Larus, eds., *Nuclear Proliferation: Phase II* (Lawrence, Kansas: University of Kansas Press, 1974), pp. 149–82; Todd Friedman, "Israel's Nuclear Option," *Bulletin of the Atomic Scientists* 30, no. 7 (September 1974): 30–36; Lawrence Freedman, "Israel's Nuclear Policy," *Survival* 17, no. 3 (May-June 1975): 114–20; Robert E. Harkavy, "The Pariah State Syndrome," *Orbis* 21, no. 3 (Fall 1977): 623–50. Also, for an extraordinarily valuable extended discussion, see Robert E. Harkavy, *Spectre of a Middle Eastern Holocaust: The Strategic and Diplomatic Implications of the Israeli Nuclear Weapons Program* (Denver: University of Denver Monograph Series in World Affairs, 1977).

For an insightful discussion of the possible impact of the Israeli nuclear weapons potential, see Steven J. Rosen, "Nuclearization and Stability in the Middle East," in Onkar Marwah and Ann Schulz, eds., *Nuclear Proliferation and the Near-Nuclear Countries* (Cambridge, Mass.: Ballinger, 1975), pp. 157–84. Also extremely valuable is Paul Jabber, *A Nuclear Middle East: Infrastructure, Likely Military Postures and Prospects for Strategic Stability*, U.C.L.A. Center for Arms Control and International Security Working Paper No. 6 (Los Angeles, 1977).

2. "How Israel Got the Bomb," *Time* 107, no. 15 (April 12, 1976): 39–40.

3. See Nicholar Valery, "Israel's Silent Gamble with the Bomb," *New Scientist* 64, no. 927 (December 12, 1974): 809.

4. See Steve Weissman and Herbert Krosney, *The Islamic Bomb* (New York: New York Times Books, 1981) for a fascinating and detailed account of alleged Libyan and Pakistani moves toward nuclear weapons.

5. A statement of concern about Iraqi suspect intentions can be found in Shai Feldman, "The Bombing of Osiraq—Revisited," *International Security* 7, no. 2 (Fall 1982): 114–42.

6. See Yair Evron, "Israel and Nuclear Weapons," in Jae Kyu Park, ed., *Nuclear Proliferation in Developing Countries* (Seoul: The Institute for Far Eastern Studies, 1979), p. 124.

7. Quoted in Ernest W. Lefever, *Nuclear Arms in the Third World* (Washington, D.C.: The Brookings Institution, 1979), p. 67.

8. See Shlomo Aronson, *Israel's Nuclear Options*, U.C.L.A. Center for Arms Control and International Security Working Paper No. 7 (Los Angeles, 1977), pp. 1–3.

9. From an American point of view, the situation would have been far better if the gauntlet had been thrown down first by the Arabs at the meeting of the ITU, thereby allowing the United States to withdraw from that less important international agency in order to teach the world a lesson. The lesson, having being learned, would then have made it possible for Israel and the United States to remain within the IAEA. But the sequence was the reverse. The gauntlet was thrown first in the September IAEA meeting; America suspended participation in the more important IAEA, which then precluded an expulsion of Israel at the subsequent meeting of the ITU. Bad luck, or bad strategic management by the United States, or bad intelligence prognosis by the Arabs may have produced an outcome that no one would have wanted.

10. The question of whether the possession of nuclear weapons would encourage Israeli moderation or intransigence toward the Arab states is discussed at greater length in Uri Bar-Joseph, "The Hidden Debate: The Formation of Nuclear Doctrines in the Middle East," *The Journal of Strategic Studies* 5, no. 2 (June 1982): 210–23; and Aronson, *Israel's Nuclear Options*, pp. 24–34.

11. *The New York Times*, July 10, 1982, p. A–1.

12. Trevor Nevitt Dupuy, *The Elusive Victory* (New York: Harper & Row, 1978), pp. 387–405.

13. See Aronson, *Israel's Nuclear Options*, pp. 10–20.

14. The allegations on the possible disappearance of sensitive nuclear materials from the Apollo, Pennsylvania facility are outlined in Weissman and Krosney, *The Islamic Bomb*, pp. 119–24.

15. With regard to uranium enrichment, Israel may have access to whatever progress South Africa has made in the jet nozzle separation process. In exchange, Israel may be contributing the services of its nuclear physicists to help the South Africans in this venture.

3 INDIA AND PAKISTAN

Richard P. Cronin

The danger of nuclear proliferation in South Asia is great and by most indications growing. India exploded a plutonium device underground in 1974 and continues to pursue an ambitious nuclear effort encompassing the entire fuel cycle. Pakistan is now close to achieving the capability to conduct a nuclear explosion. A hopeful thaw in Indo-Pakistani relations during late 1982 and early 1983 has been reversed substantially as a consequence of increasing political instability in both states and mutual charges of interference in each other's internal affairs. Both countries see a nuclear weapons option as important to their territorial integrity, independence, and national identities. Other countries argue that the nuclear activities of India and Pakistan pose grave risks to peace and stability in South Asia, and threaten the present "fire break" against the spread of nuclear weapons to regional powers. Additionally Pakistan's location and political identification with the Arab states makes its nuclear program a factor in the volatile Middle East equation.

The views put forth in this chapter are the author's own, and do not necessarily represent those of the Congressional Research Service of the Library of Congress.

Four primary considerations influence the prospects for proliferation in South Asia: (1) the technical capabilities and resources of each state; (2) the nuclear policy decisionmaking process in each country; (3) the dynamics of Indo-Pakistani rivalry and other security motivations; and (4) the susceptibility of each state to external leverage. A more difficult process is constructing policy options for the United States or other nations concerned about proliferation.

The best opportunities for deterring proliferation in South Asia slipped by before the nuclear supplier countries adopted stringent export policies. Belated punitive efforts by the United States in the last several years—such as cutting off economic and military assistance to Pakistan and unilaterally suspending the fuel supply agreement covering India's U.S.-built Tarapur Atomic Power Station—had foreign policy costs deemed unacceptable to some in light of the Soviet invasion of Afghanistan and other disturbances of the regional equilibrium. Current U.S. policies toward India and Pakistan contain both incentives to discourage proliferation and the promise of serious sanctions should either country take further initiatives to acquire nuclear weapons. These achievements, however, do not appear to deter an inexorable movement toward the development or deployment of nuclear weapons.

The primary nuclear suppliers have had limited success in slowing the development of a nuclear weapons capability in South Asia. As a result of actions taken by Canada, the United States, and the Soviet Union, India has had to accept costly delays in its nuclear program in order to avoid submitting new facilities to the inspections and safeguards of the International Atomic Energy Agency (IAEA). The United States succeeded in pressuring France to withdraw from a nuclear reprocessing facility project in Pakistan, and the United States, Canada, and various European governments have impeded Pakistan's access to technology and components for its uranium-enrichment program.

Supplier countries and security partners still can have an impact, but because of the earlier failure to control the export of critical technology the long-run prospect for proliferation in South Asia will be governed largely by the dynamics of Indo-Pakistani relations and their military aspirations.

NUCLEAR CAPABILITIES OF INDIA AND PAKISTAN

The nuclear programs of India and Pakistan reflect the different priorities and resources of each country.[1] India maintains a broad-based, energy-oriented program that envisions a three-stage effort involving: (1) natural uranium fuel reactors; (2) a fast breeder reactor program, fueled with plutonium from the first phase; and (3) a thorium-uranium fuel cycle utilizing India's large reserves of thorium sands. Except for the use of plutonium produced by a small research reactor to conduct its nuclear test in 1974, the Indian effort has not been overtly geared to a weapons program. The comprehensiveness of the Indian effort, however, provides a natural cover for developing a nuclear weapons program, especially given India's emphasis on "self-sufficiency"—a code word for the avoidance of international safeguards. Due to its security perceptions, scarce resources, and limited scientific manpower, Pakistan's efforts more clearly suggest a strategy to develop a nuclear explosive capability in advance of a balanced civil nuclear program.[2]

Indian Nuclear Capabilities

Indian nuclear activities date from the establishment of the Tata Institute of Fundamental Research in 1945 and the formation of the Indian Atomic Energy Commission in 1948 under the chairmanship of Dr. Homi Bhaba. Although Indian sources maintain that the country only has a laboratory-scale enrichment capability, India has an indigenous capability to produce its own natural uranium fuel, to fabricate the fuel, to construct CANDU (Canadian-Deuterium-Uranium) reactors, to produce the heavy water to modulate them, and to reprocess the spent fuel into weapons-grade plutonium. India also has a significant research and industrial infrastructure including: the Bhabba Atomic Research Centre, the Kalpakkam (Madras) Reactor Research Centre, the Hyderabad nuclear fuel complex, three public-sector industrial companies, a Power Products Engineering Division for designing, constructing, and operating nuclear power plants, private-sector satellite suppliers, and three government-sponsored teaching and research institutions.[3]

Research reactors are India's prime source of weapons-grade plutonium (Pu^{239}). Three of India's eight research reactors in operation or under construction are significant in terms of plutonium production. India's Canadian-supplied, forty megawatt (mw) CIRUS (Canadian-Indian-Reactor-U.S.) heavy water, natural uranium reactor, which became operational in 1960, can produce about nine kilograms of plutonium a year—enough for one bomb—and was the source of plutonium for India's 1974 blast. R–5, a 100mw unit near completion, will be able to produce two and a half to three times that amount.[4] Together, these two reactors could theoretically produce enough material for a modest weapons program. A new research reactor at Trombay, called Dhruva, was commissioned in summer 1984 and will add to CIRUS's plutonium output even before R–5 is commissioned.[5] None of these reactors is under international inspection and safeguards.

In addition to the Tarapur Atomic Power Station (supplied by the United States in the 1960s), India has four power stations, each with two 200–220mw reactors in operation, under construction, or in advanced stages of planning. These units are all CANDU-type, heavy water–modulated, natural uranium–fueled reactors. Plants completed or under construction include the Rajasthan Atomic Power Plant (RAPP–I and –II), the Madras Atomic Power Plant (MAPP–I and –II), and similar twin reactor stations at Narora, in Uttar Pradesh state, and Kakrapar, in Gujarat state.

The first unit of the Rajasthan Atomic Power Plant (RAPP–I) began operation in December 1973. Following the 1974 Indian nuclear explosion, Canada ceased cooperation with India, and RAPP–II was completed by India in April 1981, years behind schedule. Both units have suffered repeated breakdowns due to deficient engineering quality control and a shortage of heavy water. An accidental dumping of waste water closed RAPP for months, and repeated outages have resulted from problems with fuel bundles and end shields, which also result in heavy water losses.[6]

India has five heavy water plants, but only one small plant (Nangal), producing 14 metric tons a year, has been reliably operational, and half of its output is dedicated to the CIRUS research reactor. Two other units designed to produce 67 and 71 tons per year (Baroda and Tuticorin, respectively) have been plagued by breakdowns and feedstock shortages. An explosion and fire in 1977 delayed the Baroda plant by several years. A fourth plant (Talcher) is designed to produce 63 tons. A fifth plant (Kota) will produce 100 tons per year when it completes commissioning.[7] Two additional units are under construction. As of late 1981 India was only producing about 30 tons of heavy water annually.[8] Heavy water output reportedly grew significantly in 1984 based on improved performance of the Baroda and Tuticorin plants, but the government told the Indian Parliament that it was not in the public interest to reveal actual production figures.[9]

The shortages of heavy water have seriously upset India's nuclear power program. The use of Soviet-supplied heavy water resulted in RAPP–II being brought under safeguards against India's wishes. India deferred the start-up of MAPP–I from early 1982 until late 1983 in order to wait for Indian-produced heavy water and thereby avoid safeguards.[10] The heavy water shortfall could also affect the commissioning of the R-5 research reactor, scheduled for completion in 1984.[11]

These setbacks in India's heavy water program, and the resultant delays in bringing the CANDU power reactors on line, inevitably slow the breeder reactor phase of India's three-stage nuclear development program and limit its weapons option. At present India produces no substantial output of unsafeguarded spent power reactor fuel that could be reprocessed and used in the fast breeder program. As a consequence, the fast breeder test reactor might have to employ CIRUS-produced plutonium to avoid safeguards,[12] thus placing it in competition with any warhead requirements.[13]

A further limitation on India's nuclear weapons capability arises from its modest reprocessing capability. India has only two operational reprocessing facilities. They are a small pilot plant at Trombay (near Bombay), which probably reprocessed fuel waste from the CIRUS research reactor to produce the material for the 1974 explosion, and a larger, but still modest, facility at Tarapur intended to reprocess spent fuel from the Tarapur and Rajasthan reactors. Tarapur has also been used to separate uranium-233 from irradiated thorium for the very small Purnima–II test reactor, which achieved criticality on May 11, 1984.[14] A third plant at Madras—to handle waste from the Kalpakkam (Madras) and Narora (Uttar Pradesh state) reactors—is still in the planning phase.[15] During 1983 the Tarapur plant began reprocessing spent fuel from RAPP under IAEA safeguards. India has officially scorned reports in the U.S. press, presumed to be based on U.S. governmental sources, that Indian reprocessing operations could provide sufficient quantities of weapons-grade plutonium for up to twenty bombs per year.[16]

Although Pakistan claims that India possesses several nuclear weapons, there is no published evidence that India has any operational nuclear weapons capability.[17] However, there is little doubt about India's ability to develop a small nuclear arsenal. The comprehensiveness of its nuclear and space programs is such that a nuclear missile capability is theoretically achievable. In addition to the warhead requirements, which are presumably within its capability from indigenous sources, India's sizable force of Jaguar and MiG–23 aircraft, if suitably modified, could carry certain types of nuclear weapons. India has already launched three satellites into orbit, the most recent weighing 38kg, with its own rocket. The present satellite launch vehicle (SLV–3) is only comparable in payload to the U.S. Scout rocket, but a new-generation launch vehicle planned for the late 1980s will have a 800–1,000kg payload capability, enough for an intermediate-range ballistic missile (IRBM).[18] Due to delays in India's rocket program, the large payload, polar satellite launch vehicle may not be available until the 1990s.[19] Whether India can acquire the necessary guidance technology for an accurate IRBM is uncertain; however, hitting a Pakistani city would not be a difficult technological feat.

Pakistan's Nuclear Capabilities

Pakistan's nuclear program dates from about 1955, when the government formed a committee of distinguished scientists charged with drafting a comprehensive nuclear energy plan. The Pakistan Atomic Energy Commission, created in 1956 under the chairmanship of Dr. Nazir Ahmad, undertook the task of creating the requisite manpower base by sending scientists and engineers abroad under various "Atoms for Peace"-type programs. Between 1955 and 1965 several hundred Pakistanis were trained at foreign research sites, including Harwell in the United Kingdom, and the Argonne, Oak Ridge, and Brookhaven laboratories in the United States.[20]

Pakistan's one power reactor, Karachi Nuclear Power Plant (KANUPP), a small 125mw plant supplied by Canada on a turnkey basis, became operational in 1972. The KANUPP facility is a natural uranium, heavy water reactor of the CANDU-type, which according to some sources can produce as much as 55kg per year of plutonium (enough for four to six bombs) when operating at peak capacity. However, the reactor has never operated at full capacity, and since 1977 it has often operated at a sharply reduced level due to a cut-off in Canadian fuel supplies.[21] The Pakistan Institute of Nuclear Science and Technology (PINSTECH) in Islamabad also has a small U.S.-supplied, five megawatt swimming pool-type research reactor installed in the early 1960s.[22] Both reactors are under international safeguards.

Pakistan has solicited bids for construction of a 900mw light water, low-enriched-uranium–fueled power plant on the Indus River at Chasma, where it can draw hydroelectric power. Construction of the plant is subject to obtaining financing and a willing supplier. Reportedly the United States has sought to persuade potential suppliers, including the West Europeans and the Japanese, not to sell a reactor to Pakistan unless it agreed to put all of its nuclear facilities—not just the reactor in question—under international inspection and safeguards.[23] The French company, Framatome, received government authorization to prepare a bid, and French foreign minister Claude Cheysson, during a March 1983 visit to Islamabad, indicated that France would not require full-scope safeguards as a condition for supplying the reactor.[24] However, there is some speculation that France made its offer for foreign policy reasons with full knowledge that the financing of the project was so uncertain that it was unlikely to be undertaken.[25]

One source of concern about Pakistan's nuclear program is its ability to fabricate its own fuel rods using unsafeguarded uranium at the Chasma site. Pakistan reportedly possesses significant uranium deposits in the Suleiman Ranges in the vicinity of Dera Ghazi Khan and near Gilgit, and has a pilot plant for the extraction of uranium at the Atomic Minerals Centre at Lahore.[26] Pakistan has also acquired sizable quantities of "yellow cake"—the first stage of refining uranium—from Niger. This capability and limitations on the safeguards at KANUPP raised fears that Pakistan might have tried irradiating indigenous fuel rods to obtain a source of fissile material.[27] However, following complaints by the International Atomic Energy Agency, Pakistan accepted upgraded safeguards at KANUPP.[28]

The cancellation of the French reprocessing facility at Chasma did not prevent Pakistan from moving forward to acquire the capability to separate plutonium from spent fuel. First, Pakistan is apparently continuing work on the Chasma facility based on its alleged possession of 95 percent or more of the blueprints. Second, a French- and Belgian-assisted "hot cell" facility installed at PINSTECH in the mid-1970s could potentially produce small amounts of plutonium.[29] In a comprehensive assessment of Pakistan's nuclear activities on June 21, 1984, Senator Alan Cranston claimed that "well-informed observers" believed that the facilities had undergone cold tests in 1982 and had since processed radioactive material. According to Senator Cranston, the facility can produce up to fifteen grams of plutonium per year, enough for about one bomb.[30]

Pakistan is now known to be pursuing a second route to a bomb capability by constructing a clandestine centrifuge uranium-enrichment facility at Kahuta, near Rawalpindi/Islamabad. A small pilot plant at Sihala (the existence of which has been acknowledged by President Mohammad ul-Haq Zia) may also be involved.[31] In a lengthy interview with an Urdu language newspaper in February 1984, the head of Pakistan's enrichment effort, Dr. Abdul Qadir Khan, claimed that Pakistan had the capability to enrich uranium to reactor grade (i.e., about 3 percent), ostensibly for a future light water reactor.[32] According to Senator Cranston, the Kahuta plant now has a capacity to produce about 45kg of weapons-grade, highly enriched uranium (HEU) annually, and Pakistan has procured hardware to build a plant capable of producing 90–120kg of HEU annually.[33]

Pakistan is also believed to have some of the building blocks of a warhead delivery system. Reportedly this capability includes "blast wave" detonation technology and aircraft, including both the U.S. F–16's and older Mirage IIIs and Vs that can be rigged to carry a crude nuclear weapon.[34] An Indian source also claims that Pakistan has entered into a secret agreement with Otrag, the West German rocket company—once linked with a Libyan nuclear program—for a rocket launch system.[35] The arrest of three Pakistani nationals in Houston in July 1984 for attempting to illegally export fifty krytrons (high-speed switches capable of use in nuclear warheads) raised additional concerns about how close Pakistan might be to a bomb capability.[36]

Although the record of Pakistan's nuclear activities includes allegations of Libyan-supplied "yellow cake" from Nigeran, Libyan, and Saudi Arabian financing and illicit Western private technical collaboration, one of the most troubling concerns is the possibility of Chinese aid to Pakistan's presumed weapons program. Speculation centers around former President Zulfikar Ali Bhutto's visit to the People's Republic of China in May 1976. One cause for suspicion is Bhutto's cryptic reference during his testimony before the Pakistan Supreme Court. In response to the government's charges against him, Bhutto stated:

> . . . My single most important achievement is an agreement which I arrived at after an assiduous and tenacious endeavour spanning over eleven years of negotiations. In the present context, the agreement of mine, concluded in June 1976, will perhaps be my greatest achievement and contribution to the survival of our people and nation.[37]

Eleven years dates back to the 1965 India-Pakistan war, in which China threatened but failed to intervene on Pakistan's behalf. China also failed to intervene in the subsequent 1971 conflict over the emergence of Bangladesh. A more benign interpretation suggests a secret Chinese security arrangement with Pakistan against India. However, as if confirming the suspicions of Chinese cooperation with Pakistan's nuclear program, the Reagan administration reportedly suspended discussions on nuclear cooperation with China based on concern about possible Chinese assistance to Pakistan's nuclear enrichment program.[38] These concerns apparently remain a sticking point, and are reported to be holding up submission to Congress of a U.S.-Chinese nuclear cooperation agreement initialed during President Ronald Reagan's trip to China in April-May 1984.[39]

In May 1979 then assistant secretary of state for oceans and international environmental and scientific affairs, Thomas R. Pickering, estimated that Pakistan needed two to five years to acquire enough explosive material through enrichment for a nuclear explosion.[40] Five years later the estimate appears incorrect at least as far as the enrichment route is concerned, but Dr. Abdul Qadir Khan's interview implies significant progress on the centrifuge program. While less is known about Pakistan's recent progress on reprocessing, some analysts believe that Pakistan already has enough material for an explosive device by this method but not enough for a weapons program.

Indian defense experts view the enrichment program as the main focus of Pakistan's weapons-oriented activities, and profess to take seriously Dr. Khan's claim that "we have left India far behind in enriching uranium." Khan has said publicly that making a bomb was essentially a "political decision," and that if asked to do so, Pakistan's scientists "will not disappoint the country."[41]

If the claim is true, the achievement of an enrichment capability by Pakistan has been carried out despite the efforts of the United States and other Western countries to prevent Pakistan's acquisition of dual-use technology, especially electric inverters and centrifuge components. Western observers are much more skeptical about the significance of Pakistan's capability than Indian analysts who, understandably, may be inclined to take a worst case view. Mastery of the technology to enrich a small amount of material to a low degree of purity is not the same as the ability to produce quantities of highly enriched uranium for a weapons program.[42] However, the information cited by Senator Cranston, if accurate, suggests that Pakistan has made remarkable progress and can already enrich a significant amount of material to weapons-grade. Certainly the acknowledgement by Pakistan of some enrichment capability, coupled with evidence that Pakistan has sought to obtain parts for triggering devices, is cause for concern that the country is very near to an explosive capability and intends to produce a number of bombs or explosive devices.

Observations on the Indian and Pakistani Nuclear Programs

Pakistan periodically has announced ambitious plans for civilian nuclear power, but its strategy defies logical analysis except for a presumed weapons program. Pakistan had justified the Chasma reprocessing facility on the basis of an ambitious and wholly unrealizable program of adding one heavy water power reactor per year into the 1990s. There was no reasonable requirement for such a large-capacity reprocessing facility, given the existence of only the small heavy water reactor at Karachi. Likewise, Pakistan had no need for an enrichment capability, at least until it solicited bids for the light water reactor to be located at Chasma.

India has a broad-based civil power program that is plausible on paper but that clearly allows a nuclear weapons option. India's efforts to minimize its submission to international inspections and safeguards are consistent with its opposition to "discriminatory" nonproliferation regimes, but also serve to protect the nuclear option. However, self-sufficiency has led to significant delays both to India's civil power program and its ability to build a nuclear arsenal from unsafeguarded fissile materials. On the one hand, this sacrifice implies that, except for the capability to counter a limited Pakistani weapons program, India's aspirations to become a weapons power are conceived in a long-term framework. On the other hand, India simply may have overestimated its ability to carry out its plans without foreign collaboration. As R. R. Subramaniam and C. Raja Mohan have observed, "The Indian nuclear decision makers seemed to have bungled at the levels of overall strategy of production, technological choice and project management."[43]

NUCLEAR DECISIONMAKING IN INDIA AND PAKISTAN

In both India and Pakistan, as might be expected, the most sensitive nuclear decisions are made by the highest political authority. Below that level, however, the politics of nuclear decisionmaking are rather different in each country.

In India the operational decisions have always been made by the scientific and bureaucratic communities, specifically the Ministry of Atomic Energy, the Ministry of Science and Technology, the Department of Atomic Energy (DAE), the Atomic Energy Commission, and the Bhabba Atomic Research Centre.

From the beginning India's scientific leadership has guided the nuclear program under the overall direction of the political authorities. The decision to undertake a nuclear explosion in 1974 was Prime Minister Indira Gandhi's. Plans made by the scientists, politicians, and bureaucrats have been carried out amid an open public debate regarding national self-interests. There is an active lobby of defense strategists, politicians, and publicists outside the decisionmaking circle which promotes a nuclear weapons program, as well as a vocal, albeit smaller, group of nuclear weapons opponents. Thus, political and scientific policies are made against the background of a lively public discussion among the country's elites. The one unpublicized factor is the attitude of the Indian military concerning the utility of a nuclear weapons program. According to an Indian journalist, "Opinion within the armed forces alone has continued to be a professionally guarded and basically unknown factor."[44] Others see the Indian military as split over the nuclear issue, but in any event, not central to the decisionmaking process.[45]

Earlier, Pakistan's nuclear program was largely under the control of civilian scientists and bureaucrats, though the lines were certainly blurred during the administrations of generals Ayub Khan and Yahya Khan (1958–1969). Even during these periods, with the exception of a 1967–71 hiatus, Zulfikar Ali Bhutto dominated the nuclear decisionmaking process as foreign minister, minister for fuel, power, and natural resources, and minister in charge of Pakistan's Atomic Energy Commission (PAEC). After becoming prime minister in 1971 Bhutto strengthened his control of the Pakistani nuclear program. He created and headed a new Ministry of Science, Technology and Production, and made himself chairman of the PAEC.

The seizure of power by General Zia in 1977 largely eliminated what separation had existed between the military and civilians in the nuclear decisionmaking process, as military men moved into nearly every governmental department. Bhutto was thought by many to have kept the nuclear program in his own hands as one source of countervailing power against the military. After July 1977 the military became the predominant decisionmakers. In his death-cell testament Bhutto accused General Zia of acquiescing in the cancellation of the French reprocessing plant in exchange for Western backing for the military regime, and of forsaking the country's security against an Indian bomb.[46]

The effort to produce fissile material, however, may be split between the PAEC civilians and the army. General Zia himself now holds the portfolio for science and technology. Munir Ahmad Khan—a Bhutto appointee—continues as chairman of the PAEC, and was given another three-year term in March 1984.[47] The uranium-enrichment effort is still headed by Abdul Qader Khan, while the army may be running the Kahuta reprocessing project. According to one report, the army is so deeply involved in the Kahuta project that any reduction in the project's status could jeopardize the president's relations with the officer corps, which is the main basis of his support. The director of the army's Special Works Organization (more recently known as the Civil Works Organization), which built the Kahuta facility, was promoted to major-general and made adjutant-general of the army.[48] In his February 1984 interview Dr. Abdul Qadir Khan stated that both army and air force engineers had contributed to the "electronic and mechanical engineering aspects of the project."[49]

At least until the December 1984 referendum which confirmed him as president for five more years, General Zia was not thought by most analysts to wield untrammeled personal power as Bhutto could at his peak. Nuclear decisionmaking probably is still reached collectively by Zia and his senior colleagues with due regard to the technical advice of scientists and senior PAEC bureaucrats. Dr. A. Q. Khan attributed recent progress in the enrichment program to "the personal interest and efforts" of President General Mohammad Zia ul-Haq and Finance Minister Ghulam Ishaq Khan, and their friends.[50]

THE DYNAMICS OF THE INDO-PAKISTANI RIVALRY

Although India's nuclear ambitions derive from other factors—notably the Chinese nuclear capability and prestige considerations—the crux of the proliferation issue lies in the Indo-Pakistani rivalry. This adversarial relationship has communal and religious roots that are as deep and pervasive as the Arab-Israeli conflict, although softened somewhat by a common past and shared cultural traditions.

The main issue of contention is both countries' claims to the former, nominally independent state of Jammu and Kashmir, a territory of approximately 86,000 square miles at the apex of the frontiers of Afghanistan, China, India, and Pakistan. The *de facto* boundary has changed little since the 1948 cease-fire, although it was the scene of action during both the 1965 and 1971 Indo-Pakistani wars. Pakistan holds about one-third of the total area in a territory called Azad ("free") Kashmir, while the balance, including the strategic Vale of Kashmir, constitutes the Indian state of Jammu and Kashmir.

The Kashmir dispute is not an insignificant matter, as the contested territory has considerable strategic and political importance. The strategic Karakoram highway between Pakistan and China passes through the Pakistani-controlled part of the disputed area. India's loss of the fertile and populous Vale of Kashmir would make moot its claim to the Aksai Chin region of Ladakh, a northern district of Kashmir, now controlled by China,[51] and would threaten Punjab state, India's granary. Pakistan's loss of Azad Kashmir would cost it strategically important regions bordering on Afghanistan and China, and result in the loss of a land-link with its closest ally.

Beyond the territorial dispute is an even more fundamental conflict involving each country's identity and aspirations. For Pakistan, the accession of Kashmir's Hindu ruler to India in 1948 undercut Pakistan's formative concept as the homeland for the Muslims of British India. For India, the retention of Kashmir, along with large pockets of Muslims throughout the rest of the country, confirmed its secular identity, despite an overwhelming Hindu majority. At least ninety million Muslims, and possibly more than Pakistan's total population of about ninety-two million, now live in India. India's multi-religious society and its official secularism, recently tarnished by growing communal strife, remains a continuing challenge to the "two nation" theory that provided the rationale for the creation of Pakistan. While India is determined to enjoy regional predominance befitting its size and population, Pakistan continually strives to achieve equality of status.

The Military Balance

A more concrete issue is the existing power imbalance between India and Pakistan—a critical source of the nuclear rivalry. The military balance has never completely reflected the imbalance of population and economic power, partly due to Pakistan's successful exploitation of its strategic position in securing U.S. and Chinese aid, as well as an important military supply relationship with France and financial support from friendly Muslim states.

Pakistan maintains about twenty army divisions, India thirty-one. Of India's thirty-one divisions, ten are mountain divisions, nine of which are deployed along the Chinese border. The exact number of Pakistani divisions positioned near the Afghan frontier (including deployments in western Punjab) is a guarded military secret. Currently India counts approximately fourteen Pakistani divisions (twelve infantry and two armored) stretched out along the common frontier from the Arabian Sea coast to northern Kashmir.[52] These divisions are opposed by about fifteen Indian divisions (thirteen infantry and two armored).

Greater disparities exist in the numbers of tanks and combat aircraft, which are, respectively, two to one and three to one in India's favor. Given the limited logistical reserves on both sides, the marginal utility of tanks in the mountainous Kashmir region, and the existence of large irrigation canal barriers on the plains, neither side now appears in a position to make major strategic gains in a future conflict. In time, however, India's growing military preponderance and the presence of Soviet troops on Pakistan's northern border could prove decisive.

India's numerical superiority and existing nuclear lead, coupled with geographical factors (being long and narrow, all of Pakistan is within range of Indian combat aircraft), encourage Pakistan to develop a nuclear option. Acquisition of nuclear weapons by either party mandates their possession by the other, both for deterrence and the prevention of a decisive asymmetry.

Trends in Indo-Pakistani Relations

Since the Soviet invasion of Afghanistan, Indo-Pakistani relations have undergone both stress and change, and are currently more bitter than at any time since the 1971 war. Initially India's tacit acceptance of the Soviet occupation of Afghanistan and Pakistan's subsequent efforts to bolster its diplomatic and security position by acquiring U.S. weapons caused India to react with harsh words and vague warnings of "war clouds" hanging over the region. India's ire focused not on the destabilizing action of the Soviet Union but on U.S. responses, including the Indian Ocean buildup and the effort to renew security ties with Pakistan. These developments coincided with new evidence concerning Pakistan's nuclear activities.

On September 15, 1981, Islamabad offered a nonaggression pact to New Delhi as a footnote to its announcement that Pakistan had reached an agreement with the United States on a six-year $3.2 billion aid package—including the purchase of forty F–16 aircraft. The Indians reacted with suspicion and saw the offer merely as a ploy to allay fears in the U.S. Congress that American weapons would again be employed in a subcontinental war.

Ultimately, after some six months, Pakistan's persistence in pressing its suit wore down Indian objections. The Gandhi government found it increasingly difficult to explain its refusal to take up the Pakistani offer of talks, and its stance also impeded efforts to improve relations with the United States, then an important foreign policy goal.

In January 1982 Pakistan's foreign minister, Agha Shahi, went to New Delhi for discussions about normalizing relations. Prime Minister Gandhi countered Pakistan's no-war pact offer with her own proposal for a peace and friendship treaty, and for the establishment of a joint commission for resolving bilateral issues. Agha Shahi departed New Delhi with both sides having agreed in principle to establish the joint commission and to hold further discussions on alternative normalization proposals. After a temporary hiatus caused by a rift over Kashmir at a meeting of the UN Human Rights Commission in Vienna, the talks got back on track in May when India's foreign minister, P. V. Narasimha Rao, visited Islamabad and delivered a letter from Mrs. Gandhi to General Zia. The talks were resumed in Islamabad at the foreign minister's level in August.

An apparent breakthrough occurred in early November 1982 when President Zia met briefly with Prime Minister Gandhi while en route to Malaysia. Earlier, Mrs. Gandhi had rejected a summit meeting as premature, but she reversed her position and received General Zia cordially. The leaders agreed to go ahead with the joint commission proposal and to hold normalization discussions soon. In late December the Indian and Pakistani foreign secretaries met in New Delhi and reached agreement on the formation of a joint commission co-chaired by the foreign ministers of each country, which was to meet alternately in New Delhi and Islamabad on an annual basis. The agreement provided for the creation of subcommissions to promote cooperation in economic, cultural, educational, tourism, travel, information, scientific, and technical areas. The joint commission was formally ratified by President Zia and Prime Minister Gandhi in March 1983, just prior to the meeting of Non-Aligned Nations in New Delhi.

The countries failed to resolve more fundamental concerns. Key disagreements included India's insistence that bilateral issues such as Kashmir could not be raised in international or multilateral forums, and Pakistan's refusal to agree to a formula that would forbid foreign—i.e., American—bases.[53] While it has repeatedly denied any desire to grant facilities to the United States, Pakistan wants the term "foreign bases" defined so as not to foreclose its options in an emergency, such as a Soviet attack, or to yield its sovereign rights to make such agreements as suits its interests.[54]

Beginning in mid-1983 relations began to deteriorate as both countries entered periods of heightened political instability.

Pakistani charges of Indian interference during antigovernment disturbances in Sind Province[55] were followed by Indian allegations of Pakistani support to extremist groups in Punjab and Jammu and Kashmir states.[56]

Developments in 1984 brought into question whether any possibility of a rapproachement exists in the nearterm, thus underscoring the dangers posed by the introduction of nuclear weapons into the equation. In May 1984 the Indian foreign secretary visited Islamabad and resumed a high-level political dialogue. The foreign secretaries initialed agreements liberalizing travel and visa procedures, and agreed to meet in New Delhi in August to take up the alternative no-war pact and peace and friendship treaty proposals.[57] Less than a month later, in the aftermath of the Indian army's bloody assault on Sikh extremists at the Golden Temple, in the border city of Amritsar, the fragile progress received a new setback. Strains resulting from Indian charges that Pakistan had trained and armed the Sikh militants were only partly eased by Islamabad's correct and efficient handling of the subsequent hijacking of an Indian Airlines plane to Lahore. In mid-July India abruptly requested a postponement of the foreign secretary's talks scheduled for August 7 and 8 and the second meeting of the India-Pakistan Joint Commission, citing a need to "allow ourselves a little time to assess the results of recent contacts between the two countries."[58]

Prime Minister Indira Gandhi's assassination by Sikh extremists further embittered relations. Prime Minister Rajiv Gandhi has expressed a desire for better relations and welcomed President Zia's decision to bring to trial a number of Sikh hijackers. Indian policymakers, however, still see the hand of Pakistan in the ongoing Sikh insurgency in Punjab and remain deeply concerned about Pakistan's nuclear activities.

Implications of Current Trends

Recent developments show that the two countries have not by any means abandoned their thirty-five-year-long rivalry, least of all in the nuclear area. Differences over normalization procedures are not merely semantic. Pakistan seeks a no-war pact to remove the principal liability of Indian emnity—the threat of attack by superior forces while it faces a new front in Afghanistan. A no-war pact formula would also reduce the likelihood of an Indian preemptive strike on Pakistan's nuclear installations. India, obviously, has a different agenda—one that seeks to ensure Pakistan's inability to overturn the status quo by constraining its external relationships. India also seeks a broader normalization of relations regarding trade, travel, information exchange, and other subjects that could prove threatening both to Pakistan's authoritarian system and its highly protected industries.

The difficulty of the nuclear issue is that Pakistan's search for parity clashes directly with India's regional aspirations. India's weapons option initially was a response to China's entry into the nuclear club and to the Indian-Chinese border war. Over the long term, India perceives China as its primary strategic threat. China has not given up its claims to territory held by India, including Arunachal Pradesh state (formerly the Northeast Frontier Agency). Although India can probably mount a successful conventional defense of its frontier, one fear is that China would use its nuclear advantage to force an Indian capitulation. India is determined to maintain its regional preeminence over Pakistan, all the more so in view of the close Sino-Pakistani relationship. Pakistan's acquisition of a nuclear "equalizer" would undermine India's hard-won conventional superiority and cause it, at a minimum, to undertake a weapons program of its own or trump Pakistan's ace by exploding a hydrogen bomb.

OUTLOOK FOR PROLIFERATION IN SOUTH ASIA

The motives and evolution of the nuclear programs of India and Pakistan and the diminishing impact of Western nonproliferation efforts underscore the danger of nuclear proliferation in the region.

The best hope of deterring proliferation in both countries probably lies with India and Pakistan themselves. At present, both have an apparent interest in not moving beyond a certain point. Pakistan has made important progress in strengthening its military forces in the face of a serious threat to the north and a perceived, continuing threat from India. What is hard to decipher is precisely how each country perceives the utility of nuclear weapons, and under what circumstances each will reveal its hand. Statements by officials and policymakers in each country suggest that both states see nuclear weapons as part of their future defense. While A. Q. Khan's motives have been variously interpreted, his remarks have not been officially rebutted and have struck responsive chords in the government-controlled press. At this point, both countries appear set on a course of promoting a greater sense of ambiguity about their capabilities and intentions.

Neither India nor Pakistan can be forced to abandon its nuclear capabilities. India's option to destroy Pakistan's enrichment and reprocessing facilities is constrained by the high likelihood of Pakistani retaliation—possibly against India's nuclear complex at Bombay—and the unforeseeable consequences of a new subcontinental war. There are, however, indications that a preemptive attack may have been under active consideration during the summer of 1984.[59] The overall security of the region, including nonproliferation efforts, would be better served by a *modus vivendi*. This solution could encompass either an overt or a tacit agreement on the limits of these countries' respective nuclear activities. At present, however, neither seems willing to promote such an understanding.

How the nuclear capabilities of South Asian countries fit into the Middle East equation is unclear. Pakistan has certainly sought financial and other assistance from Arab states to advance its plans. Yet the main motivations regarding the Islamic countries seem to be prestige-related, in particular, to confirm Pakistan as the leading industrial power of West Asia. Pakistan is not identified closely with radical Islamic regimes, although it feels compelled for very cogent security and internal political reasons to maintain good relations with Iran. If Pakistan transferred a nuclear device or placed its nuclear capability in the service of the Arab states, Pakistan would play its card for a questionable gain and would face severe penalties from the West. Nonetheless, a Pakistani nuclear capability would have a great impact on the Middle East in view of Israeli perceptions concerning the "Islamic bomb."

U.S. and Other Supplier Options

Despite the limitations on its ability to influence the nuclear policies of India and Pakistan, the United States does have non-proliferation policy options. The current policy is legislatively enshrined in the 1978 Nuclear Non-Proliferation Act and Sections 669 and 670 (Symington and Glenn amendments) of the 1961 Foreign Assistance Act, as modified by Public Law 97–113. Section 669 prohibits U.S. aid to countries receiving unsafeguarded uranium-enrichment technology, while Section 670 requires an aid termination in the event that a nonweapons state acquires unsafeguarded reprocessing technology, transfers or acquires a nuclear weapon, or explodes a nuclear device. In 1981 Congress provided a waiver to Section 669 for Pakistan under certain conditions until September 30, 1987, thus permitting the restoration of U.S. security assistance. At the same time, Congress expanded the scope of Section 670 to include the transfer or receipt of a nuclear device and restricted the president's waiver authority in the case of a nuclear detonation by Pakistan or any other nonweapons state. The June 1982 Supreme Court decision regarding congressional veto provisions raises serious doubts about the ability of the Congress to overrule a waiver made by the president pursuant to these sections, but Congress still retains the legislative and appropriations power to end U.S. aid if it so chooses.

Essentially current U.S. policy involves both incentives and disincentives. As a practical matter the United States has terminated nuclear cooperation with India and will not carry out its 1963 obligation to provide fuel for India's Tarapur atomic power facility. In the summer of 1982 the Reagan administration decided to allow France to substitute for the United States in supplying low-enriched uranium for Tarapur, a compromise that also involved a French departure from current supplier rules on the perpetuity of safeguards. (The Tarapur agreement only addresses the period up to 1993.) During a visit to New Delhi in summer 1983, Secretary of State George Shultz committed the United States to resolving the outstanding issue of spare parts for the Tarapur reactors. These parts, which are said to be needed for its safe operation, are to be obtained by India on the open market if possible. Failing that, the United States is committed to supplying them, presumably through the president's waiver authority under the 1978 Nuclear Non-Proliferation Act.[60] Both the 1982 and 1983 agreements again highlighted the susceptibility of "global" policies such as nonproliferation to regional and bilateral policy objectives, as well as practical issues such as the safe operation of a U.S.-supplied plant.[61]

With Pakistan, the United States has employed a more ambitious version of the carrot and stick policy, having earlier severed all economic and military assistance except for humanitarian food aid. (The United States has a bilateral security agreement with Pakistan but no nuclear cooperation agreement.) The shift in U.S. nonproliferation strategy emphasizing positive support for Pakistan's security concerns was ratified by Congress, but with strong dissent by those who wanted a firm Pakistani commitment not to pursue nuclear weapons technology.[62] Political support for the new security relationship remains somewhat tenuous, but to date Congress essentially has supported the program and has not placed obstacles in the way of its continuance, despite recurring concern about Pakistan's nuclear activities.[63] New evidence about Pakistan's nuclear activities, which emerged during the summer of 1984, including detailed information provided by Senator Alan Cranston in a floor statement on June 21, could undercut congressional support.[64] How Congress will react is clouded both by the uncertainty of support for a significant curtailment of U.S. aid to Pakistan—given the potential repercussions for American regional security interests—and the key importance of Pakistan to members of Congress who wish to support more directly and extensively the Afghan resistance movement.

The long strain in U.S. relations with India and the lukewarm political support for U.S. aid to Pakistan, coupled with the low credibility of both states' proclaimed peaceful nuclear objectives, rules out direct incentives such as extending assistance to civil power programs. Moreover, both countries have shown a determination to protect the autonomy of their nuclear activities at all costs, save for individual facility or heavy water supply agreements that suit their interests.

Theoretically India and Pakistan are quite vulnerable to Western economic sanctions, including measures that deny access to World Bank and International Monetary Fund loans. However, while the United States successfully obtained nuclear supplier cooperation on stricter terms of trade, there is almost no prospect of forging unified Western support for drastic punitive measures, at least until more imminent threats arise. At the same time, India and Pakistan must seriously consider the possible international political and economic consequences of crossing new nuclear thresholds.

The United States has sought vigorously to limit Pakistan's access to dual-use technology while otherwise improving U.S.-Pakistani relations. American regional objectives thus far have not been hampered by continued efforts to block the export of sensitive technology from all sources. Theoretically, U.S. efforts could have the effect of reassuring India that Pakistan is not being permitted to carry out a nuclear weapons program under an American security umbrella—a factor that would serve Pakistani security interests as well. At present, however, Indian policymakers seem unconvinced that the United States is really serious about its efforts to deter Pakistan's acquisition of nuclear technology.[65]

In the final analysis, prospects for proliferation in South Asia are primarily dependent on the actions of India and Pakistan themselves. The actions of the United States and other supplier countries have already caused major delays in the nuclear programs of India and Pakistan, but save for drastic action that compromises other important goals, Western countries have largely exhausted new options. One obvious step is to continue to press for improvements in IAEA safeguard procedures, if only to give credibility to supplier demands for such inspections, and to prevent backsliding on export controls by countries seeking short-term economic or foreign policy gains. (This includes Soviet efforts to sell nuclear power plants to India and French consideration of supplying the proposed Chasma power plant to Pakistan.) India and Pakistan have chosen to avoid full-scope safeguards in the interest of maintaining their weapons option; there is no compelling reason why they should not have to pay the price of the inevitable delays to their nuclear programs. The best hope of keeping the nuclear weapons genie in the bottle lies in the normalization of Indo-Pakistani relations, now a distant prospect. The most realistic scenario probably includes a nuclear-armed India and quite likely a nuclear-armed Pakistan in the 1990s, if not before, or an Indian preemptive attack on Pakistan's nuclear facilities before a weapons capability is achieved. Either development would have profound negative consequences for regional stability and U.S. interests in south and west Asia.

The United States can contribute to improving relations between the subcontinental powers, but the required actions would necessitate a delicate balancing of often conflicting policy objectives. Indeed, some of these objectives may turn out to be irreconcilable. Moreover, since the American public has little awareness of the subcontinent, policymakers will experience difficulties generating consistent political support of a regional policy involving visible costs but limited, and less readily apparent, gains.

NOTES

1. For a concise assessment of Indian and Pakistani nuclear capabilities, see U.S. Congress, Senate Committee on Foreign Relations, *Analysis of Six Issues About Nuclear Capabilities of India, Iraq, Libya, and Pakistan,* Prepared for the Subcommittee on Arms Control, Oceans, International Operations, and Environment by the Environment and Natural Resources Policy Division, Congressional Research Service, Library of Congress, 97th Cong., 1st Sess., January 1982 (Washington, D.C.: Government Printing Office, 1982).

2. The annual report of the Indian Department of Atomic Energy for 1980–81 states that the Indian nuclear program employs some 18,021 scientific and technical personnel and 11,651 auxiliary and administrative staff. From 1978–79 to 1980–81 the scientific and technical staff grew by two to three thousand per year (Government of India, Department of Atomic Energy, *Annual Report, 1980–81,* p. 4). According to one source the overall requirement of the Pakistan Atomic Energy Commission is about 250 scientists and engineers per year. This figure does not give a clear indication of total personnel, but certainly Pakistan's scientific and technical staff is much smaller than India's. See Shirin Tahir-Kheli, "Pakistan," in James Everett Katz and

Onkar S. Marwah, eds., *Nuclear Power in Developing Countries: An Analysis of Decision Making* (Lexington, Mass.: Lexington Books, 1982), pp. 261–67.

3. N. Ram, "India's Nuclear Policy: A Case-Study in the Flaws and Futility of 'Non-Proliferation'" (Paper prepared for the 34th Annual Meeting of the Association of Asian Studies, Chicago, April 2–4, 1982).

4. Senate Committee on Foreign Relations, *Analysis of Six Issues, 3*; Bertrand Goldschmidt, "Indian Nuclear Problems: An Expert's Analysis," *The Hindu* (Madras), April 24, 1983. Goldschmidt credits R–5 with the capacity to produce up to thirty kilograms of plutonium per year.

5. "Atomic Energy in India," *India News* (Indian Embassy, Washington, D.C.), May 28, 1984, p. 4; K. Subrahmanyam, *The Times of India* (Bombay), Supplement, March 19, 1984, pp. 1, 4; Foreign Broadcast Information Service (FBIS), *Worldwide Report: Nuclear Development and Proliferation*, JPRS–IND–84–010, April 30, 1984, pp. 26–29.

6. "Nuclear Setback," *Tribune* (Chandigarh), September 22, 1982; K. V. Subrahmanyam, "Nuclear Energy: A Dismal Record," *Business India* (May 24–June 6, 1982): 81; A. L. Berry, "Nuclear Energy: Is Our Program Expensive?" *Economic Times* (New Delhi), July 12, 1982. The minister of state for science and technology, C. P. N. Singh, stated that RAPP–I suffered nine outages in 1978, fourteen in 1979, and nineteen in 1980 owing to technical problems and human error, while RAPP–II, commissioned in early 1981, suffered eleven outages from April to July and only operated at 36.6 percent of capacity (*Nucleonics Week* [September 10, 1981]).

7. "India, Wanting No Constraints, Loath to Seek Heavy Water from Soviets," *Nucleonics Week* (February 18, 1982): 4.

8. N. Ram, "India's Nuclear Policy," n. 78, Pt. II.

9. *The Statesman* (Calcutta), September 28, 1984, p. 6, FBIS, JPRS–TND–84–027, November 2, 1984, p. 36.

10. "India, Wanting No Constraints," p. 4.

11. "Minister Reports Heavy Water Output Adequate," *The Times of India* (Bombay), May 7, 1982, p. 5. Responding to charges that he was "hiding something" when he gave an ambiguous response to the availability of heavy water for the R–5 reactor, Minister of State for Science and Technology C. P. N. Singh stated that at the moment there was no requirement to import heavy water for the reactor and that the matter of imports would be addressed as and when necessary.

12. "India Will Run FBTR with Mixed-Carbide Fuel Next Year—Probably with CIRUS Plutonium," *Nuclear Fuel* (February 28, 1983): 9.

13. India now claims the fast breeder reactor at Kalpakkam can be started up by the end of 1984 using a newly developed mixture of plutonium and uranium carbide. See *India News*, May 24, 1984, p. 4.

14. "First Reactor Using U-233 Goes Critical," *Indian Express* (Delhi), May 12, 1984, p. 1.

15. Richard K. Betts, "India, Pakistan, and Iran," in Joseph A. Yager, ed., *Nonproliferation and U.S. Foreign Policy* (Washington, D.C.: The Brookings Institution, 1982), p. 96.

16. "India Denies Plan to Make Bomb," *Financial Express* (New Delhi), February 22, 1983; R. Chakrapani, "India Denies Reports on Bomb Fuel," *The Hindu* (Madras), February 22, 1983.

17. Stephen P. Cohen, "Pakistan: Coping with Regional Dominance, Multiple Crises, and Great-Power Confrontations," in Raju G.C. Thomas, ed., *The Great-Power Triangle and Asian Security* (Lexington, Mass.: Lexington Books, 1983), p. 53.

18. Mohan Ram and Cheah Cheng Hye, "India Reaps Prestige But Critics Query the Benefit," *Far Eastern Economic Review* (December 24, 1982): 44–45.

19. Amarnath K. Menon, "SLV–3: A Space Odyssey," *India Today* (May 1983): 153.

20. Tahir-Kheli, "Pakistan," p. 263.

21. Betts, "India, Pakistan, and Iran," p. 98.

22. Tahir-Kheli, "Pakistan," pp. 264–65.

23. Judith Miller, "Pakistan Seeking 2D Atom Reactor," *The New York Times*, December 3, 1982, p. A–6.

24. "Pakistan Postpones Tender Deadline," *News Review* (May 1983): 1?.

25. "U.S. Officials are Privately Furious Over French Foreign Minister," *Nucleonics Week* (April 7, 1983): 5.

26. P. B. Sinha and R. R. Subramanian, *Nuclear Pakistan: Atomic Threat to South Asia* (New Delhi: Vision Books, 1980), p. 35.

27. Theoretically irradiating rods for 200 to 300 days reduces the content of Pu^{240}, which otherwise makes spent fuel from power reactors less desirable for explosive purposes. The operation of reactors at low power is also said to reduce the Pu^{240} content. See S. K. Sharma, *The Times of India* (Bombay), May 1, 1982, p. 8.

28. "IAEA Completes its Desired Upgrading of Safeguards at KANUPP," *Nucleonics Week* (March 3, 1983): 1.

29. International Institute for Strategic Studies, *Strategic Survey, 1981–1982* (London: IISS, 1982), p. 21. For additional background on this facility, see Steve Weissman and Herbert Krosney, *The Islamic Bomb: The Nuclear Threat to Israel and the Middle East* (New York: New York Times Books, 1981), pp. 80–84.

30. Remarks by Senator Alan Cranston, *Congressional Record*, June 21, 1984, 98th Cong., 2d. Sess., pp. S7901–7902. Reportedly administration officials have also confirmed that Pakistan is producing weapons-grade material. See Russell Warren Howe, "Pakistanis are Closer to Producing Nuclear Weapon," *The Washington Times*, July 26, 1984, pp. A–1, A–5.

31. Mary Anne Weaver, "Zia: Pakistan's Military Ruler, Before U.S. Visit, Talks about Drugs, Arms Build-up, India, Elections, Afghanistan, and 'the Bomb'," *The Christian Science Monitor*, November 30, 1982. See also Akhtar Ali, *Pakistan's Nuclear Dilemma: Energy and Security Dimensions* (Karachi: Economic Research Unit, 1984), pp. 61–62.

32. "Scientist Affirms Pakistan Capable of Uranium Enrichment, Weapons Production," (*Nawa-i-Wakt* in Urdu, February 10, 1984), FBIS, JPRS–TND–84–005, March 5, 1984, pp. 35, 43.

33. *The Congressional Record*, June 21, 1984, pp. S7901–7902.

34. Sinha and Subramanian, *Nuclear Pakistan*, p. 88.

35. Dilip Bobb, "Pakistan: Sinister Nuclear Strategy," *India Today* (November 15, 1981): 117–18.

36. Robert Manning, "The Krytron Affair," *Far Eastern Economic Review* 125, no. 31 (August 2, 1984): 11; "3 Pakistanis Indicted on A-Arms Charges," *The Washington Post*, July 17, 1984, p. A–3.

37. Zulfikar Ali Bhutto, typescript of testimony before the Supreme Court of Pakistan, in reply to Pakistan government White Papers, pp. 192–93, quoted in P. K. S. Namboodiri, "Pakistan's Nuclear Posture," in K. Subrahmanyam, ed., *Nuclear Myths and Realities: India's Dilemma* (New Delhi: ABC Publishing House, 1981), pp. 145–46.

38. Judith Miller, "U.S. is Holding Up Peking Atom Talks," *The New York Times*, September 19, 1982, p. A–11.

39. Don Oberdorfer, "Arms Issue Snags Pact with China: U.S. Seeks Promise on Proliferation for Nuclear Deal," *The Washington Post*, June 15, 1984, pp. 1, 27.

40. U.S. Congress, Senate Committee on Governmental Affairs, *Hearing Before the Subcommittee on Energy, Nuclear Proliferation and Federal Services*, 96th Cong., 1st Sess., May 1, 1979

(Washington, D.C.: Government Printing Office, 1979), pp. 25–26.

41. A. Q. Khan interview, FBIS, JPRS–TND–84–005.
42. "Pakistan's Nuclear Chief Says It Could Build Bomb," *The Washington Post*, February 10, 1984; Robert Manning, "A Backyard Bomb?" *Far Eastern Economic Review* (August 2, 1984): 10–11. See also, Ali, *Pakistan's Nuclear Dilemma*, p. 62.
43. R. R. Subramanian and C. Raja Mohan, "India," in Katz and Marwah, *Nuclear Power in Developing Countries*, p. 173.
44. N. Ram, "India's Nuclear Policy," p. 6.
45. Betts, "India, Pakistan, and Iran," pp. 140–41.
46. Ibid., pp. 135–38.
47. *Nucleonics Week* (March 29, 1984).
48. "Zia's Road to the Bomb," *Foreign Report* (London: The Economist Newspaper Limited, August 26, 1982).
49. A. Q. Khan interview, FBIS, *Worldwide Report*, JPRS–TND–84–005, p. 39.
50. Ibid., pp. 35, 44.
51. On Indian maps the disputed Aksai Chin region is part of Ladakh, in the northeastern part of Jammu and Kashmir.
52. During a question session in the Upper House in early 1984 the Indian defense minister identified Pakistani dispositions as follows: four infantry divisions in Azad Kashmir; six infantry divisions and three independent armored brigades in Punjab; one armored brigade and one infantry division opposite India's Gujarat state; and one armored brigade and two infantry divisions adjacent to Rajasthan state. See *Defense and Foreign Affairs Daily*, May 15, 1984, p. 2.
53. H. K. Dua, "Caution Marks Peace Talks with Pakistan; Accord Reached on Joint Panel Signed," *Indian Express*, December 25, 1982.
54. A. T. Chaudhri, "A New Wind Across the Subcontinent," *Indian Express* (New Delhi), November 13, 1982.
55. Kuldip Nayar, "The 'Support' Misfires," *The Tribune* (Chandigarh), September 8, 1983; FBIS *South Asia*, September 2, 1983, pp. F–2 and F–3, and September 12, pp. E–1, F–1 and F–2; A. T. Chaudhuri, "India-Pakistan Ties Souring," *Indian Express* (Bombay), September 28, 1983.
56. "Jammu and Kashmir: Tremors of Tension," *India Today* (February 29, 1984): 24.
57. FBIS *South Asia*, May 23, 1984, pp. F–1 and F–2; Ibid., May 30, 1984, pp. F–1 and F–2; "Indo-Pak Agreement on Visa Rules," *Indian Express* (New Delhi), May 21, 1984, p. 1.

58. "Indo-Pak Talks Postponed," *The Overseas Hindustan Times* (New Delhi), July 28, 1984, p. 1.

59. The January 1985 disclosure of a major spy scandal reaching into the prime minister's office gave credence to reports that a preemptive option had been presented to Mrs. Gandhi last summer. Ashutost Handoo, "Secret Note Leak to CIA Alerted Sleuths," *Hindustan Times* (New Delhi), January 22, 1985.

60. William Claiborne, "Shultz Promises for India's Reactor," *The Washington Post*, July 1, 1983, p. 1; "Reported on Secretary of State Shultz's Visit," *Foreign Broadcast Information Service* VIII (July 1, 1983).

61. These conflicts are even more stark in regard to Pakistan, now perceived as a "front line" state. See Thomas Perry Thornton, "Between the Stools? U.S. Policy Towards Pakistan During the Carter Administration," *Asian Survey* XXII, no. 10 (October 1982): 959–77.

62. For a discussion of how Congress dealt with the proposed aid package for Pakistan in 1981 see Richard P. Cronin, "Congress and Arms Sales and Security Assistance to Pakistan," in *Congress and Foreign Policy—1981*, Committee Print. U.S. Congress, House Committee on Foreign Affairs (Washington, D.C.: Government Printing Office, 1982).

63. On March 28, 1984, during action on the foreign assistance authorization bill, the Senate Foreign Relations Committee adopted an amendment that would have forbidden military aid and arms sales to Pakistan unless the president certified to Congress that Pakistan neither possessed a nuclear device nor was acquiring, overtly or covertly, the means to produce one. This action was essentially reversed by the committee on April 4, when it adopted an amendment that would revise the Foreign Assistance Act to require an annual presidential certification "that Pakistan does not possess a nuclear explosive device and that the proposed United States assistance program will reduce significantly the risk that Pakistan will possess a nuclear explosive device" (U.S. Congress, Senate, Committee on Foreign Relations, Senate Report No. 98-400, April 18, 1984, pp. 58–59, 114).

     The amendment was defeated, however, when the bill reached the Senate floor in October 1984. This vote culminated efforts by Senate critics of Pakistan's nuclear activities to bar the transfer of F–16 aircraft and other weapons systems to Pakistan unless Congress received satisfactory guarantees that Pakistan had abandoned its presumed weapons program.

64. *Congressional Record*, June 21, 1984, S7901–7906.

65. Assessment based on author's conversations with Indian officials in New Delhi in early February 1985. The dismissal of the more serious charges and the light sentence imposed on a Pakistani national in the Houston krytron case will likely be read in India as evidence that the Reagan administration puts its security relationship with Pakistan well ahead of its desire to prevent Islamabad's acquisition of nuclear weapons. For background on the case see Seymour M. Hersh, "Pakistani in U.S. Sought to Ship A-Bomb Trigger," *The New York Times*, February 25, 1985, A1, A8.

4 ARGENTINA

Daniel Poneman

The Argentine nuclear program is riven by apparent contradictions. On the one hand, the government has refused to accept any comprehensive nonproliferation commitment. It is building a plutonium-reprocessing plant and reserves the right to conduct peaceful nuclear explosions. While both plutonium and peaceful nuclear explosions have putative civilian uses, they have far more powerful military implications. On the other hand, the Argentine government reaffirms that its nuclear objectives are exclusively peaceful. Admiral Carlos Castro Madero, president of the Argentine National Atomic Energy Commission (CNEA) during the seven years of military government, often attacked collaboration among the nuclear supplier nations as discriminatory against nuclear importers, and yet boasted of being invited to join in such collaboration. During the Malvinas Islands conflict, Castro Madero protested Britain's use of a nuclear-propelled submarine, but not the reported existence of nuclear weapons in the British naval task force.

The apparent contradictions in Argentine nuclear policy reflect a shrewd CNEA policy of touting the economic benefits of fission without compromising its military potential. By playing on Argentine hopes for independence and development, the

89

CNEA has protected its bureaucratic position despite government and economic upheavals. Rhetoric aside, however, the nuclear program has been and will remain constrained by technological dependence upon the advanced nations for at least the next dozen years.

A dependent government cannot easily conduct an independent policy, as Prime Minister Margaret Thatcher roughly reminded General Leopoldo Galtieri. CNEA leaders have been more adroit than their governmental superiors in protecting their image without sacrificing their accomplishments. This success has derived from a nuclear policy that is unlike any other in the world.

This chapter will explore the sources and features of this policy in relation to nuclear weapons proliferation. The explanation requires, first, that Argentine policy be placed in the context of other approaches to nuclear power in the developing world.

Approaches to Nuclear Power

Though the governments of many developing countries conduct some nuclear research, most lack a commercial-scale nuclear power program. Their reticence to continue down the nuclear path has several causes. Most powerful is cost: the price of a commercial-scale reactor is more than $1 billion. Of that sum, about 70 percent represents capital, much of which must be paid in foreign exchange. Both capital and foreign exchange are painfully scarce commodities in the developing world, particularly during the present debt crisis.

The complexity and dangers of nuclear technology also deter its pursuit in the developing world. Moreover, nuclear technology development places a premium on scarce, skilled manpower resources, while threatening to establish a technical enclave so highly developed that few if any other industries would be advanced enough to benefit from the imported technology. Finally, the large scale required to make the heavy capital investment in a nuclear power reactor worthwhile creates problems for the many developing countries with small electrical grids.[1] In short, the handful of developing countries that do pursue the nuclear power option must marshal their capital and manpower with care, and attend constantly to the program to secure its success.

Those developing countries with active nuclear power programs can be divided into two categories. One group concentrates on the introduction of nuclear-generated electricity, and usually accedes (though often reluctantly) to binding pledges against the acquisition of nuclear weapons to ensure that nonproliferation concerns do not lead their suppliers to restrict nuclear commerce. Brazil, Egypt, South Korea, Mexico, and Taiwan are illustrative of this approach, even though all these nations have curtailed their nuclear power plans. The other group is more concerned with the security benefits nuclear technology affords, seeks to acquire sensitive nuclear technologies (such as uranium enrichment and plutonium reprocessing), and will usually sacrifice the economic benefits of efficient nuclear-electric generation in order to preserve political autonomy. India, Israel, Pakistan, and South Africa lead in this category. For ease of description these two groups may be called "dependents" and "independents," respectively.

Argentine policy tends toward the independent, yet remains cooperative enough to maintain a steady stream of supplies from all but those nations most zealously opposed to nuclear proliferation, such as the United States and Canada. Argentina has a serious nuclear power program, like the dependents, but rejects the Treaty on the Non-Proliferation of Nuclear Weapons (NPT) and the Treaty for the Prohibition of Nuclear Weapons in Latin America (the Treaty of Tlatelolco). The government has successfully resisted pressures to sign what it deems to be discriminatory agreements to abjure nuclear weapons, while avoiding supply cut-offs that have crippled the power reactors already in operation in India and Pakistan. Atucha I, in its first decade, operated at about 90 percent capacity, according to Argentine sources, compared to the 20 to 40 percent rating of the Tarapur and Rajasthan nuclear power stations, and the pathetic 5 to 10 percent rating typical of the Karachi nuclear power plant in recent years.[2]

The following section will consider the motivations that led Argentina to adopt this unique policy, its execution, and its effects from a proliferation perspective.

MOTIVATIONS

In Argentina, political, security, and economic concerns converge in a powerfully pronuclear way. Domestically, transient governmental leaders of all political persuasions have leaned on the relatively stable and successful CNEA for support. The CNEA also lends the Argentine program international esteem. Meanwhile, security considerations have attracted Argentine leaders to the military potential of fission. Economically the Argentine nuclear program is justified both as a hedge against possible future reliance on foreign energy supplies, and as a vehicle for growth and development. These respective motivations will be treated in turn.

Political Motivations

Political motivations underpinned the original Argentine nuclear commitment.[3] This is understandable since a developing country's nuclear research effort offers prestige and little else. As Argentina's program grew in scale and expense, so did the need for economic justification. The nuclear plan approved in 1979 called for the construction of five power reactors and an integrated nuclear fuel cycle by the year 2000.[4] But economic crisis and the $45 billion foreign debt forced the government to impose severe austerity measures. The continued government commitment to the $1.25 billion and $2.5 to $3 billion reactors, Embalse and Atucha II, as well as the $800 million Sulzer Brothers heavy water plant, attests to the political appeal of Argentina's nuclear program.

Political motivations are not addressed to an exclusively domestic audience. Argentine leaders have long sought to advertise their nuclear achievements internationally. In Latin America, Argentina's rise to preeminence resulted from its development of the first research reactor, the first indigenously conducted, power reactor feasibility study, the first power reactor, the first fuel-element fabrication plant, and the first plutonium-reprocessing facility on the continent. Argentina has actively participated in the International Atomic Energy Agency (IAEA) since its inception, hosting numerous nuclear conferences and supplying experts and technical assistance to other developing countries, including its Latin American neighbors.

To the enormous satisfaction of Argentine officials, the CNEA has become a nuclear supplier. Argentina supplied two research reactors and related facilities to Peru and is negotiating to supply similar assistance to Colombia and Uruguay. No other developing nation has ever exported a nuclear reactor.

Ironically this new phase of the Argentine nuclear program has created an identity crisis. Is Argentina a part of the developing world or superior to it? Traditionally Argentina has criticized the advanced nations for their discriminatory behavior toward the developing world. As Argentina's nuclear program has progressed, however, the prospect of joining the ranks of the advanced nations that formerly sought to muscle Argentine policy has become more appealing. The political motivations behind the nuclear program are the attainment of prestige and independence; having achieved prestige, inclusion in the Nuclear Suppliers Group (NSG) would clearly help Argentina to secure independence.

Thus far, Argentine officials have not had to choose decisively. The military government exploited anticolonialist rhetoric for all its moral and political worth. Castro Madero rejected the NPT as a "neocolonialist treaty," arguing that technology imports create "a potential risk of economic dependence, or of a kind of scientific and technical colonialism."[5] When the opportunity arose, however, Argentine officials could not resist self-congratulation over their new status. Commenting on the significance of his attending a meeting in Japan, in which all other participants were NSG members, Castro Madero declared: "It is a distinction conferred upon Argentina, by inviting us to participate along with advanced countries such as France, England, Russia, the United States and Japan. . . . Argentina's advanced position in nuclear development was recognized."[6]

Political motivations, inevitably, will continue to play a seminal role in Argentina's nuclear development.

Security Motivations

Security motivations, as used here, refer to the desire to protect Argentine borders from foreign attack, to promote Argentine nationalism, to maintain a technological edge over Brazil in the nuclear field, and otherwise to enhance the government's image. Conflicting signals complicate the assessment of how important security motivations have been to the Argentine nuclear program. Ambiguity can result from either muddled objectives or intentional obfuscation. In Argentina the consistency and simultaneity of pronuclear and antinuclear weapons signals suggest that such ambiguity is intended. If this is true, then it is reasonable to conclude that security motivations do play an important role in driving the Argentine nuclear policy, even without serious effort to build or acquire nuclear weapons.

From a military standpoint nuclear technology can fulfill one or more of the following options: (1) maintaining (without pursuing) a weapons option; (2) threatening to acquire nuclear weapons; (3) acquiring nuclear weapons; (4) testing nuclear weapons; and (5) using nuclear weapons militarily. As the options become increasingly menacing, they suggest stronger foreign responses. The CNEA has openly practiced option one and implicitly indulged in option two, while steadfastly maintaining its firm opposition to options three, four, and five. Under the current government of President Raúl Alfonsín, hints that Argentina may acquire nuclear weapons have ceased. The weapons option encourages military support for CNEA programs. When combined with peaceful assurances, it also curries foreign respect without provoking embargoes or retaliation from CNEA backers or potential adversaries.

Declaratory policy provides the first insight into security motivations. Every leader of the Argentine nuclear program has affirmed its strictly peaceful intentions. Admiral Oscar Quihillalt, CNEA head from 1955 until 1973, declared straightforwardly, "We never thought of making a nuclear device in the country."[7] Perón's CNEA chief, Admiral Pedro Iraolagoitia, stated that "the country has no project for, nor conditions to develop, an atomic bomb."[8] Castro Madero reaffirmed Argentina's intention not to develop nuclear weapons, even after the military defeat in the South Atlantic.[9] After his election in 1983, President Alfonsín quickly emphasized that the Argentine program would be directed exclusively toward peaceful ends.

Yet past Argentine leaders have refused to ratify their peaceful declarations through comprehensive commitments, such as the NPT and the Treaty of Tlatelolco. They have also reserved the right to conduct "peaceful nuclear explosions," and resisted the application of international safeguards on Argentine nuclear activities. (The purpose here is merely to explore motivations. These policies will be treated more fully below.)

A peaceful policy can easily be discarded, but a militarily useful technology cannot easily be unlearned. Even if CNEA pacifism continues, it could be overruled by a future Argentine government eager to exploit fission technology to produce nuclear weapons. Also, the possible disingenuity of declared policies suggests that a prudent assessment of intentions should give great weight to the development of technologies that irrefutably enhance nuclear weapons potential.

Argentine technological development has been well suited to possible use for military purposes. Argentina selected the natural uranium fuel cycle, which is a better plutonium producer than is the light water cycle. Argentina briefly operated a laboratory-scale reprocessing plant in the late 1960s and is now building a larger version. In November 1983 Admiral Castro Madero announced that Argentina had acquired the ability to enrich uranium in the content of the uranium–235 (U–235) isotope.[10] Although peaceful justifications for these technological choices are plausible, the military implications cannot be ignored.

In short, ambiguous declaratory policy, together with the selection and sedulous development of weapons-usable technologies, suggests an earnest Argentine interest in a nuclear weapons option. This option is desired to maintain domestic political support for the nuclear program, and to exert leverage throughout Latin America and the world.

Economic Motivations

Economic motivations are also critical to the Argentine nuclear program. Political concerns alone could justify a research-scale effort, but not the large commercial commitment that has been undertaken in Argentina. One power reactor is approaching its tenth year of operation, a second is now producing electricity, a third is under construction, and three more reactors are planned by the end of the century. Fuel cycle facilities are also in various stages of development, and a significant private sector in the nuclear field has emerged. Both security and growth strategies support the Argentine economic interest in nuclear power.

Resentment cultivated by a century of dependence on and perceived exploitation by foreigners in the energy sector sensitized Argentinians to energy as a security as well as an economic matter. Classical economists treat energy as an economic good, like any other, supplied in quantities dictated by demand. But where the classically assumed free markets and easy substitution of production inputs are absent, the critical role of energy as an input to most other economic factors justifies governmental concern. This message was brought home by the history of energy shortages in Argentina. Until 1945 Argentina relied almost exclusively on England for the coal that stoked locomotives, steam engines, and electrical generators. Drastic British export cutbacks during the two world wars forced Argentinians to burn wood, charcoal, corn, and straw instead.

After the Second World War, a population explosion in Buenos Aires created severe electrical shortages. The country possessed large oil reserves, but poor management and governmental policy reverses troubled the oil sector through the mid–1960s. (Now Argentina imports less than 10 percent of its oil.) By this time, the perceived promise of nuclear power as a reliable source of energy had reached its zenith. President Arturo Illia, encouraged by a decade of nuclear research under Quihillalt's direction, authorized the construction of the nation's first nuclear power plant.

Economic development strategy, as well as security concerns, drove Argentine nuclear policies. The nuclear program from the outset was a lodestone, attracting talent and technology. The CNEA has trained and employed thousands of Argentinians. Professional personnel at the CNEA rose from a few dozen in 1956 to more than 6,000 by 1981. The commission has used the program as a vehicle for learning engineering and construction skills that are useful in other economic sectors. The technologies imported as part of the nuclear plan are intended to raise the overall capabilities of the Argentine economy. The electricity to be generated from the reactors is also expected to stimulate growth, but the 3,000 megawatt (mw) nuclear capacity projected by 1995 is dwarfed by the projected 20,000mw hydro contribution.[11] The unique nuclear contribution will not be to megawattage but to advances along the national learning curve. These advances are used to justify Argentina's investment of more than $5 billion in nuclear power.[12]

Of all of these motivations, political considerations emerge as the most important. Security motivations could argue against the Argentine policy by provoking an unpleasant nuclear competition with Brazil and alienating the North Americans and Europeans with whom the Argentinians feel a strong cultural affinity. With Argentina's vast natural wealth—including oil, coal, and hydroelectric resources—a strong case could be made that greater technology transfer and training could be had for less trouble and expense in other economic sectors.

This is not to say that the security and economic appeal of nuclear power in Argentina is contrived, but merely to note that powerful arguments contrary to the traditional pronuclear stance exist. Indeed, these arguments have convinced the governments of most developing countries to abstain from major nuclear commitments and seem to carry weight in the new Argentine government. The purpose here is to suggest that politics underscore the commitment.

ARGENTINE NUCLEAR CAPABILITIES

By invoking the unassailable desire for independence, the Argentine government has preserved all possible nuclear options: a complete fuel cycle, a self-sufficient reactor industry, exports to other developing nations, and peaceful nuclear explosions. Since a peaceful nuclear explosive has obvious military applications, one may conclude that the government wishes to retain the nuclear weapons option. While preserving the option, the Argentinians are not visibly or actively pursuing a nuclear weapons capability. The following sections discuss how Argentina has technologically and politically maintained its hybrid nuclear policy.

The Nuclear Power Program

Argentina's nuclear program has been developed according to the following precept: import when necessary, build when possible. The first Argentine research reactor, for example, was manufactured and assembled in Argentina using U.S. plans. Most of the remaining five research reactors were indigenously designed and built. Early on, the CNEA began to manufacture research reactor fuel elements, though enriched uranium always came from abroad. The newest research reactor, RA–6, was inaugurated in 1982.

The first nuclear power plant, Atucha I, began delivering electricity (two years behind schedule) on March 17, 1974. Located about 110 kilometers up the Paraná River from Buenos Aires, Atucha is fueled by natural uranium, and moderated and cooled by heavy water. It was built under a $70 million contract with the West German manufacturer Siemens AG, which provided for 100 percent financing and 35 percent local participation. Reportedly, cost overruns increased the price of the station to $140 million. Siemens apparently absorbed the loss without complaint. The 317mw rating was later increased to 335mw.

The second Argentine nuclear power plant project was more troubled. Bidding was even more competitive than it had been for Atucha I, as the light water reactor (LWR) manufacturers made a last stand against the heavy water reactor (HWR) vendors, hoping to gain a toehold in what promised to be an important nuclear export market. Despite undercutting the HWR bids by 10 percent, however, the LWR promoters lost out to Atomic Energy of Canada, Limited (AECL). Three critical advantages probably account for AECL's victory. First, the CANDU (Canadian-Deuterium-Uranium) reactor uses natural uranium, permitting Argentina to continue to avoid dependence on enriched uranium. Second, the CANDU reactor core consisted of many pressure tubes instead of one large pressure vessel. Argentine engineers hoped that they could more easily manufacture these tubes than to cast an enormous, thick-walled vessel—a process requiring high quality control and difficult seamless welding. Third, and perhaps most important, AECL sweetened the reactor offer by including, at a bargain price, a technology transfer agreement that would have provided the CNEA with the analytical tools necessary to design its own future reactors without foreign assistance.

Subsequent annoyance with the Canadians reinforced Argentine desires for independence. Two figures reflect a decade of financial grief: The reported original price was $250 million; the ultimate cost of the now complete reactor has been estimated at $1.25 billion. The Canadians drastically curtailed their participation at Argentina's Embalse reactor and reneged on the technology transfer agreement. Moreover, sensitized by the use of the Canadian-supplied Cirus research reactor to produce the plutonium used in the Indian nuclear test of May 1974, the Canadian government threatened to cancel the deal unless Argentina accepted additional safeguards on the Embalse agreement.

Haggling over refinancing the project and increasing safeguards continued into 1976. The CNEA finally accepted an agreement barring not only Argentina's reexport of any materials produced in the reactor without Canadian permission, but also the use of supplied technology or materials for the manufacture of any nuclear explosive, peaceful or otherwise. The agreement also extended safeguards coverage from fifteen years to the approximate thirty-year lifetime of the reactor.[13] The 600mw Embalse reactor finally went critical in March 1983—three years behind schedule.

A third, 745mw reactor—Atucha II—is now under construction. Atucha II and all reactors planned for the future will be of the heavy water variety, as mandated by presidential decree.[14] Financial problems and safeguards disputes have slowed the Atucha II project as well. Projected start-up has been delayed three years, until 1990. The remaining three reactors were to be completed by 1997, according to the nuclear plan approved in 1979.[15] The Alfonsín government, however, has indicated that it has no plans to begin any power reactors beyond Atucha II before the end of its term, in December 1989.

At the same time that the CNEA ordered Atucha II, it agreed to buy a 250-ton-per-year heavy water plant from the Sulzer Brothers of Switzerland. This plant was the keystone of the Argentine effort to complete the front end of the fuel cycle. Once complete, this plant would enable the CNEA to perform all the steps required from uranium mining to reactor start-up without dependence on foreign suppliers. This capability would free the government from concern that outside political leverage could force the Argentine reactors to shut down for want of fuel or moderator.

The Argentine government expressed a preference for the heavy water, natural uranium fuel cycle as early as 1964, at the United Nations Conference on the Peaceful Uses of Nuclear Technology.[16] Argentina argued that it did not wish to become vulnerable to disruption of nuclear fuel supplies. (At that time, the United States held a monopoly in the international uranium-enrichment business.) This reason later lost cogency due to several developments: (1) Natural uranium reactors were vulnerable to disruption in heavy water supplies; (2) the United States lost its enrichment monopoly, with the Soviet Union and Western Europe emerging as competitors; and (3) deep cuts in many nuclear programs left the market glutted with excess enrichment capacity, to the advantage of enriched uranium buyers.

These factors, all apparent by the time of the Embalse light water versus heavy water reactor debate, did not alter Argentina's initial preference. Perhaps the Argentine attachment to natural uranium was reinforced by its advantage over low-enriched uranium as a source of fissile material. To increase the concentration of the uranium–235 isotope from a reactor grade of 3 percent to weapons grade of at least 40 percent and, ideally, over 90 percent is extremely difficult technologically. Separating weapons-grade plutonium chemically from irradiated reactor fuel is easier. Natural uranium reactors are better weapons sources than are enriched uranium reactors; they produce more of the weapons-usable plutonium–239 isotope and less of the nonfissile plutonium–240 contaminant. The Argentine choice of natural uranium reactors, then, facilitated later acquisition of weapons-grade material. Thus, the Argentine reactor choice leads directly to consideration of the nuclear weapons option.

The Nuclear Weapons Option

Since 1967 official Argentine policy has called for the achievement of nuclear fuel cycle independence. (See Table 4–1.) This policy has dual implications for nuclear weapons acquisition. First, by definition, once independence is attained, the nuclear program will be insulated from outside pressure. Thus, should Argentina edge closer to nuclear weapons capability, its nuclear reactors could not be held hostage to embargoes on nuclear assistance. Lest this security be considered unimportant, recall the miserable operating performances of the Pakistani and Indian power reactors once they were cut off from Western assistance.

Table 4–1. Argentine Nuclear Fuel Cycle Activities.

Category	Status
Uranium resources	At up to $100/lb., 30,363 tons of reasonably assured resources, plus 18,000–25,000 tons of estimated additional resources.
Uranium milling	Three plants are in operation with three more planned. Currently, 180–220 tons of "yellow cake" (U_3O_8) are milled annually.
Uranium conversion (from U_3O_8 to UO_2)	One West German-supplied plant has a 150-ton annual capacity. The project to build an Argentine plant of equal capacity has been delayed.
Fuel-element fabrication	A 1976 Argentine pilot plant at Constituyentes fabricated 240 elements for use at Atucha I. An industrial-scale plant is operating at Ezeiza, producing all the elements for Atucha I and some for Embalse.
Zirconium production	A 1-ton-per-year pilot plant at Bariloche has been in operation since 1978, producing zirconium sponge. A plant at Pilcaniyeu in Rio Negro is planned to produce metallic zirconium from either local minerals or imports.
Zircaloy production	An alloys factory and a tube plant have been built at Ezeiza.
Heavy water production	The $800 million, 250-ton-per-year Sulzer Brothers plant at Arroyito in Neuquen Province is scheduled for start-up in 1985.

Table 4–1 continued.

Category	Status
	An Argentine, 2-ton pilot plant is over 60 percent complete but has been delayed. This pilot plant was originally intended to form the basis for an indigenously designed, industrial scale heavy water plant. Construction on the larger plant has begun at Atucha.
Uranium enrichment	Success in pilot-scale enrichment, by the gaseous diffusion method, announced. The plant at Pilcaniyeu is to have a 500 kg capacity to produce 20 percent U–235, with start-up in 1986. An 180-ton line of 1 percent U–235 enrichment is also planned.
Spent fuel	A second spent-fuel storage pool at Atucha I is complete and received its first irradiated elements in May 1982.
Plutonium reprocessing	The plant will have a yearly output of 10–15 kg of plutonium. The originally scheduled August 1982 completion date has been pushed back to 1988.
Waste disposal	Field study underway for underground geological storage at Sierra de Media, about 50 km from Gastre (northwest of Rawson, in Chubut Province). The study includes preliminary engineering work.

Second, and more directly, nuclear independence includes the ability to produce materials usable as the critical mass of a nuclear explosive. In November 1983 the CNEA unexpectedly announced that it had successfully demonstrated the enrichment of uranium, using gaseous diffusion technology. The spectre of nuclear weapons raised by the announcement was balanced by the usual assurances of peaceful motives. Despite the alarmed reaction in many quarters, whether the enrichment plant will be able to produce weapons-grade U–235 with facilities now planned remains unclear.

The CNEA built and operated a small reprocessing plant in the late 1960s, which may produce perhaps a few grams of plutonium before its dismantlement in the early 1970s.[17] In 1979 Castro Madero announced that the CNEA would begin to "produce" plutonium in a new, expanded reprocessing facility. The planned capacity of this plant is around ten to fifteen kilograms of plutonium output per year.[18]

Admiral Castro Madero offered three justifications for plutonium reprocessing: First, the plutonium extracted from spent fuel could be recycled in Argentine power reactors, reducing uranium needs by 50 percent; second, plutonium could eventually be used as breeder reactor fuel; third, in order to compete effectively against other nuclear suppliers in the Latin American market, Argentina must be able to provide equivalent services, including plutonium reprocessing.[19] Although there has been no trade in plutonium-reprocessing plants since the cancellation of the French contracts with South Korea and Pakistan, Castro Madero argued that the CNEA should be ready to compete should that market revive.

These arguments were weak. At foreseeable uranium prices, mining fresh uranium will be cheaper than recycling plutonium in thermal reactors, especially since Argentina has large indigenous reserves. Plutonium reprocessing will be necessary to fuel breeder reactors, but the breeder will not be introduced for several decades, if at all, in Argentina. With regard to Argentina's ability to compete with other reprocessing suppliers, the moratorium on such trade is unlikely to end in the near future. Plutonium reprocessing, however, makes eminent sense when these declared interests are bolstered by two other motives—the desires for independence and a nuclear weapons option.

The CNEA has not been in a hurry to reprocess plutonium. After the first Argentine reprocessing facility shut down, desultory planning for a second facility led nowhere. Nearly a decade lapsed before construction began on the present Ezeiza plant. Indeed, the slow pace of the reprocessing project suggests that separated plutonium is not urgently desired. During the recent financial crisis the project was suspended and operation is not expected to begin until at least 1988. In 1983, when the 500 percent peso devaluation essentially halved the CNEA budget, Castro Madero placed highest priority on completing the

Embalse station and the heavy water plant supplied by the Sulzer Brothers, while proceeding more slowly on Atucha II.[20] Work on the indigenous plutonium-reprocessing and heavy water production plants was suspended.

Though the militarily sensitive programs may sometimes have a lower priority, the CNEA never forecloses the option to move toward a weapons program. Haste is not essential; the CNEA derives leverage from the prospect of producing weapons-grade material. If it actually begins to reprocess and gather a plutonium stockpile, the CNEA may provoke hostility in the Northern Hemisphere and fear in Latin America. The country's security, then, may be better served by the imminence than the attainment of a reprocessing capability.

Of course, if Argentine reprocessing commences, the government will enjoy a new form of leverage. Perhaps the government could obtain concessions from others in return for Argentine pledges to limit reprocessing, contribute its plutonium to an international storage program, or refrain from exporting reprocessing technology to other countries. Should Argentina use the plutonium to conduct a peaceful nuclear explosion, as the government maintains is its right, it will attain another sort of leverage. But the advantages are speculative and may be offset by other countries' negative reactions. While the Argentine government might be willing to run the risk to gain influence, under its present philosophy Argentina is unlikely to do so until its nuclear program has become self-sufficient in all respects. By Argentine accounts that will not happen until the end of the century.[21]

Should the Argentines decide to exploit that technology, they can choose between two routes. One route would not violate IAEA safeguards. The CNEA would build the long-discussed RA–7 research reactor, uranium oxide and heavy water plants, and plutonium-reprocessing facility. The uranium ore could be mined, processed, and converted from "yellow cake" (U_3O_8) to the more usable uranium dioxide (UO_2) form. The CNEA could fabricate uranium dioxide fuel elements for the large RA–7 reactor. This research reactor could be moderated partly by heavy water produced in Argentina's two-ton pilot plant, though several more tons would be needed. When irradiated, the transformed plutonium–239 isotopes could be separated at the Ezeiza facility from the residual uranium and newly created fission products contained in the spent fuel. Interestingly, the projected spent-fuel output of the RA–7 would just match the planned spent-fuel intake of the Ezeiza reprocessing plant. Allowing for waste, the whole process could produce about enough plutonium for one or two nuclear explosives per year.

The other route could provide more plutonium, but would require Argentine abrogation of IAEA safeguard commitments. The key would be to obtain more spent fuel by using the output from the commerical reactors at Embalse (1,800mw) or Atucha I (375mw) instead of the 70mw RA–7. The same uranium-milling and conversion steps would be followed. A new, 400-element-per-year fuel-fabrication plant could supply the Embalse and Atucha I reactors. Heavy water for these reactors could be produced at the Swiss-built, safeguarded Arroyito facility. The spent fuel would contain more plutonium—enough for several explosives per year—than could be produced in the RA–7.

In conclusion, the CNEA has the ability, within a relatively short time, to begin producing fissile material of at least the quality required for a crude nuclear fission device. One cannot say that Argentina is a given number of months or years away from a bomb, because the timing depends on political decisions as well as technical constraints. The important point is that Argentina's nuclear weapons program is close enough to worry about, but neither so close nor so invulnerable to foreign pressures to consider unstoppable.

POLITICS

Politics shape the Argentine nuclear program at the domestic, bilateral, and international levels.

Domestically, until 1983 the CNEA had cornered the nuclear market. For example, in 1979 the Peronists attacked the Sulzer Brothers contract and in 1975 introduced congressional legislation calling on the government to manufacture a nuclear weapon for national defense.[22] The CNEA repudiated the bill and the Peronists' efforts proved feckless. While nuclear policies arouse popular and media debate, they have imposed no perceptible mark on CNEA policy.

Even the military has played a circumscribed role. To the extent that there has been speculation concerning nuclear weapons research, the supposed locales have been military bases, not CNEA laboratories. Beyond that, military involvement has centered on bureaucratic infighting. For instance, army officers backed the light water reactor bid in the Embalse competition, probably less because of that model's intrinsic virtues than because they wanted to break the navy monopoly on one of the country's most successful programs. (Good army relations with Westinghouse Corporation, the leading LWR bidder, may also have played a role.)

The Alfonsín government is trying through legislation to bring the CNEA under congressional control. This reform could transform CNEA nuclear policies, since civilian politicians traditionally have had little effect in the nuclear field.

Bilateral Relationships

Despite the stability of the program, Argentine efforts in closing the fuel cycle, coupled with the government's rejection of full-scope safeguards and the NPT, already have jeopardized imports from some quarters, notably North America. In the 1950s and 1960s the United States was a leading supplier, but deteriorating political relations between the two countries undermined nuclear cooperation. The coup de grâce was supplied when U.S. officials indicated some reluctance to supply heavy water for Atucha I. This reluctance angered the CNEA, perhaps tipping the balance decisively in favor of Siemens over the Westinghouse bid. Within a few years the mutual antagonism had ripened. In 1975 the United States charged that Argentina had removed reactor waste containing unseparated plutonium from Atucha I without IAEA knowledge.[23]

The Argentine government deplored the restrictive approach to nuclear commerce practiced by the Carter administration. Although relations improved somewhat with the inauguration of the more sympathetic Reagan administration, the Nuclear Non-Proliferation Act of 1978 precluded the resumption of nuclear commerce with Buenos Aires. Castro Madero confirmed that "as far as the letter of the law is concerned . . . no exchange of technology between the two countries will be possible."[24] The Canadians also shared the strong U.S. concern over nonproliferation, and forced the Argentines to renegotiate the safeguards covering the Embalse project.

Experience with the North Americans confirmed the necessity for Argentina to diversify its supply sources. The West Germans, with their long commercial experience in Argentina, were prime candidates. As expected, they proved to be more accommodating. When Argentina looked as though it would have to accept full-scope safeguards in order to acquire the Atucha II plus heavy water plant package, the West German government helped the CNEA wriggle free. The West German and Canadian governments had agreed to require Argentine acceptance of IAEA safeguards for all Argentine nuclear facilities, present and future, as required of all NPT nonnuclear weapons state parties. But when the CNEA divided the deal into separate competitions for the heavy water plant and the Atucha II power station, the West Germans were willing to sell only the reactor and to drop the requirement to accept NPT-type (full-scope) safeguards.[25]

Meanwhile, the selection of Sulzer Brothers of Switzerland over the Canadians to build the heavy water plant appeared to reflect diversification for its own sake. Many Americans considered the Canadian heavy water technology superior in quality and reliability. Criticism focused on the Sulzer Brothers' past performance. A heavy water plant at Baroda, India, was heavily damaged by an internal explosion. Another one, in France, could not be put into operation. Further concern arose because the Argentine plant was to produce ten times more heavy water than the largest existing Sulzer Brothers' facility.[26]

In the early 1980s the CNEA looked eastward for supplies. From the Soviet Union the CNEA purchased heavy water to replace operating losses at Atucha I, and contracted to purchase 100 kilograms of 20 percent enriched uranium for its research reactors. The Soviet Union also supplied some rolling presses and laminating equipment to the Argentine zirconium alloy plant.[27] In addition, China agreed to sell 20 percent enriched uranium to the CNEA.[28]

Finally, in Latin America, rivalry with Brazil has long spurred Argentine nuclear efforts. The competition dates back to the 1950s, when the two governments raced to become the first to build a research reactor in Latin America. Argentina has been winning ever since, largely due to the high priority accorded the nuclear program in Buenos Aires.

To be sure, Brazil leads Argentina in many other gauges of power and sophistication. But that only intensifies the Argentine commitment to nuclear superiority. The Brazilians at times have sought to catch up, most notably in 1975 with a multibillion dollar deal to import nuclear assistance from West Germany. The package included up to eight 1,300mw reactors, as well as facilities for uranium enrichment, fuel fabrication, and plutonium reprocessing. The deal soured, though, as endless construction difficulties and cost increases coincided with a drastic decline in both oil prices and the Brazilian economy. Whether more than two of the proposed reactors will be built is still unclear, while the much heralded and feared transfer of sensitive facilities remains a distant prospect. As in the old tale, the Brazilian hare could not defeat the Argentine tortoise, showing that there is no easy substitute for patience and diligence in nuclear technology development.

In the mid–1970s the Argentine-Brazilian rivalry softened. Brazilian accusations of Argentine nuclear weapons plans were at least temporarily forgotten, as increasingly restrictive export policies by nuclear suppliers, particularly the North Americans, gave the two a common, anticolonialist cause. In May 1980 the two governments concluded a nuclear cooperation agreement. Pursuant to that accord, Argentina was to lend Brazil 240 tons of uranium and deliver up to 160,000 meters of zircaloy tubes. In return, Brazil was to weld and assemble the lower part of the Atucha II pressure vessel. Alarmism and contentiousness gave way to greater understanding and expression of common interests.

These bright hopes for Latin American cooperation soon faded. Recession and declining oil prices deflated the economic incentives. The Malvinas-Falklands war alarmed the Brazilians, as Argentine nuclear ambitions and irascibility became more apparent. Latent mistrust revived. At present, the mutual return to civilian rule has restored each government's confidence in the nuclear pacifism of the other.

Bilateral relationships involve safeguards as well as contracts. Since these safeguards are now administered almost entirely by the IAEA, a discussion of Argentina's international posture is necessary.

International Relationships

Argentine governments have firmly opposed full-scope safeguards agreements, which would commit them to submit indigenous as well as imported facilities to international control. The CNEA accepts IAEA safeguards on facilities transferred from abroad, but objects to "any additional requirements, such as restrictions to the transfer of technology in certain fields, or conditions such as the so-called (prior) consent"[29] on subsequent uses of safeguarded materials. It considers such additional requirements arbitrary and discriminatory. The CNEA has resisted the imposition of full-scope safeguards even though this has entailed financial costs. Disputes are not limited to the North Americans; safeguards renegotiations with the West Germans have at various times threatened to shut down Atucha I and arrest the Atucha II deal. Disagreement in the latter case reportedly involved technology transfer provisions in the IAEA safeguards agreement, as well as Argentina's right to conduct peaceful nuclear explosions.[30]

The Argentines have not always succeeded in fending off unwanted safeguards provisions. The supplemental safeguards at Embalse were forced upon them under the threat of Canadian withdrawal from the project. So long as Argentina remains dependent on outside suppliers, it will remain vulnerable to such ultimatums. Nevertheless, so far the CNEA has been able to keep indigenously-constructed heavy water and plutonium-reprocessing plants free from safeguards.

Argentina has not acceded to the Non-Proliferation Treaty, the Treaty of Tlatelolco, or the Limited Test Ban Treaty. Objection to the NPT centered on the alleged invidious discrimination favoring the nuclear weapons states. To the Argentine military government, the South Atlantic conflict confirmed the wisdom of rejecting the NPT for a second reason: It offers no protection against the nuclear weapons states' actions, such as Great Britain's use of a nuclear-propelled submarine.[31]

This action by the British, Castro Madero contended, also violated the "spirit" of the 1967 Treaty of Tlatelolco.[32] Argentina refused to join the other Latin American countries (including Brazil and excepting Cuba) in ratifying this nuclear-weapon-free zone. Argentina could not accept the U.S. interpretation of the treaty's definition of "nuclear weapons" as also prohibiting "peaceful nuclear explosives."[33] A decade after the treaty's submission for signature, the Argentine delegation to the United Nations Special Session on Disarmament promised to ratify Tlatelolco. That pledge was never fulfilled.

The military defeat inflicted by Great Britain ossified Argentine opposition to the global nonproliferation regime. In May 1982 Argentina formally lodged a protest with the IAEA against the British use of a nuclear submarine to sink its only cruiser, the *Belgrano*, with 1,048 men aboard. In Vienna, Castro Madero declared that Argentina would be free in the future to develop a nuclear submarine without violating any previous commitments.[34] In February 1983, after the IAEA board of governors affirmed that IAEA and NPT safeguards are compatible, Castro Madero reacted by reserving the right to withdraw material that Argentina wishes to use for naval propulsion from IAEA safeguards.[35]

Analyzed closely, these baleful Argentine pronouncements did not accomplish much. The attack on the NPT "non-proscribed uses" loophole seemed curious. Why focus on *propulsion*, rather than Britain's nuclear *weapons* (some of which allegedly were sent, albeit mistakenly, to the South Atlantic conflict)? If retaliation was desired, the construction of nuclear weapons would have been easier as well as more militarily threatening.

Why then did Castro Madero emphasize nuclear propulsion rather than nuclear weapons? One cannot be certain, but possibly he wished to vent domestic political pressure on the CNEA to act without moving toward nuclear weapons acquisition. The war had exposed the latent contradictions between Argentina's hope of independence and the reality of its subservience. The national humiliation of losing a local conflict to a distant colonial adversary could not be suffered in silence.

Argentina had to respond; inaction would confess impotence. Open pursuit of nuclear weapons, however, could provoke supplier cut-offs like those that have crippled the Pakistani and

Indian nuclear power stations. Moreover, a nuclear weapons push would divert money and energy from the major CNEA projects. If Castro Madero wanted to protect the Argentine nuclear power program from both domestic tampering and foreign embargo, it would have been canny politics to threaten a relatively harmless form of nuclear retaliation—a nuclear naval propulsion program. This retaliatory proposal could divert attention away from more drastic measures and permit the CNEA to carry on with its traditional priorities.

Some evidence supports this hypothesis. When Castro Madero first threatened Argentine use of nuclear submarines, he added that Argentina was not about to build nuclear weapons. Madero insisted that "it has nothing to do with nuclear explosives."[36] He elaborated his position two weeks later:

> The priorities established by the CNEA will be maintained. But [there is a new factor] . . . . This factor is the possibility of Argentina developing nuclear submarines. We must be cautious on this issue and we will begin by conducting feasibility studies to determine the cost of the project, the time that will be required and whether we will need foreign aid to carry it out.[37]

Afterward, Castro Madero has repeatedly reaffirmed Argentina's lack of interest in nuclear weapons. The Alfonsín government immediately canceled the Argentine nuclear submarine proposal.

CONCLUSION

Summing up capability and policy, what does Argentina's nuclear program provide? Economically the program generates electricity and employment. It serves as a conduit for acquiring more advanced technologies from abroad, and supports training for related scientific programs. At the same time, however, the progam has been expensive, and many Argentines believe it has claimed too large a share of the public fisc.

Politically the program yields prestige to the government both domestically and regionally. The government's self-esteem grows alongside its nuclear sophistication, to the point where it now perceives itself to be both a solid contributor to Latin American anticolonialism and a rightful member in the ranks of the nuclear suppliers.

The Argentine government also enjoys security benefits from encouraging continued suspicions that it might be developing a nuclear arsenal. So long as Argentina refrains from testing or moving toward an explosives program, it can avoid the harshest diplomatic and economic costs incurred by flouting the international consensus against proliferation. Argentina's ambiguous nuclear objectives can also be used to pry concessions from those nuclear suppliers who wish to retard nuclear proliferation. The Argentine government may bargain for concessions outside the nuclear field as well.

Argentine nuclear policy cannot be understood simply as an expression of national will: It also reflects bureaucratic competition within the government and military. Ambiguities are carefully nurtured not only to keep foreigners interested yet cautious, but also to offer something for everyone in the Argentine bureaucracy, be it economic promise, military strength, or political stature. Though no one's panacea, the nuclear program is successful enough to have earned widespread respect. That adds luster to the government and helps the CNEA maintain its preferred position among Argentine agencies.

This policy of purposeful ambiguity will continue to serve Argentina well so long as the government can continue to exploit mixed signals for these advantages. Should the Nuclear Suppliers Group revive and concertedly act to throttle supplies to Argentina pending acceptance of full-scope safeguards, or should Brazil feel so threatened as to move significantly toward a nuclear weapons option, Argentina may be forced to show its hand. Whether that hand would reveal a weapons program or not will depend on where Argentine politics stand at that moment, how much bureaucratic clout the CNEA can muster to protect its power program, and what sort of threat forces the government into the open. The Nuclear Suppliers Group or Brazil will probably not exert enough pressure to force these events. Therefore, the Argentine government will probably continue to combine two elements: (1) a weapons option and opposition to international nonproliferation accords; and (2) generally responsible behavior and disavowal of weapons intentions.

This policy may eventually afford Argentina its long-sought nuclear independence. The transition from rhetorical to actual independence is likely to be dangerous. As Argentina edges closer to the threshold, its leverage over those governments opposed to nuclear weapons proliferation will increase. Tlatelolco could remain unratified, while CNEA officials reassert the sovereign right to conduct peaceful nuclear explosions. Anxious Brazilians could respond with an indigenous nuclear development program that would be militarily threatening. In view of these sobering prospects, the rare opportunity presented by the Radical Party's accession to power should be seized. President Alfonsín has recently suggested that he would sign the NPT at once if Argentina were guaranteed access to peaceful nuclear technology and if the nuclear-weapons states were to undertake effective measures to control or disarm existing nuclear stockpiles. His forthcoming attitude presents a rare opportunity. If it is missed, the Argentine program could continue to be shrouded in purposeful ambiguity, its leaders excused from ever having to choose irrevocably between nuclear power and nuclear weapons.

NOTES

1. Following the rule of thumb that no unit should provide more than 10 percent of overall capacity, a 600 megawatt unit should not be introduced into grids below 6,000 megawatts.
2. Capacity factor calculations vary significantly according to assumptions. See G. MacKerron's criticism of more favorable estimates for the Karachi station, in *The New Scientist* (March 19, 1981): 765.
3. As early as September 1945 the Argentine junta proclaimed that the "exceptional importance" of uranium affected the "general interest of the nation" (El Poder Ejecutivo Nacional, *Decreto No. 22.855*, September 1945). Six years later, President Juan Perón startled the world by announcing that Ronald Richter (an Austrian emigré from the Nazi fusion project) had mastered nuclear fusion through indigenously developed Argentine technology. Within hours of the announcement, leading physicists throughout the world registered their skepticism. Soon, however,

Richter's quackery became so apparent that Perón had to dismiss him.

The Richter incident is important because it spawned two salient aims which later characterized Argentine nuclear efforts. One was independence. The other was nonpartisanship. See Daniel Poneman, *Nuclear Power in the Developing World* (London: Allen & Unwin, 1982), pp. 68–70.

4. República Argentina, El Poder Ejecutivo Nacional, *Decreto No. 302*, January 29, 1979.

5. *Energía* (June 1982): 594–95; and *La Prensa* (Buenos Aires), April 10, 1982.

6. *Convicción* (Buenos Aires), March 17, 1982, p. 11.

7. This response by Quihillalt to Brazilian charges that Argentina was embarking upon a nuclear weapons program appeared in the *The Christian Science Monitor* (London ed.), August 5, 1967.

8. *Nucleonics Week* (June 26, 1975): 9.

9. *Buenos Aires Herald*, December 11, 1982; and *Telam* (Buenos Aires), June 11, 1982.

10. Edward Schumacher, "Argentina Claims Nuclear Capacity," *The New York Times*, November 19, 1983, p. A–1.

11. República Argentina, Ministério de Economía, Secretaria de Estado de Energía, *Plan nacional de equipamiento para los sistemas de generación y transmisión de energía eléctrica; período 1979-2000: resumen*, September 1979, p. 41.

12. It is difficult to estimate the CNEA budget in dollar terms because of the peso's instability. From a 1980 estimate of $956 million, it declined to $773 million in 1983 and $503 million in the first year of the Alfonsín administration. CNEA officials hope for an increase in the 1985 budget. "¿Hacia donde va el plan nuclear?," *Clarin* (Buenos Aires), January 27, 1985, p. 20.

13. *Buenos Aires Herald*, December 11, 1982.

14. El Poder Ejecutivo Nacional, *Decreto No. 3183*, October 19, 1977.

15. El Poder Ejecutivo Nacional, *Decreto No. 302*, January 29, 1979.

16. J. L. Alegría et al., "La contribución de la energía nuclear a la solución del problema energético argentino," in *Peaceful Uses of Atomic Energy: Proceedings of the Third International Conference*, Vol. 1 (New York: United Nations, 1965).

17. CNEA, *Centro Ezeiza Atómica* (1967); Victoria Johnson and Carlos Astiz, "Latin America," in Frederick C. Williams and David A. Deese, eds., *Nuclear Nonproliferation: The Spent Fuel Problem* (New York: Pergamon Press, 1979), p. 79.

18. *Nucleonics Week* (March 3, 1983): 4.

19. *Jornal do Brasil* (Rio de Janeiro), January 10, 1982, p. 26.

20. The finance ministry was expected to cut 20 percent from the proposed 1983 CNEA budget (*Nucleonics Week* [March 3, 1983]: 4).

21. *Telam* (Buenos Aires), August 30, 1982.

22. Jonathan Kandell, "Argentina Assay Their Atom Potential," *The New York Times*, April 2, 1975, p. A-2.

23. Edward Milenky, *Argentina's Foreign Policies* (Boulder, Colo.: Westview Press, 1978), p. 120.

24. *Mercado* (Buenos Aires), July 30, 1981, pp. 2–26. Translated in FBIS, *Worldwide Report: Nuclear Development and Proliferation*, no. 113, JPRS 78971.

25. "Europe's Boost for Latin Bomb," *The International Herald Tribune*, April 8, 1980, p. 4.

26. *Noticias Argentinas* (Buenos Aires), October 15, 1979. See also Castro Madero's rebuttal to these charges in "Statement at the Signing of Decreto No. 2441"(n.d.), pp. 21–24.

27. *Nucleonics Week* (November 11, 1982): 1; *Mercado* (Buenos Aires), July 30, 1981, pp. 2–26; and *Telam* (Buenos Aires), April 6, 1982.

28. *Nucleonics Week* (November 11, 1982): 1.

29. Castro Madero, quoted in *Nucleonics Week* (March 11, 1982): 10.

30. *Mercado* (Buenos Aires), July 30, 1981, pp. 2–26; and *Nucleonics Week* (February 5, 1981): 6.

31. Castro Madero, quoted in *Convicción* (Buenos Aires), July 11, 1982, p. 23.

32. Text of speech reprinted in *Energía* (June 1982): 594–95.

33. "Treaty for the Prohibition of Nuclear Weapons in Latin America," Article V; and "A Proclamation by the President of the United States of America concerning Additional Protocol II to the Treaty for the Prohibition of Nuclear Weapons in Latin America, June 11, 1971," Section II.

34. *Telam* (Buenos Aires), June 11, 1982.

35. *Nucleonics Week* (March 3, 1983): 4. IAEA safeguards prohibit the use of covered material for "military purposes," while NPT safeguards prohibit use of covered material specifically for nuclear weapons or explosive devices. Argentina's complaint was that, while it was constrained by the more restrictive IAEA safeguards, Britain was free under the NPT to remove material from safeguards for "non-proscribed"—i.e., nonexplosive—military purposes, such as nuclear propulsion of submarines.

36. *Telam* (Buenos Aires), June 11, 1982.

37. Interview on Buenos Aires Argentina Televisora Color Network, June 25, 1982.

5 BRAZIL

David J. Myers

Brazilians believe that they have a special destiny. Their country ranks fifth in size and eighth in population in the world. Brazil's economy also ranks eighth. The military leadership, in power since 1964, anticipates that during the twenty-first century Brazil will dominate South America. Economically Brazilian industries will have to master advanced technologies and become competitive in the international arena. Politically Brazil must secure recognition and acceptance of its central role in South America from its neighbors and from the industrialized countries of the world. In reaching these latter objectives the military leadership foresees national security challenges: These challenges may propel Brazil to produce nuclear weapons.

While Brazil's drive to acquire nuclear power technology is related to complex political and economic considerations, its attitude toward developing nuclear weapons is shaped largely by Argentina's nuclear program. The 1982 Malvinas Islands conflict between Argentina and Great Britain renewed Argentine efforts to acquire a nuclear weapons capability. Doubtless, Brazil will never allow Argentina to be the only South American country with such weapons. An Argentine nuclear capability would frustrate Brazilian regional aspirations and would intensify apprehensions regarding the security of Brazil's southern frontier. Also, Argentina's decision to reoccupy the Malvinas Islands (territory it had not controlled for 150 years) reinforced suspicions that Argentina might use a nuclear monopoly in South America to resurrect old dreams of uniting its "lost territories": the Spanish colonial viceroyalty of the Rio de la Plata. Not only do these territories include the present-day buffer states of Uruguay, Paraguay, and Bolivia's Santa Cruz province, they also encompass parts of the Brazilian states of Rio Grande do Sul, Santa Catarina, and Parana.

The "lost territories" issue remains very real to Buenos Aires and Brasilia. War games in the Brazilian armed forces typically focus on frustrating Argentine efforts to recover its former territories along the southern Brazil border.[1] At the zenith of President Juan Domingo Peron's power in Argentina during the early 1950s, Peron played to nationalistic aspirations associated with regaining the "lost territories." In the North Atlantic these declarations were either ignored or dismissed as jingoistic bombast; after all, the United States opposed the forcible transfer of territory between countries in the Western Hemisphere. However, since the late 1970s the United States has encountered great difficulties projecting power internationally, even in its relations with small countries in the nearby Caribbean Basin. Consequently Brazilians and Argentines have grown increasingly skeptical that Washington would or could impose its preferences on the relatively distant South America.

Old territorial grievances and new political realities thus provide the backdrop for an analysis of Brazil's nuclear program. In undertaking this task, this chapter will focus on four questions: (1) What are Brazil's nuclear intentions? (2) What are Brazil's nuclear capabilities? (3) What kind of nuclear policy will the interplay of capabilities and intentions lead Brazil to pursue in the future? (4) What are the most important implications for the United States of Brazil's nuclear program? This final question leads to a discussion of U.S. policies regarding the problems of nuclear proliferation in South America.

BRAZILIAN INTENTIONS

Although the industrial countries expressed misgivings when Brazil and West Germany signed their famous nuclear accord on June 27, 1975, the United States reacted with a mixture of outrage and anguish. That two important allies would make an agreement circumventing the United States on a matter as vital as transferring the entire nuclear fuel cycle confirmed Washington's fear that its international influence was on the decline. Demonstrating independence from the United States, however, played an important part in the Brazilian government's decision to opt for West German nuclear technology. Brazil was tired of U.S. indifference, annoyed at its refusal to support its drive for upward international mobility, and resentful over continuing U.S. paternalism. The Brazilian–West German nuclear agreement thus gave Brazil a high-prestige technology and at the same time reduced dependence on the United States.

The importance attached to the June 1975 Agreement for the Peaceful Uses of Nuclear Energy is an ideal starting point for assessing Brazilian nuclear intentions. There are three important aspects to the agreement: (1) Brazil's determination to keep open both a nuclear power and a nuclear weapons option; (2) the basic components of the accord itself; and (3) Brazil's political, national security, and economic motivations underlying the agreement. Exploration of these three areas provides an overview of what Brazil hopes to accomplish with its nuclear program; it also sets the stage for examining Brazilian capabilities.

Keeping Open the Nuclear Option

The atomic bomb's decisive role in ending World War II in the Pacific made it obvious to Brazilians interested in attaining great power status that eventually their country would have to master nuclear technology. However, Argentina's ill-fated efforts to create a nuclear explosion in the early 1950s provided the impetus for Brazil's development of its own nuclear program. In 1953 President Getulio Vargas sent Admiral Alvaro Alberto, president of Brazil's National Research Council (NRC), to West Germany to obtain gas centrifuges. After a promising reception, the admiral arranged for Brazilian scientists to receive special training in the handling of heavy gases. For one brief moment President Vargas believed that

Brazil would soon possess the capability to produce its own enriched uranium.[2]

This early attempt to acquire nuclear technology was uncovered by John J. McCloy, the U.S. high commissioner to Germany. Under pressure from Washington the deal was canceled, and Admiral Alberto resigned as president of the NRC. The abortive Brazilian effort was but one example of attempts by excluded states to break the Anglo-Soviet-U.S. monopoly over nuclear technology. President Dwight D. Eisenhower recognized, however, that the monopoly could not be sustained. In a creative attempt to control the dissemination of nuclear technology, Eisenhower initiated the Atoms for Peace program, which made nuclear information and technology available and provided the training for foreign nationals.[3] Brazil received its first nuclear research reactor under the Atoms for Peace program, agreeing in return to obey international controls and to buy U.S.-enriched uranium fuel. Argentina, however, decided not to accept an internationally controlled research reactor. Buenos Aires had no intention of tying its nuclear program to a technology dominated by the United States.

Fluctuations in U.S.-Brazilian relations, domestic politics, and concerns over Argentina's growing nuclear capabilities influenced Brazilian nuclear policy from the mid–1950s to the early 1970s. President Juscelino Kubitschek (1956–61) favored close relations with Washington and promised to adopt the U.S.-controlled light water technology for Brazil's nuclear-powered electric industry. Presidents Janio Quadros (1961) and João Goulart (1961–64) championed an "independent" Brazilian foreign policy. They also preferred the French heavy water nuclear reactors, which were fueled by natural uranium, to the light water reactors whose enriched uranium fuel was sold only by the United States at that time. Following the military coup of April 1964, however, pro-U.S. officers broke off negotiations with the French for a heavy water reactor and placed a moratorium on all negotiations for nuclear technology transfers to Brazil.[4]

During the late 1960s Argentine efforts to acquire a commercial nuclear generating facility refocused Brazilian attention on the nuclear technology transfer issue. In 1968 Argentina signed a contract with Siemens A.G. of West Germany for its first nuclear power reactor. Although the U.S. firm of Westinghouse Corporation made the lower bid, Argentina chose West Germany's heavy water technology.[5] This development led to speculation in Brasilia that Buenos Aires selected the Siemens reactor because its natural uranium fuel could produce more weapons-grade plutonium than the enriched uranium fuel used by its light water competitor. In addition, the continuous refueling capability renders monitoring natural uranium reactors more difficult than enriched uranium reactors.[6]

Brazil's initial response to the Argentine reactor selection was to negotiate its own agreement with France. The Franco-Brazilian understanding called for joint research in thorium technology, uranium exploration, and power plant construction.[7] Nevertheless, Brazil's most significant response was its 1972 purchase of an enriched uranium reactor from Westinghouse. However, the Brazilian-U.S. project was beset with problems. Brazil desired the complete nuclear fuel cycle, which included the technology for uranium enrichment and spent-fuel reprocessing—important parts of nuclear weapons production. Since Brazil had not signed the Treaty on the Non-Proliferation of Nuclear Weapons (NPT), the U.S. government prohibited Westinghouse from including uranium-enrichment and spent-fuel reprocessing capabilities as "sweeteners" in the contract to purchase nuclear power plants.[8]

Unhappiness with these prohibitions, which the West German–Argentine agreement did not include, was one reason why Brazil moved away from the United States as a supplier of nuclear technology. In July 1974 the United States returned the deposit on enrichment services contracted by Brazil for its nuclear reactor. Accompanying the returned deposit was notification that the contract was conditional because the U.S. government could not legally accept firm contracts for enrichment beyond its available capacity at the time. Washington's action apparently propelled Brasilia toward development of a domestic enrichment capability as well as toward modifying the course of its nuclear programs.[9]

Two other factors influenced Brazil's decision to explore European alternatives for nuclear power. First, the successful oil embargo of 1973 argued for a reduction in dependence on petroleum as an energy source. Brazil imported 80 percent of its petroleum needs and possessed minimal reserves.[10] Because petroleum prices were expected to rise indefinitely following the embargo, a shift toward nuclear-generated electricity was economically justified at that time. Second, in 1974 India exploded a nuclear device. Entry into the nuclear club by an Asian developing country convinced Brazil's recently inaugurated president, General Ernesto Geisel, that the military dimension of nuclear power could not be ignored, especially given Argentina's interest in nuclear weapons. This latter consideration strengthened the case of those who argued that Brazil should move away from dependence on safeguarded U.S. nuclear technology.

The Brazilian–West German Nuclear Power Agreement: An Overview

The June 27, 1975, agreement between Bonn and Brasilia provided for the unprecedented sale of a complete nuclear fuel cycle. It also mandated the creation of several West German–Brazilian companies to implement the agreement and to train Brazilian technicians and scientists.

Provisions for uranium enrichment and spent-fuel reprocessing facilities generated the most controversy. Consequently, in response to intense pressure from the United States and from their European neighbors, the West Germans insisted on safeguards even more stringent than those recommended by the International Atomic Energy Agency (IAEA). Nevertheless, what was demanded were not "full-scope" safeguards; as the Indian explosion demonstrated, less than "full-scope" safeguards provide no guarantee against nuclear weapons development.[11] Therefore, West Germany extracted a pledge from Brazil not to produce explosives, and not to copy West German technology except under certain conditions. The history of technology transfers, however, suggests that the latter pledge is impossible to enforce.[12] Thus, the West German nuclear agreement allowed Brazil to gain access to a wide range of nuclear technology and, with it, nonmilitary and military options.

Motivations

Similar to its Argentine rival, political, national security, and economic motivations underlay Brazil's interest in and agreement to the West German proposal. (See Poneman, Chapter 4.) Political motivations, particularly the issues of prestige and increasing independence from the northern industrial countries, were primary.

Internationally Brazil aspired to become the hegemonic power in South America. As a strong regional power Brazil could then counteract U.S. paternalism and intervention. Brazil's foreign ministry increasingly saw ties with Asian and African countries as a means to strengthen Brazil's bargaining position with the United States and Western Europe. Since Brazilian culture contained both European and African elements, Brazil sought to play the role of an intermediary between the industrial north and the underdeveloped south. While this cultural diversity resulted on occasion in confusion about how Brazil wished to be viewed internationally, in the context of this discussion the important point is that Brazil actively sought an international leadership role. Thus, Brazil's possession of nuclear technology could enhance national prestige and, by implication, its capacity to exercise leadership.

Mastery of nuclear technology was and is a matter of prestige for Brazil's military regime in its relations with the country's people. The generals came to power promising economic growth, competent administration, and social peace. They claimed that by setting aside the divisiveness of partisan politics and by pursuing orderly development, Brazilians would propel their country toward its rightful place as a regional hegemon and world power.[13] Because nuclear technology was perceived as a significant indicator of national power, the military regime assumed that creation of the Brazil they had promised mandated acquisition of a nuclear power capability.

The 1968 nuclear accord between Argentina and West Germany, especially because it lacked significant international safeguards, convinced the Brazilian government that access to the complete nuclear fuel cycle was a matter of urgent national security. President Costa e Silva's concern reflected the Brazilian military's continuing suspicion and distrust of ultimate Argentine intentions. As noted earlier, dismemberment of the former La Plata viceroyalty during the turbulent post-independence decades made Argentina a territorially dissatisfied state.

Argentina's nuclear decisions, and Brazilian perceptions concerning Argentina's motivations, must be understood in the context of events along the Argentine-Brazilian frontier during the late 1960s and early 1970s—a period of increased Brazilian activity. In 1971, for example, the Brazilian military assisted one faction of the Bolivian military in its successful campaign to oust the leftist government of General Juan Torres.[14] Subsequently Bolivia permitted Brazil to expand its presence throughout the potentially energy-rich province of Santa Cruz. In Paraguay, Brasilia joined with Asuncion in building the gigantic Itaipu hydroelectric project; this undertaking directly affected the flow of water into Argentina's Plata River Basin. Also, thousands of Brazilian peasants migrated to Paraguay hoping to benefit from the economic development that Itaipu would set in motion.[15] In some zones Brazilians outnumbered Paraguayans, and the Paraguayan government appeared oblivious to the dangers of separatist movements by expatriate Brazilians.

Uruguay also moved politically and economically closer to Brazil during the late 1960s and early 1970s.[16] Trade with Brazil increased, and Brazilians purchased additional land on the Uruguayan side of the Brazilian-Uruguayan frontier. Even more important, Brazilian advisers were invited by the Uruguayan military to assist in liquidating the urban Tupamaro guerrillas. Tensions associated with the antiguerrilla struggle led to a military seizure of power, and ties between the Uruguayan and Brazilian military strengthened. During this time of Brazilian regional advances, domestic political turmoil paralyzed Argentine foreign policy.

Mastery of nuclear technology, from the Argentine perspective, in a single stroke could provide Argentina with the power and prestige necessary to challenge Brazil's influence in the buffer states of Uruguay, Paraguay, and Bolivia. Argentina's subsequent pursuit of nuclear technology was, therefore, partly driven by the perception that Argentina must find a counter to

Brazil's growing ability to project power beyond its borders. The greater Argentina's success in obtaining nuclear technology, however, the more Brazil felt compelled—for reasons of national security—to do the same.

Economic considerations also entered into the Brazilian-West German nuclear agreement. Between 1968 and 1974 the Brazilian "miracle" had created one of the world's largest economies; but it assumed secure supplies of low-cost energy. After the 1973 oil embargo and subsequent price increases made shambles of this assumption, Brazil began exploring alternative energy sources. The prospect that petroleum needs could be supplied domestically appeared grim. Even the most optimistic studies doubted that Brazil could ever supply more than one-third of its petroleum requirements from domestic sources.[17] Brazil did possess important uranium reserves. Consequently during the early 1970s nuclear power appeared as a reasonably priced and dependable source of energy for Brazil's growing economy. Indeed, when the agreement was signed, supporters boasted that in the year 2010 nuclear energy would generate 41 percent of Brazil's total electric power.[18]

Brazil also hoped to export nuclear power reactors and enriched uranium fuel to other Third World countries, and perhaps even to Western Europe.[19] In so doing, Brazil would earn critical foreign exchange. At the same time, Brazil sought to break the industrial North's monopoly—particularly that of the United States—of a technology that could enable the developing countries to reduce their economic and military dependence on the developed world. The justification of Brazilian access to a complete fuel cycle was, to be sure, a potent political, national security, and economic issue.

BRAZILIAN CAPABILITIES AND THEIR DETERMINANTS

Following the June 1975 nuclear agreement, Brazil made significant progress in creating a nuclear power infrastructure. Nevertheless, much that was promised remains unfulfilled. Financial constraints and the limited availability of highly trained technicians proved more troublesome than did other obstacles. In addition, government policymaking was often paralyzed because of disagreements over the cost-benefit ratio of specific investments. Still, Brazil remains in a position to take advantage of technological breakthroughs for both military and peaceful purposes.

Accomplishments

Projects exist in varying states of completion for each dimension of the landmark agreement with West Germany. These include: (1) uranium mining and exploration; (2) uranium enrichment; (3) fuel fabrication; (4) spent-fuel reprocessing; and (5) power plants. Other Brazilian nuclear and nuclear-related projects range from the creation of electricity by means of fusion to the testing of ballistic rockets, which could carry Brazilian nuclear weapons to potential targets throughout South America.

Between 1975 and 1984 considerable progress was made in locating and classifying Brazilian uranium reserves. The Brazilian government set its uranium reserves at 300,000 tons late in 1983. Of these reserves, 190 tons were classified as "measured and indicated," thus giving Brazil the fifth largest reserves in the world. In addition, estimated Brazilian reserves of thorium are 80,000 tons. Thorium, however, is most useful for breeder reactors, and thorium breeders are unlikely to have any commercial significance until the twenty-first century.[20]

Brazilian uranium-enrichment technology is based on Germany's Becker jet-nozzle enrichment process. When the Brazilian–West German agreement was signed in 1975, the Becker technique was not operational on an industrial scale.[21] While mechanically simpler than either gaseous diffusion or the new gas centrifuge enrichment technology, the jet-nozzle process consumes more electricity—nearly twice as much as gaseous diffusion and twenty times more than the centrifuge. However, because the Becker jet-nozzle process was the single enrichment technology that the West Germans controlled, it was the only one available for transfer under conditions acceptable to the Geisel government.

The 1975 agreement called for Brazil to receive jet-nozzle technology capable of enriching uranium from 0.7 percent to 3.2 percent. At Resende, in the state of Rio de Janeiro, a plant with this capability is under construction. When it begins producing commercially, with a planned capacity of 300 tons of enriched uranium annually, Resende will consume 1.5 million kilowatt hours of electricity—equivalent to the entire output of a medium-sized hydroelectric plant. However, Resende will not reach the threshold of even industrial-scale production—60 tons of enriched uranium annually—until 1986. A definitive judgment as to whether the Becker jet-nozzle process is economically competitive with other technologies cannot be made until 1990.[22]

The Resende complex also contains a plant for converting enriched uranium into fuel elements. This facility began operation in October 1982 and incorporatestechnology transferred from the Kraftwerk Union (KWU) consortium of West Germany. Between 1980 and 1982 KWU trained many Brazilians for work at the Resende fuel-fabrication plant. The Resende fuel-fabrication plant is considered capable of operating close to its planned production capacity of 100 tons of fuel elements annually. Production includes the manufacture of forty structural elements to recharge Brazil's first nuclear power plant, Angra I, and the supply of initial loads for Angra II and Angra III. Officially Resende's fuel-fabrication facility is estimated to have cost $31 million.

Although in July 1982 President Paulo Nogueira Batista of the state nuclear energy corporation (Nuclebras) publicly stated that work on the reprocessing plant will begin in 1983, Brazil has yet to initiate any construction. The location of the reprocessing plant has not been decided; still, Nogueira Batista maintains that the plant will commence operation in 1988. His estimation assumes that, despite international concern over the military capability of spent-fuel reprocessing equipment, West Germany will proceed with technological transfers as outlined in the June 1975 accord.[23] There is a high probability that the West Germans will not change their minds. Not only has Bonn resisted pressure to retract the terms of the 1975 agreement, but within West Germany itself reprocessing has been promoted by the government as a procedure for detoxifying nuclear waste. Denying technology for waste detoxification might be read by many as indifference to the health of people in the developing world. Also, a West German denial might discredit the government position that the benefits of spent nuclear fuel reprocessing far outweigh its military dangers.[24]

Brazil purchased its first commercial nuclear reactor to generate electricity from Westinghouse. Construction on this turnkey project, located in the state of Rio de Janeiro at Angra dos Reis, began in 1972. Designated Angra I, the reactor was scheduled to come on line in 1977. However, the plant did not generate electricity until March 1982, and even then, vibrations in the generator prevented Angra I from producing more than a fraction of its planned capacity of 626 megawatts (mw). The problem intensified, and Nuclebras subsequently shut down the plant. Although scheduled to resume generating electricity by late 1983, scientists seriously doubt whether Angra I will ever operate at more than half of its planned capacity.[25]

Brazil's other nuclear power reactors are part of the West German package. The original agreement foresaw up to eight nuclear generating facilities. The first of these, Angra II, is also located at Angra dos Reis. Its installed generating capacity will be 1,300mw. Currently under construction, Angra II is experiencing many of the same difficulties encountered in the building of Angra I.[26] The cumulative effect of difficulties with the Angra reactors undermined confidence in Nuclebras and its president Nogueira Batista. Nogueira Batista gave the national government an opportunity to move against Nuclebras when in mid–1982 he asked for bids on contracts involving a third Angra reactor and two additional nuclear power plants along the São Paulo coast, at Iguape. These contracts committed billions of dollars in foreign exchange at a time when Brazil was negotiating with the International Monetary Fund to reschedule its debt. Moreover, Batista resorted to procedures of questionable legality in awarding contracts for the two Iguape reactors, jeopardizing his position still further.[27]

Following the November 1982 elections, President João Figueiredo removed Nogeira Batista as president of Nuclebras and named his own man, Hervasio Carvalho, as head of the National Nuclear Energy Commission (CNEN). Nuclebras also suffered a 40 percent budget cut. In addition, the two Iguape reactors were postponed indefinitely, and Figueiredo stretched out completion of Angra III until 1990. Given this shift in priorities, the Brazilian nuclear power industry of 1995 will consist of three commercial plants with an operational capability of less than 3,226mw of electric generation.

Brazil's nuclear priorities include activities related to nuclear power and weapons. In the former area, for example, Nuclebras entered into a joint venture with the West Germans and Austrians in order to manufacture heavy equipment for the 1,300mw reactors projected in the June 27, 1975, deal. Known as Nuclebras Equipamentos Pessados (NUCLEP), the joint venture began operation in May 1980. NUCLEP was to produce the reactor vessel and steam generator for the now indefinitely postponed Iguape I reactor. In addition, NUCLEP was to supply nuclear generating equipment for export, and Argentina did order one reactor vessel for its Atucha II nuclear power plant. As of 1984, however, the future of NUCLEP still appears precarious. The Malvinas Islands conflict forced Brazil to rethink relations with Argentina, and the weakened financial position of Third World states raised questions about these countries' ability to pay for nuclear power plants. Finally, within Brazil, how reductions in the Nuclebras budget will affect NUCLEP remains unclear.

A number of Brazilian research centers are working on other nuclear-related technologies, including lasers, fusion, fast breeders, and ultra-centrifuge enrichment. None of these research efforts is under international safeguards. A CNEN project, Campos de Roma in the state of Rio de Janeiro, is probably the most important of these research programs. Initially the project concentrated on fast breeder reactors, which use thorium as fuel. The technology for this research is provided by Italy, and the CNEN has also attracted French, Italian, and West German scientists to work at Campos de Roma and on other projects. Additional activities planned for Campos de Roma include research on plasma physics and nuclear fusion. The rising costs of all nuclear technology, however, have delayed plans to expand Campos de Roma. Instead, the CNEN is concentrating available resources on the IPEN (Instituto de Pesquisas Energeticas e Nucleares) in São Paulo.

Located at the University of São Paulo, IPEN's activities constitute the bulk of Brazilian nuclear weapons research.[28] The facility also employs the best physicists and nuclear engineers in Brazil. In the post-November 1982 electoral shakeup of Brazilian nuclear policy, President Figueiredo appointed a leading advocate of nuclear weapons acquisition, Colonel Durvaldo Concalves, as head of IPEN. Prior to Concalves's appointment, President Figueiredo placed all nuclear research facilities, including IPEN, under control of the national government.

Other centers for nuclear weapons and related research exist. Among the most important is the air force's Centro Technico Aerospacial at Saõ Jose dos Campos. Also, at the submarine research facility in Rio de Janeiro, the navy is upgrading its capability to absorb nuclear technology. Finally, the army's Centro Technológico de Exercito (CENTEX) is conducting a broad range of research at the Marambai missile base.[29] One of the CENTEX projects involves studying the use of nuclear energy in the propulsion of satellites.

To summarize, Brazil has created an infrastructure that allows its scientists and technicians to become acquainted with a broad range of rapidly evolving nuclear technologies. Despite reductions in Nuclebras in early 1983, Brazil has the capability to expand its nuclear power industry. Weapons research, as suggested above, has received increased emphasis, reflecting Brazilian concern that Argentina may accelerate its efforts to produce and deliver nuclear weapons as a consequence of the Malvinas conflict.

The Influence of Internal Conditions

Brazil's nuclear program has remained a high-priority item since the late 1960s. Four characteristics of the domestic political economy explain what has been accomplished during these years: (1) the continuing dominance of the military in politics; (2) bureaucratic and personal rivalries involving the most important national public corporations and political leaders; (3) difficulties in adapting to the exacting technical standards necessary to develop and operate a successful nuclear program; and (4) conflicting pressure for balancing investment in infrastructural buildup against short-term demands by the poor for a better life. Political, economic, and national security factors, therefore, have conditioned accomplishments at least as much as they have influenced motivations.

The armed forces participate in nuclear policymaking and traditionally give final approval to major decisions in this area. The interest of the armed forces derives from the military applications of nuclear energy, and since 1964 control of the government has facilitated direct military control of all nuclear and nuclear-related policy.

General Ernesto Geisel, president between 1974 and 1979, personally oversaw negotiation of the nuclear technology agreement with West Germany and supervised the creation of Nuclebras. Paulo Nogueira Batista, first president of Nuclebras, was Geisel's trusted confidant. When General João Figueiredo took over as president in late 1979, he also involved himself in nuclear energy policy. Figueiredo consulted with the chiefs of each military service late in 1982 to determine the magnitude and division of resources between the civilian and military dimensions of the nuclear program. In January 1983 Figueiredo placed all nuclear research installations under national government control, in a hierarchy where military authority would be unchallenged.[30] This action suggests that even should the Brazilian military return to the barracks, it would continue to rule supreme in all aspects of nuclear research.

Bureaucratic infighting continues to impede the adaptation and development of nuclear technology in Brazil. In 1975 the Brazilian government addressed this problem by decreeing that all research teams operating in fields other than those favored by the West German agreement were to be dismantled.[31] As a first step, Nuclebras insisted on terminating nuclear research at the army-run Instituto Militar de Engenharia in Rio de Janeiro. The institute was engaged at that time in work on heavy water production and fast breeder reactors. Nuclebras also moved to impose its priorities on Electrobras, the state electric corporation. Electrobras was developing a master plan for electric power generation that would satisfy Brazilian needs well into the twenty-first century. Intense competition developed between those who favored reliance on hydroelectric power generation and others who argued for nuclear power.

Nogueira Batista of Nuclebras and General Costa Caval-canti of Electrobras maneuvered against each other for the better part of three years. The latter had the ear of President Figueiredo, and the former received backing from ex-President Geisel. Eventually Costa Cavalcanti prevailed. Nogueira Batista's last-ditch effort to save the West German agree-ment, as suggested earlier, involved negotiating contracts for the Iguape nuclear power plants against the wishes of President Figueiredo. This challenge provided the president with the excuse he wanted to diminish Nuclebras and reduce the influence of the West German nuclear lobby. While the role of Nuclebras, without Nogueira Batista, is presently being rede-fined, it will probably be limited to overseeing the dramati-cally shrunken nuclear power generating program. Other nuclear activities, mostly related to military objectives, now fall under the jurisdiction of the National Security Council. Research facilities are operated either by an individual mili-tary service or by the CNEN.

Difficulties in adapting to the exacting technical standards necessary to develop and manage nuclear power have plagued the Brazilian program since its inception. These difficulties became highly visible in association with the Angra I nuclear power plant. For example, technical considerations were largely ignored when the bay at Angra dos Reis was selected as the site for the initial commercial nuclear reactors. The bay at Angra dos Reis lacks the solid geologic substrata necessary to build stable foundations for nuclear power plants. In addition, a large fault runs under the bay. These conditions forced a long delay in the construction of Angra I while supports for its foundations were redesigned.

The redesigned support system and foundations demanded special techniques for the pouring of concrete, but these proce-dures were ignored. Consequently Nuclebras had to remove even the redesigned foundation supports and pour them a sec-ond time, using stricter standards. Angra I thus began generat-ing electricity almost five years behind schedule; it will never operate at its installed generating capacity of 626mw.[32]

The sites chosen for Angra II and Angra III—the two remaining nuclear power plants planned for in the West Ger-man agreement—are even more swampy than the one on which Angra I was constructed. Even if all goes as planned, the Angra II and Angra III plants—only two out of the nine proposed—will not come on line until the late 1980s and early 1990s. These facilities are unlikely to reach their planned generating capacity of 1,300mw. Finally, shortages of qualified personnel remain a significant obstacle in Brazil's efforts to master both the military and peaceful dimensions of nuclear technology.

Political demands associated with the average Brazilian's desire for a better life invariably constrain the government's ability to invest in nuclear technology. Resources are scarce, resource allocation is highly competitive, and the nuclear energy program has become ever more costly. Initially expenditures associated with the June 1975 agreement were estimated at $10 billion. In 1980 Brazilian officials hinted that implementation would cost more than double the initial estimate. However, the secretary general of the Brazilian Physics Society places the real long-term implementation costs at $40 billion. Given the Brazilian debt of $95 billion, the world economic recession of 1981–83, and persistent malnutrition and unemployment, an expenditure of this magnitude for nuclear programs far exceeds the financial capability of the Brazilian state.[33]

Inputs from the International Environment

Historically the course of Brazilian economic and technological development has been influenced by decisions made in the North Atlantic countries. Developments in nuclear power reflect this pattern. All operational Brazilian nuclear facilities employ North American or West European technology. Therefore, Brazilian nuclear capabilities depend on the willingness of these governments to allow the necessary technology transfers and to provide Brazil the funds needed to pay for the desired nuclear technology.

Apprehensions about nuclear weapons proliferation have led to U.S. opposition to any sale of a complete nuclear fuel cycle to a nonnuclear power. This concern has profoundly influenced the course of Brazilian nuclear policy. Even under the most cordial of conditions, the Geisel government would not obtain U.S. approval for purchasing a complete fuel cycle. Brazil's refusal to sign the NPT ensured that presidents Gerald Ford and Jimmy Carter would not consider an exception to this policy in the negotiations between Nuclebras and Westinghouse pertaining to the Angra I nuclear reactor. This U.S. policy led directly to the Brazilian–West German agreement and to additional Brazilian efforts to secure nuclear technology from other West European states.[34]

The growing power of the antinuclear lobby in the United States made the transfer of any nuclear technology to Brazil extremely unlikely after the June 1975 agreement was signed. Opponents of nuclear power, as well as other liberals in the United States, saw Brazil as a pariah state. Even conservatives remained uneasy about Brazilian intentions. In 1981, for example, the Reagan administration stepped in to nullify an accord between Princeton University and Brazil that would have involved Brazilians in a joint research project to explore the potential of nuclear fusion in generating electricity.[35]

The willingness of West European countries to supply manufacturing processes and training denied by the United States has allowed the Brazilian nuclear program to become more than the operation by locals of turnkey facilities. In addition to providing the technology transfer envisioned in the June 1975 agreement, the West Germans have displayed a willingness to assist the Brazilian military in establishing various nuclear research facilities. West Germany's position acknowledges that its participation in future Brazilian nuclear projects depends on continued responsiveness to the needs and priorities of the Brazilian armed forces. If the West Germans were seen as inflexible about the international safeguarding of transferred nuclear technology, then the Brazilian market could be lost to the Swiss, the French, or the Italians. Loss of the Brazilian market, because of an unwillingness to comply with the wishes of the Brazilian government, would damage West Germany's position as a nuclear supplier throughout the developing world. Competition among North Atlantic suppliers, therefore, has increased Brazil's leverage with West Germany and has provided Brazil with a greater nuclear capability than it otherwise could have acquired.

While international supplier rivalry has assisted Brazil in procuring sensitive elements of the nuclear fuel cycle, bureaucratic infighting and economic difficulties have caused the government to revise its ambitious plans for Brazil's nuclear industry.[36] Differences between Nogueira Batista and President Figueiredo played an important part in the former's exit from Nuclebras and in the 40 percent cut in the Nuclebras budget in 1983. Another equally important factor was the liquidity crisis relating to repayment of the Brazilian debt during 1982 and 1983. In order to avoid default on the U.S. $95 billion owed to foreign creditors, Brazil was forced to implement some of the measures recommended by the International Monetary Fund. These measures included scaling down many economic infrastructural investment programs. Given the escalating costs of nuclear power and the greater return on investment in hydroelectric power, reducing the Nuclebras budget became an irresistible option. In this light, developments in the Brazilian nuclear power program appear as but one more manifestation of Brazilian dependence on northern financial institutions.

THE FUTURE OF BRAZILIAN NUCLEAR POWER

Brazilian nuclear policy during the 1980s and 1990s will revolve around three broad issues: (1) the generation of electricity and other civilian, nonexplosive purposes; (2) the supply of nuclear technology to other countries, especially in the developing world; and (3) the military use of nuclear power, encompassing the development of nuclear weapons and their deployment by the Brazilian armed forces.

Brazil as a Peaceful Nuclear User

The National Nuclear Energy Commission has emerged as Brazil's most important nonmilitary source of nuclear energy policy. President Figueiredo intends for the CNEN to oversee programs in uranium exploration and mining, uranium enrichment, fuel fabrication, spent-fuel reprocessing, and nuclear power generation.[37] Each of these programs formed part of the

West German accord. The CNEN also will coordinate experimental nuclear research and make recommendations to the president concerning the fate of NUCLEP. As indicated earlier, NUCLEP was to have produced reactor vessels for the indefinitely postponed Iguape I and Iguape II nuclear reactors.

While Brazil's nuclear program will be reduced, future governments seem likely to honor President Geisel's commitment to absorb nuclear technology. Abandonment of the nuclear power program would be a significant blow to Brazilian political prestige throughout the developing world, particularly to Brazilian hegemonic aspirations within South America. Abandonment of nuclear power by Brazil would lead to recalculation by its neighbors of the political and technological balance between Brazil and Argentina, especially given the comparatively smooth development of the latter's nuclear power program. The obvious military implications of Brazil's inability to master peaceful nuclear power could not be ignored.

Additional political and technological benefits will keep Brazil's nuclear power program alive during the coming decades. A capability to tap diverse energy sources gives Brazil valuable leverage in bargaining with energy suppliers, particularly the Organization of Petroleum Exporting Countries. Demonstrated mastery of nuclear technology provides an element of national pride and supports official efforts to legitimate the government in the eyes of nationalistic Brazilians; it also reinforces the view Brazilians have of themselves as a people capable of advanced technological achievements. Finally, current investments in nuclear technology will allow Brazil to take full advantage of possible future cost-reducing breakthroughs.

Brazil as a Nuclear Supplier

Upon signing the June 1975 Agreement for the Peaceful Use of Nuclear Energy, the Geisel administration believed that the way had been opened for Brazil's emergence as an important exporter of nuclear technology. In the final year of his presidency, Geisel entered into a nuclear agreement with Iraq, one of Brazil's major oil suppliers. This accord called for Brasilia to supply Baghdad with low-enriched uranium, with safety technology, with the nuclear information system of the IAEA, and to undertake the training of Iraqi personnel.[38] It also raised questions as to whether President Geisel had violated the Brazilian–West German agreement which stipulated that no sensitive materials or technology, including highly enriched uranium and reprocessing equipment, would be transferred. Israel was obviously displeased with the Iraqi transaction, as it enabled Iraq to continue stockpiling.

Argentina has been the only other important customer for Brazilian nuclear technology. Brazilian-Argentine relations took a turn for the better during the late 1970s, when the two countries resolved longstanding differences over water rights in the Plata River Basin. Resolution was followed in May 1980 by a nuclear cooperation agreement, under which Argentina agreed to sell zircaloy tubing and transfer technology for fuel assembly and quality control to Brazil. In return, Brazil would supply Argentina with the pressure vessel and vapor generators for its Atucha II nuclear power generator. In addition, the agreement pledged cooperation in uranium mining and processing, fuel cycle and nuclear station research, and radioisotope production. However, both sides were slow to implement these accords, and in April 1982 Argentina's invasion of the Malvinas Islands revived Brazilian mistrust of Argentina. Subsequently Brasilia has been reluctant to participate in cooperative nuclear power ventures with Buenos Aires.[39]

Despite setbacks in its programs to export nuclear technology to Iraq and Argentina, Brazil has not abandoned its desire to become a nuclear supplier. Future exports are to include uranium, both in its natural and enriched forms, and products from the heavy equipment complex operated by NUCLEP. The minister of mines and energy, Cesar Cals, unveiled a long-range plan in 1982 that called for the export of 3,000 tons per year of uranium concentrate and 500 tons per year of enriched uranium. While no timetable for reaching these goals was advanced, the minister anticipated that the uranium concentrate would come from Brazil's processing center currently under construction at Itataia, where more than half of the country's known uranium reserves are located. However, the Itataia processing center will not begin operation until the mid–1990s, and, as indicated earlier, the jet-nozzle enrichment plant at

Resende cannot produce enriched uranium in commercial quantities until 1988.[40]

Whether Brazil will realize its 1975 dream of becoming an important nuclear exporter to Africa, Asia, and South America remains problematical.[41] In these highly competitive markets, experience, innovation, and proven reliability are important. Nuclebras has proven itself only marginally competent in constructing the Angra reactors in Brazil. It cannot compete internationally with such giants as Westinghouse and Kraftwerk Union. Although Nuclebras might become a subcontractor in some specialized areas, it still faces the problem of competing with established firms from the industrialized countries. Brazil apparently made a major mistake in negotiating the 1975 agreement when it failed to press Kraftwerk Union for assured subcontracting roles in the consortium's international reactor construction business.

Brazil as a Possessor of Nuclear Weapons

Evidence has been accumulating that Brazil is committed to the acquisition of some nuclear weapons. In 1982 West Germany succumbed to Brazilian pressure and began providing nuclear technology not covered by the June 1975 agreement. The Instituto de Pesquisas Energéticas e Nucleares (IPEN) received radiation protection equipment that enabled its reprocessing plant to extract plutonium safely. Other West German technology assisted in the purification of uranium. In addition, the government announced its intention to upgrade the nuclear research facility at Campo de Roma, where an Italian-French consortium is involved in transferring breeder reactor technology.[42]

Conceivably Brazil has the potential to develop a "small nuclear force"—the ability to launch a credible first strike against a regional power but insufficient to threaten a second strike against the strategic targets of either superpower. However, Brazil would have to adapt or acquire new delivery systems, devise survivable basing modes, and develop reliable and secure command, control, and communication systems. While nuclear weapons could be carried on Mirage III interceptors presently included in the air force inventory, any decision to create a "small nuclear force" would mandate the purchase of newer, more capable delivery systems. While programs to develop and test Brazilian ballistic missiles have made impressive progress, any "small" Brazilian nuclear force of the 1990s will utilize tactical aircraft as its primary means of delivery. Export models of most available aircraft, like the Anglo-French Jaguar, do not contain nuclear wiring and delivery hardware. However, Brazilian industries are capable of reconfiguring such aircraft with simple but reliable nuclear arming, fusing, and firing mechanisms.[43]

Whether Brazilian progress toward the creation of a "small nuclear force" accelerates or stops short of developing weapons and acquiring a delivery system will depend on Brazilian perceptions of Argentine intentions. Argentina retains a significant lead, perhaps of five or more years, in any all-out race to acquire an operational "small nuclear force." Brazil would prefer not to become involved in such a race, because it could not win. However, the Argentine military understands that if it acquires a "small nuclear force," Brazil eventually will do the same. Argentina and Brazil would then possess expensive nuclear armed forces that would serve as mutual deterrents. For this reason, at least until the Malvinas Islands conflict, both countries avoided programs to acquire a "small nuclear force."

Great Britain's reconquest of the Malvinas Islands during May and June of 1982 had a profound effect on Argentine thoughts about the desirability of developing a "small nuclear force." In Buenos Aires, after the British victory, a primary concern has become to make military intervention in the South Atlantic prohibitively costly. Consequently acquisition of a "small nuclear force" has become more attractive. One certain result of this policy, however, would be the generation of irresistible pressure on Brazil to do the same.[44] Brazilian distrust of Argentine designs on the "lost territories" is stronger than ever. Recent attention by the Figueiredo government to the military dimension of its nuclear program reflects this heightened distrust. Thus, even skillful diplomacy will be hard-pressed to prevent the proliferation of nuclear armaments from becoming a major problem in South America.

Reducing the Weapon Incentive: The Leverage of U.S. Technology and the Military Umbrella for Brazil

Prestige, economic benefits, and national security considerations have been identified as motivations for Brazil's effort to acquire a complete nuclear fuel cycle. Neither Washington's offer of turnkey projects nor its use of pressure on its North Atlantic Treaty Organization (NATO) allies has proved effective in deterring Brazilian efforts to master this technology.

Events from 1975 to 1984 suggest that the United States cannot prevent a complete nuclear fuel cycle from being transferred to Brazil. Directing how Brazil employs transferred technology is also extremely difficult. Nevertheless, the United States may be able to exert some influence on selected, high-priority issues. Washington obviously does not want Brasilia to develop its own nuclear weapons. Leverage reducing the attractiveness of so doing can be applied with a reasonable probability of success along two dimensions: facilitating Brazilian acquisition of sophisticated peaceful nuclear technology if it foreswears the nuclear weapons option; and offering protection under a nuclear deterrent so powerful that Brazilians would have little incentive to develop their own nuclear armed forces.

Problems with the Angra II and Angra III reactors, along with President Figueiredo's shakeup of Nuclebras, present an opportunity for the United States to reemerge as a significant factor in the Brazilian nuclear program. However, leverage can be acquired only if the United States withdraws its opposition to Brazilian acquisition of elements in the nuclear fuel cycle, such as uranium enrichment and spent-fuel reprocessing. Additional influence would be forthcoming if Washington sanctioned participation by a U.S. private corporation in Brazil's breeder reactor program and reversed its veto of a Brazilian presence in fusion research at Princeton University.

Any decision to participate in the Brazilian nuclear program along the lines indicated above would require the United States to reverse nuclear technology transfer policies that have been in place for more than two decades. Brazil is well on its way to acquiring the very elements of the nuclear fuel cycle that existing nonproliferation policies were designed to block. The United States should convince Brazilians not to use their cycle for weapons purposes. In this context, the United States may want to take the lead in transferring a complete fuel cycle, if ιe cycle could be managed by a public corporation controlled by the most important South American states. The United States should insist on full-scope safeguards for the nuclear fuel cycle of any such South American public corporation, even though safeguards may be violated without being detected. The impact of having a safeguarded nuclear fuel cycle, even given the demonstrated limitations of detecting equipment, will be movement toward creating a nonthreatening international environment.

The United States must foster the evolution of a nonthreatening international environment for Brazil. Bilateral agreements that reinforce Washington's commitment under the Rio Pact would be an important step in this direction. In addition, the United States might agree to sell Brazil a number of sophisticated weapons systems, such as the F–15 and F–18 aircraft, which have not been available because of restrictive arms transfer policies.

Brazilian fears of Argentine designs on southern Brazil merit special attention from U.S. policymakers. They could be allayed by restating Washington's opposition to the forcible transfer of territory within the Western Hemisphere. Also, Brazilian fears of Argentina would be greatly reduced by a U.S. plan for jointly deploying military forces with Brazil if Argentina developed its own "small nuclear force." However, should Brasilia test its own nuclear device, U.S. assistance in any confrontation with Buenos Aires would not be forthcoming. In the meantime, Brazilian insecurity might also be lowered if Brazilian military services, in addition to the navy, were encouraged to participate in periodic Unitas-like maneuvers. These maneuvers presumably would include Argentina, providing a forum in which Argentina and Brazil could work together for common purposes. Finally, indirect pressure on the United Kingdom to negotiate some form of joint sovereignty over the Malvinas Islands might lead to a reduction inBrazilian apprehensions about Argentina. If Argentina did not feel compelled to reconquer the Malvinas, it would have little justification for upgrading its military capabilities. Tensions throughout South America would be lowered, and the region's two most important states would feel less need to acquire nuclear weapons.

In regard to Western Europe, Washington should not openly oppose its NATO allies when they transfer elements of the nuclear cycle to Brazil, or if the option should develop, to a South American multistate agency. Washington should, however, continue to press for the inclusion of full-scope safeguards in all nuclear technology transfers. Additionally some of the previously mentioned mechanisms for strengthening ties between Brazil and the United States might be similarly adapted to Brazil with NATO. Integration into the Western defense system, especially if supplemented by economic incentives, would lend support to elements in Brazil opposed to exercising the independent nuclear weapons option.

The 1960s and 1970s made Brazilians increasingly conscious of their national interests, and some of these interests differ from those of the United States. Many, however, remain compatible, and given the economic and political realities of the 1980s, nuclear policy falls within the "largely compatible" category. While taking advantage of the many opportunities to develop a common nuclear policy with Brazil, therefore, Washington must not act as if it is being betrayed when Brasilia pursues nuclear policies of which the United States disapproves. The overall compatibility of the two countries' nuclear interests dictates that differences be expressed as friendly disagreement.

NOTES

1. Interview by the author with a high-ranking Brazilian naval officer in Rio de Janeiro on October 15, 1981. Also, Frank D. McCann, "Brazilian Foreign Relations in the Twentieth Century," in Wayne Selcher, ed., *Brazil in the International System: The Rise of a Middle Power* (Boulder, Colo.: Westview Press, 1981), p. 6.

2. Juarez Tavora, *Atomos para O Brasil* (Rio de Janeiro: José Olympio, 1958), pp. 346–47.

3. The liberalization represented in the Atoms for Peace program has been characterized as "exploiting the inevitable" (Depart-

ment of State, Bureau of Public Affairs, *The Export of Nuclear Technology*, Special Report no. 9 [1974], p. 3). Also see Office of Technology Assessment, Congress of the United States, *Nuclear Proliferation and Safeguards* (New York: Praeger Publishers, 1977), p. 5.

4. Reflections of domestic political changes in nuclear policy are profiled in Victoria Johnson, *Brazilian Nuclear Development: Intent and Capabilities* (Ann Arbor: University Microfilms International, 1979), pp. 70–74. A useful overview from the Brazilian perspective is provided by Eduardo Pinto, "Brasil—Os dificeis Caminhos Da Energia Nuclear," *Jornal do Brasil* (Rio de Janeiro), June 16, 1974.

5. Johnson, *Brazilian Nuclear Development*, pp. 73–75.

6. The significance of this "advantage" of natural uranium reactors over enriched uranium reactors, from the Brazilian perspective, is discussed in Norman Gall, "Atoms for Brazil, Dangers for All," *Foreign Policy*, no. 23 (Summer 1976): 183–84.

7. Elve Monteiro de Castro, "A Energia Nuclear do Brasil," *A Defensa Nacional* (Rio de Janeiro), January-February 1974, pp. 63–64.

8. Johnson, *Brazilian Nuclear Development*, pp. 73–74.

9. Subcommittee on Arms Control, International Organizations and Security Agreements of the Committee on Foreign Relations of the U.S. Senate, *Nonproliferation Issues Hearings* (Washington, D.C.: Government Printing Office, 1977), pp. 124–25.

10. "Política Nuclear: Os projectos, as alternatives e o misterio," *Visão*, September 9, 1974, pp. 27–28.

11. Edward Wonder, "Nuclear Commerce and Nuclear Proliferation: Germany and Brazil, 1975," *Orbis* 21, no. 2 (Summer 1977): 285–86.

12. A useful popular analysis of the unworkability of the IAEA safeguards, including how they have been circumvented, is contained in James N. Miller, "The Peaceful Atom Bares its Teeth," *Reader's Digest* (June 1983): 93–98.

13. The best discussion of the motivations of those staging the April 1964 coup is Alfred Stepan, *The Military in Politics: Changing Patterns in Brazil* (Princeton: Princeton University Press, 1971).

14. Carlos J. Monera and Rolf Wichmann, "Brazil and the Southern Cone," in Selcher, ed., *Brazil in the International System* (Boulder, Colo.: Westview Press, 1982), pp. 159–159.

15. Ibid., pp. 174–75; and Martin T. Katzman, "Translating Brazil's Economic Potential into International Influence," in Selcher, ed., *Brazil in the International System*, pp. 99–122.

16.   Thomas E. Weil et. al., *Area Handbook for Brazil* (Washington, D.C.: D.A. Pam 55020, 1974), pp. 299–300.

17.   Government of Brazil, *National Energy Balance*, pp. 7–8.

18.   William H. Courtney, "Brazil and Argentina: Nuclear Choices for Friendly Rivals," in Joseph A. Yager, ed., *Nonproliferation and U.S. Foreign Policy* (Washington, D.C.: The Brookings Institution, 1980), pp. 271–72.

19.   Gall, "Atoms for Brazil," p. 157.

20.   *Estado de São Paulo* (São Paulo), July 4 and August 22, 1982.

21.   Ibid., June 15, July 2, and August 7, 1982. For a detailed analysis of commercial-type, jet-nozzle uranium-enrichment technology, see "Nuclear Proliferation: India, Brazil and Germany May Accelerate the Process," *Science* (May 30, 1975): 911–14. See also *Jornal do Brasil*, June 25, 1982, as translated in *Joint Publication Research Service (JPRS)*, July 28, 1982, pp. 18, 19.

22.   *O Globo* (Rio de Janeiro), July 2, 1982 (*JPRS*, August 5, 1982, p. 9).

23.   *Gazeta Merchantil*, April 28, 1982 (*JPRS*, July 8, 1982, p. 35); and *O Globo*, July 2, 1982.

24.   Allen L. Hammond, "Brazil's Nuclear Program: Carter's Nonproliferation Policy Backfires," *Science* (February 18, 1977): 657–59. See also *Der Speigel* (March 15, 1976), and "Atomwirtshaft: 12.000.000 Mark für Deutschland," *Wirtschaftswoche* (June 27, 1975): 13.

25.   *Latin American Regional Report: Brazil* (London: Latin America Newsletters Ltd.), February 11, 1982, pp. 6–7.

26.   *Nucleonics Week* (January 6, 1983): 3; and *O Estado de São Paulo*, September 24, 1982.

27.   *Latin American Regional Report: Brazil*, February 11, 1983, pp. 6–7.

28.   *Nucleonics Week* (December 2, 1982): 4; and *O Estado de São Paulo*, July 3, 1982.

29.   *Latin American Regional Report: Brazil*, February 5, 1982, pp. 5–6.

30.   Ibid., February 11, 1983, pp. 6–7.

31.   Ibid., February 5, 1982, p. 5.

32.   *Nucleonics Week* (March 10, 1983): 3; and *Latin America: Weekly Report: Brazil*, April 22, 1983, p. 4.

33.   *Latin American Regional Report: Brazil*, May 30, 1980, p. 7. See also Warren Hoge, "Brazilians, Once So Buoyant, Succumb to Burdens," *The New York Times*, October 21, 1983, p. A–17.

34.   George H. Quester, *Brazil and Latin American Proliferation: An Optimistic View*, ACIS Working Paper no. 17 (Los Angeles:

Center for International and Strategic Affairs, 1979), pp. 2–19; and Hammond, "Brazil's Nuclear Program," pp. 658–59.

35. *Latin American Regional Report: Brazil*, April 29, 1983, p. 5.

36. *Latin America Weekly Report*, June 10, 1983, pp. 1, 2.

37. *Latin American Regional Report: Brazil*, February 11, 1983, pp. 5–6.

38. *Jornal do Brasil*, September 27, 1979.

39. *Nucleonics Week* (April 17, 1980): 4–5; Ibid. (February 18, 1982): 5, 6.

40. *Correio Brasilienese* (Brasilia, Federal District), June 10, 1982, p. 9; and *Latin American Regional Report: Brazil*, April 23, 1982, p. 5.

41. Leslie H. Gelb, "Nuclear Nations to Tighten Export Controls," *The New York Times*, July 6, 1984, pp. A–1, A–4. The article names Brazil, along with China, as one of two new supplier countries causing concern among members of the London Suppliers Club.

42. *Latin American Regional Report: Brazil*, February 5, 1982, pp. 5–6.

43. William H. Courtney, "Brazil and Argentina: Strategies for American Diplomacy," in Yager, ed., *Nonproliferation and U.S. Foreign Policy*, pp. 377–96. See also *Latin American Regional Report: Brazil*, June 3, 1983, pp. 6–7.

44. "Argentina Pushes Nuclear Program," in Council on Hemispheric Affairs, *Washington Report on the Hemisphere*, June 26, 1983, p. 5.

6 SOUTH AFRICA

Robert S. Jaster

Seven years have passed since the Soviet Union alerted Western governments to its discovery of a suspected nuclear test site under construction in a remote corner of South Africa. That discovery led to a concentrated and sophisticated intelligence collection effort by the United States, and to a flurry of diplomatic activity by Western officials. The quest for intelligence has continued. So has diplomatic activity, in the form of occasional low-key discussions between the United States and South Africa.

Despite such efforts, the United States knows little more today than it did six years ago about South African activity in the Kalahari Desert in the summer of 1978. The state of knowledge is no better—perhaps worse—about the mysterious flash that occurred over the South Atlantic in the early hours of September 22, 1979. Technical experts agreed that the Kalahari site more closely resembled a nuclear test site than it did anything else. The South Atlantic incident, however, provoked sharp disagreements within the U.S. scientific and technical communities. Some experts were strongly convinced that the flash could have been caused only by a nuclear explosion. Others, including a presidential panel, considered natural phenomena a more likely explanation. Nor did political analysts agree on the most likely suspect, assuming it was a nuclear

147

explosion. The smoking gun was seen variously in the hands of India, South Africa, Israel, and the latter two in collusion. The only explanation dismissed out-of-hand was a suggestion from South Africa that an old, errant Soviet missile might have blown up on the South Atlantic seabed.

On one aspect of South African nuclear development, however, there is near unanimity: South Africa is judged to have the capability to design, produce, and deliver a nuclear weapon. Have the South Africans developed a weapon? If so, have they tested it? In the absence of conclusive technical evidence, the answers to these and other questions must be found in South African politics; in particular, the leadership's shifting perception of threats to South Africa, and of the country's strategic importance in the world.

This chapter will examine briefly the technical evidence of South African nuclear development, and then will analyze major political factors defining South African nuclear strategy. Among the questions to be addressed are: Would South Africa want a nuclear weapon? What military use might such a weapon have? Why, and under what conditions, might South Africa test a weapon? Under what circumstances might it be deployed? What are the implications of a South African nuclear capability for long-range Western interests in regional security and nonproliferation?

CAPABILITIES AND INTENTIONS: A LOOK AT THE TECHNICAL EVIDENCE

South Africa's nuclear weapons potential can be assessed only within the framework of its general nuclear development program. The first stage of that program, which began in the late 1940s, focused on the extraction of uranium ore for export. In the scramble to secure reliable sources of uranium for the anticipated boom in world demand, the United States and Great Britain turned to South Africa (then a Commonwealth member), which was estimated to have as much as 25 percent of the noncommunist world's total reserves.[1] The United States and Great Britain invested in uranium-processing facilities in South Africa, which opened its first processing plant in 1952.[2]

Between 1953 and 1971 the United States imported more than 40,000 tons of South African uranium oxide, valued at $450 million.[3] (U.S. government purchase contracts with South Africa ended in 1966.) South African production accounted for 13 to 14 percent of noncommunist countries' uranium output in the mid–1970s.[4] In the past few years, diminishing world demand and falling prices for uranium have reduced South African export receipts and have removed potential South African leverage over the international uranium market.

Stage two—establishing the technological base for further nuclear research, including the development of an indigenous enrichment capability—occurred during the late 1950s and 1960s. In 1957 South Africa and the United States signed a twenty-year agreement under the Eisenhower administration's Atoms for Peace program. The agreement authorized South Africa to purchase its first research reactor, the U.S.-designed Safari I, and the highly enriched uranium (HEU) needed to run it. Under the terms of the agreement, South Africa sent ninety-four of its nuclear scientists and technicians to train at various U.S. nuclear installations, including the Oak Ridge and Argonne laboratories of the Atomic Energy Commission (AEC).[5] South Africa also initiated a nuclear research and development program at Witwatersrand University and became a charter member of the International Atomic Energy Agency (IAEA).

In 1965 the Safari I research reactor, at Pelindaba, went critical. From the start, the reactor had been subject to IAEA safeguards; safeguards, however, would not have prohibited the use of Safari I for experiments directed toward acquiring a weapons capability.[6] An example would be experiments involving the generation and control of neutrons and the properties of materials under neutron bombardment—experiments critically important to the development of a "clean" tactical weapon.[7] South Africa later designed and built a second research reactor, Pelunduna Zero, which was not subject to IAEA safeguards.[8] This reactor, known as Safari II, has since been decommissioned.

These earlier developments—the processing of indigenous uranium ore, access to Western nuclear technology, and the acquisition of a research reactor—enabled South Africa to take the most important step toward achieving independent nuclear capability: acquiring the means to enrich uranium. In July 1970 Prime Minister John Vorster announced the indigenous development of a unique and allegedly economical process for the commercial enrichment of uranium. Five years later a pilot enrichment plant at Valindaba was operational, though with a small capacity.

The decision to develop an independent enrichment capability had a plausible commercial basis. South Africa had initially hoped to enhance the foreign exchange potential of its uranium by converting it to low-enriched uranium (LEU) for use in nuclear power plants. In 1975 Dr. Abraham Roux, then head of South Africa's Atomic Energy Board (AEB), confidently announced that South Africa was ready to build a large-scale enrichment plant. There was talk of a 5,000-ton-per-annum enrichment facility that would earn $250 million a year from exports of nuclear fuel.[9]

By 1978, however, conditions had changed. The slowdown in the growth of global nuclear generating capacity raised serious doubts about the future demand for nuclear fuel. In South Africa's case, such doubts were heightened by the fact that a large-scale plant probably would cost over $2 billion—more than double the original estimate, and too much long-term capital foreither foreign investors or local capital markets to digest.[10]

Also of serious concern was the Carter administration's 1977 decision to suspend the U.S. long-term contract to supply LEU unless South Africa signed the Treaty on the Non-Proliferation of Nuclear Weapons (NPT). That contract provided for the supply of LEU for two nuclear power reactors under construction at Koeberg, near Capetown. The two plants, bought from France, were scheduled to be operational in 1982–83, well before South Africa would be able to run the French plants with its own indigenously enriched fuel. The U.S. Nuclear Non-Proliferation Act of 1978 formalized the ban on nuclear fuel supply to those refusing to sign the NPT.

In light of these factors—rising construction costs, uncertain export markets, and the suspension of U.S. fuel deliveries for Koeberg—South African leaders chose a smaller enrichment facility. A smaller plant could be built more quickly, thereby assuring that the nuclear power plants would not stand idle for want of fuel.

But doubts emerged concerning South Africa's near-term capacity for uranium enrichment. In 1979 Dr. Roux maintained that within three years the enlarged enrichment facility at Valindaba would be able to meet the LEU needs of Koeberg,[11] and "after the necessary modifications" could provide enough highly enriched uranium to keep the Safari I research reactor running.[12] Less than a year later this estimate was revised downward in a report by the government-owned Uranium Enrichment Corporation (UCOR).[13] It would take up to five years, UCOR reported, before Valindaba could produce fifty tons of LEU annually—barely enough to meet Koeberg's estimated annual consumption of forty-eight tons.

In 1981 South Africa announced its success in producing "small quantities" of uranium–235 enriched to 45 percent.[14] The press, however, reported that a shortage of LEU might delay the start-up of the first Koeberg power station "for several years," that is, well beyond Roux's original target date of 1982.

American and South African officials have continued intermittent and low-key talks. Consistent with its policy of constructive engagement toward South Africa, the Reagan administration has loosened restrictions on exports of so-called dual-use items with potential nuclear application.[15] South Africa, however, has not been persuaded to sign the NPT or to accept full-scope safeguards, arguing that this would risk revealing the technical secrets of its unique enrichment process. Since the Reagan administration has shown no inclination to seek repeal of the ban on nuclear fuel deliveries, the impasse continues.[16]

How do these developments relate to South Africa's technical capability to produce a nuclear weapon? A country's weapons capability rests on three basic requirements: sufficient quantities of weapons-grade material; scientific and technical skills to design a weapon; and a means of delivery.

Leaving aside the arcane question of whether South Africa might have received weapons-grade material through covert diversion of another country's supply, or through diverted U.S. supplies of HEU (104 kilos of which were received between 1962 and 1975), there is little reason to doubt that South Africa has had the capability to produce small quantities of weapons-grade uranium since the late 1970s.[17] Roux acknowledged in May 1977 that the pilot enrichment plant at Valindaba could be used for this purpose.[18] Could the facility produce enough weapons-grade plutonium? According to U.S. intelligence estimates, by 1979 Valindaba might have produced as much as forty kilos of HEU, which is less than the estimated forty-eight kilos needed to detonate the crude fission devices used in other countries' first tests.[19] Yet, if the South Africans were able to duplicate or acquire recent Western techniques in warhead design—for example, to encase uranium–235 in a four-centimeter sphere of uranium–238—forty kilos would have been more than sufficient.[20]

As to South Africa's design capabilities, one can only speculate. Its mining industry has developed expertise in the technology of explosives for many years. Indeed, this achievement was one of the first areas in which South Africa's growing armaments industry achieved virtual self-sufficiency. South African scientists and engineers have had access, until very recently, to U.S. and European nuclear laboratories, graduate faculties, research institutes, and professional conferences. Undoubtedly they have endeavored to maintain contacts abroad in spite of the decrease in technical exchanges at the state level.

There are a number of instances of South Africa's energetic efforts to overcome deficiencies in priority areas. One example is South Africa's covert acquisition of a long-range artillery shell of U.S. manufacture to meet the threat of Soviet 122mm rockets during South Africa's military incursions into Angola in 1981–82. Moreover, there is no reason to think South Africa would have neglected so crucial an area as weapons design, once a decision had been made to acquire the bomb. South Africa also has been involved in what appears to be a growing, trilateral, nuclear relationship with Israel and Taiwan. American intelligence officials are said to have expressed concern that scientists from Israel and Taiwan are helping the South Africans build nuclear weapons and produce weapons-grade uranium.[21] There has been speculation, for example, that South Africa's nuclear cooperation with Taiwan may have provided access to metal-fusing processes that would be applicable to weapons design.

South Africa's possession of a means of delivery—the third requirement for a weapons capability—is certain. Its Canberra and Buccaneer bombers and Israeli-designed Jericho missiles are suitable delivery vehicles.[22] The Mirage III fighter/bomber, with a maximum weapon load of 4,000 kilos, is another example. Observers like Robert Harkavy have long assumed that there is "little reason for Pretoria to anticipate problems in penetrating the urban airspace of surrounding nations, not to mention the possibilities of sea-borne delivery."[23]

Available evidence on South Africa's technical capabilities clearly points to possession of all the prerequisites for developing a nuclear weapon. On this point, at least, virtually all observers agree. Whether, in fact, South Africa has acquired such a weapon is frequently debated within scientific and technical communities. The discovery of the Kalahari site and the atmospheric event in the South Atlantic have aroused more than academic interest in the question.

Kalahari Revisited

Available facts concerning South Africa's suspected nuclear test site in the Kalahari Desert have been analyzed at length in the press and professional literature. In this discussion, therefore, the topic will be only briefly summarized and major implications drawn.

On August 6, 1977, the Soviet Union first called U.S. attention to what it claimed were preparations for an imminent nuclear test by the South Africans. A U.S. review of high-resolution satellite photography, much of it taken soon after the Soviet warning, disclosed a cluster of sheds and other buildings around a prominent tower, along with a solidly built structure somewhat removed from the others. These were clearly visible in a remote and desolate stretch of desert. Various U.S. specialists are said to have been unable to match the structures with any other sort of known activity. American officials were quoted as being 99 percent certain that the structures represented preparations for a nuclear test, though ambiguity remained. The anomalies at the site led some analysts to suspect a hoax. The following weeks witnessed intense diplomatic activity. The United States and France, as scheduled suppliers of enriched uranium and nuclear power stations, respectively, made strong demarches to the Vorster government on the basis of this leverage. The South Africans' ambiguous response is discussed later.

Several observations regarding the Kalahari episode are worth making. Senior U.S. officials appeared convinced that the Kalahari complex was designed as a nuclear test site. The site design was compatible with those of other countries' first tests, which were surface tests of a crude device, as opposed to a more fully developed weapon. Although a number of senior South African officials offered reassurances concerning their government's intentions, no plausible explanation of the site has been offered by the South Africans.[24] Construction activity at the site continued until at least December 1977, more than four months after the site had been discovered and monitored. The Kalahari activity thus appears to have been a deliberate, phased construction program.

The South Atlantic Incident

Two years after the Kalahari episode, an intense burst of light, lasting less than a second, was detected by a U.S. air force intelligence satellite, the Vela, as the satellite passed over a remote expanse of ocean between South Africa and Antarctica. The alarming feature of this flash was its double pulse, a signature unique to nuclear explosions. As in the Kalahari case, the incident has been extensively analyzed.[25] Treatment here will be limited to a brief account and observations as to what the Vela incident may suggest about South Africa's technical progress toward acquiring and testing a nuclear weapon.

The Vela's recording of a small, two- to four-kiloton explosion was convincing evidence. In each of the forty-one previous cases where the Vela had registered a double pulse, independent sources confirmed that the disturbance had been a nuclear explosion. In this case, however, the usual corroborating evidence, such as the recording of seismic disturbances and collection of radioactive debris, was lacking. A panel of scientific experts convened by the White House reviewed the evidence for two months. The panel concluded that the case for a nuclear explosion remained unproven, but that it could find no other plausible explanation.[26]

Other experts challenged these findings. A Los Alamos scientist pointed out that the fallout from a low-altitude, low-yield blast would have stayed at low altitudes. Within twenty-four hours, the fallout would have been brought down and dispersed into the ocean by local rains and winds.[27] Such an explosion, therefore, might easily have escaped detection.

Scientists elsewhere claimed that the panel had dismissed corroborating evidence of a nuclear explosion. A radio telescope at Arecibo, Puerto Rico, registered an ionospheric disturbance at the same time as the Vela recording. Unlike most previous disturbances, this moved from southeast to northwest, placing it in the approximate area of the Vela flash. No natural disturbance could be found to account for the "Arecibo ripple." A detailed study by the Naval Research Laboratory (NRL) analyzed a hydroacoustic signal, whose timing and possible direction seemed to link it with the flash. The NRL claimed the pulse was the strongest yet recorded, comparable to signals produced by earlier nuclear tests in the Pacific.[28]

The White House panel, however, found flaws in this evidence. Other observers, also, remained skeptical. The area covered by the Vela at the moment of the flash had a diameter of some 3,000 miles, extending from the Indian Ocean across the southern tip of Africa to the South Atlantic and southward to the northern edge of Antarctica. One analyst suggested that, if there had been a nuclear explosion, India was the most likely suspect.[29]

Similarly the intelligence community lacked consensus. The Central Intelligence Agency initially found that acoustic evidence from widely scattered listening posts indicated a nuclear explosion. Later the agency decided that background noise could have been responsible.[30] A classified Defense Intelligence Agency report, however, concluded that the Vela had indeed recorded a nuclear event.[31]

Circumstantial evidence heightened suspicions that South Africa had secretly conducted a test. An inquiry by a U.S. Senate aide disclosed that the U.S. National Technical Information Service had received only one request for literature on the detection of seismic disturbances. The client was South Africa's defense and naval attaché.[32] In April 1980 it was disclosed that an Oxford-trained South African scientist, Dr. Renfrew Christie, had been detained in South Africa since October 1979 under the Terrorism Act for giving a foreigner classified data on sites that the AEB considered seismologically safe for detonating a nuclear device.[33] A South African naval exercise allegedly took place in the South Atlantic at the time of the Vela sighting.[34] Western sources, however, report that only a port security exercise was known to be in progress at that time.

Assuming that the September 1979 event was a South African nuclear test, what does the technical evidence suggest about South Africa's capabilities and intentions? Dr. Richard Betts of the Brookings Institution said that such a two- to four-kiloton explosion "would represent either a 'fizzle' of a normal first-generation weapon or . . . a highly sophisticated 'trigger' device."[35] One recent analysis accepts the latter explanation, stating that a clean, low-yield thermonuclear device requires only a small quantity, eight to ten kilos, of fissionable material, and minimizes radioactive fallout.[36] This figure is consistent with estimates of South Africa's limited capacity to produce weapons-grade fuel. It is also consistent with the failure of U.S. global monitoring devices to detect radioactive debris following the event. Physicist Charles Kennard notes that, unlike suspected preparations for a test in the Kalahari, the later incident was an atmospheric explosion; thus, if it was a nuclear detonation, the device was one of advanced design.

All the technical and circumstantial evidence, taken together, suggests a number of propositions. There is virtually no doubt that South Africa has the capability to design, produce, and deliver a small nuclear weapon. There is an equally high probability that the Kalahari complex was designed to be, or to appear to be, a nuclear test site. Either case clearly implies that a weapons option entered into South Africa's nuclear strategy and calculations. And though serious reservations and ambiguities shroud the Vela incident, there are too many indications of a South African nuclear test to dismiss this explanation. More importantly, however, a covert South African test would have had grave policy implications for the Carter administration's nonproliferation policy. These political realities weighed heavily on the White House. Thus, a staff member of the president's Office of Science and Technology Policy noted that the technical data were useless unless they produced an airtight case.[37] In the absence of a "smoking gun," the White House panel could only reach the verdict it did: case unproven.

An assessment of South Africa's nuclear intentions—how a nuclear weapons capability might or might not fit into its military strategy—cannot be deduced from technical evidence alone. In the following section, the politics of a nuclear weapon will be explored from the standpoint of the South African leaders' unique threat perceptions and their strategy for the survival of white rule.

POLITICS AND THE BOMB: UNDERSTANDING PRETORIA'S NUCLEAR STRATEGY

South African whites have considered themselves to be under a state of siege for more than thirty years, as opposition to apartheid both in and outside the country has become more widespread and more effective. During the past several years, this siege mentality has been used by leadership and refined into an official ideology of threat and survival.

With the collapse of Portuguese dominion over Angola and Mozambique in 1974, and the end of white settler rule in Rhodesia in 1979, cross-border guerrilla attacks into South Africa and Namibia increased, leading to growing tensions and conflict between South Africa and its neighbors. Pretoria's leaders saw a need to mobilize support among South Africa's whites—not only fellow Afrikaners, and Coloureds and Asians as well. Afrikaner nationalism could no longer suffice as a unifying ideology for such an enlarged *laager*. Hence, Heribert Adam, a leading authority on Afrikaner politics, notes the need for a new formula: "The ideology of survival implies an unquestioned threat. An enemy exists by definition, regardless of the specifics that are under attack. . . . Survival means countering a challenge to life itself. . . ." Furthermore, "the secret of successful mobilization with survival politics lies in creating anxieties in the first place, and then offering the way out for the frightened."[38] And, in the words of a pro-National Party newspaper:

"The National Party is the guarantor of white survival in a turbulent subcontinent, and the opposition and other enemies will exploit every little crack."[39]

The Botha leadership has defined the threat to survival in terms of a "total onslaught" allegedly being waged against South Africa.[40] In 1981 Defense Minister Magnus Malan described the onslaught to Parliament as: "Communist inspired, Communist planned, and Communist supported. [The aim is] to gain control over southern Africa. On their way [to world domination] Russian leaders have selected certain interim objectives, and southern Africa is one."[41] Prime Minister Pieter W. Botha earlier had outlined for Parliament the Soviet objectives in South Africa: "The main object . . . under the guidance of the planners in the Kremlin, is to overthrow this state and to create chaos in its stead, so that the Kremlin can establish hegemony here."[42] The onslaught is "total," said General Malan, "not only in terms of ideology, but also as regards the political, social, economic and technological areas."[43] The enemy, he said, employs a wide range of measures in the political, diplomatic, religious, psychological, cultural, social, and sports spheres.

The military threat is seen as the most serious. The government is confident that it can handle the immediate guerrilla problem. Though South African leaders claim to see no imminent danger of direct Soviet attack, they have continued to warn that, once the Soviet Union's indirect strategy has succeeded, "the final conventional confrontation will take place."[44] Foreign Minister R. F. Botha, in a confidential discussion with U.S. officials, described the Soviet plan as "first Namibia, then Botswana, Lesotho, and Swaziland, followed by the final attack on South Africa. The government can't ignore this reality."[45]

More immediately, Pretoria's leaders have expressed alarm over the buildup of sophisticated weapons in nearby states. Prime Minister Botha told Parliament that such equipment could be "converted almost overnight into a credible instrument of Russian aggression."[46] In 1982 a Defence White Paper was even more alarmist: "The presence of Soviet armaments in the neighboring countries of the RSA [Republic of South Africa], which include heavy and advanced equipment, increases the possibility of a conventional threat to the RSA and SWA [Namibia], *even in the short or medium term.* If the Soviet Union wishes to become involved, Soviet personnel is all that would be required"[47] [emphasis added]. In 1979 Deputy Defense Minister H. M. J. Coetzee claimed that 4,000 to 6,000 East German troops had been "deployed" in Angola and Mozambique, and that units of this "Afrika Corps" were preparing to intervene directly in support of the South West Africa People's Organization (SWAPO).[48] In 1981 the defense minister told Parliament that the presence of 300 Soviet tanks, 350 armored personnel carriers (APCs), and 400 infantry vehicles just beyond South Africa's borders meant that the country must prepare to face a conventional attack.[49]

The threat of conventional attack and the role it plays in defense planning have been largely ignored by outside observers.[50] The military leaders' public concern is clearly self-serving, but that of the political leadership is quite genuine. These attitudes have influenced defense strategy and battle tactics. They also appear to have been accepted by the white community. In a recent poll of white South Africans, 80 percent disagreed with the statement that "the Communist threat against the country is exaggerated by the government." Among Afrikaners, almost 87 percent disagreed.[51] Even an opposition member of Parliament expressed the conviction that:

> In Africa as things stand we are not going to have to deal with a purely African situation. . . . We must unfortunately expect to see more foreign troops on our borders. [We already have the Cubans; now something else has been added]: a second Afrika Corps . . . composed of East Germans . . . highly trained and experienced . . . paratroopers equipped with the most modern weapons, who are poised to the north of Southwest Africa.[52]

The adoption of the "total onslaught" concept was undoubtedly influenced by South Africa's growing international isolation, particularly after 1975. Widespread international condemnation followed the Soweto student uprising, in which some 600 blacks and 4 whites were killed. Soweto occurred when South Africa's white leadership already had been shaken by the scale and intensity of black protest. Prime Minister Vorster struck a somber note in his 1977 New Year's Day address to the nation: "If therefore a Communist onslaught should be made against South Africa, directly or under camouflage, South Africa will have to face it alone, and certain countries which profess to be anti-Communist will even refuse to sell us arms. . . . This is the reality of our situation."[53] This growing sense of isolation was reflected in then Defense Minister P. W. Botha's statement to a National Party congress in 1977 that South Africa was "moving more and more in the direction in which the state of Israel has already been since 1948."[54]

The threat and ideology of survival also have a vital link to domestic politics. Afrikaners, who comprise the large majority of National Party supporters, have traditionally looked for strong, authoritarian leaders. In Afrikaner history, the heroes are tough, unyielding leaders who conquered a hostile environment and prevailed in battle over the fierce Zulu impis and the superior forces of the British invaders. In opinion polls, Afrikaners have continued to ascribe toughness as an admired leadership trait, particularly toughness in the face of outside provocation.

P. W. Botha, South Africa's current prime minister, fits this mold. As defense minister, he expanded and modernized South Africa's armed forces and won sharp increases in defense spending. His colleagues have dubbed him *Piet Wapon*—Pete the Gun—and close subordinates have described him as a "superhawk." A progovernment newspaper welcomed his selection as prime minister: "Mr. Botha is tough . . . and toughness as opposed to weakness is an essential prerequisite if South Africa is to survive the unremitting pressures which it faces."[55]

Yet P. W. Botha is politically vulnerable. He is personally and politically committed to a program of race reform designed to give some political voice to Coloureds and Asians, and to improve the economic lot of urban blacks. Botha has declared these reforms to be an essential part of the national plan for survival. Modest as these reforms may appear to outsiders, they have aroused a storm of protest from conservative Afrikaners. In March 1982 sixteen members of Parliament defected from the National Party over the reform issue and joined the official opposition. This is the first time since the National Party came to power in 1948 that it has had a formal opposition on its right. Botha sees these reforms as critical to the survival of white rule, but his critics charge him with making concessions that will weaken white control and lead ultimately to black majority rule.

If Botha is to win the necessary support for his reforms, he must demonstrate to the electorate that he is in control of events, is not yielding to outside pressures for change, and is deliberately pursuing a course thought to be in the best interests of white survival. His reform proposals thus are hostage to his success in demonstrating intransigence to foreign criticism and belligerency to armed provocation. Botha's awareness of this challenge already has been shown in the execution of his "Total National Strategy."

Implementing a "Total National Strategy"

The Botha government's answer to total onslaught is the "Total National Strategy," defined as "a comprehensive plan to utilize all the means available to a state according to an integrated pattern . . . to achieve national aims."[56] Those aims were elaborated by Prime Minister Botha in a twelve-point plan for domestic and foreign policy. Two points directly relate to security strategy: the ninth, "South Africa's firm determination to defend itself against interference from outside in every possible way"; and the eleventh, "the maintenance of effective decision-making by the State, which rests on a strong Defence Force to guarantee orderly government as well as efficient, clean administration."[57]

Botha already has streamlined the cabinet committee system in a way that stresses and concentrates decisionmaking on security issues.[58] He has reduced the number of permanent cabinet committees from twenty to five. The committees meet regularly and frequently rather than occasionally as they did under the Vorster administration. The State Security Council (SSC), established in 1972, is the most important policymaking body. It is the only committee established by law and given fixed membership: the prime minister, who is chairman; the ministers of defense, foreign affairs, justice, and peace; and the senior cabinet minister (if not one of the three above). Other ministers and department heads serve occasionally. The SSC is believed by some sources to have become a super-cabinet under Botha, concentrating security decisionmaking in fewer hands than before. South African sources claim, for example, that a decision to undertake a major military operation must first be given SSC approval. At the sub-cabinet level, military representatives now sit on the fifteen interdepartmental committees covering all the main aspects of government.[59] As part of the "Total National Strategy," Botha also appointed top-level industrialists and bankers to a thirteen-member Defence Advisory Board, which advises the South African Defence Forces (SADF) on matters such as business methods and arms manufacture.[60]

Botha had earlier made changes in the SADF structure to reflect the shifting threat. He divided SADF ground forces into a Conventional Force and a Force for Counterinsurgency and Terrorism. To develop "a deterrent able to resist a fairly heavy conventional attack on South Africa,"[61] the SADF in 1978 established a school for conventional combat training.[62] In September 1977 the SADF held its first large-scale conventional warfare exercise, Operation Blitz: artillery, tanks, APCs, and mortar units repulsed an "enemy" armored division supported by aircraft that had invaded South Africa from Namibia and was moving toward Kimberly.[63] By late 1981 South Africa's armaments industry had begun shifting priorities to conventional weapons such as artillery, armored vehicles, and naval equipment.[64] So far there is no evidence that regional peace initiatives in 1984, including South Africa's cease-fire with Angola and its nonaggression pact with Mozambique, have altered this threat perception. In announcing a planned 21 percent rise in military spending for 1984–85, South African leaders said it would be "unrealistic" to expect these developments to allow a near-term defense cut, although they expressed hope for a "downward trend" if the peace initiatives should prove lasting.[65]

The leadership's need to reassure South African whites and demonstrate to nonwhites its will and ability to crush any armed aggression has led to a belligerent and high-risk policy toward neighboring states, especially Angola. This neighbor has provided sanctuary and an arms conduit for SWAPO, the guerrilla movement operating against South African control of Namibia. During the past six years, as SWAPO hit-and-run attacks increased, South Africa conducted heavy counterinsurgency operating inside Angola. Ground and air attacks were launched against missile sites and SWAPO guerrilla bases 175 miles deep inside Angolan territory. On at least one occasion South African forces attacked a mechanized column of the Angolan army, apparently to capture or destroy heavy weapons. South Africa also established a battalion of dissident Angolan ex-guerrillas to carry out overt and covert operations inside Angola. In its efforts to seal the Angola-Namibia border against SWAPO incursions, the SADF has occupied a border strip thirty miles inside Angola.

But preemptive and punitive cross-border strikes by the SADF have not been limited to Angola. South African officials have repeatedly accused Mozambique, Lesotho, and Zimbabwe of allowing guerilla attacks to be launched from their states by the African National Congress (ANC), the oldest and most prominent black nationalist movement operating against South Africa. The years 1980–1984 witnessed a resurgence of ANC guerrilla sabotage and isolated attacks on symbolic targets. The ANC has not been able to mount the sort of guerrilla campaign launched by Rhodesian nationalists in the early 1970s. But its success in 1981 in blowing up oil storage tanks at Sasol, an oil-from-coal complex, its effective sabotage in 1983 against the Koeberg nuclear power station, and its bombing of an air force headquarters building in downtown Pretoria offer dramatic evidence ("political graffiti" said one observer) to black and white South Africans that the armed resistance is alive and well inside the country.

These occasional and isolated events are taken extremely seriously by the government. In January 1981 a SADF armored column, driving Soviet-made vehicles with Mozambican markings, crossed the border and drove to Maputo, Mozambique's capital, where the South Africans attacked and destroyed an ANC-occupied building. That act led to condemnation by the United Nations Security Council and to Soviet warnings that it would not fail to uphold its obligations under the Soviet-Mozambican friendship treaty. Neither action, however, deterred South Africa from launching an almost identical strike into Lesotho in December 1982,[a] in which ANC members and several innocent Lesotho citizens were killed.

How have South African whites reacted to this blatantly aggressive posture? Have they, like most observers, been critical of South African belligerence against nearby states? On the contrary, one indication of the destabilization policy's popularity is that South Africa's major right-wing opposition party accused Botha of trying to win votes by launching heavy attacks into Angola a short time before South Africa's general election in 1981. A 1982 survey of white attitudes found that 81 percent agreed with the statement, "South Africa should militarily attack terrorist bases in neighboring states (like the ANC base near Maputo)." Among National Party supporters, over 86 percent were in agreement.[66]

What are the implications of the "total onslaught" and "Total National Strategy," which the Botha government has offered as the means of white survival? Once the notion of a total, communist-inspired onslaught became the general perception of white South Africans, the leadership found it relatively easy to win public acceptance for mobilization to meet that threat. Higher military budgets, greater demands on civilian manpower and on other scarce resources, and longer and more frequent military service periods are among the attendant costs that the white public has shown itself ready to bear.

Moreover, the government enjoys overwhelming white support for its boldly aggressive military policy in the region. This support remains, though the policy has not so far ended ANC attacks or the SWAPO insurgency. There is no evidence that any substantial element of the white public would favor military restraint, or that it is seriously concerned about adverse world opinion on this issue. Indeed, South Africa's whites would probably applaud harsh measures against the "total onslaught." Only if the government were perceived as not sufficiently tough or aggressive would it run the risk of serious criticism from the electorate.

a. Critics of the U.S. decision to abstain from condemning the Maputo raid argue that the Botha government was given a green light to repeat such attacks. While the U.S. abstention was undoubtedly pleasing to the South Africans, it is extremely unlikely that a U.S. vote would have had any significant impact on a policy decided on the basis of perceived internal political imperatives.

ALTERNATIVE NUCLEAR STRATEGIES: VAN DER MERWE VERSUS SLIM JAKHALS

The technical evidence suggests that for several years South Africa has had the capability to design, produce, and deliver a low-yield nuclear weapon. There is also strong evidence that South Africa may already have tested a weapon. The analysis of domestic political imperatives suggests that South Africa's leaders would not close off the option of possessing a nuclear weapon. The chances are that the present leadership would want a reliable "bomb in the basement" that could be deployed on short notice. If, in fact, that has been South Africa's goal, what is its strategy?

In assessing South African nuclear strategy—in particular, whether it is the open policy claimed by South African officials, or one of secrecy and deception as widely suspected—one should be aware that each of these characteristics is consistent with a different aspect of Afrikanerdom. One is represented in Afrikaans folklore by the character Van der Merwe, the credulous country bumpkin, forever the victim of his own ignorance and of tricks played on him by city sophisticates. The other is Slim Jakhals, the sly jackal who is another rustic; but in this case his air of innocent gullibility masks an alert and devious mind, enabling him to outsmart those who would do him in. In its statements on nuclear weapons policy, as well as in its Kalahari diplomacy, the South African government has on various occasions appeared in each of these guises.

South African officials have generally maintained that they are pursuing peaceful nuclear development, not seeking a weapon. Typical is the denial of weapons intention by AEB chairman Roux, who told a correspondent from *The New York Times* in May 1977, "We are not making nuclear weapons. Tell me, what would South Africa do with a nuclear weapon?"[67] Frequently, however, their statements have been far less unequivocal. Some have asserted South Africa's ability to produce a weapon and have suggested that circumstances could cause the government to change course. The occasional threatening statement has usually been followed by one designed to tone down the previous one.

In 1965, at the inauguration of Safari I, South Africa's first research reactor, Prime Minister Hendrik F. Verwoerd noted the government's obligation to "consider" the military aspects of nuclear energy.[68] Roux quickly played down the notion of any official interest in nuclear weapons. A few years later a statement by the army chief of staff, General H. J. Martin, that South Africa was prepared to produce nuclear arms, was repudiated by then Defense Minister P. W. Botha.[69]

In 1970 a newspaper close to the National Party leadership hinted at the government's thinking:

> Mr. Vorster has not yet said categorically that South Africa will never make an atom bomb. In view of this fact, people will have to look at us in a new light. South Africa now becomes an altogether different proposition. . . . This bargaining power can be used in various fields in the difficult years that lie ahead. America, for example, would have to revise its strategy toward us.[70]

In May 1976 Vorster told a *Newsweek* correspondent, "We are only interested in the peaceful application of nuclear power. But we can enrich uranium, and we have the capability. And we did not sign the nuclear nonproliferation treaty."[71]

Probably the most threatening statement was made by Connie Mulder, a senior National Party leader in the 1970s and minister of information in the Vorster cabinet. In 1977 he said: "Let me just say that if we are attacked, no rules apply at all if it comes to a question of our existence. We will use all means at our disposal, whatever they may be. It is true that we have just completed our own pilot plant that uses very advanced technology, and that we have major uranium resources."[72] Such statements would probably not have been coordinated and orchestrated. Equally unlikely, however, is that senior government and party officials would publicly express purely personal views, or views that did not reflect the leadership's agreed strategy, particularly with regard to the sensitive nuclear weapons issue.

These statements then must be assumed to represent the official public position of the government. It would seem to be a position designed to reassure (or lull) the international community about South Africa's current nuclear intentions, while reminding the world that South Africa has the means to produce a weapon and should be accorded the respect due a threshold nuclear state—in short, the policy of "calculated ambiguity" discussed by Betts and others.

The questions of South African credibility and underlying policy interests emerged during the Kalahari episode. Assuming that the consensus of the U.S. technical, scientific, and intelligence communities was correct—that the Kalahari site was probably designed as a nuclear test site—then there still are various alternative explanations.

One is that South Africa in fact planned to test a device. South African leaders may have acted in the belief that a nuclear device could be detonated without discovery. This seems unlikely in view of South Africa's access to knowledge of satellite photography. For example, a NASA tracking station in the republic was manned by South African personnel working for the South African Council for Scientific and Industrial Research.[73] Or perhaps South Africa was about to test a device in defiance of global opinion, and in the mistaken belief that foreign reaction would not be so strong. Then, as the sharpness of the Western demarche exceeded South African expectations, Vorster was forced to cancel the test in order to preserve important relationships with the United States and Western Europe. This explanation, however, assumes that the Vorster leadership was extremely naive and underestimated Western reactions. Could the government really have been ignorant of the priority that the Carter administration attached to nonproliferation?

The most plausible explanation appears to be that South Africa was, indeed, prepared to test a device, but its chief objective was to provoke a U.S. reaction. South Africa's leaders saw the opportunity to use nuclear test preparations as a bargaining chip to win important concessions from the proliferation-sensitive Carter administration, which had been pursuing a hard line toward the Vorster government. The South Africans also recognized the need to maintain a basis for plausible denials, but made the denials ambiguous to keep the West anxious. In addition to giving U.S. officials false explanations of the purpose of the Kalahari site, South African leaders played a sort of mirrors game in their denials. Officials referred to "firm denials" that they had given previously, but the earlier denials, on close inspection, appeared to have virtually no substance.

Arguably, the first categorical denial was contained in Vorster's letter to U.S. president Jimmy Carter in October 1977, two months following the Western demarche.

At the height of the Kalahari crisis, an editorial in the government mouthpiece, *Beeld*, reflected official testiness on the issue:

> The great powers which have nuclear weapons have adopted an odd attitude. *One would have thought that it would have been tactically more profitable for them to draw closer a potential member of the nuclear club, which South Africa is. Their bullying attitude could result in making us a maverick bull in the nuclear herd*, and that is surely not a sound situation from their point of view. South Africa will go its own way and its own interests will be decisive[74] [emphasis added].

South Africa's readiness to enter negotiations with the United States and to present its list of specific demands in return for signing the NPT lend credence to this explanation. Vorster personally responded to the Carter initiative, saying South Africa would "consider" signing the NPT, but needed guarantees of future U.S. deliveries of enriched uranium. When Carter sent Gerard Smith, special ambassador for Nuclear Non-Proliferation Affairs, to discuss the NPT issue with South Africa, Pretoria's demands included: resumption of U.S. deliveries of HEU for Safari I; guaranteed supply of LEU for the Koeberg power station; relaxation of U.S. exports of nonsensitive technology for the Valindaba uranium-enrichment plant; and U.S. support for reinstating South Africa in its seat on the IAEA Board of Governors.[75]

Intermittent discussions, held from June to November 1978, ultimately broke down because South Africa was unwilling to submit its enrichment facility to IAEA inspection under the NPT. The South Africans maintained that such inspection might disclose the secret of their enrichment process, which others might then exploit commercially. The U.S. Nuclear Non-Proliferation Act of 1978 prohibits the sale of any enriched fuel to countries not applying IAEA safeguards to all nuclear facilities. While in November of that year the United States suspended a contract to supply HEU for Safari I, Roux said the LEU deliveries for the Koeberg plant would not be affected.

Any attempt to assess Pretoria's intentions in the Kalahari should also take into account the suspected South African nuclear test in the South Atlantic two years later. It is possible that South Africa had moved toward the open testing of a presumably crude device in the Kalahari until it ran into unexpectedly heavy pressure from the Western powers to call off the test. In the weeks following the discovery, South African leaders would have debated whether or not to proceed. In this scenario, the government would have decided that a test at Kalahari would incur excessive foreign relations costs, and therefore postponed testing a weapon until it could do so secretly. Thus, South Africa took another two years to design and produce a clean, low-yield weapon that could be tested without detection.

In a more Machiavellian variant, South African leaders possibly were disappointed when blatantly obvious test preparations failed to extract substantial concessions from the United States. They decided to move ahead with a second option: the covert testing of a finished weapon. But since they could not acquire HEU from the United States, South Africa's extremely limited enrichment capabilities would have to supply all the country's HEU needs. This constraint could have delayed the covert test until September 1979.

The "hoax" hypothesis—namely, that the Kalahari was a fake test site, constructed to gain nuclear concessions from the United States—seems the least plausible. It ignores the evidence that South Africa has wanted to develop a weapons capability. In addition to the inevitable storm of international criticism, South African leaders would also have risked public embarrassment and humiliation at being caught. Furthermore, such an elaborate hoax was unnecessary: discreetly planted official leaks that South Africa was considering a test, followed by ambiguous denials, would have been enough to secure U.S. attention.

If South Africa's Kalahari strategy was designed to extract nuclear concessions from the West, it must be counted a failure. In terms of the delayed start-up of the Koeberg power station through cancellation of U.S. supplies, the costs have been substantial. But in a larger sense the strategy probably is seen in Pretoria as a partial success. It brought convincing evidence that the Western powers now consider South Africa a threshold nuclear state and must take its new status into account. This recognition enhances South Africa's importance in the eyes of the world, and it may open the way for future negotiations on issues of mutual strategic interest. As Betts points out, the strategy demonstrated to South Africa's leaders "the value of the nuclear threat as diplomatic leverage, an option to be forgone *in exchange* for reciprocal favors"[76] [emphasis in original].

The most puzzling aspect of South Africa's nuclear strategy is the absence of an obvious military target. Professor J. E. Spence finds it "difficult to see any military utility for nuclear weapons, either as deterrent or defence."[77] He notes that nuclear threats are unlikely to deter guerrillas. Both he and Betts argue that South Africa's conventional military power is overwhelming compared to that of all the nearby states combined.[78]

Their skepticism is well-taken. On relatively short notice, South Africa can muster an armed force of 800,000 men—experienced, well-led, and armed with advanced weapons.[79] The notion that the SADF, backed by a united white community and the strongest economy in Africa, would require a nuclear deterrent against weak, crisis-ridden neighbors like Angola, Zimbabwe, or Mozambique is absurd. Nor is there any reason to think a bomb would be useful against guerrillas. What use, then, for a bomb?

Spence says "the spectre of Soviet/Cuban conventional support for guerrilla struggle in South Africa might constitute a quickening incentive"[80] to acquire a tactical weapon. Betts, too, sees its possible military use only in a worst-case scenario, involving a massive Soviet intervention in support of groups opposing the government while the West remains uninvolved. Both Betts and Spence view this scenario as a remote contingency.

Their analysis is sound from the viewpoint of an objective assessment of the balance of forces in southern Africa. But the key to the question of a bomb's use lies in South Africa's *perception* of military threat. As argued previously, South Africa's national leadership and its white electorate believe that communist states have been preparing for a massive, communist-supported conventional assault and that such an assault could occur in the short or medium term, according to a recent Defence White Paper. Furthermore, South Africa has been responding to this perceived threat by training its forces for conventional warfare, and by redirecting the focus of its arms industry from counterinsurgency weapons to conventional weapons. In short, South Africa has been preparing for exactly the sort of "remote contingency" in which Betts and Spence see the most likely use for a nuclear weapons force.

Kenneth Adelman and Albion Knight take the discussion further.[81] They state that South Africa's leaders might use a bomb as a "weapon of last resort" if the survival of Afrikanerdom were threatened, or as a demonstration deterrent—for example, exploding a weapon in a remote area as a warning to aggressors. The first situation is not implausible, assuming that South Africa's leaders are imbued with what one author has termed the "Samson complex," bringing destruction on their own people as well as on their enemies.[82] But it errs by limiting the survival mandate to Afrikaners. At the least, white survival would be the issue, and the white community might weigh in on the fateful ultimate decision.

Using a nuclear detonation as a demonstration deterrent, the second situation Adelman and Knight describe, would be unlikely to stop an assault long-planned and already in progress. For example, a Mozambican leader who realized that Maputo was about to become a nuclear target still might not be able to call off a scheduled attack already in progress against South Africa.

Adelman and Knight also suggest two more limited uses for nuclear weapons by the South Africans. Such a weapon might be employed to "break up any concentration of conventional forces against South Africa's industrial and population centers"; and a small, relatively clean, tactical weapon could be used in battlefield situations.[83] These suggested uses are compatible with South African threat perceptions. They are also compatible with the type of weapon South Africa is suspected of having tested in 1979.

Evidence of South African military attitudes toward a nuclear weapon is understandably scarce, and mostly indirect. In 1972 the SADF chief Admiral Birman warned that South Africa, even in cooperation with local states, could not successfully defend the Southern Hemisphere against a "large-scale enemy infiltration or invasion," but must seek protection through "the deterrent strategy based on nuclear terror and the fear of escalation."[84] His statement is significant on several counts. It acknowledges that South Africa's conventional military power would be inadequate against large-scale, conventional attack and suggests that South Africa seek the protection of a Western nuclear umbrella. By 1972 there was already little or no chance of achieving this protection; thus, his statement may have suggested indirectly that South Africa consider acquiring its own nuclear deterrent.

Several years earlier, South Africa's army chief of staff had stated that his country was prepared to manufacture nuclear arms.[85] A senior South African naval officer, Commodore H. F. Nel, said that South Africa could "ward off a combined onslaught by African states, even if this involved limited intervention by outside powers."[86] He then warned that South Africa reserved the right to put its nuclear expertise to practical use.

Although these statements offer few clues to the anticipated use of nuclear weapons, they do suggest that South Africa's military, far from dismissing the need for such weapons, has from the early stages of their country's nuclear development favored a nuclear weapons program.

Other evidence that nuclear weapons have played a part in South African defense strategy for some time is contained in an alleged 1972 AEB classified report. In the report several maps indicated areas that would be seismologically "safe" for exploding nuclear devices of varying sizes. One map showed that a ten-kiloton device could be detonated along South Africa's northern border without causing seismic damage, and that some border areas could withstand a 100-kiloton blast.[87]

IMPLICATIONS FOR U.S. POLICY

At least three factors combine to make South Africa a difficult case for U.S. nonproliferation interests. South Africa is a pariah state. As Betts points out, U.S. opposition to apartheid, as well as the need to keep official distance from South Africa's apartheid government, rules out the option of offering South Africa a credible security umbrella that might dissuade it from developing a nuclear deterrent.[88] Consequently the United

States and South Africa do not have the sources of reciprocal leverage that exist, for example, in the U.S.-Korean relationship.

Continuing uncertainty over the status of South Africa's nuclear weapons development makes it difficult for policymakers to judge the next South African move. South Africa's official ideology of survival through a "Total National Strategy" against "total onslaught" also strains nonproliferation interests. Since these concepts have been accepted by both the leadership and the electorate, to persuade South Africans to modify or abandon their underlying threat perception would be extremely difficult.

This factor leaves the United States with few carrots and sticks. Betts notes that a U.S. nuclear embargo, or the threat of one, might prevent South Africa from developing a nuclear weapon, but only if its desire for one were marginal. Betts concludes, however, that cooperation in the nuclear field, where energy and weapons policies are linked, offers the only feasible source of U.S. leverage.[89] The feebleness of this lever already has been demonstrated by South Africa's willingness to endure a cut-off in U.S. enriched-fuel supplies in order to keep its nuclear facilities free of international inspection.

What alternatives are left the United States? The 1977 Report of the Nuclear Energy Policy study group suggests that countries suspected of having a nuclear weapon should not be treated as nuclear weapons states, but should be allowed to renounce weapons ambitions.[90] This point would seem particularly valid in regard to South Africa. The United States must allow South Africa a basis for continuing plausible denial. To accuse South Africa, publicly or privately, of possession might be cathartic for U.S. anti-apartheid feelings, but it would lead only to a hardening of South Africa's position, would increase regional frictions and long-term prospects for expanded conflict. To confront South Africa would remove its already shaky basis for plausible denial and would weaken constraints against blatantly open testing, or deploying or threatening to deploy tactical nuclear weapons. In addition, a public U.S. statement that South Africa had the bomb would lead to Soviet and African pressure for economic sanctions, and to strained U.S. relations with Africa and perhaps with its European allies. It might lead

Nigeria to make good its threat to acquire its own nuclear weapons.

The United States must walk a fine line. It must assume South Africa has the bomb, while officially accepting the South African claim that it does not. American policy might be directed toward preventing the South Africans from the open declaration, testing, deployment, threat, or use of nuclear weapons. Specific policy prescriptions are always hazardous, but the following propositions may be applicable to the South African case.

1. South African whites should be encouraged to modify their paranoid view of the external threat. The chances of success are slim, but the effort should be made. Among specific approaches, the United States could express general approval of any real shifts away from apartheid. The continuation of a regular, low-key dialogue with Pretoria's leaders on general global and regional issues would expose them to an outside point of view. Such dialogue might calm their fears, or at least give them a more realistic perspective on the prospects of attack by outside powers. American government and business leaders could use various public and private forums to suggest that the military threat to the republic is not as great as most South African whites fear. If the peace initiatives begun by South Africa and its neighbors in the early months of 1984 should lead to a general lessening of regional tensions, that in itself would help modify South African threat perceptions.

2. The United States must avoid reassuring South Africa too much, or sending ambiguous signals about U.S. readiness to support South Africa against external threats. Any hint that the United States and South Africa are in a common struggle against communism would encourage South African leaders to increase preemptive or punitive strikes—including the possible deployment of nuclear weapons—against nearby states. The United States should convey vague hints of the repercussions that would follow if South Africa were to escalate the scale of attacks. The rationale could be that neither global nor domestic opinion would allow the United States to avoid taking harsh measures in response to such attacks.

3. The United States should also continue to conduct frequent and low-key dialogues with southern African states, and to

warn them of the intensity of South African fears (if, indeed, they need such warnings), and to urge increased dialogue with South Africa and peaceful solutions to regional conflicts. The Front Line states' leaders provide the most useful focal point for such U.S. initiatives. The risks taken by inviting Soviet military personnel or by acquiring large stocks of heavy weapons should be emphasized to southern African states. Finally, these countries could be reminded that neither the Soviet Union nor Cuba could expect to prevent or rollback a South African invasion. Indeed, the most appropriate U.S. nonproliferation initiatives are those that would be normally pursued to reduce tensions and conflicts in the region.

NOTES

1. Richard Betts, "A Diplomatic Bomb for South Africa?" *International Security* 4, no. 4 (1979): 94.
2. Ibid.
3. Ronald Walters, "Uranium Politics and U.S. Foreign Policy in Southern Africa," *Journal of Southern African Affairs* (July 1979): 286.
4. Betts, "A Diplomatic Bomb for South Africa?" p. 94.
5. Kenneth Adelman and Richard Knight, "Can South Africa Go Nuclear?" *Orbis* 23, no. 3 (Fall 1979): 634.
6. Under the 1978 U.S. Nuclear Non-Proliferation Act, U.S. deliveries of enriched uranium have been terminated pending South African acceptance of full-scope safeguards, including IAEA inspection of all nuclear facilities.
7. Charles Kennard, "Valindaba—the Talking is Over" (Research paper, Monterey, Calif.: Naval Postgraduate School, 1983), p. 6. (Unpublished.)
8. Betts, "A Diplomatic Bomb for South Africa?" p. 92.
9. *Financial Mail*, February 17, 1978.
10. Ibid.
11. Uranium enriched to 3 percent would be sufficient to meet Koeberg's requirements. See Joseph Lelyveld, "South Africa Struggles to Build a Nuclear Industry," *The New York Times*, June 24, 1981, p. A–2.
12. *The Weekly Star* (Johannesburg), July 14, 1979.
13. Ibid., October 4, 1980.
14. Lelyveld, "South Africa Struggles," p. A–2.

15. Since 1980 the administration has granted export licenses for the sale to South Africa of helium–3, vibration test equipment, multichannel analyzers, and a hot isostatic press, all of which have potential use in nuclear weapons development. In each case, South Africa has assured the United States that the item would not be used for nonpeaceful purposes. For detailed discussion, see Judith Miller, "U.S. Easing Policy on Nuclear Sales to South Africa," *The New York Times*, May 19, 1982, p. A–7.

16. Ibid.

17. Walters, "Uranium Politics and U.S. Foreign Policy in Southern Africa," p. 286.

18. John F. Burns, "South Africa's Secret Atom Plant Suspected of Working on a Bomb," *The New York Times*, April 30, 1977, pp. 1, 6.

19. Ibid.

20. Kennard, "Valindaba—The Talking is Over," citing H.C. Paxton, *Los Alamos Critical Mass Data* (LAMS 3067), Los Alamos Scientific Laboratory, 1980.

21. Judith Miller, "3 Nations Widening Nuclear Contacts," *The New York Times*, June 28, 1981, p. A–15.

22. Ronald Walters, "U.S. Policy and Nuclear Proliferation in South Africa," *U.S. Military Involvement in Southern Africa* (Boston: Southend Press, 1978), p. 182.

23. Robert Harkavy, "The Pariah State Syndrome," *Orbis* 21, no. 3 (Fall 1977): 643.

24. Bernard Gwertzman, "Report of A-Blast off Africa is Called Indecisive by U.S.," *The New York Times*, October 27, 1979, pp. 1, 5.

25. See in particular, Eliot Marshall, "Flash Not Missed by Vela: Still Veiled in Mist," *Science* (November 30, 1979): 1,051; Eliot Marshall, "Navy Lab Concludes the Vela Saw A-Bomb," *Science* (August 29, 1980): 996–97; John J. Fialka, "Underwater Sensors Felt Blast Near South Africa," *The Washington Star*, November 2, 1979, p. A–4; Thomas O'Toole, "Only 3 Vela Satellites Now Scout for Nuclear Blasts in Atmosphere," *The Washington Post*, November 3, 1979, p. A–9.

26. Thomas O'Toole, " 'A-Blast' Was No Lightning Bolt," *The Washington Post*, January 1, 1980, p. A–8.

27. Ibid.

28. Marshall, "Navy Lab," p. 997.

29. Arnold Kramish, "Nuclear Flashes in the Night," *The Washington Quarterly* (Summer, 1980).

30. Thomas O'Toole, "Experts Explore Cause of Flash Near S. Africa," *The Washington Post*, November 2, 1979, p. A–23.

31. *Science* (August 1, 1980): 572.

32. Thomas O'Toole, "Atomic Fallout Examined for Proof of Blast Report," *The Washington Post*, November 14, 1979, p. A–18.

33. *The Telegraph* (London), April 14, 1980.

34. Richard Betts, "South Africa's Nuclear Potential," in Joseph Yager, ed., *Nonproliferation and U.S. Foreign Policy* (Washington, D.C.: The Brookings Institution, 1980), p. 304.

35. Ibid.

36. Kennard, "Valindaba—The Talking is Over," citing *inter alia* John Cane, "The Technology of Modern Weapons for Limited Use," *Orbis* 22, no. 1 (Spring 1978).

37. Marshall, "Navy Lab," p. 997.

38. Heribert Adam and Hermann Giliomee, *Ethnic Power Mobilized* (New Haven: Yale University Press, 1979), pp. 132–35.

39. Ibid.

40. For a comprehensive analysis of the threat and South Africa's response, see Robert Jaster, *South Africa's Narrowing Security Options*, Adelphi Paper no. 159 (London: IISS, 1980); and Deon Geldenhuys, *Some Foreign Policy Implications of South Africa's Total National Strategy* (Braamfontein: SAIIA, March 1981).

41. *Hansard 1981*, col. 4,674.

42. *Hansard 1980*, vol. 85, cols. 3,316–24.

43. Cited in Geldenhuys, *Some Foreign Policy Implications of South Africa's Total National Strategy*, p. 4.

44. Jaster, *South Africa's Narrowing Security Options*, citing P.W. Botha's statement in 1971.

45. *Covert Information Bulletin*, no. 13 (Washington, D.C.: Covert Action Publications, July-August 1981).

46. *Hansard 1980*, vol. 86, col. 5,294.

47. Republic of South Africa, Department of Defence, *White Paper on Defence and Armaments Supply*, 1982.

48. *The Telegraph* (London), August 28, 1979.

49. *The Times* (London), February 18, 1981.

50. See *South Africa: Time Running Out*, Report of the Study Commission on U.S. Policy Toward Southern Africa, Foreign Policy Study Foundation (Berkeley: University of California Press, 1981), ch. 11.

51. Deon Geldenhuys, *What Do We Think? A Survey of White Opinion on Foreign Policy Issues* (Braamfontein: South Africa Institute of International Affairs, November 1982), p. 6.

52. H. H. Schwarz (PFP), in House of Assembly Debate, March 2, 1979. (See *Hansard 1979*, cols. 1,710– 11.)
53. *Rand Daily Mail*, January 2, 1977.
54. *Die Transvaaler*, August 26, 1977.
55. *The Citizen* (South Africa), cited in *P. W. Botha: A Political Backgrounder* (London: South African Embassy, 1978).
56. Republic of South Africa, *White Paper on Defence*, p. 5.
57. Geldenhuys, *Some Foreign Policy Implications of South Africa's Total National Strategy*, pp. 10–40 and 60–63.
58. Ibid., pp. 37–38.
59. *The Times* (London), September 1, 1980.
60. *Hansard 1976*, February 2, 1976, col. 6,218.
61. Jaster, *South Africa's Narrowing Security Options*, p. 28.
62. *Hansard 1978*, April 18, 1978, col. 4,817.
63. Jaster, *South Africa's Narrowing Security Options*, p. 28.
64. *Financial Times*, December 22, 1981.
65. Alan Cowell, "South African Military Outlays to Grow," *The New York Times*, March 29, 1984, p. A–3.
66. Geldenhuys, *What Do We Think? A Survey of White Opinion on Foreign Policy Issues*, pp. 9–10.
67. Burns, "South Africa's Secret Atom Plant."
68. Betts, "A Diplomatic Bomb for South Africa?" p. 96.
69. Ibid.
70. *Beeld* (South Africa), July 26, 1970.
71. Betts, "A Diplomatic Bomb for South Africa?" p. 92.
72. Jim Hoagland, "S. Africa, with U.S. Aid, Near A-Bomb," *The Washington Post*, February 16, 1977, p. A–12.
73. Walters, "U.S. Policy and Nuclear Proliferation in South Africa," p. 195.
74. *Beeld*, August 24, 1977.
75. Jaster, *South Africa's Narrowing Security Options*, p. 46.
76. Betts, "A Diplomatic Bomb for South Africa?" p. 107.
77. J. S. Spence, "South Africa: the Nuclear Option," *African Affairs* 80, no. 321 (1981): 445–46.
78. Betts, "A Diplomatic Bomb for South Africa?" pp. 97–101.
79. For a comprehensive analysis of South Africa's military power and development, see *South Africa: Time Running Out*, ch. 11; and Jaster, *South Africa's Narrowing Security Options*.
80. Spence, "South Africa: the Nuclear Option."
81. Adelman and Knight, "Can South Africa Go Nuclear?" pp. 642–43.
82. Harkavy, "The Pariah State Syndrome," p. 644.
83. Adelman and Knight, "Can South Africa Go Nuclear?"

84. Jaster, *South Africa's Narrowing Security Options*, p. 12.
85. Betts, "A Diplomatic Bomb for South Africa?" p. 97.
86. *South African Digest*, October 24, 1980.
87. *The Observer* (London), February 25, 1979, citing a document obtained by the ANC and submitted to a UN seminar on outside nuclear cooperation with South Africa.
88. Betts, "South Africa's Nuclear Potential," pp. 397–98.
89. Ibid., p. 401.
90. Report of the Nuclear Energy Policy Study Group, *Nuclear Power: Issues and Choices* (Cambridge, Mass.: Ballinger Publishing Co., 1977).

II THE NONPROLIFERATION REGIME

7 U.S. NUCLEAR EXPORTS AND THE NONPROLIFERATION REGIME

Peter A. Clausen

Previous chapters in this volume have dealt with the political, technical, and regional security dynamics of proliferation in countries that have acquired nuclear weapons or seem in the process of doing so. With this chapter, attention shifts to the nonproliferation regime and the American nuclear export policies that historically have both shaped and unsettled that regime.

The opening section traces the development of U.S. policy from World War II through the Treaty on the Non-Proliferation of Nuclear Weapons (NPT). It emphasizes America's political and commercial role in the building of the nonproliferation regime, and identifies the roots of later conflicts with European suppliers and with countries like India and Brazil.

We will then review the developments of the early and mid–1970s that led to a recasting of U.S. nonproliferation strategy, and examine the efforts of the Carter and Reagan administrations to adapt U.S. export policy to a changed proliferation environment. The main theme of this section is the recurrent tension between the introduction of new restrictions on nuclear supplies and the preservation of America's reputation as a "reliable supplier."

The final section of this chapter assesses future prospects for U.S. export policy as a tool of nonproliferation. Against the

183

background of historical experience and the nature of the current nuclear market, it attempts to identify the sources and limits of U.S. influence on behalf of a strong international supply regime.

U.S. EXPORT POLICY AND THE BUILDING OF THE NONPROLIFERATION REGIME

American policy on peaceful nuclear cooperation dates from President Dwight D. Eisenhower's Atoms for Peace initiative in 1953. Nonproliferation policy was at this point already a decade old, having originated with the wartime efforts of the United States and Great Britain to deny Germany access to uranium and their agreement at Quebec in 1943 not to transfer information regarding the atomic bomb project to third parties. Wartime atomic collaboration with Britain gave way to a uniform U.S. policy of secrecy and denial with the passage of the 1946 Atomic Energy Act.[1] This policy reflected the conclusions of the Acheson-Lilienthal Report that, in view of the close connection between military and peaceful nuclear technologies, the spread of nuclear energy under national control posed an inherent proliferation threat.

By 1953, however, the Soviet Union and Great Britain had transformed the U.S. weapons monopoly into a club, and several other countries were embarked on civil nuclear programs. These developments seemed to indicate the futility of the denial approach, and encouraged the shift to a more liberal policy of controlled cooperation. Yet the merits of the issue are not clear-cut, since one cannot know how an earlier policy of peaceful nuclear cooperation, or a continuation of denial after 1953, would have affected the process of proliferation.[2] This is essentially a question (still very relevant to nonproliferation policy) of the relative influence of two competing effects of denial—the stimulus it may give to national nuclear programs on the one hand and the obstacles it places in their way on the other.

In any event, there were other reasons besides nonproliferation strategy for a shift toward nuclear cooperation in the early 1950s. These included the alliance tensions caused by the 1946 Atomic Energy Act, the political and commercial attractions of a world nuclear market, and the hope that peaceful nuclear cooperation could be turned to American advantage in the U.S.-Soviet nuclear arms race.[3]

Atoms for Peace and the Nuclear Bargain

Following Eisenhower's proposal in 1953, the Atomic Energy Act was amended to allow U.S. cooperation with other countries in nuclear research and power programs. The nonproliferation logic of Atoms for Peace was centered on the manipulation of incentives through a "nuclear bargain." In return for access to nuclear technology and materials from supplier countries, recipients would give assurances of peaceful use and would accept safeguards (inspections and accounting of nuclear materials) to verify their compliance with these assurances. Safeguards were initially administered on a bilateral basis by the United States, then transferred to the International Atomic Energy Agency (IAEA) after the agency's inspection procedures were established in the 1960s.

The new policy assumed that while the United States could not prevent the development of nuclear programs in other countries, it might nevertheless gain influence over such programs through cooperation. Nuclear cooperation could elicit peaceful use commitments and, it was hoped, steer nuclear programs in cooperating countries away from military activities.

However, the Atoms for Peace policy did not directly constrain national nuclear programs. Participating countries were free to pursue military nuclear programs in conjunction with externally assisted peaceful ones, as did France. No renunciation of the weapons option, or acceptance of what later became known as "full-scope" safeguards, was required as a condition of U.S. exports until the Nuclear Non-Proliferation Act of 1978 (NNPA), twenty-five years after the Atoms for Peace proposal. The linkage between peaceful cooperation and nonproliferation, then, was contingent on assumptions about supplier influence and customer incentives.

In practice, the bargain was hedged on both sides. If recipients of nuclear aid were not required to give nonproliferation assurances, it was also true that there were limits to cooperation on the supplier side. Most importantly, the U.S. continued a policy of denial where enrichment technology was concerned. This policy helped perpetuate an international division of labor in the nuclear fuel cycle that gave the Atoms for Peace system a safety net in two ways—directly by retarding the spread of enrichment technology, and indirectly by reinforcing American leverage over countries using light water reactors (LWRs), for which the United States was the only supplier of low-enriched uranium.

Early U.S. Exports and Safeguards Development

Exploiting its control of fuel supplies and its technological leadership position, the United States nurtured and soon came to dominate the world nuclear market. Cooperation agreements were signed with most of the industrial countries and with several developing nations. Cooperation initially involved training and research, including U.S.-supplied research reactors and fuel. With the growth of the nuclear power industry, the U.S. light water reactor (LWR) emerged as the preferred technology, prevailing over the gas-cooled reactor types developed by Great Britain and France.[4]

American ascendancy was given an important early boost with the establishment of the European Atomic Energy Community (EURATOM) and the recommendation that Europe adopt the LWR as the basis of its reactor programs. The LWR proposal was opposed by France, which argued for a EURATOM independent of U.S. technology and fuel. France proposed construction of an enrichment plant as the keystone of European nuclear cooperation. Swayed by U.S. guarantees of enriched uranium at heavily subsidized prices, EURATOM opted for dependence on the United States.

Thus, in an early test of "reliable supply" policy, the United States successfully used market incentives to undercut the spread of sensitive technology. At the same time, the episode illustrates the limits of that policy where political and security incentives outweigh market logic. France, determined not to jeopardize its military nuclear options through foreign fuel dependence, proceeded with a national enrichment plant.[5]

Over the next few years, EURATOM became a "proving ground" for U.S. LWR technology.[6] After breakthrough exports to Italy in 1958 and the Federal Republic of Germany (FRG) in 1961, U.S. vendors—led by Westinghouse Corporation and General Electric Company—established their dominant position through direct sales and licensing arrangements with overseas firms. By the end of the 1960s, these two companies were supplying 90 percent of the world market.[7]

In conjunction with the opening up of international nuclear commerce, the basic IAEA safeguards system was developed. As the leading nuclear supplier and chief sponsor of the agency, America took the initiative in this process, and IAEA safeguards were in large part modelled after the U.S. bilateral agreements. Nevertheless, because of the unprecedented abridgment of national sovereignty implied in granting broad rights of access and inspection to an international agency, the negotiations establishing the IAEA system were protracted and contentious. American approaches encountered considerable resistance, in particular from India, France, and (until later in the 1960s) the Soviet Union. As a result, several important issues were resolved through compromises that weakened the system (for example, the decision to permit national stockpiles of fissile material) or were left ambiguous. The question of "critical time"—the frequency and intensity of inspections needed to provide useful warning of diversions—proved too controversial to be dealt with rigorously and was sidestepped.[8]

Much of the early history of U.S. policy is reflected in microcosm in the 1963 Tarapur reactor export to India.[9] Tarapur was the first power reactor export to a developing country and was regarded as an important breakthrough for the United States, both for commercial and security reasons (as a channel for countering Soviet influence in India). Typically for early reactor exports, the sale was approached as a "loss leader" by the vendor (General Electric), and was financed on generous concessionary terms under a forty-year loan at three-quarter percent, provided by the Agency for International Development. Normal commercial criteria were subordinated to the prospective economic and political rewards of breaking the Indian market.

The Tarapur safeguards negotiations were especially difficult, as India sought to keep outside controls on its program to an absolute minimum. A key issue was whether the reactors would intrinsically be subject to safeguards (as the United States maintained) or only when they were being operated with U.S.-supplied fuel (the Indian view). Unable to resolve this difference, the parties resorted to a formula that seemed to render it moot: During the thirty-year life of the agreement, the United States would be the exclusive fuel supplier for Tarapur. This solution allowed each side to retain its own interpretation (indeed, the difference of opinion was formally recorded in the text of the agreement), but begged the question of the reactor's safeguards status in the event the agreement was terminated at some point.[10]

The Non-Proliferation Treaty

The negotiation of the 1968 Non-Proliferation Treaty was a major step in the evolution of U.S. nuclear export policy and of the international regime. Building upon the logic of the nuclear bargain, the NPT enlarged and made more explicit the obligations of both sides. Recipients of nuclear equipment and fuel were for the first time asked to renounce the development of nuclear explosives and, under Article III of the treaty, to accept safeguards on their entire nuclear programs (that is, on indigenous as well as foreign-assisted activities and facilities). Nuclear suppliers, under Article IV, undertook to provide "the fullest possible exchange of equipment, materials, and scientific and technological information for the peaceful uses of nuclear energy."

The treaty both moved the nonproliferation regime forward and left a legacy of new problems and ambiguities. Two questions of interpretation were especially important. First, what should be the policy of suppliers toward cooperation with nonparties to the treaty such as India, Pakistan, Brazil, and Argentina? Cooperation with these countries, while not prohibited by the treaty, would in effect discriminate against NPT parties, since the latter would have to accept full-scope safeguards while the former would not.

The United States decided against imposing the NPT safeguards requirement on all its cooperating partners. To do so would have jeopardized continued U.S. nuclear relations with the EURATOM countries and Japan, whose ratification of the treaty was still in doubt in 1970 when the treaty came into force. The result was an anomalous situation—hardly helpful to the credibility of the nonproliferation regime—in which countries refusing to renounce the weapons option could benefit from foreign cooperation on more lenient safeguard terms than those that did.

The second question of interpretation concerned the Article IV reference to the "fullest possible" peaceful nuclear cooperation. Did this wording create a right of nonnuclear weapons states (NNWS) to the full range of nuclear technology, including fuel enrichment and reprocessing? Or was cooperation in these sensitive technologies excluded on the grounds that it would constitute indirect assistance in the acquisition of nuclear explosives, which was prohibited under Article I? The second view was rejected, but the precise extent of the obligation, if any, to make sensitive technologies available remained unclear.

This issue was doubly important to advanced civil nuclear powers such as West Germany and Japan. A strict line against sensitive fuel cycle activities in the NNWS would jeopardize their domestic fast breeder reactor programs as well as their ability to compete as nuclear suppliers against nuclear weapons states like the United States and France.[11] Despite U.S. reassurance on these points, the possible adverse effect of the NPT on peaceful nuclear development was a major concern of America's nonnuclear allies during the negotiations, and an issue on which they sometimes made common cause with nonaligned states like India.[12]

These debates on peaceful uses underscored the larger political wrenching the NPT negotiations caused for the Atlantic Alliance and U.S.–West Germany relations in particular. As the centerpiece of U.S.-Soviet detente in the 1960s, the NPT was widely perceived in Europe as reflecting a downgrading of the alliance in U.S. priorities—the appearance of what West Germany's chancellor, Kurt Kiesinger, called "nuclear complicity" between the superpowers over Europe's head. The handling of the negotiations, in which the United States seemed to surrender the alliance's Multilateral Force (MLF) option as a concession to the Soviet Union, added to this perception. For West

Germany, the symbolism of the NPT was especially unpleasant given that the treaty, from the Soviet standpoint, was aimed above all at West Germany.[13]

Conclusions

After the turbulent events of the 1970s, a tendency developed to reflect upon the 1950s and 1960s as a kind of golden age—a time when the United States, largely by virtue of its preeminence in nuclear commerce, was able to forge and progressively upgrade an international consensus that served both its own self-interest and the general welfare.

This image, as the previous pages have suggested, distorts the reality of regime-building in the early years. Consensus was considerably more fragmented than the retrospective wisdom would have it. Despite a steady upgrading of international rules on nuclear trade and safeguards, important states remained outside the consensus, and agreement was often reached by papering over differences and deferring difficult issues. At each stage, the seeds of later problems and disputes were sown.

In particular, by 1970 the divisive impact of nonproliferation issues on Atlantic relations was well-established. France in the 1950s and West Germany a decade later had reasons to feel that they were the victims of U.S. nonproliferation policy, and to be suspicious of U.S. initiatives on political and commercial grounds. Given this legacy of mistrust, new tensions inevitably arose when France and West Germany emerged in the 1970s as leading suppliers in their own right.

This rather fragile consensus suggests that U.S. influence was more limited than often assumed. No doubt U.S. market power conferred important leverage, particularly in the development of safeguards, where "recognition of the U.S. role as a principal supplier of nuclear materials, equipment, and technology ... underlay the entire negotiating process."[14] Nevertheless, in light of U.S. commercial dominance, what is striking is not American success but the extent to which others were able to resist or blunt American purposes.

Yet this should not be surprising. The building of the regime was a political process, bringing into play stakes and interests beyond the commercial and economic realm. For states like France and India, nuclear negotiations engaged basic values of national security and independence. In this bargaining context, U.S. market power alone was not likely to be decisive. Moreover, U.S. purposes were ambiguous. Nonproliferation competed for priority with other concerns, and the international nuclear regime served as a vehicle for the promotion of diverse American interests, including European unity, Third World influence, and superpower detente. The United States was not prepared to jeopardize these other policy stakes by mobilizing all its potential influence on behalf of a rigorous safeguards system or other strictly nonproliferation objectives.

AMERICAN POLICY REVISED AND EMBATTLED

In the early and mid–1970s, a series of developments transformed both the internal dynamics and the external environment of the nonproliferation regime. Structural changes in the world nuclear market brought European suppliers into competition with the United States for reactor exports and, with the emergence of the Urenco and Eurodif consortia, ended the American enrichment monopoly. The oil crisis, meanwhile, underscored the advantages of energy self-sufficiency, and in particular, nuclear development. Energy-poor countries acquired a new interest in national fuel cycle facilities, and European and Japanese plans for the transition to plutonium-based nuclear economies gained added urgency.

These changes eroded the regime's margin of safety, creating the prospect of widespread access to technologies and materials of direct relevance for nuclear weapons, and altering the patterns of influence and incentives on which the regime had rested. The new realities were dramatized by the 1974 Indian nuclear explosion, and by the 1975 West German sale to Brazil of enrichment and reprocessing technology as part of a nuclear cooperation agreement. At the same time, France contracted to export reprocessing facilities to South Korea and Pakistan.

This transition was a period of relative inattention to nonproliferation issues on the part of the United States. During the early 1970s U.S. nuclear policy was almost entirely preoccupied with the Nixon administration's enrichment privatization initiative. This clumsily handled (and unsuccessful) attempt to interest private industry in the running of American enrichment facilities was undertaken without much sensitivity to its international ramifications, and seriously damaged foreign confidence in U.S. fuel supplies.[15] In support of the initiative, the United States modified its enrichment contracts, shifting a large burden of risk from the supplier to the customer, abruptly closed U.S. order books in July 1974, and retroactively classified forty-five existing contracts, including two with Brazil, as "conditional."

The episode accelerated America's loss of control over the world enrichment market—as Urenco, Eurodif, and the Soviet Union all profited from the crisis of confidence in U.S. supplies—and helped crystalize Brazil's 1975 decision in favor of West German reactors over Westinghouse. As such, it left a powerful imprint on the assumptions and attitudes of U.S. nuclear policymakers, creating a preoccupation with America's reputation for supply reliability as the key to U.S. nuclear influence.

Hence, the lessons of this period were mixed and ambiguous—pointing toward tighter export controls and stricter safeguards on the one hand and toward reliable supply on the other. This somewhat schizophrenic legacy pervaded subsequent U.S. policymaking, as attempts to restore confidence in the traditional nuclear bargain coexisted uneasily with attempts to redefine and abridge the bargain. The tension between cooperation and constraint formed the axis of the subsequent policy debate as the United States sought a balance consistent with nonproliferation effectiveness and with the requirements of supplier consensus.

The Carter Policy

As reformulated by the Ford and Carter administrations and the Nuclear Non-Proliferation Act of 1978 (NNPA), U.S. policy sought to come to grips with the growing overlap between the peaceful and military atoms by tightening the rules of nuclear cooperation and revising the conventional wisdom about nuclear power development.[16] The strategy involved both unilateral U.S. actions and an elaborate diplomatic effort, including the Nuclear Suppliers Group and the International Nuclear Fuel Cycle Evaluation (INFCE). There were three main strands: supplier restraint in the export of sensitive nuclear technologies; a full-scope safeguards requirement for cooperation with nonnuclear weapons states, whether NPT parties or not; and a deferral of reprocessing and other steps toward the commercial use of plutonium fuels in the industrialized countries. This agenda was ambitious and diplomatically sensitive because it required America to treat its allies both as part of the problem and part of the solution. Tactically the policy leaned heavily on supply leverage—of the suppliers as a group to constrain the spread of sensitive technologies, and of the United States to shape the nuclear program's choices of its fuel and reactor customers.[17]

The use of supply leverage proved especially controversial in connection with the Carter initiative against the plutonium economy. This policy brought the United States into direct confrontation with Europe and Japan, where the use of plutonium fuels was regarded as essential to future energy security, and where reprocessing and breeder reactor programs were well advanced. The immediate point of friction was the exercise of U.S. consent rights over the reprocessing of U.S.-supplied fuel. Such rights were a standard feature of American agreements for nuclear cooperation, with the notable exception of the U.S.-EURATOM agreement, but had not previously seemed of great importance given the strong presumption on all sides in favor of reprocessing and a transition to plutonium fuel cycles. With the change in U.S. nuclear policy, though, these rights took on a new significance as a lever against allied plutonium plans.

Japan was particularly vulnerable, since it required American approval to start up its pilot reprocessing plant at Tokai Mura and to ship spent fuel from Japanese utilities to Great Britain and France for reprocessing. The EURATOM countries, in turn, were subject to the NNPA provision requiring the United States to renegotiate its agreement with the community to obtain consent rights. (Continued U.S. fuel supplies to EURATOM, in the absence of such renegotiation, have required an annual presidential waiver.) In addition, control over the spent fuel sent to Great Britain and France for reprocessing gave the United States leverage over the economic viability of those countries' facilities.

Bringing consent rights to bear against allied plutonium plans was a delicate policy problem, and there were strong disincentives to the full use of the leverage theoretically available to the United States. Not only did strong pressure carry disproportionate political costs in U.S. relations with Europe and Japan (whose cooperation was needed on tightening export policies), but it risked hastening the decline of U.S. influence by driving customers to alternate fuel suppliers.

In practice, the Carter administration wielded the lever of consent rights with great ambivalence. Criteria were developed that in effect "grandfathered" reprocessing contracts signed prior to 1977, thereby enabling America to approve all requests from Japan and several non-EURATOM European countries to ship fuel to Britain and France. However, requests were subject to an extended case-by-case review and the United States retained a veto on the return and use of the separated plutonium. While a limited agreement was reached on the operation of the Tokai Mura plant, America reserved its position on longer-term reprocessing plans in Japan and other nonnuclear weapons states. Meanwhile, the United States attempted to define an "evolutionary" approach to nuclear development that would accommodate allied breeder research and development while holding the line against early commercialization. The Carter administration especially sought to deter the recycling of plutonium in existing thermal reactors, which would set a broad precedent for plutonium use by any country with a nuclear program.[18]

By the end of the Carter administration, this effort had shown mixed results. The INFCE reports—though not generally supportive of the U.S. position on reprocessing—did contain helpful statements on the marginal economic merits of thermal recycling, the technological feasibility of disposing nuclear wastes without reprocessing, and the formidable technical and economic base needed for a breeder program. At the same time, the downturn in nuclear power programs in the West lent support to the U.S. argument for reduced commitments to plutonium fuels. Despite modest signs of convergence, however, there remained a substantial gulf between the United States and its allies on the plutonium question in general and the unresolved consent rights issue in particular.

American policy met with considerably greater success on the issue of sensitive technology exports. After a bitter confrontation with West Germany over its sales to Brazil, a *de facto* supplier embargo on further exports of fuel cycle facilities was in effect through the late 1970s. West Germany announced a moratorium on new reprocessing exports in June 1977, thereby coming into line with a similar French declaration the previous fall.[19] The United States also succeeded in rolling back reprocessing plans in South Korea and Taiwan, and persuaded France to suspend the export of reprocessing technology to Pakistan. (Pakistan continued to pursue indigenous reprocessing and enrichment projects, causing a cut-off of U.S. foreign aid.) On the other hand, French and Italian cooperation with the highly suspect Iraqi nuclear program showed the limits of U.S. influence.

On the question of full-scope safeguards, the Carter administration came close but ultimately failed to achieve supplier consensus. West Germany was unwilling to jeopardize future sales (especially in Latin America where it was emerging as the dominant supplier) by making full-scope safeguards a requirement for its exports. As a result, in 1979 Argentina acquired a reactor and heavy water plant under a joint agreement with West Germany and Switzerland without accepting safeguards on its indigenous nuclear activities. This acquisition moved Argentina closer to its goal of nuclear self-sufficiency and was a disquieting signal of the potential for supplier backsliding in an increasingly competitive but depressed market.

During the last year of the Carter administration, nonproliferation policy was caught in the geopolitical backlash of the Iranian crisis and the Soviet invasion of Afghanistan. Renewed interest in containing Soviet influence in South Asia and improving America's strategic position in that region led the administration to reconsider its sanctions-oriented nonproliferation policy toward India and Pakistan. Accordingly the administration decided to resume military assistance to Pakistan and to continue fuel shipments to India despite the NNPA's

March 1980 cut-off date for cooperation with countries not accepting full-scope safeguards.

Whether these decisions represented a subordination of nonproliferation to more pressing security interests, or a reformulation of policy designed to pursue both sets of interests more effectively, was open to debate. In the case of Pakistan, the issue became moot when President Mohammed ul-Haq Zia rejected the U.S. aid offer as insufficient. With respect to India, President Carter had better success when his authorization of new fuel exports for Tarapur—against the advice of the Nuclear Regulatory Commission—was narrowly upheld by the Senate.

While impressive as a display of presidential influence, Carter's victory on the Tarapur fuel issue did little to dispel the impression that the United States had awkwardly trapped itself in a no-win situation. To continue fuel shipments would undercut U.S. policy on safeguards and tarnish the NNPA. A cut-off, however, would not only jeopardize improved U.S.-Indian relations but would carry proliferation risks. Termination of U.S. exports, the administration argued, would be cited by India as a violation of the 1963 agreement, freeing it to abrogate IAEA safeguards at Tarapur and to reprocess the accumulated spent fuel at will. However valid this argument (for India might have been bluffing), it carried overtones of yielding to blackmail and raised in a pointed way the question of who had gained leverage over whom. In effect, by accepting carefully circumscribed obligations in return for U.S. assistance, India had acquired hostages against a future U.S. cut-off. The threat to renounce those obligations, in the final analysis, trumped the U.S. threat to terminate cooperation.

The Reagan Policy

The Reagan administration assumed office signaling a major shift in nuclear export policy away from the emphasis on restraint, denial, and universalism of the past several years.[20] Arguing that overly restrictive policies had undercut U.S. influence and harmed the prospects for nuclear power growth, administration officials promised a more cooperative and pragmatic approach to export policy.

Beyond this shift in the direction of export policy, the new administration regarded export policy *per se*, with its focus on the capabilities of potential proliferators, as having been overemphasized relative to the security factors that shape nuclear incentives. The Reagan administration proposed to redress this imbalance, giving greater attention to the security dimension of proliferation through alliance policies, conventional arms sales, and a generally more assertive U.S. foreign policy. This approach was most clearly expressed in policy toward Pakistan, where the United States resumed military assistance under a $3.2 billion aid package, including the sale of forty F–16s.[21]

As it evolved in practice, U.S. nuclear export policy under President Ronald Reagan showed more continuity with the 1970s than the early statements of administration nuclear philosophy suggested.[22] The administration decided not to seek new legislation to liberalize the framework for U.S. nuclear cooperation (for example, by removing the retroactive provisions of the NNPA). It continued the policy of nuclear denial toward Pakistan and opposition to sensitive technology transfers to potential proliferators, and worked with the other suppliers to upgrade export controls on dual-use technologies.[23] While these elements of continuity were in part explained by strong congressional opposition to a weakening of U.S. nonproliferation policy, they also reflected some recognition by the administration of the logic of restraint.

However, in both tone and substance the Reagan policy deemphasized some of the "revisionist" themes of the recent past, such as the preoccupation with the risks of plutonium fuel cycles, and harked back to the earlier tradition of the nuclear bargain. This thrust was particularly evident in the administration's emphasis on "reliable supply" and the strong correlation it assumed between the U.S. role in nuclear commerce and U.S. influence on behalf of nonproliferation objectives.[24] In keeping with this orientation, the Reagan administration was less ambivalent than its predecessor about nuclear power development and more energetic (though not more successful) in promoting American nuclear exports.

Both for reasons of nuclear philosophy and alliance harmony, the Reagan administration attached a high priority to breaking the impasse on U.S. consent rights and allied plutonium programs. The administration declared that it would not "inhibit or set back" the breeder reactor and reprocessing programs of the industrial countries, and proposed to accommodate those programs by negotiating "programmatic" arrangements under which the United States would give long-term advance approval for reprocessing of U.S. fuel and for use of the resulting plutonium.[25]

This approach was not a radical departure from previous policy; the Carter administration, also, had been groping toward a programmatic consent formula for Japan and Europe during its final year. However, the Reagan policy was less self-conscious about proposing an overt double standard for plutonium use (acceptable in some countries but not in others), and more confident of its ability to manage the regime-level legitimacy problems this might entail. In effect, the new approach rejected the Ford-Carter thesis that plutonium inherently poses serious problems for the nonproliferation regime and that there is a need for consistent criteria governing its use in the industrialized countries and elsewhere. This impression was reinforced by the willingness of the Reagan administration to approve thermal recycling of U.S.-origin plutonium and by its strong advocacy, despite the indifference of the private sector, of domestic reprocessing and plutonium use.

On the issue of sensitive technology exports, the Reagan policy again substituted a flexible standard for the previous rule of restraint. It announced that it would "continue to inhibit" such exports "where the danger of proliferation demands," and subsequently moved to lift the longstanding U.S. embargo on exports of reprocessing and enrichment technology. The administration declared that it would consider requests from American firms to cooperate with European and Japanese reprocessing ventures, and offered to share U.S. centrifuge technology with Australia in a joint enrichment project in that country.

The question of sensitive technology exports also arose in connection with the bidding for reactor sales to Mexico in 1981–82. In soliciting bids for its now-suspended nuclear expansion program, Mexico announced an interest in acquiring fuel cycle technologies as well as reactors. The Reagan administration tried to walk a fine line to keep U.S. firms competitive without making commitments on technology that could trigger a wholesale collapse of supplier restraint. In the end, the United States maintained a studied ambiguity about near-term technology transfer, while suggesting that over the longer term nothing was ruled out. It offered U.S. assistance in assessing Mexico's requirements for reprocessing and enrichment, held out the prospect of future cooperation in these fields, and invited Mexican participation in nonsensitive areas of the U.S. breeder and reprocessing programs.[26]

The Mexican case underscored both the difficulty of drawing clear lines to support a discriminatory supply strategy and the delicacy of any American effort to recapture nuclear influence through a stronger presence in the commercial market. Indeed, the Reagan policy essentially begged the question of how, in a highly competitive market, U.S. commercial success would translate into nonproliferation leadership. While its rhetoric tended to treat a U.S. "return to the game" as a kind of public good, the administration's approach to Mexico and to the competition with European enrichers for the Australian partnership (ultimately lost to Urenco) showed a keen appreciation of the zero-sum aspects of the game. In this respect, despite its frequent allusions to restoring the historic U.S. role in nuclear cooperation, the Reagan administration sometimes seemed ambivalent about that role: nostalgic for the era of U.S. predominance but tempted by the attractions of being an "ordinary supplier," relieved of special responsibilities for defining and defending regime norms.

Ambivalence also marked the Reagan administration's approach to the issue of full-scope safeguards. The administration affirmed support in principle of a full-scope safeguards requirement for significant new supply commitments, and lobbied the other suppliers to boycott Pakistan's effort to purchase a new reactor while the latter's indigenous, weapons-related facilities remained free of safeguards. However, it shared the Carter administration's doubts about the wisdom of applying this condition to existing supply relationships. Therefore, faced with the cut-off provision of the NNPA (the grace period then having expired), the United States sought to apply the NNPA in a nonpunitive manner by arranging or acquiescing in surrogate supply sources for the countries most affected.

Tarapur was again the critical case. As in 1980, America's main concern was that a cut-off of U.S. fuel would cause India to renounce safeguards on its reactors. This outcome was averted by arranging for France to assume America's supply role under the 1963 agreement, with all other provisions—and ambiguities—of that agreement remaining unchanged. Hence, India remained uncommitted to continuing safeguards after the expiration of the agreement in 1993, and asserted its right to reprocess U.S. fuel already supplied.[27]

Two other countries subject to the NNPA cut-off, Brazil and South Africa, also arranged alternative fuel supplies with American help. Brazil was granted a suspension of its U.S. enrichment contract so that it could acquire fuel elsewhere without financial penalty, and South Africa obtained surplus uranium on the European market in a deal brokered by U.S. firms with implicit government assent.

PROSPECTS: U.S. EXPORT POLICY AND THE REGIME

The bumpy course of U.S. nuclear export policy over the last ten years reflects the frustrations of adapting policy to changes in markets and in proliferation dynamics. Essentially the United States has attempted to answer two persistent questions: How, and to what extent, can export policy be brought to bear effectively against the threat of proliferation? How can U.S. influence in this process be maximized?

These questions do not have definitive answers. The optimum balance points between cooperation and restraint, and country-specific and regime interests, are inherently elusive and changing. Moreover, two constraints complicate the search for a coherent policy: the inevitable tensions between nonproliferation policy and other foreign policy and security interests; and, since the 1970s, a volatile and polarized domestic nuclear policy environment.

The importance of the latter factor as an impediment to the reestablishment of stability in nuclear export policy should not be underestimated. The erosion of bipartisan consensus on nonproliferation policy in the last ten years is closely related to the domestic nuclear power controversy and the broadening of participation in nuclear decisionmaking beyond the formerly dominant nuclear establishment. One result has been an oscillation of nonproliferation policy in accordance with the influence of different constituency groups in successive administrations. Thus, the Carter policy felt the gravitational pull of environmentalist groups and the Reagan policy that of the domestic nuclear industry. A more effective nonproliferation policy would seem to require better integration of the nonproliferation policy process with foreign policy at large, and better insulation of it from the claims of domestic interest groups on both sides of the nuclear power debate. The following assessment of prospects for U.S. export policy should be considered against the background of these broader policy imperatives.

Nuclear Markets and Supply Strategies

Three features of the world nuclear market are of particular importance to nonproliferation efforts. The structure of supply is pluralistic, demand is severely depressed, and a high proportion of the customers, outside of Europe and Japan, have moderate to high nuclear weapons incentives. America's share of the market has declined dramatically since the early 1970s. France and West Germany compete on terms equal or better than U.S. reactor firms for export sales, and Canada, Sweden, and the Soviet Union are additional sources of supply. Japan may also enter the reactor export market soon. Supply of enrichment services is similarly diversified. The U.S. share of the noncommunist market has fallen from almost 100 percent as late as 1976 to about 35 percent in the early 1980s. Eurodif and Urenco supply about half the market, and the Soviet Union the remainder. In addition, a number of Third World states—including Argentina, Brazil, and the People's Republic of China—are emerging as suppliers of at least a limited range of nuclear technology and materials.[28]

The contraction of demand is equally dramatic. The export market for reactors has shrunk radically. At best only a dozen or so importing countries are likely to expand their programs over the next several years, and these countries will probably confine their orders to one or two reactors each.[29] This outlook parallels the situation in many of the industrialized countries, where nuclear power growth has virtually stopped except for the completion of plants already substantially constructed.[30]

Finally, the shrinkage of the export market has skewed its composition disproportionately toward countries whose record of behavior or security situations suggest an interest in keeping open a nuclear weapons option. Thus, the most prominent Third World customers are South Korea, Taiwan, Argentina, and Brazil. Other problem countries with an interest in reactor purchases over the next few years are Pakistan and Israel.

Taken together, these market characteristics create an inhospitable environment for supply policies in support of nonproliferation. On the one hand, the diversity of suppliers and the diffusion of technological capabilities limit the effectiveness of "denial" strategies. On the other hand, the logic of restraint and compliance that was implicit in the traditional nuclear bargain is also weakened. As a result, strategies of "reliable supply" and "control through cooperation," which essentially depend on the effects of the web of nuclear dependence to moderate proliferation risks, are devalued.

For example, the downturn of nuclear power in theory should dampen the momentum of sensitive nuclear activities. It undercuts the economic case for moving to plutonium fuels (since uranium is cheap and abundant) and supports a supplier strategy employing market incentives and fuel assurances to slow the spread of fuel cycle facilities.[31] In practice, however, the scope for realizing such a strategy is relatively narrow, both because the logic of competition tempts suppliers to offer technology sweeteners and because customers of sensitive technology are motivated in most cases not by market economic calculations but by political and security factors.

Morever, the current buyer's market may tempt even countries with low proliferation incentives (like Mexico) to play suppliers against one another in a quest for fuel cycle technologies, even though the very diversity of fuel sources should in principle reduce their appeal. Indeed, if fuel supply insecurity were the main motive for the acquisition of fuel cycle technologies, the problem would be virtually solved, given the current glut of uranium and enrichment services. "Front end" fuel assurance, once considered a key institutional measure for reducing incentives for reprocessing, has become academic. ("Back end" assurances, such as international arrangements for spent fuel and waste management, would still be helpful from a nonproliferation standpoint, but the domestic political sensitivities associated with these schemes have frustrated their implementation.)

The current market also limits the use of nuclear cooperation to obtain nonproliferation commitments from customer states. This situation is partly a function of the nuclear recession: The buyer's market weakens inhibitions against dealing with countries with dubious records (as evidenced by the recent interest in reactor sales to Pakistan and China), and helps the latter to resist pressures to provide nonproliferation guarantees as a price of entry into the market.[32] The more fundamental problem is that nuclear cooperation is an inherently weak lever when weighed against the security calculations of countries that deliberately keep open a weapons option. Experience suggests that where supply dependence is reinforced by a heavily dependent security relationship, as in the U.S.-Korean case, supplier leverage can be exploited for nonproliferation gains. However, where the nuclear relationship exists in a relative vacuum, or where the broader political-security context is unfavorable to the supplier, the nuclear link is a slender reed.

Thus, with countries like India, South Africa, Argentina, and Brazil, nuclear supply has proven largely unsuccessful either in eliciting nonproliferation assurances or in creating dependencies that can be exploited to deter steps toward proliferation. While suppliers have obtained safeguards on portions of these countries' programs, on balance nuclear cooperation has served the customers' purposes better than those of nonproliferation policy. The recipients have received cooperation essentially on their terms, using it as a bridge to progressively greater nuclear independence while keeping their own options open. Moreover, their progress toward self-sufficiency not only insulates these countries against supply sanctions but may actually (as in the Indian case) provide counterleverage to deter cut-offs. The logic of "control through cooperation" is turned on its head. This kind of reverse leverage can take other forms as well, such as oil power. The very factors that allow a country like Iraq, for example, to gain access to nuclear cooperation cast doubt on the ability of suppliers to use that cooperation for nonproliferation leverage.

This said, however, to dismiss the importance of efforts to maintain and strengthen the supply regime would be a mistake. The nuclear programs of most of the problem countries continue to rely in varying degrees on links with the suppliers. Accordingly export restraint offers some hope of gaining time with these countries and of adding to the technical, economic, and political price of weapons programs. The experiences of Pakistan and of India suggest that withholding cooperation can raise barriers and impose costs. Conversely the permissive record of supplier assistance to Argentina, Brazil, and Iraq has aggravated the proliferation threat posed by these countries.

Strong diplomatic efforts are required to prevent an erosion of export controls, especially on the transfer of sensitive technologies; to upgrade the supplier consensus regarding noncooperation with countries that refuse full-scope safeguards or that are engaged in weapons-related activities; and to expand supplier cooperation in the area of sanctions against safeguards violations, nuclear tests, or other steps toward proliferation. Identifying the agenda of supplier diplomacy is of course easier than demonstrating how consensus can be achieved and maintained. Clearly, however, the United States remains the essential leader and catalyst in this process.

Supplier Relations and U.S. Influence

In considering the scope and conditions of U.S. influence in this area, one should recognize America's declining share of the nuclear market. This factor constrains U.S. leverage and renders a cooperative approach to supply policy necessary. The United States cannot unilaterally set the terms of international nuclear relations either through the power of its own example or through the wasting asset of its fuel supply role.

But, as discussed in the first section of this chapter, the historical American domination of nuclear markets, while important, was not a decisive factor in the development of the nonproliferation regime. To overstate the role of this factor is to miss the essentially political nature of the regime-building process and the importance of nonmarket factors in determining outcomes at key junctures. The experience of the past several years confirms this pattern. The United States has sometimes succeeded despite a lack of significant market leverage (e.g., France's suspension of the sale of reprocessing technology to Pakistan), or failed despite a theoretically commanding supply position (e.g., the use of consent rights to steer Japan away from reprocessing).

The critical determinants in such cases have been the larger political and economic stakes and their relative valuation by the states concerned. America's most conspicuous failures have occurred when the costs to the other party of acceding to the U.S. position, or to the United States of imposing it, have been perceived as excessive. Note the cases of the West Germany-Brazil agreement (where the economic stakes were dominant for West Germany), and of French and Italian cooperation with Iraq (where access to oil was decisive). In contrast, the French economic stake in the reprocessing export to Pakistan was relatively modest. Similarly the United States, generally, has had more success with France than with West Germany, notwithstanding the former's greater nuclear independence from the United States, because of the West German nuclear industry's far greater reliance on exports.[33] (The recent French economic crisis, which has increased the importance of exports to the economy at large, may change this situation.)

A comparison of the cases of France-Pakistan and West Germany–Brazil indicates two other factors that influence the persuasiveness of U.S. arguments on behalf of supplier restraint. First, America demonstrated convincingly that Pakistan posed a concrete, near-term proliferation threat, while the Brazilian threat was more distant and speculative. Second, the United States had no evident economic stake in the outcome of the Pakistan case, while the interest of American firms in the Brazilian export made it possible (if not fair) for West Germany to suspect that U.S. policy was commercially motivated.

From this perspective, attempting to increase U.S. nuclear influence by improving the American market position is a blind alley, and could in fact put serious pressure on the nonproliferation regime. In the present market, export success is unlikely to strengthen the U.S. position in nonproliferation diplomacy. The reverse is more likely—other suppliers, determined not to be outbid in the future, might become less receptive to U.S. leadership. This outcome is all the more likely if the United States itself appears opportunistic or ambivalent about nonproliferation standards.

A good first principle, then, is that the United States should be "above suspicion" in its own export policy and avoid sending mixed signals on questions of safeguards or technology transfer that allow other suppliers to justify a relaxation of standards. Accordingly there is merit to an across-the-board U.S. restriction on sensitive exports, even though it offers no guarantee of being emulated by other suppliers. In this area, U.S. restraint would appear to be a necessary, though hardly sufficient, condition of restraint by others. For the same reason, the erratic course of the last two administrations on the full-scope safeguards issue—and particularly the reluctance to end cooperation with India, South Africa, and Argentina—has been unfortunate.

While a determined U.S. bid for exports is an unpromising route to supplier cooperation, an accommodation on the question of plutonium use and American consent rights is desirable. Both the Carter and Reagan administrations have been attracted by the idea of a trade-off between the liberalization of U.S. policy on plutonium and greater supplier cooperation on nonproliferation issues. Whether a direct linkage exists is doubtful, but an end to the debilitating impasse on plutonium would ease the strained atmosphere of supplier relations. Moreover, by demonstrating American sensitivity to allied energy security interests, such accommodation would allow the United States to press more vigorously the security argument for strict nuclear export policies.

Expanded cooperation in nuclear research and development would also be welcomed by Europe and Japan, both for symbolic reasons and because U.S. technological leadership still commands respect. Although cooperation in breeder reactor development would be most dramatic, other areas—especially waste and spent-fuel management and reactor safety—are more relevant to the health of supplier nuclear industries and therefore to dampening export pressures.

Nevertheless, whatever marginal impact such cooperation might have, to look to a general revival of the industry as a way of relieving the current pressures on suppliers is unrealistic. Severe overcapacity in the supplier countries will persist, and strategies to maintain export restraint must emphasize ways of coping with the consequences of this fact. In other words, one of the main tasks of supplier cooperation is to minimize the "rogue effects" of the nuclear recession on the nonproliferation regime.

This task may require more radical forms of cooperation than those so far attempted. One possibility that has been proposed is a market-sharing arrangement whereby prospective exports would be allocated among the suppliers on a geographical basis.[34] Even this solution would be precarious in the present market, however. Like the existing supplier guidelines, it would attempt to reduce the scope of competition but would not address the root of the problem—that there are too few sales in prospect to keep the industry, as now constituted, alive. Market sharing might therefore have to be supplemented by a kind of adjustment-assistance program or other mechanisms to ease the domestic impact of the industry's decline and to compensate especially vulnerable suppliers for sales foregone.

The Broader Context of Supplier Relations

Insulating the supply regime from competitive pressures and from the effects of recession in the nuclear industry is central to the maintenance of export restraint. To a significant extent, however, the prospects for supply policies are shaped by forces outside the realm of nuclear energy relations. This larger context affects the possibilities of supplier cooperation in two respects.

First, as this chapter has frequently noted, nuclear export policies are driven by many factors in addition to commercial motives. The use of nuclear exports to advance national economic, political, and security interests has always constrained supplier cooperation—as demonstrated in recent years by the cooperation of European suppliers with Iraq and, more generally, by the use of nuclear sales to promote stronger political and economic relations with important Third World states like Brazil, China, and Mexico. In addition, reactor exports have been viewed as a means of stimulating national economies and improving trade balances during the world recession.

Second, the prospects for rigorous supply policies are related to the persuasiveness and coherence with which nuclear proliferation is linked to the framework of security relations among the supplier countries: An effective supply regime is more likely if proliferation is taken seriously as a security issue by the United States and its allies. If the priority of nuclear supply issues is to be sustained and U.S. influence maximized, lifting supplier politics out of the sphere of nuclear energy relations and onto the "high politics" agenda is necessary. This task is not simply one of consciousness-raising, important as that may be. It is a question of demonstrating U.S. seriousness by anchoring nonproliferation objectives more firmly into the Western security equation.

NOTES

1. For a recent analysis of U.S. policy development during this period, see Gregg Herken, *The Winning Weapon: The Atomic Bomb in the Cold War, 1945–50* (New York: Alfred A. Knopf, 1981).

2. Whether a continuation of *military* nuclear collaboration after the war might have forestalled the British bomb program is another matter. See Andrew Pierre, *Nuclear Politics: The British Experience with an Independent Strategic Force 1939–1970* (London: Oxford University Press, 1972), pp. 75–77.

3. On the U.S.-Soviet context, see Henry Sokolski, "Atoms for Peace: A Non-Proliferation Primer?" *Arms Control* (September 1980).

4. On the "reactor wars" and U.S. penetration of the European nuclear market, see Irvin C. Bupp and Jean-Claude Derian, *Light Water: How the Nuclear Dream Dissolved* (New York: Basic Books, 1978); and Henry Nau, *National Politics and International Technology: Nuclear Reactor Development in Western Europe* (Baltimore: Johns Hopkins University Press, 1974).

5. On EURATOM, French policy, and the enrichment issue, see Lawrence Scheinman, *Atomic Energy in France Under the*

Fourth Republic (Princeton: Princeton University Press, 1965), pp. 176–84.

6. Bupp and Derian, *Light Water*, p. 29. Exports in these early years were especially important to the U.S. nuclear industry because of the relatively late blooming of the American domestic market: "The cooperative arrangements the 'Atoms for Peace' program made possible . . . provided an enormous opportunity for Americans to undertake projects abroad that were precluded by political and economic constraints at home" (Ibid., p. 35).

7. Paul Joskow, "The International Nuclear Industry Today," *Foreign Affairs* 54, no. 4 (Summer 1976): 792. The crowning triumph for the LWR was the French decision, after the departure of President De Gaulle, in favor of U.S. reactor technology—a choice long urged by Electricité de France but opposed by the French Atomic Energy Commission.

8. A good review of the development of the system from an American perspective is the statement by Myron Kratzer in *The International Atomic Energy Agency (IAEA): Improving Safeguards*, Hearings, 97th Cong., 2d Sess., March 3 and 18, 1982, pp. 19–53. See also Atlantic Council, *Nuclear Power and Nuclear Weapons Proliferation* (Boulder, Colo.: Westview Press, 1978), Vol. 1, pp. 57–68. For a French perspective on the same events, see Bertrand Goldschmidt, *The Atom Complex* (La Grange Park: American Nuclear Society, 1982), pp. 277–88.

9. For a fuller discussion of U.S.-Indian nuclear relations, see Peter Clausen, "Nonproliferation Illusions: Tarapur in Retrospect," *Orbis* 27, no. 3 (Fall 1983).

10. See Joint Committee on Atomic Energy, *International Agreements for Cooperation*, Hearings, 88th Cong., 1st Sess., Sept. 5, 1963; 2d Sess.; April 22 and June 30, 1964, p. 64.

11. See Peter Pringle and James Spigelman, *The Nuclear Barons* (New York: Rinehart and Winston, 1981), p. 301 ff.

12. On the politics of the NPT negotiations, see Elizabeth Young, *A Farewell to Arms Control* (Hammondsworth: Penguin Books, 1972); and George Quester, *The Politics of Nuclear Proliferation* (Baltimore: Johns Hopkins University Press, 1973).

13. For an excellent treatment of the tensions between U.S. alliance and nonproliferation policies, see William Bader, *The United States and the Spread of Nuclear Weapons* (New York: Pegasus Books, 1968).

14. Atlantic Council, *Nuclear Power and Nuclear Weapons Proliferation*, p. 68.

15. For a full treatment of this episode, see Michael Brenner, *Nuclear Power and Non-Proliferation: The Remaking of U.S. Policy* (New York: Cambridge University Press, 1981), Part I. See also Edward Wonder, *Nuclear Fuel and American Policy* (Boulder, Colo.: Westview Press, 1977). Brenner argues that the privatization initiative was "the outstanding miscalculation, from a nonproliferation standpoint, that has been made in the nuclear energy field since the United States started down the road marked by Atoms for Peace" (p. 224).

16. On the process of U.S. policy revision under presidents Ford and Carter, see Brenner, *Nuclear Power*. On the Carter policy, see also Joseph Nye, "Maintaining a Nonproliferation Regime," in George Quester, ed., *Nuclear Proliferation: Breaking the Chain* (Madison: University of Wisconsin Press, 1981), pp. 20–29; and Joseph Nye, "Nonproliferation: A Long-Term Strategy," *Foreign Affairs* 56, no. 3 (Spring 1978). The NNPA set a rigorous standard for U.S. approvals which, if interpreted strictly, could virtually rule out reprocessing and plutonium use in nonweapons states. For a discussion of the consent rights issue, see Victor Gilinsky, "Plutonium, Proliferation, and the Price of Reprocessing," *Foreign Affairs* 57, no. 2 (Winter 1978–79).

17. A good critical analysis of this aspect of the Carter policy is contained in Thomas Neff and Henry Jacoby, "Nonproliferation Policy in a Changing Nuclear Fuel Market," *Foreign Affairs* 57, no. 5 (Summer 1979).

18. See Nye, "Nonproliferation: A Long-Term Strategy."

19. On the shift in French policy, see Pierre Lellouche, "France in the International Nuclear Energy Controversy," *Orbis* 22, no. 4 (Winter 1979). The London (or Nuclear) Supplier Guidelines, published in 1978, stopped short of formalizing an embargo, calling instead for "restraint" in the transfer of sensitive techologies and materials.

20. This section draws from Peter Clausen, "The Reagan Nonproliferation Policy," *Arms Control Today* (December 1982).

21. The resumption of aid required congressional action since Pakistan refused to give assurances against proliferation as required by the Symington Amendment to the Foreign Assistance Act. The administration hoped nonetheless that the aid relationship would moderate the pace of the Pakistani weapons program and deter a nuclear test that would in all likelihood cause a new cutoff. See House Committee on Foreign Affairs, *Security and Economic Assistance to Pakistan*, Hearings, 97th Cong., 1st Sess., April 27, Sept. 16, 22, and 23, and Nov. 17 and 19, 1981.

22. "United States Non-Proliferation and Peaceful Nuclear Coopera-
    tion Policy," Office of the Press Secretary, White House, July 16,
    1981. This statement is considerably more moderate than
    reports during the transition period which indicated a wholesale
    dismantling of the Carter policies.
23. See, for example, Milton Benjamen, "More Curbs Sought on A-
    Materials," *The Washington Post*, January 3, 1983, p. 1;
    "Enhanced Trigger List Encompassing Centrifuge Technology
    Set for Accord," *Nucleonics Week* (February, 3, 1983): 1; and Les-
    lie Geld, "Nuclear Nations Agree to Tighten Export Controls,"
    The New York Times, July 16, 1984.
24. The Reagan administration tended to attribute the decline of
    U.S. nuclear leadership to restrictive nonproliferation policies
    rather than to structural factors, such as the rise of competing
    suppliers and downturn in nuclear energy. See statement of
    Deputy Energy Secretary Kenneth Davis, quoted by Milton
    Benjamen, "Administration Becomes Flexible on Gray Area
    Nuclear Exports," *The Washington Post*, August 8, 1982, p. 11.
25. "Administration's Plutonium Policy Finally Materialized,"
    Nucleonics Week (June 12, 1982): 2; and "Reagan Alters Policy
    on A-Fuel Recycling," *The Washington Post*, June 9, 1982, p. 3.
    For a critique, see Victor Gilinsky, "The Adminstration's
    Risky Plutonium Policy," *The Wall Street Journal*, July 15,
    1982, p. 30.
26. See "Mexican Participation in U.S. Reprocessing, Enrichment
    Ventures Possible," *Inside Energy* (March 26, 1982): 1; "U.S. to
    Stress New Flexibility on Nuclear Exports in Talks with Mex-
    ico," *Inside Energy* (December 4, 1981): 1; "White House Lends
    an Ear to Industry's Export Sales Problems," *Nucleonics Week*
    (January 7, 1982): 1.
27. See "Tarapur Situation Settled for Present; Major Conflict Still
    Unresolved," *Nucleonics Week* (December 2, 1982): 1. During
    1983 Tarapur surfaced yet again to bedevil U.S. nonproliferation
    policy, this time over the issue of spare parts for the reactors.
    Secretary of State Shultz announced that the United States
    would supply needed components, which are not subject to the
    NNPA safeguards requirement, if other suppliers were unable to
    do so. This and other administration actions, including approval
    of a large heavy water transfer to Argentina, prompted several
    congressional initiatives to tighten further restrictions on U.S.
    dealings with full-scope safeguards hold-outs so as to prohibit
    virtually any direct or indirect nuclear cooperation with such
    countries.

28. On the "third tier" nuclear suppliers, see Lewis Dunn, *Controlling the Bomb* (New Haven: Yale University Press, 1982), p. 41–43.

29. For a careful country-by-country review of the nuclear export market, see William Walker and Mans Lonnroth, *Nuclear Power Struggles: Industrial Competition and Proliferation Control* (London: George Allen and Unwin, 1983).

30. See Irvin C. Bupp, "The Actual Growth and Probable Future of the Worldwide Nuclear Energy Industry," in Quester, ed., *Nuclear Proliferation.*

31. Such a strategy is proposed by Ted Greenwood and Robert Haffa, Jr., "Supply-Side Non-Proliferation," *Foreign Policy* 24 (Spring 1981).

32. See "France and Pakistan Discuss a Nuclear Deal," *The New York Times*, March 30, 1983, p. 7. The United States is prevented by the NNPA from nuclear cooperation with Pakistan. It has, like the other suppliers, shown strong interest in nuclear sales to China, and signed a nuclear cooperation agreement with that country in 1984. However, controversy over China's apparent assistance to the Pakistani nuclear weapons effort has held up implementation of the agreement. See Lena Sun, "U.S.-China Energy Pact Faces Delay," *The Washington Post*, July 29, 1984, p. 1.

33. See Lellouche, "France in the International Nuclear Energy Controversy"; and Ervin Hackel, "The Politics of Nuclear Exports in West Germany," in Robert Boardman and James F. Keeley, eds., *Nuclear Exports and World Politics* (London: Macmillan, 1983).

34. See, for example, Walker and Lonnroth, *Nuclear Power Strategies*; and Abraham Ribicoff, "A Market-Sharing Approach to the World Nuclear Sales Problem," *Foreign Affairs* 54, no. 4 (July 1976). For a good discussion of related issues, see Steven Backer, "Monopoly or Cartel," *Foreign Policy* 23 (Summer 1976).

8 SOVIET NUCLEAR EXPORT POLICY

William C. Potter

Prevention of the spread of nuclear weapons has long been a theme of Soviet arms control declaratory policy. It also has found concrete expression in Moscow's endorsement of the 1963 Partial Test Ban Treaty, the 1967 Treaty for the Prohibition of Nuclear Weapons in Latin America (Treaty of Tlatelolco), the Treaty on the Non-Proliferation of Nuclear Weapons (NPT) of 1968, and since 1958, the Soviet Union's own stringent nuclear export policy. Although much of Moscow's nonproliferation rhetoric and elements of its nonproliferation behavior can be explained in terms of narrow self-interest (e.g., prevention of nuclear accession by traditional adversaries), the range and consistency of Soviet nonproliferation efforts, as well as certain specific actions, indicate a genuine appreciation by Soviet leaders of the dangers posed by the diffusion of nuclear weapons.

I wish to thank Anya Kroth and Sergei Zamascikov for their research assistance. I also wish to acknowledge the valuable advice provided by Gloria Duffy, Thomas Graham, Stephen Meyer, Arthur Steiner, Robert C. Tucker, Charles Van Doren, Richard Williamson, and numerous U.S., Soviet, and Indian government officials. My research was supported by the UCLA Center for International and Strategic Affairs, the UCLA Center for Russian and East European Studies, Lawrence Livermore National Laboratory, and the Ploughshares Fund.

213

Notwithstanding its overall commendable record on non-proliferation, the Soviet Union in the past decade has undertaken several nuclear export initiatives that are not easily reconciled with its image as an ardent nonproliferation advocate and consistent practitioner of stringent nuclear export controls. These initiatives pertain to Soviet nuclear trade with Argentina, Cuba, India (all non-NPT states), and with Libya (generally assumed to covet nuclear weapons). The purpose of this chapter is twofold: to analyze Soviet nuclear transactions with the aforementioned states; and to assess the extent to which recent Soviet behavior represents a revision in Soviet nonproliferation policy and a departure from prior Soviet support for stringent export controls and a strong IAEA (International Atomic Energy Agency) safeguards system.

SOVIET NUCLEAR EXPORT POLICY: THE HISTORICAL CONTEXT

An appraisal of the possible reorientation of Soviet nuclear export policy in recent years requires familiarity with the prior record of Soviet export behavior. One can discern at least three different periods in the development of Soviet perspectives on nuclear exports.[1]

Secrecy and Denial (1945–1954)

During the period between 1945 and 1954, Soviet concern with the issues of nuclear exports and nonproliferation was peripheral to the major security problem of countering U.S. nuclear weapons superiority.[2] Not surprisingly, therefore, the Soviet Union was unreceptive to U.S. initiatives such as the Baruch Plan, which would have created an International Atomic Development Authority with "managerial control over all atomic activities potentially dangerous to world security." At a time when the Soviet Union had yet to test a nuclear device, the Baruch Plan was seen by Moscow as a strategy to perpetuate Soviet nuclear inferiority. The inspection procedures called for by the Baruch Plan also raised in Stalin's mind the spectre of Western intelligence operations within the Soviet Union and possible espionage directed at Soviet military industrial facilities. Soviet non-proliferation policy, consequently, sought to reverse the sequence of control and disarmament that characterized the U.S. approach. Whereas the Americans envisioned the creation of inspection and control machinery first and then nuclear disarmament, the Soviet Union insisted that the destruction of all atomic weapons precede introduction of an international control system.[3] In effect, the Soviet proposal meant nuclear disarmament by the United States alone and no prospect for U.S.-Soviet agreement on the control of atomic energy.

The one aspect in which Soviet nuclear policy resembled that of the United States prior to 1954 was in its emphasis on secrecy and denial. Soviet research and development efforts in the nuclear field at this time were primarily oriented toward military purposes and were conducted in great secrecy and in isolation from other countries. No serious consideration appears to have been given to the export of Soviet nuclear expertise or technology. This policy of nuclear secrecy, however, did not preclude the USSR from exploiting the uranium deposits of the socialist countries in Eastern Europe.

Atoms for Peace (1954–1958)

President Dwight D. Eisenhower, in his famous December 1953 "Atoms for Peace" speech before the United Nations, signaled a change in U.S. nuclear export policy from secrecy/denial to active global promotion of the peaceful applications of atomic energy. The Soviet response to the U.S. initiative was to launch its own international crusade for nuclear energy.[4]

One of the first steps in the campaign was sponsorship of a series of meetings during 1954 in the Soviet Union and Eastern Europe for invited physicists and engineers from Western Europe as well as the Third World. When in December 1954 the U.S. Atomic Energy Commission decided to declassify information on the Argonne (Illinois) atomic pile, the Soviet Union responded in January 1955 by announcing its readiness to share technical data collected during operation of its first atomic power plant.[5] Shortly thereafter, scientists from forty-one nations were invited to a conference on the peaceful uses of atomic energy in Moscow in July 1955. This conference preceded by one month another international nuclear energy conference in Geneva and marked the escalation of a nuclear information export race in which "the nuclear giants lifted their skirts of secrecy, each challenging the other to reveal more evidence of dedication to the peaceful atom."[6]

By the mid–1950s this race had taken the form of exporting not only nuclear power information and technical experts but also research reactors. The first recipients of Soviet nuclear exports were the East European states and the People's Republic of China (PRC). Each of these countries in 1955 was offered a two megawatt (mw) research reactor with a small amount of uranium enriched to 10 percent.[7] Czechoslovakia was also promised a 150mw natural uranium, heavy water–moderated, gas-cooled reactor, and Hungary and East Germany, smaller pressurized water reactors fueled with enriched uranium.[8] These intra-bloc agreements were followed in early 1956 by a nuclear cooperation agreement with Yugoslavia and an offer to establish a nuclear research laboratory in Egypt.

By far the most extensive and significant nuclear assistance provided by the Soviet Union in the mid–1950s was to China. Between 1955 and 1958 the Soviet Union delivered a 6.5mw heavy water research reactor, announced a "First Five Year Plan for Foreign Aid" for the development of thirty-nine atomic centers in China, and likely delivered (or at a minimum, assisted the assembly of) a gaseous diffusion uranium-enrichment plant at Lanchow.[9]

Significantly the Soviet Union failed to apply safeguards to any of these nuclear exports, perhaps because of their confidence in controlling the nuclear programs of their allies. Soviet laxness may also have been due to their failure to appreciate fully the ease with which these exports could be used for military purposes.[10] The latter explanation is supported by the failure of the Soviet Union to insist on safeguards on nuclear exports during this period even to countries outside of the bloc, such as Egypt. The lack of Soviet attention in the mid–1950s to the issue of nuclear safeguards also reflects the absence of a coherent and consistent nonproliferation strategy. Indeed, precisely at the time when the allied decision to rearm West Germany raised the issue of nonproliferation in Moscow to importance, the Soviet Union proceeded to supply the PRC with substantial nuclear assistance.

Only in 1958, after the Chinese indicated publicly that they intended to produce their own nuclear weapons, did the USSR fully recognize that the proliferation danger which they heralded in the West, in fact, existed in the South and was acute primarily because of the USSR's own nuclear largess.[11] This recognition prompted Moscow to suspend its nuclear aid to China and to persuade Beijing that nuclear nonproliferation in general, and Chinese nuclear abstinence in particular, were in the best interests of China. Unsuccessful in its efforts at persuasion, Moscow withdrew its nuclear advisors and technicians from China in August 1960.

Technology Control (1959–Present)

The termination of Soviet nuclear assistance to the PRC marks a significant shift in Soviet nuclear export policy away from reliance on political (as opposed to technological) controls. As Gloria Duffy notes, "The ease with which the Chinese transformed Soviet nuclear aid into a weapons program seemingly was taken by the Soviets as an ill presentment of the way Soviet nuclear exports might be manipulated in the future by other recipient countries."[12] Having been victimized once, the USSR noticeably retrenched its nuclear exports. The promise to Hungary of a 100mw reactor, for example, was not fulfilled; nor was the pledge to assist Czechoslovakia in developing a natural uranium (and high-plutonium-producing) power plant. The Soviet Union also restricted nuclear reactor exports to the light water reactor variety and instituted a serious safeguards system, well in advance of any comparable safeguards adopted by other nuclear suppliers.[13] Moscow insisted that all recipients of its nuclear reactors obtain the nuclear fuel from the Soviet Union and return the spent-fuel rods to the USSR. The East European states also were prevented from developing their own uranium-enrichment and plutonium-reprocessing facilities.[14]

Soviet efforts to impose more stringent controls on nuclear exports after 1958 coincided with the rise of nuclear nonproliferation in the hierarchy of Soviet foreign policy objectives. The serious negotiation undertaken by the Soviet Union with the United States and Great Britain over a nuclear test ban treaty reflected this increased priority.[15] Following the successful conclusion of the Partial Test Ban Treaty in 1963, Soviet foreign policy efforts in the nuclear field were directed primarily toward preventing West German acquisition of nuclear weapons.[16] The major vehicle for promoting this objective was the NPT which, after extensive negotiations, was opened for signature in July 1968.

Most Western observers of Soviet nuclear policy agree that Soviet concern over proliferation diminished significantly following West German adherence to the NPT. Certainly there was a decline in the perceived urgency and magnitude of the proliferation threat expressed in Soviet nonproliferation pronouncements. This change may have corresponded to altered assessments among Soviet foreign policy elites as to the nature of the proliferation threat. A decline in the priority of nonproliferation as a Soviet foreign policy objective, however, should not be confused with its abandonment as a policy goal or a necessary divergence between declaratory policy and actual behavior.[17] Indeed, if one focuses on nonproliferation behavior rather than rhetoric, one observes a subtle shift in Soviet policy in the mid–1970s in the direction of more pragmatic and cooperative behavior. This change entailed movement away from their post–1958 approach to proliferation, which was characterized by the notion that "there would be no proliferation problem if all countries would follow the policy of the USSR and 'each take care of its own.'"[18] Soviet involvement in the Zangger Committee, the Nuclear Suppliers Group (NSG), the 1975 and 1980 NPT Review Conferences, and the International Nuclear Fuel Cycle Evaluation (INFCE), for example, reveals increasing Soviet recognition of the complexity of proliferation problems and the utility of coordinated, multinational action.[19] In these and other international forums the United States and the Soviet Union often worked closely to tighten nuclear export controls and to gain greater adherence to the NPT. (See Table 8–1.) At the NSG meetings the Soviet Union regularly aligned itself with the supplier state proponents of strict nuclear export controls—a group usually including the United States, Canada, and Great Britain.

Table 8–1. Forums for U.S.-Soviet Consultation on Nonproliferation Issues during the Ford, Carter, and Reagan Administrations.

Forum	Administration	Frequency	Focus	Remarks
Zangger Committee	Ford Carter Reagan	1/yr.[a]	Export guidelines	Set up in 1970. Last met in June 1983. Continues to be chaired by Zangger. Relatively dormant between 1977 and 1981. More active in 1982 and 1983.
Nuclear Suppliers Group	Ford (1975–76) Carter (1977–78)		Export guidelines	First met in 1975. Has not met since 1978.
INFCE	Carter (1977–80)	3 plenary conference meetings and 61 working group meetings.	Nuclear fuel cycle	
Threshold Test Ban and PNE Negotiations	Ford (1974–76)		Nuclear test limitations	

Table 8–1 continued.

Forum	Administration	Frequency	Focus	Remarks
CTB	Carter (1977–80)		Nuclear test limitations	
IAEA Board of Governors	Ford (1974–76) Carter (1977–80) Reagan (1981–84)	4/yr.		Usually involves lower-level representation than General Conference.
IAEA General Conference	Ford (1974–76) Carter (1977–80) Reagan (1981–84)	1/yr.		Very important forum for U.S.-Soviet consultation. Usually involves lengthy review of wide range of proliferation issues.
IAEA Experts Consultant Groups[b]				
1. International Spent-Fuel Management	June 1979 to July 1982			
2. International Plutonium	First convened September 1978;			

Storage	concluded at end of 1982		
3. Committee for Assurances of Supply	First convened June 1980		
Scientific Advisory Committee of the Director General of IAEA	Ford (1974–76) Carter (1977–80) Reagan (1981–84)	Discussions of technical issues	
Joint Committee established by the U.S.-Soviet Agreement for Cooperation in Atomic Energy	Carter (1977–79) Reagan (1983–84)		Meetings ceased after 1979 Soviet invasion of Afghanistan. Agreement was renewed in summer 1983.
UN General Assembly and First Committee of the UN (Political and Security)			
NPT Review Conference	Ford (May 1975) Carter (August 1980)		

Table 8–1 continued.

Forum	Administration	Frequency	Focus	Remarks
Ad hoc	Carter (March 1977)			Vance discussed holding meeting on proliferation with Soviets when he presented Carter's comprehensive arms control proposals.
	Carter (June 1977)			First meeting held to follow-up March 1977 proposal. Chaired by Warnke and Nye (U.S.), Morokhov (USSR).
	Carter (August and September 1977)		South Africa	Exchange of intelligence information regarding South African nuclear

		test site. Discussions at ambassadorial level.
Carter (May 1978)	South Africa	Nye and Timerbaev met in Geneva.
Reagan (December 1982)	IAEA, Export controls	Kennedy and Morozov met in Washington, D.C.
Reagan (June 1983)	IAEA, Export controls	Kennedy and Petrosyants met in Moscow.
Reagan (February 1984)	NPT review conference	Kennedy and Petrosyants met in Vienna.
Reagan (November 1984)	NPT review conference	Kennedy and Petrosyants met in Moscow.

Embassy to Embassy (in some Nth countries)

Notes: a. Chairman may call additional meetings and has done so in past.
b. The United States ceased to participate in these meetings following the IAEA vote to withdraw Israel's credential at September 1982 General Conference. In February 1983, after a five-month reassessment of its participation, the United States announced its intention to resume participation at an "early, appropriate date." It resumed participation that same month.

Probably the most unusual example of Soviet cooperation with the United States on nonproliferation measures occurred in the summer of 1977 when the USSR shared intelligence information with the United States regarding possible South African construction of a nuclear test site in the Kalahari Desert.[20] The Soviet Union subsequently agreed not to jeopardize a U.S. initiative in the United Nations to gain South African adherence to the NPT and international safeguards.[21] This form of cooperation in the United Nations is particularly significant as an indicator of Moscow's genuine interest in nonproliferation since it occurred outside the public domain and did not enable the Kremlin to exploit for propaganda purposes their nonproliferation vigilance or anti–South African stance.

Less dramatic than the South African incident, but still indicative of Soviet interest in cooperative nonproliferation measures, was Soviet support for the Western idea of multinational fuel cycle facilities where spent fuel might be reprocessed safely. As expressed by I. G. Morozov, deputy chairman of the State Committee for the Utilization of Atomic Energy:

Multinational regional fuel cycle centers under the effective control of the IAEA might serve as one of the factors contributing to the resolution of the problem of nonproliferation during the development of nuclear energy production. The plans worked out by the agency for these centers provide for the satisfaction of the energy needs of a large group of nations and for simultaneous localization and reliable monitoring of the more dangerous consequences of nuclear energy production.[22]

The Soviet-proposed model for such a regional fuel cycle arrangement was the regional fuel cycle system operating within the Council for Mutual Economic Assistance framework.[23]

A Possible Shift in Soviet Policy: Standards of Evidence

The current place of nonproliferation on the Soviet agenda is difficult to discern. On the one hand, the USSR continues to be a vocal supporter of the NPT and a more quiet advocate of nuclear restraint through the Zangger Committee. The Soviet Union has supported recent U.S. efforts in the Zangger Committee to gain acceptance of more precise definitions of the items affected by the nuclear suppliers' "trigger list" (those items whose export would trigger the application of IAEA safeguards to the facility for which items were supplied). The lack of precise definitions is presently a problem since the trigger list specifies the affected technologies but not all their component parts.[24]

Consistent with the Soviet stance in the Zangger Committee is the enactment of the "Export of Nuclear Materials, Technologies, Equipment, Installations, Special Non-nuclear Materials and Services," approved by the USSR Council of Ministers on January 13, 1982.[25] This legislation, in fact, is broader in some respects than the Nuclear Suppliers Guidelines. Also indicative of fairly high-level Soviet support for strengthening the nonproliferation regime is the Soviet offer in July 1982 to place some of its nuclear facilities under the IAEA inspection system. This action appears to have been taken despite the opposition of the State Committee for the Utilization of Atomic Energy.[26] One additional sign of continued Soviet interest in preventing the spread of nuclear weapons was resumption in late 1982, after a hiatus of four years, of high-level U.S.-Soviet consultations on nonproliferation. These talks, the most recent of which were held in November 1984, were nonpolemical and focused on a wide range of proliferation problem areas, including the role of the IAEA, the international system of nuclear export controls, specific problem countries, and the 1985 NPT Review Conference.

On the other hand, certain aspects of recent Soviet nuclear export policy seem to conflict with a serious commitment to nonproliferation. Most frequently cited as examples are Soviet trade in heavy water with India, trade in heavy water and highly enriched uranium with Argentina, and provision of nuclear power reactor assistance to Cuba and Libya. Before examining these cases in detail, however, it is useful to identify the standards of evidence one might apply in assessing Soviet nuclear export conduct. In other words, what kinds of behavior should be judged as indicative of Soviet support for or indifference/opposition to strengthening the nonproliferation regime?

Behavior indicative of a nation's genuine commitment to stringent export controls might include: (1) insistence on full-scope safeguards for recipients of nuclear trade; (2) requirement of NPT party status as a precondition for nuclear assistance; (3) strict adherence to the Zangger Committee and Nuclear Suppliers Group Guidelines for nuclear trade; (4) refusal to provide nuclear assistance to "high-risk" Nth countries; (5) insistence on the return of spent nuclear fuel; (6) active support for the tightening of supplier state export guidelines; (7) readiness to sacrifice political gains for nonproliferation objectives; and (8) the universal application of stringent export controls (i.e., without respect to the political leaning of the recipient country). In addition, one may assess a nation's nuclear export behavior in relative terms, that is, in comparison with other nuclear supplier states. Alternatively one can identify forms of behavior that indicate a disregard for stringent nuclear export controls and nonproliferation. Such behavior is the obverse of the forms listed above.

The next section of this chapter applies the standards of evidence noted above to recent Soviet nuclear export policy vis-à-vis Argentina, Cuba, India, and Libya. An effort is then made to determine the extent to which Soviet behavior in these four cases is representative of recent Soviet nonproliferation policy and the extent to which it signals a departure from Soviet nuclear export policy in the period of "technology control."

FOUR CASE STUDIES

India

On May 18, 1974, India detonated an underground nuclear explosion in the Rajasthan Desert. The public Soviet reaction to the Indian nuclear test, which was at most politely noncommittal, was not what one might have expected from a sponsor of the NPT. (In fairness to the Soviet Union, the initial U.S. response was also restrained.) According to the TASS report the day of the explosion, India conducted "a peaceful explosion of a nuclear device" and "reaffirmed its strong opposition to the use of nuclear explosions for military purposes."[27] Subsequent reports in the Soviet press generally reiterated this position, although on occasion one could find reference to an Indian bomb.[28]

The initial Soviet public response to the Indian explosion, while seemingly at odds with Moscow's stance on nonproliferation, could nevertheless be explained in terms of the high political costs the USSR probably would have incurred had it adopted a disapproving posture. The uncritical Soviet response may also have been influenced by Moscow's continuing support domestically for peaceful nuclear explosions as a significant economic resource.[29] Finally, the Soviet Union could point to the fact that their nuclear export policy, unlike that of Canada and the United States, had not contributed significantly to the Indian explosion. (The only Soviet contribution was possibly the supply of eighty tons of heavy water in 1972, a shipment that was made because of a temporary shortage in Canadian supply.)[30]

More difficult to reconcile with the Soviet Union's post–1958 policy of stringent nuclear export controls was news in late 1976 that the USSR planned to provide India with a large quantity of heavy water. Heavy water supplied by the United States and Canada had been used by India to produce plutonium for their first atomic explosion, and U.S. observers were fearful that the Soviet Union had agreed to the heavy water sale without assurances from India that it would not explode another nuclear device.[31] This fear was reinforced by information that the USSR had violated the nuclear export guidelines endorsed by the Nuclear Suppliers Group by not requiring India to accept, as a precondition for the heavy water sale, international safeguards on the transferred material as well as on all facilities in which the material was to be used. The Soviet sale was especially disturbing and confusing to U.S. nonproliferation advocates who had cooperated with the Soviet Union during the NSG deliberations in which the USSR had regularly supported strict nuclear export controls.

Some aspects of the 1976 sale of heavy water remain unclear and one can identify at least two accounts, based on published reports and interviews, which, at first glance, seem contradictory.[32] Further examination, however, suggests an explanation that may account for the apparent discrepancy.

The prevalent Western interpretation, supported ironically by a Soviet official at the IAEA, suggests that in September 1976 Prime Minister Indira Gandhi sought and secured a Soviet commitment to provide 200 tons of heavy water for the Rajasthan Atomic Power Station, which consisted of two reactors (RAPP–I and RAPP–II) of the CANDU (Canadian-Deuterium-Uranium) type. Approximately one-quarter of the Soviet heavy water shipment was to be delivered immediately without any safeguards in effect. When appraised of the Soviet-Indian deal, the United States and Canada reportedly reminded the Soviet Union of its obligations under the 1974 Zangger Committee and 1976 Nuclear Suppliers Group "trigger list" guidelines and stated that the Rajasthan nuclear facility was in jeopardy. The Soviet Union then, allegedly, pressed the Indians to abandon their long-term opposition to multiple-point safeguards and to accept the principles of pursuit and perpetuity.[33]

One variant of this account, provided by a former employee of the Soviet State Committee for the Utilization of Atomic Energy, is that the USSR initially did not press for safeguards in the heavy water sale. This posture, however, is explained not in terms of a lack of concern about proliferation, but due to the lack of familiarity with the terms of the Zangger Committee and Nuclear Suppliers Group "trigger lists" on the part of the foreign ministry officials engaged in the initial discussions with the Indians.[34]

The prevalent Indian interpretation differs from the preceding account. It alleges that from the outset the Soviet Union pressed for Indian acceptance of stringent safeguards.[35] Indian sources acknowledge, however, that the USSR technically violated the Zangger Committee and the NSG guidelines since a substantial portion of the 200 tons of heavy water was delivered to India prior to the conclusion in November 1977 of a nuclear safeguards agreement between India and the IAEA. According to this account, the delivery of the first installment of Soviet heavy water was based on "good trust and faith" that a safeguards agreement would be concluded before India would actually use the heavy water.

Although the prevalent Indian and Western accounts are at odds, they are in fact reconcilable if one assumes that Moscow initially believed its heavy water shipment to Rajasthan would be covered by existing safeguards at that facility. According to one participant-observer, this is precisely what occurred. The Soviet Union believed that it was honoring the Zangger commitment by shipping heavy water to Rajasthan, which was then safeguarded under the terms of a 1971 trilateral agreement among Canada, India, and the IAEA. What they appear not to have appreciated and what the United States conveyed to them was the possibility that India might circumvent the existing safeguards by: (1) using Soviet heavy water at RAPP–I to free Indian heavy water from that facility for unsafeguarded use (since the tripartite safeguards agreement had no pursuit clause); (2) declaring the 1971 agreement void because of an alleged Canadian breach of the agreement; and (3) using Soviet heavy water at RAPP–II, which was not then on the Rajasthan safeguards inventory.[36] When informed of these circumvention possibilities and when reminded that under Article 1 of the NPT each nuclear weapons state had a responsibility that went beyond an obligation to honor the Zangger guidelines, the Soviet Union concurred.

The terms of the 1977 IAEA agreement, though falling short of the professed Soviet objective of full-scope safeguards, went well beyond the controls previously in effect at India's nuclear facilities.[37] Its provisions, which the Indians were reluctant to publish, include the application of safeguards to:

- any nuclear material, including subsequent generation of special fissionable material produced, processed, or used in the Rajasthan Atomic Power Station; and
- any nuclear material, including subsequent generations of special fissionable material produced, processed, or used by the use of the heavy water supplied by the Soviet Union.[38]

The agreement also specifies that the heavy water will be used exclusively for peaceful purposes and will not be used for the manufacture of any nuclear explosive device. The agreement, therefore, encompasses the important safeguard principles of "perpetuity," "pursuit," and "no PNE [peaceful nuclear explosion] use."

Although Prime Minister Morarji Desai approved the safeguards agreement that had been initiated by Mrs. Gandhi's government, it declined to use the purchased heavy water. Under Section 25 of the 1977 IAEA agreement, India thereby avoided the application of safeguards to the Rajasthan reactors. At the time of Mrs. Gandhi's return to power in January 1980, however, a much more pessimistic appraisal of the Indian heavy water program was made. In February 1980, therefore, India accepted an offer by the Soviet Union to supply another 256 tons of heavy water and, later in the year, decided to use the Soviet water to commission RAPP–II.[39] As far as can be discerned, the same safeguards that had been negotiated for the 1976 sale were in effect for the 1980 deal. As of July 1983 the following amounts of Soviet heavy water apparently were shipped to India:

1976	55 tons
1977	75 tons
1978	70 tons
1980	41 tons
1981	40 tons
1982	40 tons
1983 (July)	20 tons[40]

In addition to trade in heavy water, the Soviet Union has on several occasions offered to supply India with enriched uranium for the Tarapur reactor and a large nuclear power plant.[41] Both the initial offer of enriched uranium and the large power plant (made by Premier Aleksei Kosygin during his 1979 visit to India) were declined by the Indian government. A subsequent Soviet offer to build a 1,000mw reactor, broached in September 1982 during a visit to the USSR by Mrs. Gandhi, received greater consideration. Lack of Indian enthusiasm for the reactor, however, went beyond the question of safeguards—which the Soviet Union insisted upon. A more fundamental issue was the size of the reactor—regarded by the Indians as much too large for the Indian grid—and the type of reactor—a light water, enriched uranium variety that would require Indian dependence on an external fuel supplier. In order to meet the first Indian objection, the USSR in 1983 offered to provide two 440mw light water reactors instead of a single 1,000mw reactor.[42] The Soviet Union made clear, however, that it thought India had made a mistake in selecting heavy water, natural uranium reactors and offered to provide only the light water reactor model exported to other socialist countries.

Having briefly described Soviet-Indian nuclear trade, what conclusions can one draw regarding Soviet adherence to stringent export controls? The Soviets clearly did not require and, most likely, never pressed for Indian acceptance of full-scope safeguards as a precondition for the heavy water sale. Furthermore, NPT party status was never made a prerequisite for nuclear assistance. However, at the time of the 1976 sale, only Canada, among all the nuclear supplier states, made full-scope safeguards a precondition for the supply of materials on the Zangger list, and it did so in reaction to its own unwilling contribution to India's nuclear explosive program. Although the Soviet Union was in technical violation of the Zangger Committee "trigger list" guidelines and those of the nonbinding Nuclear Suppliers Group, the safeguards ultimately insisted upon by the USSR (i.e., perpetuity, pursuit, and no PNE use) were more stringent than any previously applied to India. The Soviet action represented the first instance in which a separate safeguards agreement was negotiated for the international sale of heavy water. Even if one accepts the interpretation that Soviet insistence on stringent safeguards for the 1976 sale was a consequence of U.S. and Canadian intervention, the nature of the intervention was very restrained and limited to a reminder. Moreover, it is difficult to conceive of any leverage the United States or Canada could have exercised had the USSR chosen to disregard its nonproliferation obligations.

One cannot easily discern from Soviet commentary whether or not Kremlin decisionmakers perceived India as a high-risk proliferation threat. As previously noted, the Soviet press generally referred to India's 1974 nuclear test as a "peaceful nuclear explosion," in keeping with Indian parlance. Soviet readiness to insist on stringent safeguards, including a no-PNE-use provision, however, suggests a more somber Soviet assessment of the Indian nuclear program, especially in light of the political costs Moscow was ready to incur with a leading, friendly member of the Non-Aligned movement. While the imposition of safeguards on the heavy water sale to India does not demonstrate the universality of Soviet nuclear export policy, it does indicate that Soviet nonproliferation policy is not directed exclusively against Soviet military and political adversaries (e.g., West Germany, South Africa, Taiwan, South Korea, and Israel) or neighboring client states (i.e., the East European countries).

Libya

On May 26, 1975, Libya ratified the NPT, nearly seven years after it signed the treaty. Four days later the Soviet Union and Libya signed an intergovernmental protocol on the utilization of atomic energy for peaceful purposes.[43] According to most Western accounts, these two events were connected and involved Soviet pressure on Libya to ratify the NPT in return for the promise of nuclear assistance.[44] The Soviet motive for the nuclear accord, which included provision of a small research reactor with a capacity up to ten megawatts, however, is unclear.[45]

The simplest explanation for the Soviet initiative is one of political opportunism and influence. According to this interpretation, Soviet nuclear assistance was a means to draw Libya closer to the Soviet Union and to increase Soviet influence in the region. The protocol signaled to other developing nations the tangible benefits of Soviet friendship. The major difficulty with this explanation is that the Soviet Union had already cultivated a close relationship with Libya by means of substantial arms sales. Moreover, any additional leverage acquired by nuclear assistance had to be balanced against the risks posed by the possible diversion of nuclear technology and material for military purposes. Since 1958 the Soviet Union had judged those risks to be high enough to merit stringent export controls.

Another possible interpretation, suggested by Gloria Duffy, is that the Soviet Union was concerned about Colonel Muammar el-Qaddafi's nuclear ambitions but offered the research reactor to preempt the sale to Libya of nuclear technology by less scrupulous nuclear suppliers. The offer probably was influenced by the Iraqi nuclear trade requests during the 1973–1974 period. At that time, the Soviet Union reportedly was approached by Iraqi president Saddam Hussein for the purpose of acquiring a high-plutonium-producing reactor. Consistent with its post–1958 nuclear export policy, the Soviet Union declined the request. Nuclear salesmen from France, Italy, West Germany, and Canada, however, showed no similar restraint and competed with one another for the deal. In 1975 the Soviet Union may well have anticipated that France, Italy, and West Germany would again fill the order should Moscow decline Libya's request.

Commercial considerations also may have prompted Soviet interest in the sale of the nuclear reactor to Libya. By the mid–1970s the Soviet Union was marketing nuclear technology and services abroad more aggressively. The Libyan deal, therefore, may have been regarded by Moscow as an important step in establishing Soviet viability as a nuclear supplier for developing nations. Payment in hard currency was another attraction for the Soviet Union, which was later accused by the Libyans of selling the reactor for three times the world market price.

A third, more malevolent, explanation for the Soviet deal is that Moscow sought to counter Israel's nuclear potential in the Middle East by providing Libya with a nuclear weapons option.[46] This interpretation, however, is at odds with most other behavioral indicators of Soviet nuclear export and nonproliferation policy since 1958. It is also contrary to Soviet declaratory policy, which rejects the argument made by some Western analysts that an overtly nuclearized Middle East might stabilize the region.[47] Moreover, the small research reactor actually sold to Libya—capable of producing no more than 1.2 kilograms of weapons-grade plutonium per year—is hardly the kind of reactor Moscow would have supplied had it sought to provide Libya with the technical means to emulate Israel's nuclear program.[48]

Whatever the initial motivation for the Soviet sale, nuclear trade between the two countries after 1975 proceeded slowly. Although public accounts of the dates and substance of these nuclear discussions vary considerably, apparently plans for Soviet construction of a nuclear power station in Libya were discussed in February 1976 during the visit to Moscow of the Libyan minister of electricity, Ju'mah Salim al Arbash.[49]

Since that date, there have been numerous press reports that the Soviet Union promised to supply Libya with as many as three 300–400mw power reactors. Indeed, almost annually since 1977 reports have appeared that a contract to that effect had been or was about to be signed. *The Washington Post*, for example, in December 1977 reported that the Soviet Union had signed a contract with Libya to build a 440mw nuclear power plant for the price of $330 million.[50] No announcement about the deal, however, was made at that time by either country.

In October of the following year the Soviet Union again reportedly agreed to provide Libya with a 400mw power reactor[51] or, depending on one's sources, a 300mw nuclear power station, nuclear research center, and laboratories.[52] More recently the Atomic Industrial Forum listed a Libyan order in 1979 of a 440mw Soviet reactor,[53] and the Soviet publication, *Komsomolets*, reported the planned construction of Libya's first nuclear power plant on the shore of the Gulf of Sidra. According to the Soviet report, the plant will be equipped with a 440mw unit of the VVER (pressurized water reactor) type and will be used to desalinate salt water.[54]

The International Herald Tribune cited a similar sale reported to have been negotiated in 1980.[55] In March 1981 the Arab language weekly, *Al-Mustagbal*, also described the pending agreement on Soviet installation of a Libyan nuclear research center.[56] In May 1981, however, rather than announcing the conclusion of that agreement Soviet sources only reported that the USSR and Libya had agreed to speed up the signature of a contract for the construction of an 880mw nuclear power station in Libya.[57] Three years later, no construction of any nuclear power reactor site in Libya has begun, and uncertainty remains whether the contract has even been signed. Indeed, the interminable delays in the Soviet-Libyan nuclear power project were cited by the Finnish state electric utility, IVO, as the reason for its loss of interest in participating in the project.[58]

Although it is difficult to determine from public sources the sequence and significance of events in Soviet-Libyan nuclear negotiations since 1975, one can nevertheless draw a number of conclusions regarding Soviet nuclear export policy vis-à-vis Libya. Consistent with its obligations under the NPT, Libya concluded a safeguards agreement with the IAEA on July 8, 1980.[59] As a consequence of this agreement, full-scope safeguards are in effect for all Libyan peaceful nuclear activities, including those involving Soviet materials and assistance. With the exception of the provision of the small research reactor at Tajura, Soviet nuclear assistance to date has been quite modest. More difficult to determine, however, is the extent to which the modest level of support provided is due to Soviet restraint or Libyan dissatisfaction with the terms of the deal and the implementation of prior agreements.

As early as August 1978 John Cooley of *The Christian Science Monitor* reported that the Soviet Union was reluctant or at least slow to provide the nuclear aid promised in 1976.[60] The continued delays in finalizing and implementing the power reactor transactions, especially until Libya concluded its safeguards agreement with the IAEA in 1980, may be an indication of Moscow's hesitancy to supply even relatively low-risk technologies to a high-risk Nth country. If this is the case, there is less evidence for Duffy's thesis that Soviet-Libyan nuclear trade in the 1970s signals "a shift back to the pre–1960 [Soviet] nonproliferation philosophy"[61] in which emphasis is on political rather than technical controls in managing nuclear exports.

An alternative interpretation—more consistent with Duffy's thesis—is that while the USSR initially may have dragged its feet, by 1980 or 1981 the Libyans were a less than enthusiastic partner.[62] Although this interpretation is difficult to substantiate, it is consistent with reports of Libyan dissatisfaction with Moscow's demands for cash payments at higher than world market prices and a *Nucleonics Week* report that implementation of the 440mw reactor deal awaited the go-ahead from Libya, not the Soviet Union.[63] Also, there are indications that Libya sought alternative nuclear suppliers to the Soviet Union and actually signed nuclear assistance agreements with Argentina in 1974, France in 1976, and India in 1978.[64] Since 1978, however, when Belgonucleaire signed a consulting agreement with the Libyan Atomic Commission, Belgium has emerged as the most serious contender for the development of Libya's nuclear program.[65] Due in part to their contacts with Belgian nuclear advisors, Libyan officials have become increasingly skeptical about Soviet nuclear assistance and believe that they have been "used" by the USSR.

Whatever the reasons for the slow development of Soviet-Libyan nuclear trade, there are no indications that Moscow has reversed its post–1958 policy of stringent nuclear export guidelines with respect to Libya. As far as can be discerned, the nuclear trade rules that apply to the East European countries and Finland similarly govern Soviet-Libyan trade. If this is correct, the Libyan case is another indication that Soviet nonproliferation policy, while perhaps not universal in character, is not directed exclusively against Soviet military and political adversaries.

Unlike the Indian case, there are no indications that the Soviet Union was prepared to sacrifice political gains for nonproliferation objectives. Such a trade-off probably was not necessary given the leverage the Soviet Union exercised over Libya as its principal arms supplier. Soviet insistence on Libyan ratification of the NPT as a condition for its nuclear assistance, therefore, probably was regarded in Moscow as a prudent measure that would provoke little resistance. One can also argue, however, that Libyan ratification of the NPT was recognized by Soviet policymakers as a hollow pledge, given prior Libyan efforts to acquire a nuclear weapons capability.[66] If this was the case, Moscow either was intentionally more relaxed in its nuclear export policy than had been the case since 1958— although formally living up to its NPT obligations—or, more likely, believed that it retained sufficient control over the Libyan nuclear program to assure that Qaddafi would not violate the safeguards agreement. Although the latter assumption, if it were made, may have been a questionable one, the Soviet Union could reasonably have concluded that if they did not respond favorably to Libya's request for nuclear assistance, Western suppliers would.

Cuba

Soviet-Cuban collaboration in the field of nuclear energy dates back to 1967 when an agreement for scientific cooperation in that area was signed by the Soviet and Cuban Academies of Sciences.[67] According to this agreement, the Soviet Union promised to train Cuban nuclear service personnel and to donate a nuclear physics laboratory and a small research reactor.[68] Subsequent to the delivery of the zero power reactor around 1969, Soviet-Cuban nuclear cooperation developed slowly but steadily. By far the most significant and controversial joint project has been the planned nuclear power facility near Cienfuegos.

Announcements of the proposed nuclear power plant first appeared in the Cuban press in late 1974.[69] That same year, Soviet deputy minister of energy and electrification, Nikolai Malsev, also announced the start of design work for the Cuban plant.[70] As was the case with Libya, however, a great deal of time elapsed between the first reported signing of an agreement to build the nuclear facility (April 1976) and the implementation of the agreement. Indeed, despite reports in the Soviet, Cuban, and international press in the late 1970s and early 1980s, final approval for the plans was not given until 1982, and preliminary construction has only recently begun.[71]

One cannot identify with much certainty the primary reason or reasons for the lengthy delay. Contributing factors probably include unanticipated geological conditions at the original site location, a lack of trained Cuban personnel to operate and maintain the power plant, inadequate financing for the project, competing demands on available funds, and overcommitment of Soviet reactor production capability.[72] The delay may have resulted, at least in part, from Soviet dissatisfaction with Cuba's nonproliferation posture.

Evidence for the latter interpretation is mostly circumstantial and includes the fact that since the NPT came into effect the Soviet Union has not provided nuclear power reactors to non-NPT parties. Not only has Cuba refused to ratify the NPT, but it was one of only four countries in the United Nations General Assembly to vote against the Soviet cosponsored resolution commending the treaty in June 1968.[73] Despite its opposition to the NPT, Cuba in September 1976 announced its intention to conclude a safeguards agreement with the IAEA.[74] However, the agreement was not concluded until May 1980—a delay that may have been due in part to Soviet and Cuban differences over the extent of safeguards to be applied.

Some analysts also suggest that during the four-year interval the USSR may have pressed Cuba to sign and ratify the NPT as well as the Treaty of Tlatelolco.[75] Consistent with this interpretation was the Soviet decision in April 1978 to sign Protocol II of the Treaty of Tlatelolco, a protocol that the Soviet Union previously had refused to accept, perhaps in deference to the Cuban stance.[76] The Soviet Union also appears to have been aware of the proliferation implications posed by the Cuban reactor deal and would have preferred Cuban accession to the NPT and the Treaty of Tlatelolco. The best the USSR could obtain was Cuban agreement to stringent safeguards incorporating the same principles of no PNE use, perpetuity, and pursuit as were found in the 1977 Indian-IAEA agreement.[77] Similar safeguard provisions are in effect in connection with the Soviet supply to Cuba of a ten megawatt research reactor, reportedly scheduled to begin operation by December 1985.[78]

As was the case with respect to India, the Soviet Union did not make full-scope safeguards or NPT party status a condition for its nuclear assistance to Cuba. The USSR did, however, adhere to its Zangger Committee obligations and insisted upon the conclusion of a stringent safeguards agreement between Cuba and the IAEA before it would make available any power reactors. It is also noteworthy that on May 10, 1980, ten days after the Cuban-IAEA safeguards agreement entered into force, the Soviet Union signed a new cooperative agreement with Cuba in the field of nuclear energy. Nevertheless, the Cuban stance vis-à-vis the NPT and the Treaty of Tlatelolco must be an embarrassment for the Soviet Union as it is directly at odds with Moscow's policy.

More difficult to discern is the extent to which Soviet decisionmakers themselves perceive Cuba as posing a real proliferation risk, if only in the distant future. Soviet insistence on stringent safeguards, including no PNE use, pursuit, and perpetuity, appears to reflect a genuine Soviet concern about the proliferation potential of Cuba's nuclear program. The slow pace at which nuclear aid has been provided also is consistent with a benevolent interpretation of Soviet nonproliferation policy. The failure of the Soviet Union to insist upon NPT or Treaty of Tlatelolco party status, however, is more difficult to reconcile with the argument that Moscow is prepared to sacrifice considerable political capital in the pursuit of nonproliferation objectives, given the substantial leverage (especially in the economic arena) the Soviet Union exercises over Cuba.

The Soviet decision not to press harder on the issue of Cuban opposition to the nonproliferation regime may also be a rare example of the nonuniversalist nature of Soviet nuclear export policy. The reluctance of the Soviet Union to guarantee the return of spent fuel from future Cuban reactors to the USSR for reprocessing further differentiates Soviet nuclear trade with Cuba from that with other countries. Still, this variation should not be exaggerated and may be explained in terms of Cuba's geographic location (i.e., greater costs associated with the return of spent fuel and less risk of future Cuban military threat to Soviet territory because of the distance involved), and greater Soviet confidence in its ability to exercise political control over Cuba's nuclear program.

Argentina

Soviet involvement in Argentina's nuclear program is more recent and limited than its nuclear dealings with India, Libya, and Cuba. Although some heavy water of Soviet origin may have been purchased by Argentina in 1972, direct Argentine-Soviet nuclear negotiations were not initiated until 1980. These talks, held during a four-day visit to Moscow in March 1980 by Jorge Coll, general secretary of Argentina's National Commission for Atomic Energy (CNEA), dealt with the possibility of Argentine purchases of heavy water and technology for the manufacture of zirconium tubes, as well as for the training in the Soviet Union of Argentine nuclear specialists.[79] The initiative for the talks appears to have been taken by Argentina in response to the U.S. cut-off of nuclear exports as required by the 1978 Nuclear Non-Proliferation Act. In addition, Soviet-Argentine nuclear cooperation discussions were part of a growing number of joint business ventures in 1980, which elevated the Soviet Union to the position of Argentina's leading trade partner.[80]

The first tangible products of the March 1980 discussions were agreements for the sale of five tons of heavy water,[81] the supply of technology (a machine for shaping fuel rods), and technical experts for a zirconium-tube production facility.[82] In March 1982 Argentina also confirmed that the Soviet Union would provide uranium-enrichment services. Under the terms of the agreement, about 4,000 kilograms of uranium concentrate were to be sent to the USSR for enrichment and returned to Argentina for use in radioisotope production reactors.[83]

One month later, a contract for the supply of 100 kilograms of 20 percent enriched uranium was signed between the CNEA and the Soviet foreign trade company, Tekhsnabeksport.[84] A separate contract was concluded for an additional one ton of heavy water and an "open agreement" was reached for further purchases. At the time of these transactions, CNEA chairman Carlos Castro Madera indicated that Argentina was forced to turn to the Soviet Union because the United States had refused to supply Argentina. He also said, however, that he did not foresee any significant increase in Soviet-Argentine commercial nuclear dealings.[85]

Significantly, although Argentina is not a party to the NPT or the Treaty of Tlatelolco, stringent safeguards are in effect for both the heavy water and enriched uranium provided by the Soviet Union. Although there is no discussion of the safeguard provisions in either the Argentine press or secondary sources, an examination of the safeguard agreements reveals restrictive terms with respect to no PNE use, pursuit, and perpetuity closely resembling the terms of the 1977 Indian-IAEA agreement. The text of the October 14, 1981, "Agreement Between Argentina and the Agency for the Application of Safeguards to Heavy Water Supplied by the Union of Soviet Socialist Republics," for example, specifies that the Agency will apply its safeguards system to "any nuclear material, including subsequent generation of special fissionable material, which has been produced, processed, or used in any of the nuclear facilities in which the heavy water [from the Soviet Union] is used. . . ."[86] A similar provision exists in the "Agreement of July 8, 1982 Between Argentina and the Agency for the Application of Safeguards in Connection with the Supply of Nuclear Material from the Union of Soviet Socialist Republics."[87] Although the Argentine-IAEA agreements differ from the Indian-IAEA agreement in the lack of specificity as to the reactor facility likely to be affected (i.e., the Rajasthan Atomic Power Station is mentioned by name, but no mention is made of Atucha I), the effect of establishing the principles of pursuit and perpetuity appears to be the same.

Having sketched an outline of Soviet-Argentine nuclear trade, what conclusions can be drawn regarding Soviet nuclear export policy? As was the case with India, the Soviet Union did not require Argentina to accept full-scope safeguards as a precondition for the sale of heavy water. Nor did it press for full-scope safeguards prior to the sale of enriched uranium. NPT party status was also not an issue in Soviet-Argentine nuclear negotiations. Interestingly, as was the case with India, the Soviet Union technically violated the Zangger Committee "trigger list" guidelines by shipping five tons of heavy water to Argentina a number of months before a safeguards agreement covering the shipment was actually in effect. Nevertheless, the safeguards ultimately accepted by Argentina—for both the Soviet heavy water and enriched uranium—were very stringent and conformed closely to the model established in 1977 between India and the IAEA.

Little in the Soviet press suggests that Moscow regards Argentina as a high-risk proliferation threat—perhaps due to Argentina's geographic location, which, like Cuba, is far removed from Soviet territory.[88] The Soviets, however, have expressed greater public and private concern over Brazil's less developed nuclear program, harshly criticizing the 1975 Brazilian–West German "deal of the century" and, more recently, raising the issue of Brazil's nuclear intentions in one of the private U.S.-Soviet governmental meetings on nonproliferation.[89] Whatever its private assessment of the Argentine proliferation risk, the USSR's insistence on the application of stringent safeguards indicates no relaxation in Soviet nuclear export policy.

CONCLUSIONS

The profile of Soviet nuclear export policy that emerges from a comparative analysis of the USSR's nuclear trade with India, Libya, Cuba, and Argentina is a mixed but generally positive one. In terms of nuclear export behavior, the Soviet Union earns high marks for its adherence to the Zangger Committee and Nuclear Suppliers Group guidelines, its support of tighter guidelines, and the application of stringent export controls without respect to the political leanings of the recipient country. This steadfastness of policy is most striking with respect to India, with whom the Soviets were prepared to sacrifice important political capital in pursuit of nonproliferation objectives.

Soviet nuclear export behavior also looks particularly admirable when compared to that of other nuclear supplier states in the post–1958 period. The United States, for example, even after the restrictive Nuclear Non-Proliferation Act of 1978, continued to supply enriched uranium fuel to India's Tarapur reactor. More recently the Reagan administration arranged for France to serve as an alternative supplier.[90]

Since the mid–1970s, Soviet involvement with Libya's nuclear program has been eclipsed by other, more lax nuclear supplier states eager to offer Libya technology assistance. France reportedly signed an agreement with Libya to provide a nuclear power plant,[91] Belgium firms have sought spin-off contracts from the Soviet-Libyan deal (in addition to advising the Libyan Atomic Commission), a West German firm, Otrag, has helped develop a rocket-launching facility in the Libyan desert,[92] and the United States has trained hundreds of Libyan students in the fields of nuclear engineering and physics.[93]

With regard to nuclear supplier involvement in Argentina, even Canada was prepared to sell Argentina a CANDU reactor without insisting on full-scope safeguards.[94] Far less circumspect than the Canadians were the Swiss, who in 1979 agreed to sell Argentina a heavy water production plant.[95] The Reagan administration has also adopted a less stringent approach to heavy water sales and in 1983 allowed 143 tons of heavy water of U.S. origin to be exported to Argentina from West Germany.[96]

Doubtless, the Soviet nuclear export record is an imperfect one—as evidenced by Soviet failure in the cases of India, Cuba, and Argentina to insist upon full-scope safeguards and NPT party status as a precondition for nuclear assistance. This policy omission is most difficult to explain with respect to Cuba over whom Moscow exercises considerable leverage. To the extent that Soviet decisionmakers assessed India, Libya, Cuba, and Argentina as serious proliferation threats—something not addressed in this study—the Soviet Union also fails the test of denying nuclear assistance to "high-risk" Nth countries. Soviet willingness to provide nuclear aid to countries such as Cuba and Libya, however, probably reflects Soviet confidence in its ability to exercise political control over the recipient's nuclear program rather than diminished support for the international nuclear nonproliferation regime.

One must be careful not to overgeneralize about Soviet non-proliferation policy on the basis of four case studies. The finding that Soviet nuclear export policy generally is cautious, however, is consistent with the conclusion of most other analyses. Particularly noteworthy about this study is that it was derived from an analysis of the four cases most often cited as examples of Soviet nonproliferation misbehavior.

The Soviet Union in the past often has criticized the Western supplier states for letting economic interests take precedence over nonproliferation considerations.[97] By expanding its international nuclear material and services market, the Soviet Union may soon experience difficulty avoiding similar economic considerations. Economic interests, for example, now appear to have prompted the USSR to enter negotiations with its long-time *bête noir*, China, over the sale of a large nuclear power plant.[98] Economic factors also are probably responsible for recent Soviet decisions to request Soviet nuclear power plant customers in East Europe and Finland (and perhaps also in Cuba) to expand their onsite spent-fuel storage capacities, and to delay the return of spent fuel to the Soviet Union for reprocessing.[99] These developments, in themselves, do not constitute dramatic change in Soviet nuclear export behavior. They serve notice, however, that Soviet policy—although more circumspect and constant over the past twenty-five years than that of the other nuclear suppliers—is not immutable. The United States and its Western allies, therefore, should reinforce Soviet nonproliferation restraint and cooperate with the Soviet Union to retard the spread of nuclear weapons.[100]

NOTES

1. For a more comprehensive study, see William Potter, "Nuclear Export Policy: A Soviet-American Comparison," in Charles Kegley and Pat McGowan, eds., *Foreign Policy: USA/USSR*, Sage Yearbook of Foreign Policy Studies (Beverly Hills: Sage

Publications, 1982), pp. 291–313. Alternative periodizations are provided by Christer Jönsson, "Building a New Nonproliferation Regime: Soviet and American Perspectives" (Paper presented at the World Congress of the International Political Science Association, Rio de Janeiro, August 1982).

2. See Joseph C. Nogee, "Soviet Nuclear Proliferation Policy: Dilemmas and Contradictions," *Orbis* 24, no. 4 (Winter 1982): 753, on this point.

3. For a detailed examination of Soviet nuclear policy during this period, see Nogee, *Soviet Policy Toward International Control of Atomic Energy* (Notre Dame: University of Notre Dame Press, 1961).

4. The Soviet campaign is described by Harold Neiburg, *Nuclear Secrecy and Foreign Policy* (Washington, D.C.: Public Affairs Press, 1964), pp. 90–101.

5. See *Izvestia*, January 18, 1955.

6. Neiburg, *Nuclear Secrecy*, p. 93.

7. The most detailed analysis of Soviet nuclear exports during this period is provided by Lesley J. Fox, "Soviet Policy in the Development of Nuclear Power in Eastern Europe," University of Paris, 1982. (Unpublished.) See also Gloria Duffy, *Soviet Nuclear Energy: Domestic and International Policies*, R–2362–DOE (Santa Monica: RAND Corporation, 1979), pp. 3–5; Jaroslav G. Polach, "Nuclear Power in East Europe," *East Europe* (May 1968): 3–12; and Joseph Wilczynski, "Atomic Energy for Peaceful Purposes in the Warsaw Pact Countries," *Soviet Studies* (October 1974): 568–90.

8. See Fox, "Soviet Policy," pp. 14–19.

9. Arnold Kramish, "The Great Chinese Bomb Puzzle—a Solution," *Fortune* (June 1966): 246–48.

10. Arthur Steiner has called to my attention a recently declassified document in which Molotov expresses concern in May 1954 that Eisenhower's "Atoms for Peace" initiative might increase the availability of fissile material for military purposes. The extent to which Molotov's comments reflected genuine Soviet concern about the peaceful-military nuclear power linkage, as opposed to efforts to obstruct the appeal of U.S. proposals, is difficult to determine.

11. Soviet fear about Chinese nuclear weapons was also intensified during the summer of 1958 as a consequence of the Taiwan Straits crisis and Mao's display of indifference toward the prospect of nuclear escalation. On this point see Benjamin Lambeth, "Nuclear Proliferation and Soviet Arms Control Policy,"

in Roman Kolkowicz et al., *The Soviet Union and Arms Control* (Baltimore: Johns Hopkins University Press, 1970), pp. 88–89.

12. Gloria Duffy, "Soviet Nuclear Exports," *International Security* 3, no. 1 (Summer 1978): 86.

13. Duffy, *Soviet Nuclear Energy*, p. 7.

14. See Karel Bocek, "Czechoslovak Uranium and the USSR," *Radio Liberty Dispatch*, July 9, 1974, p. 3.

15. See Chister Jönsson, *Soviet Bargaining Behavior: The Nuclear Test Ban Case* (New York: Columbia University Press, 1979); and Glenn T. Seaborg, *Kennedy, Khrushchev, and the Test Ban* (Berkeley: University of California Press, 1981).

16. See Gerhard Wettig, "Soviet Policy on the Proliferation of Nuclear Weapons, 1966–1968," *Orbis* (Winter 1969): 1,058–84.

17. Toby Trister Gati, for example, maintains that in practice the Soviets have not adopted a strong antiproliferation stance despite their declaratory policy. Her interpretation is not supported by the present study. See Gati, "Soviet Perspectives on Nuclear Nonproliferation," California Seminar on Arms Control and Foreign Policy Discussion Paper, No. 66 (November 1975), pp. 4–5.

18. Emelyanov cited by Duffy, *Soviet Nuclear Energy*, p. 12.

19. See, for example, A. Mikhailov, "Effective Control Over Nuclear Exports," *International Affairs* (June 1982): 19–25; V. Emelyanov, *Problems of the Nonproliferation of Nuclear Weapons* (Moscow: Nauka Press, 1982); I. Dmitriyev, "To Create a Reliable Barrier," *Pravda*, July 8, 1977; and V. F. Davydov, *Nerasprostranenie Yadernogo Oruzhiya i Politika* (Moscow: Nauka Press, 1980).

20. See Murrey Marder and Don Oberdorfer, "How West, Soviets Acted to Defuse South African A-test," *The Washington Post*, August 28, 1977. For a Soviet account of the episode, see V.F. Davydov, "Nuclear Threat in the Cape of Good Hope," *SShA* (December 1977): 48–49.

21. On this point see Joseph Nye, "The U.S. and Soviet Stakes in Nuclear Nonproliferation," *P.S.* (Winter 1982): 36.

22. "Technical and Sociopolitical Aspect of Nuclear Power Production," *SShA* (September 1978): 90. Morozov's comments are in a review of the Ford/MITRE report, *Nuclear Power: Issues and Choices* (Cambridge, Mass.: Ballinger, 1977).

23. See A.M. Petrosyants, "International Forum of Nuclear Power Engineers," *Atomnaya energiya* (August 1977): 83–88; Emelyanov, *Problems of the Nonproliferation of Nuclear Weapons*, pp. 65–66 and 81; K. Borisov, "An Effective Barrier to the Spread

of Nuclear Weapons," *SShA* (March 1980): 25; and I.G. Morozov, "Statement at the Second Review Conference of the Parties to the Treaty of the Non-Proliferation of Nuclear Weapons," August 12, 1980, p. 10. Duffy (*Soviet Nuclear Energy*, p. 26) suggests that one reason for Soviet interest in MFCFs is that it would promote the movement to a plutonium-based fuel cycle—a development the USSR strongly supports.

24. The issue of shoring up the trigger list was addressed at a series of unpublicized meetings in June and November 1982 and January and July 1983, involving some but not all of the members of the Nuclear Exporters (Zangger) Committee. Although not invited to the June meeting, the Soviets participated in the November and January sessions and supported the U.S. initiative to plug gaps related to gas centrifuge technology. The November meeting is described in "Centrifuge Suppliers Meeting Privately to Shore Up Trigger List," *Nucleonics Week* (November 25, 1982): 1. See also "Agreement Hearing on More Comprehensive Trigger List Covering Centrifuge," *Nucleonics Week* (June 9, 1983): 2.

25. See "Export of Soviet Nuclear Materials, Technology Enacted," *Vneshnaya torgovlya* (April 1982): 48–49.

26. This information was obtained through interviews with U.S. government and IAEA officials who were in contact with representatives of the State Committe.

27. See *TASS*, May 18, 1974, as reported in *Foreign Broadcast Information Source Daily Report* (Soviet Union), May 20, 1974, p. J–1.

28. See F. I. Kozhevnikov and V. A. Mazov, "Scientific and Technical Progress and Certain Problems of International Law," *Voprosy istorii* (January 1974): 58–74.

29. Ironically, Moscow embraced many of the premises of the early U.S. PNE program (Project Plowshare) although the project was subsequently discredited and disbanded by the United States. For the Soviet views on PNEs, see V.S. Emelyanov, "On the Peaceful Use of Nuclear Explosions," in SIPRI, *Nuclear Proliferation Problems* (Cambridge, Mass.: MIT Press, 1974), pp. 215–23; Igor Dmitriyev, "Nuclear Blasting for Peaceful Purposes," *New Times* (February 1975): 18–20; A. K. Kruglov, "Atomic Science and Technology in the National Economy of the USSR," *Atomnaya energiya* (February 1976): 113–16; and I. D. Morokhov et al., "Peaceful Uses of Nuclear Energy and the Problem of Nonproliferation of Nuclear Weapons," *Atomnaya energiya* (February 1976): 90–102.

30. See G. G. Mirchandani and P. K. S. Namboodiri, *Nuclear India: A Technological Assessment* (New Delhi: Vision Books, 1981), pp. 67, 142. See also "Soviet Heavy Water for RAPP–II," *Nuclear Engineering International* (November 1977): 11. It is unlikely that the Soviet heavy water was under any safeguards, as the 1972 sale predates the Zangger and London Suppliers Group "trigger lists." The Soviet Union, incidentally, also is reported to have supplied Canada with fifty-five tons of heavy water in 1970 (Wilczynski, "Atomic Energy," p. 590).

31. See Thomas O'Toole, "Soviet Sale Raises Questions on India's Nuclear Plans," *The Washington Post*, December 2, 1976, p. F–7; and Don Oberdorfer, "Soviets Agree to Sell India Heavy Water for Reactors," *The Washington Post*, December 8, 1976, p. 1.

32. This section relies heavily on interviews the author conducted in Washington, D.C., in June 1983, in Vienna in July 1983, and in New Delhi in September 1983.

33. This account is consistent with that provided by Duffy, *Soviet Nuclear Energy*, p. 24, and Ravindra Tomar, "The Indian Nuclear Power Program: Myths and Mirages," *Asian Survey* (May 1980): 529.

34. This interpretation was deemed plausible by a senior Indian official in the ministry of external affairs who acknowledged that his ministry also lacked technical expertise in the nuclear field and relied upon the Atomic Energy Commission for guidance in this field.

35. This point was emphasized by a high-ranking Indian official engaged in the negotiations. See also "Heavy Water Deal with USSR in Difficulties," *Indian Express*, March 18, 1977.

36. The author was told by one U.S. participant in the discussions with the Soviets in 1976 that initially neither the foreign ministry nor the State Committee for the Utilization of Atomic Energy was aware of these three circumvention possibilities.

37. See Paul Power, "The Indo-American Nuclear Controversy," *Asian Survey* (June 1979): 574–96.

38. See IAEA, "The Text of the Agreement of 17 November 1977 Between the Agency and India for the Application of Safeguards in Connection with the Supply of Heavy Water from the Soviet Union," *INFCIRC*, 260 (July 1978). Details of the agreement were only made public in India's parliament following a lecture on the subject by Ashok Kapur which received widespread coverage in the New Delhi media.

39. An offer of an additional 200 tons of heavy water was first made in March 1979 by Kosygin during a visit to India. At that time, the Soviet Union also offered to build a 1,000mw power plant. RAPP–II went critical in October 1981 but did not begin commercial operation until April 1982. For a good account of India's heavy water production difficulties, see "Heavy Water Moderates India's Path to Independence," *Nuclear Engineering International* (July 1981): 26–27; and Mirchandani and Namboodiri, *Nuclear India*, pp. 58–69.

40. These figures are derived from responses to questions raised in the Indian parliament, Lok Sabha, Question 1,543, October 13, 1982; Rajya Sabha, Question 61, July 28, 1983; and Mirchandani and Namboodiri, *Nuclear India*, p. 142.

41. Rajya Sabha, Question 79, July 12, 1979.

42. "Soviets Offer of A-Power Plants Being Examined," *Patriot* (September 24, 1983); and "Indo-Soviet Talks on A-Plants in October," *Indian Express* (September 24, 1983).

43. *Pravda*, May 31, 1975, p. 4.

44. See, for example, Duffy, *Soviet Nuclear Energy*, p. 22.

45. The 1975 agreement reportedly called for construction of an atomic research center, provision of a small research reactor, and training in the Soviet Union of Libyan technicians for the center. See Joseph V. R. Micallef, "A Nuclear Bomb for Libya?" *Bulletin of the Atomic Scientists* (August/September 1981): 14–15.

46. Duffy, *Soviet Nuclear Energy*, p. 84.

47. See, for example, N. Zagladin, "Atomic Blackmail," *New Times*, no. 37 (1978): 21–22. See also Yu Tomilin, "Non-Proliferation of Nuclear Weapons—An Imperative of Time," *Mirovaia ekonomika i mezhdunardonaia otnosheniia* (December 1980): 48; and V. F. Davydov, "Problems of Nuclear Nonproliferation: The Positions of American Politologists," *SShA* (September 1980): 96–104.

48. An estimate of the plutonium production capability of the Soviet reactor is provided by Micallef, "A Nuclear Bomb for Libya?" p. 14.

49. British Broadcasting Corporation, "Summary of World Broadcasts: Soviet Union," February 18, 1976.

50. Thomas O'Toole, "Libya Said to Buy Soviet A-Power Plant," *The Washington Post*, December 12, 1977, p. A–39.

51. Press release of the Federation of American Scientists, "Libyan Government Charged with False Adherence to Nuclear Non-

proliferation Treaty: Scientists Urge Cancellation of Soviet Reactor Sale," November 30, 1978, p. 1.

52. "Nuclear Power Agreements," *The Washington Post*, October 4, 1978. The article quotes Andronik Petrosyants, Chairman of the Soviet Committee on the Utilization of Atomic Energy. The 300mw figure, however, is odd since it does not correspond to the size of any Soviet-produced reactor. The most commonly exported reactor is the 440mw VVER (pressurized water reactor).

53. "INFO News Release," Atomic Industrial Forum, February 6, 1980, p. 7.

54. *Komsomolets* (Erevan, USSR), reported in "Soviet Nuclear Plant for Libya Seems to be Going Ahead," in *Energy in Countries with Planned Economies* (August 2, 1979):16.

55. Dennis Redmont, "Qaddafi Move Sparks New Nuclear Fears," *The International Herald Tribune*, January 21, 1981, p. 2.

56. Cited in "USSR-Libya Nuclear Pact," *Worldwide Report: Nuclear Development and Proliferation*, no. 91 (April 15, 1981).

57. *Tass Daily Economic and Commercial News Service* (Moscow), May 15, 1981, reported in "Soviet-Libyan Energy Cooperation," *Energy in Countries with Planned Economies* (May 1981): 9–10.

58. See "Finland's Iantran Voina 'Loses Interest' in Soviet-Libyan Power Project," *Energy in Countries with Planned Economies* (September 1981): 17. The Finns had been asked by Libya to provide an emergency cooling system for the Soviet-built plant since they had previously modified Soviet 440mw units for the Louiisa power plant in Finland.

59. IAEA, INFCIRC 280 (October 1980). Libya was in technical violation of Article 3 of the NPT by not concluding a safeguards agreement within two years of the entry into force of the treaty. A large number of NPT parties, however, have been delinquent in this respect.

60. John Cooley, "Libya Shopping for Nuclear Fuel?" *The Christian Science Monitor*, August 29, 1978, p. 1.

61. Duffy, *Soviet Nuclear Energy*, pp.84–85.

62. See "Moscow to Libya: Pay Your Bills," *Newsweek* (October 4, 1982): 9.

63. *Nucleonics Week* (March 31, 1983): 11.

64. See Congressional Research Service, Analysis of Six Issues About Nuclear Capabilities of India, Iraq, Libya, and Pakistan

(Washington, D.C.: Government Printing Office, January 1982), pp. 11–12.

65. See "Percée Possible pour la Cooperation Nucleaire Belge avec les Pays Arabes," *Le Soir*, August 8, 1981.

66. See Micallef, "A Nuclear Bomb for Libya?" pp. 14–15; Press Release of the Federation of American Scientists (November 30, 1978); Weissman and Krosney, pp. 53–65; and Amos Perlmutter, Michael Handel, and Uri Bar Joseph, *Two Minutes Over Baghdad* (London: Vallentine, Mitchell, 1982), pp. 36–38.

67. See Jorge F. Perez-Lopez, "The Cuban Nuclear Power Program," *Cuban Studies/Estudios Cubanos* (January 1979): 1.

68. Ibid., pp. 4–5.

69. *Granma*, December 7, 1974, p. 2, cited by Perez-Lopez, "The Cuban Nuclear Power Program," p. 13.

70. Cited by Perez-Lopez, p. 15.

71. Illustrative news reports include: "USSR to Build Atomic Power Plant in Cuba in 1977," *TASS*, April 8, 1977; *Sotsyalisticheckaya Industrya* (February 2, 1979), quoted in *Energy in Countries with Planned Economics* (February 16, 1979): 14; "Cuba Signs Agreement on Nuclear Research Center," *TASS*, May 16, 1980; *Ekonomicheskaya Gazeta* (April 28–May 4, 1980), quoted in *Energy in Countries with Planned Economics* (May 1980); A. Castro Bias, "CMEA Role in Promoting Nuclear Service, Technology in Cuba," *Ekonomicheskoye Sotrudnichestro Stran-chlenov SEV* (May 1980): 5–19; *Ekonomicheskoye Sotrudnichestro Stran-chlenov SEV* (October 1980), quoted in *Energy in Countries with Planned Economies* (November 1980): 19.

72. It is likely that the reactor vessels eventually shipped to Cuba will be produced at the Skoda Works in Czechoslovakia since the Soviet Union is phasing out production of 440mw pressurized water reactors in favor of the 1,000mw variety. See Jorge F. Perez-Lopez, "Nuclear Power in Cuba: Opportunities and Challenges," *Orbis* (Summer 1982): 505. See also *Nucleonics Week* (March 24, 1983): 10.

73. William Epstein, *The Last Chance: Nuclear Proliferation and Arms Control* (New York: The Free Press, 1976), p. 83.

74. Perez-Lopez, "The Cuban Nuclear Power Program," p. 12.

75. Ibid., p. 27.

76. Ibid., p. 28.

77. See IAEA, "The Text of the Agreement of 5 May 1980 Between the Agency and Cuba Relating to the Application of Safeguards

in Connection with the Supply of a Nuclear Power Plant," INFCIRC 291 (June 1980).

78. See IAEA, "The Text of the Agreement of 25 September 1980 Between Cuba and the Agency for the Application of Safeguards in Connection with the Supply of a Nuclear Research Reactor from the Union of Soviet Socialist Republics," INFCIRC 298 (August 1982).

79. See "Official Reports," *Izvestia*, March 29, 1980, in *FBIS Worldwide Report*, April 9, 1980, p. K–2, and "1st Step On the Way to Nuclear Cooperation Between Argentina and USSR," *Tass News Agency*, April 14, 1980, in *Energy in Countries with Planned Economies* (April 1980): 25.

80. Trade between the Soviet Union and Argentina almost quadrupled in 1980. Argentina, which shunned the Washington-led grain embargo of the Soviet Union, made almost one-quarter of its 1980 export earnings from the sale of grain to Moscow. See Edward Schumacher, "Argentina and Soviet Are No Longer Just Business Partners," *The New York Times*, July 13, 1981, p. E–4.

81. Ibid.

82. See John Redick, "The Tlatelolco Regime and Nonproliferation in Latin America," *International Organization* (Winter 1981; 118; *Nucleonics Week* (November 11, 1982): 1, and "Soviet Experts Aid in Argentina Nuclear Tube Manufacture," *FBIS Worldwide Report*, March 28, 1980, p. 11.

83. "Soviet Enrichment Services Procurred," *Nuclear Engineering International* (June 1982). Schumacher (op. cit.) cites an erroneous report that the Soviets also sold Argentina twelve tons of enriched uranium in June 1981. The author has found no other reports of a Soviet sale of enriched uranium to Argentina in 1981.

84. "CNEA Official, Soviet Comment on Uranium Deal," *FBIS Worldwide Report*, April 18, 1982, p. B–14.

85. *Nucleonics Week* (November 11, 1982): 1.

86. IAEA INFCIRC 297 (February 1982), p. 2.

87. IAEA INFCIRC 303 (July 1983), p. 3.

88. Indeed, there is little reference in Soviet writings on nonproliferation to Argentina's nuclear program. The most extensive coverage is provided in the journal *Latinskaya Amerika*.

89. For critical Soviet commentary on Brazil's nuclear program, with specific reference to the German deal, see Yuri Kharlanov, "Controversial Deal," *Pravda*, July 6, 1975, p. 6.

90. See Peter Clausen, "The Reagan Nonproliferation Policy: A Critical Midterm Look," *Arms Control Today* (December 1982).

91. Micallef, "A Nuclear Bomb for Libya?" p. 14; and *Analysis of Six Issues*, p. 17.

92. Zivia Wurtele et al., *Nuclear Proliferation Prospects for the Middle East and South Asia*, Report prepared by Pan Heuristics for the U.S. Department of Energy, Washington, D.C., June 1981, pp. 2–24.

93. Micallef, "A Nuclear Bomb for Libya?" p. 15. *The Mid-East Report* (September 1, 1983) points out that when Libya in the summer of 1979 sought to recruit nuclear exports to come to Al Fatah University, about twenty-five notably came from the United States and Europe (p. 2).

94. Stringent safeguards, however, were required. See Douglas Tweedale, "Argentina," in James Everett Katz and Onkar S. Marwah, eds., *Nuclear Power in Developing Countries* (Lexington, Mass.: Lexington Books, 1982), p. 89.

95. Ibid. The 250-tons-per-year plant was sold by the Swiss firm of Sulzer Brothers. Unlike Canada, which offered Argentina two alternative heavy water plants conditional on the application of full-scope safeguards, no such precondition was set by the Swiss. See *Nucleonics Week* (August 25, 1983): 7.

96. David Willis, "Argentina's Ranking Nuclear Physicist Denies His Country Has Designs on the Bomb," *The Christian Science Monitor*, October 26, 1983, p. 8. In return for approval of this reexport, the Argentines reportedly have agreed to place seven tons of heavy water presently in the reactor of Atucha I on the safeguards inventory. See also "Reagan Administration Approves Sale of Heavy Water to Argentine," *Latin America Energy Report* (August 30, 1983): 136.

97. See, for example, I.G. Sinel'schikova, "Foreign Capital in Latin American Nuclear Energy," *Latinskaya Amerika*, no. 5 (1981): 57–68 and A.I. Utkin, "Transatlantic Rivalry Over Nuclear Energy," *SShA* (May 1978): 33–44.

98. "China Is Open to Proposals from All Vendors," *Nucleonics Week* (November 3, 1983): 4.

99. "East Bloc Adds Spent Fuel Storage Space As Soviet Reprocessing Sags," *Nucleonics Week* (September 22, 1983): 1.

100. On this issue, see William Potter, "Managing Proliferation: Problems and Prospects for U.S.-Soviet Cooperation," in Dagobert Brito, Michael Intriligator, and Adele Wick, eds., *Strategies for Managing Nuclear Proliferation* (Lexington, Mass.: Lexington Books, 1983) pp. 247–63.

III MANAGEMENT STRATEGIES AND POLICY ALTERNATIVES

9 RESTRAINING THE SPREAD OF NUCLEAR WEAPONS: A WALK ON THE SUPPLY SIDE

Victor Gilinsky

Soviet Foreign Minister Molotov startled John Foster Dulles in 1954 with the suggestion that the worldwide civilian nuclear expansion then contemplated under America's Atoms for Peace proposal would make it easier for additional countries to obtain nuclear weapons. The following year, the United States invented the safeguards system of the International Atomic Energy Agency (IAEA) to restrain any moves in this direction based on nuclear materials and equipment obtained in commerce. As it became clear in succeeding decades that additional protection was needed because of the widening availability of nuclear technology, new instruments were created: the comprehensive safeguards provisions of the Non-Proliferation Treaty (NPT) in the 1960s and the London Suppliers' export control agreements in the 1970s.

Unfortunately each of these elements of protection was checked at the start by the political and commercial forces behind nuclear power. These resisted controls that threatened any of the basic assumptions underlying nuclear power development and nuclear commerce. A central assumption was that plutonium, the very nuclear explosive material that was of most security concern (its production inevitably accompanies power reactor operation), would become the primary nuclear

255

fuel in the future. Tough international controls on plutonium in national hands might have dampened these commercial prospects. Moreover, giving up national control over the separation and use of this substance to an international body seemed tantamount to giving up control over an important future source of electricity. No one was prepared to do that.

It seemed for many years that no one in authority was even willing to acknowledge the dilemma inherent in planning for wide use of plutonium fuel. Official pronouncements exaggerated what could be achieved through international safeguards and played down any concerns.[1] As a consequence, not only did we end up with inadequate controls over dangerous materials, but in some cases the application of such international inspections allowed questionable projects to gain the legitimacy without which they could not have proceeded. When serious problems with the way this system functioned could no longer be swept aside, it became a commonplace that while the safeguards were not perfect they were the best that could be negotiated, and that there really was no alternative.[2]

None of this history would be worth disinterring now were it not for the fact that there are some positive new features in an otherwise gloomy picture. The chief of these is that the anticipated displacement of uranium-fueled commercial reactors by plutonium-fueled breeder reactors, which once seemed all but inevitable, now appears merely futuristic. There is much more uranium, and there are many fewer power reactors to burn it, than was predicted years ago. The consequent decline in the price of uranium combined with a much higher than expected cost of extracting plutonium from spent fuel have caused plutonium's commercial prospects to sink. These developments make the notion of effective control worth talking about again.

A good place to start is with the beginnings of the various elements of the "nonproliferation regime": the IAEA safeguards, the NPT, and the supplier guidelines. As we understand their origins and their frailties, some ideas emerge on what to do next.

INTERNATIONAL ATOMIC ENERGY AGENCY SAFEGUARDS

Central to this regime are the safeguards—the inspections and controls—of the International Atomic Energy Agency, later incorporated into the Non-Proliferation Treaty. The international agency was part of the original Atoms for Peace proposal. The international inspections were an afterthought, and I cannot help thinking that this has diminished their status up to the present.

The Atoms for Peace proposal itself tended to subordinate nuclear trade controls to commercial and foreign policy objectives. Before this, under the Atomic Energy Act of 1946, even exchanges of information on the industrial uses of nuclear energy were banned until such time as Congress should find that "effective and enforceable international safeguards against the uses of atomic energy for destructive purposes have been established."[3] Under Atoms for Peace, exports were not only authorized, but encouraged. Control measures were left to catch up with them.

President Eisenhower, in announcing the Atoms for Peace program, did say that the IAEA could be made responsible for the protection of the nuclear material contributed to the agency.[4] However, he seems to have had in mind some form of intrinsic protection which obviated the need for intrusive inspections: "The ingenuity of our scientists will provide special safe conditions under which a bank of fissionable material can be made essentially immune to surprise seizure."[5] Whether this was more than a hope, I cannot tell, but apparently the president regarded the absence of inspections in his original scheme as a definite advantage.[6]

Inspection and control functions were injected shortly before the agency was created.[7] The technological scope of the Atoms for Peace program had expanded very quickly and the implications of that had begun to sink in. Conversations with the Russians also played a role in this. The Soviet Union's initial view was that the Atoms for Peace program would have little impact on reducing weapons stocks, but that the spread of nuclear materials around the world posed a military risk.[8] The Russian decision to participate in the IAEA also meant that the organization would be a less "clubby" affair, and informal checks on security of nuclear materials would not suffice.

If controls were needed, the United States saw an advantage in having them administered by the international agency. American officials thought this approach would avoid competition with other exporters (primarily with the United Kingdom) in offering easier terms, and would make inspections more palatable to importers.[9] It also gave the agency something to do. As most American exports were expected to be under bilateral arrangements with friendly states, the new institution would have been badly undercut if member states carried out their own inspections. The agency was therefore given the role of inspecting its members' bilateral agreements. But the scientific and technical agency seems never to have shaken the feeling that monitoring its members for cheating was not entirely consistent with its high-minded purposes and hopes.

Internal U.S. documents of that period do not suggest much confidence in the protection to be gained from international inspections of agency projects. The notion was already prevalent that if countries wanted nuclear weapons badly enough they would in time, perhaps a decade, be able to get them on their own. Their indigenous activities were, after all, not covered by any sort of inspection.

Looking back to the 1950s, when the Atoms for Peace proposal was being fleshed out, the IAEA statute was being drafted, and bilateral agreements for technology and equipment were being concluded with dozens of countries, one is struck that we apparently had no sense of the strength of our position in guiding the long-term development of commercial nuclear power. We felt, even then, that American bargaining power was slipping away, and that we had better use our technological advantage while we had it to gain maximum influence for larger purposes.[10] A proposal within the U.S. government for an agreement among the "haves" to require comprehensive IAEA inspection of all nuclear activities in "have-not" countries was thought not to be achievable.[11] A National Security Council directive did require that our bilateral agreements include provisions that any extraction of plutonium from spent fuel take place in the United States or under international auspices acceptable to us. This provision was incorporated in early agreements, but it was opposed in the Atomic Energy Commission on the grounds that it would breed resentment abroad, undermining the purpose of Atoms for Peace.[12]

Plutonium's explosive property was the root of the security problem posed by nuclear commerce. An American proposal for an even stronger agency role in actually controlling, rather than merely verifying, the separation and use of plutonium covered by agency agreements was incorporated into the "Twelve Nation" draft IAEA statute presented to the 1956 Conference on the IAEA Statute.[13] This was opposed by other countries, especially India, France, and the Soviet Union (which had retreated from its earlier position).[14] Plutonium was already viewed as an important nuclear fuel for the future, presumably because uranium was then thought to be scarce. And reprocessing of spent fuel to extract the unused uranium and plutonium was thought to be a necessary adjunct of reactor operation.

Threatened with an impasse if it continued to insist on international control of plutonium stockpiles, the United States gave in.[15] The statute made it clear that the authority given the agency over reprocessing was only for the limited purpose of ensuring that reprocessing would "not lend itself" to the diversion of materials and that the applicable health and safety standards would be observed.[16]

The agency's authority over the disposition of plutonium was similarly watered down.[17] The IAEA's authority to require its members to deposit their plutonium with the agency was sharply limited by the provision that any plutonium deposited with the agency would have to be "returned promptly," at the request of the depositor.[18]

In presenting the U.S. case for a strong interpretation of what was left, Ambassador James Wadsworth said that agency control over plutonium was the "most crucial of all" safeguards, and that investing the agency with the right to control reprocessing was "indispensable":

... The agency must guard against the undue amassing or collecting of dangerous amounts of special fissionable material.... Since a stockpile honestly intended for future peaceful use is indistinguishable from one intended for future military use and, in fact, might be quickly turned to military use, the agency cannot permit the accumulation of any stockpiles of fissionable materials derived from agency supported projects other than stockpiles under agency control.[19]

But the IAEA never exercised the control Wadsworth suggested, and it is only now getting around to contemplating a pale version of it.[20] And even that is apparently getting nowhere. In this and other respects, the proposals and debates of those early years on plutonium control anticipated much of what was to come.

Plutonium is, of course, not the only nuclear explosive; it shares that status with highly enriched uranium. It is interesting that, from the start of Atoms for Peace, the United States drew a distinction between reprocessing (the technology for plutonium production) and uranium enrichment (necessary to make bomb-grade uranium–235). Both technologies had commercial applications, with enrichment being, if anything, more important, as it was needed to produce the low-enriched fuel used by most reactors. Yet reprocessing technology was shared liberally while enrichment was held tightly. This may have stemmed from a feeling that reactor plutonium was less dangerous than highly enriched uranium, although that would have been inconsistent with allowing export of highly enriched uranium for research reactors, as we did in the late 1950s. Perhaps enrichment technology was thought to be based on a real secret (barrier manufacture) whereas reprocessing was "just chemistry." Or, perhaps it was a matter of trying to preserve the commercial enrichment monopoly. In any case, as a result of this early version of technology control, uranium-enrichment technology spread more slowly than plutonium-separation technology. This situation may, however, be changing.

THE NON-PROLIFERATION TREATY: "INALIENABLE" RIGHTS TO PLUTONIUM?

In the 1960s the technology of plutonium separation and use played an important role in the lengthy debates over the next step toward tighter international control—the Non-Proliferation Treaty, which extended safeguards to cover all the nuclear activities of signatories, including indigenous ones.[21] The weapons states were exempt from this requirement, and this led the Federal Republic of Germany and Japan to complain that the arrangement would put them at a competitive disadvantage and to insist, successfully, on certain limitations to IAEA inspection of fuel facilities.[22] What their negotiators had in mind was future competition with the United States in the plutonium fuel trade.

The treaty was not universally accepted: Two weapons states and some of the countries high on everyone's worry list—India, Israel, South Africa, Pakistan, Argentina, and Brazil—stayed out. Since most suppliers required of these countries only that individual exports to them be covered by IAEA inspections, putting no conditions on their other imports and indigenous activities, the treaty hold-outs were in effect given a preferred status. In the United States that concession persisted until the passage of the Nuclear Non-Proliferation Act of 1978, which banned major U.S. nuclear exports to these countries until they accepted comprehensive safeguards.[23]

There was also a more fundamental problem: The original idea of the treaty, as embodied in the 1961 Irish Resolution in the United Nations,[24] was that it was in the interest of all countries, especially those without nuclear weapons, that the number of states with such weapons not increase. The resolution urged that the nuclear weapons states agree not to transfer weapons or their technology to nonweapons states, and that these states agree not to receive or manufacture weapons. Near the end of the long negotiations, however, the treaty was turned into a different sort of bargain, one in which most of the adherents gave up the right to manufacture nuclear weapons in exchange for what they regarded as unimpeded access to "peaceful" nuclear technology. Article IV encouraged "the fullest possible exchange" of peaceful technology between the advanced countries and the less advanced.[25] In this spirit, President Johnson went so far as to promise after the signing of the NPT that the United States would share its technical knowledge in peaceful nuclear research fully, and "without reservation."[26] What many countries had in mind on this score was, again, technology related to future use of plutonium in fast breeder reactors, whose future prospects were then in their heyday. (Curiously, no one really seems to have expected us to share uranium-enrichment technology.)

The continuing difficulty is that, should its owner so decide, a plutonium stockpile can be put to weapons use too easily for international inspections to present much of an obstacle. The danger inherent in the treaty's common interpretation is therefore that it legitimizes nuclear activities arbitrarily close to nuclear weaponry. As national rivalries are bound to drive countries to match each others' near-weapon status, this has the makings of a very unstable state of affairs. With rivals poised on the edge of acquiring nuclear weapons capabilities, it might not take much to put them over the edge.[27]

The difficulty was created by the elastic definition of "peaceful" uses. Unlike the 1946 Acheson-Lilienthal report's "safe/dangerous" distinction, which depended on the closeness—technologically speaking—of a material or an activity to bombmaking, the peaceful/nonpeaceful distinction incorporated in the IAEA charter and the NPT turns largely on the stated intentions of the nuclear materials' owner.[28] Just how elastic the peaceful label could be was demonstrated by the Indian nuclear explosion in 1974.[29]

A way out of this difficulty would have been to obtain collective agreement that the term "peaceful" covers only those materials and activities sufficiently removed from bombmaking that they can reasonably be protected by international inspections. Those whose status is more ambiguous would have to be protected by other means or conducted under international auspices. It would have been entirely consistent with the purpose of the treaty—preventing the spread of nuclear weapons—if plutonium separated from commercial fuel were placed in the ambiguous category. It was not, however, consistent with the industrial commitments of the advanced suppliers, which ran heavily toward future use of plutonium as a fuel, and which might have been at risk if plutonium were properly labeled. It was also not consistent with the technological appetites of their less advanced customers, however implausible the possible application for plutonium in their countries. Nor did anyone want to question the value of IAEA safeguards in any context.

Too much commerce had been legitimized on the basis of their putative efficacy. And officials who were working hard to gain worldwide support for the NPT and its safeguards were understandably not inclined to entertain criticism of them.

ATTEMPTS AT PLUTONIUM CONTROL BEYOND THE NPT

It was more difficult to indulge in the illusions of hope after the 1974 Indian explosion and subsequent revelations that a number of countries—some NPT parties, others not—were in the process of buying small reprocessing plants from France and the Federal Republic of Germany for what appeared to be dubious reasons. It was clear that additional control was essential if further spread of nuclear weapons was to be avoided. Although the Indian activities had not been subject to IAEA inspection, the problem lay elsewhere. As Secretary Kissinger told the UN in September 1975, the problem was easy national access to plutonium: "The greatest single danger of unrestrained nuclear proliferation resides in the spread under national control of reprocessing facilities for the atomic materials in nuclear power plants."[30]

The United States proposed the establishment of multinational regional nuclear fuel cycle centers as a "major step to reinforce all other measures." In the meantime, diplomatic pressures were brought to bear and, as a result, the export to South Korea of a small French reprocessing plant was put on ice.[31]

At American initiative, the major nuclear suppliers met in London to discuss "Guidelines for Nuclear Transfers" to set limits on commercial competition in "sensitive" materials, equipment, and technology. The meetings were secret because of the extreme nervousness of some of the participants about the reaction of their own nuclear industries and their Third World customers. After a good deal of compromise, the final guidelines urged sellers to require from recipients assurances excluding any nuclear explosive uses, and also to require IAEA safeguards on all sales.[32] The voluntary and permissive character of the guidelines, as well as the sensitivity of the participants to their commercial interests, is reflected in the mild admonition to "exercise restraint" in the transfer of "sensitive facilities, technology and weapons-usable materials."[33] If a customer is believed to have violated the rules, say, by exploding a bomb, the suppliers agreed to work through diplomatic channels on an "appropriate" response, which "could include" termination of nuclear transfers to the offending customer.[34]

The guidelines point generally in the right direction. But even the provisions that uranium-enrichment facility sales be conditioned on operation below 20 percent enrichment, or that there should be mutual agreement between supplier and recipient on "arrangements for reprocessing, storage, alteration, use, transfer or retransfer of any weapons-usable material,"[35] are only advisory. "Suppliers should endeavor," say the guidelines, "to include such provisions whenever appropriate and practicable."[36]

In the meantime, thinking in the United States went much further. A few days before the 1976 election, President Ford announced a major U.S. policy shift: He said there should not be further commitments to commercial use of plutonium unless "there is sound reason to conclude that the world community can effectively overcome the associated risks of proliferation."[37] He went on to say that nuclear power could develop and expand without plutonium use and that the United States would no longer regard reprocessing of spent fuel to obtain plutonium "as a necessary and inevitable step in the fuel cycle."[38] That is, we would ourselves accept the standards we were urging on others: "Common standards must be developed and accepted by all parties. If this is not done, unrestrained trade in sensitive nuclear technology and materials will develop—with no one in a position to stop it."[39]

The Ford policy perspective on controlling plutonium was lost in the bitter struggles between the Carter administration, tagged as being "anti-nuclear," and its critics. The administration's erratic style gave the impression of ineptitude and irresolution, and encouraged domestic and foreign opposition from those who felt threatened by a U.S. move away from commercial use of plutonium. They stamped technology "control" as technology "denial," both inconsistent with U.S. obligations under the NPT and unrealistic. In the end, the heat at home and abroad got so intense over plutonium control that the administration tossed the decision to a forty-nation International Nuclear Fuel Cycle Evaluation. Predictably, this convocation of nuclear bureaucracies came up with an only slightly qualified endorsement of plutonium and the adequacy of IAEA inspections to safeguard it. The United States, having created the enterprise, more or less went along with the result.[40]

The Reagan administration was anxious to differentiate itself from its predecessors in its plutonium policy both internationally and domestically. It retreated from the common-standards approach of previous administrations and announced it will not oppose the reprocessing and breeder programs in the advanced countries—many of them our allies and the very countries whose support we need to control the flow of dangerous technology to the Third World. The approach instead has been to try to draw the line at those countries.

This "discriminatory" approach also fit in with the administration's enthusiasm for domestic plutonium-based programs, which ironically have come to naught. The Office of Management and Budget declined to support the subsidies needed for the Barnwell Reprocessing Plant, and the Congress, balking at the price tag, killed the Clinch River Reactor Project. In a sense, this cleared the air of political obligations and allowed a fresh look at the problem of controlling plutonium.

Despite the contentiousness, confusion, and unfortunate ambivalence of U.S. policy during the post–Indian-explosion period, there were advances. In 1978 the Nuclear Non-proliferation Act spelled out for the first time in law what was expected of safeguards over plutonium: "timely" warning of wrongdoing so that the would-be bombmaker could expect to be intercepted before he could build bombs.[41] And cooperation on technology control did become more frequent, although the suppliers have not met as a full group since the issuance of the guidelines through the IAEA in 1978. There was also more continuity than appeared from administration to administration in the practical execution of this policy. The suppliers' efforts at technology control, controversial and inconsistent as some of them were, slowed down some questionable projects at a crucial time when the economics of plutonium fuel were changing. The suppliers have become more alert to the dangers of, and have more frequently cooperated to prevent, exports not subject to IAEA inspection and which are directly related to possible bomb programs.

Still, much continues to leak through as importers have become more sophisticated. And the guidelines, which were intended to extend controls beyond IAEA safeguards, have, in effect, become merely a trigger list for such safeguards. Moreover, these controls remain an almost surreptitious extralegal activity which the suppliers are reluctant to discuss. What is missing in this policy is a public rationale for restricting those technologies for which the IAEA inspections cannot provide adequate protection. For fear of "undermining" IAEA safeguards, as any criticism of the inspection is labeled, the best argument has not been presented for additional international control over plutonium and highly enriched uranium—that IAEA inspections cannot adequately protect such explosive material.

IS POWER REACTOR PLUTONIUM REALLY POTENTIAL BOMB MATERIAL?

The arguments over the need for tough controls on commercial sales have been clouded by assertions that the plutonium commonly produced in power reactors is so contaminated with unwanted isotopes that, as a practical matter, it is not usable for weapons.[42] This notion goes all the way back to the 1946 Acheson-Lilienthal report, and may have influenced some of the permissive steps taken during the Atoms for Peace period.[43] Indeed, if power reactor plutonium were not usable for weapons the entire safeguards situation would be much simpler. That is, in fact, what the IAEA believed for many years when its safeguards were under development.

Unfortunately, while the plutonium produced in power reactor fuel is not the ideal nuclear explosive—and the longer the fuel stays in the reactor the less desirable the plutonium becomes—it is a nuclear explosive all the same. Had it been used in our first nuclear device, the minimum yield would have been about a kiloton—a result that can undoubtedly be improved upon—and the likely yield something above that.[44] In

1970 Carson Mark, then director of the theoretical division at Los Alamos, elaborated on this point:

> ... I would like to warn people concerned with such problems that the old notion that reactor-grade plutonium is incapable of producing nuclear explosions—or that plutonium could easily be rendered harmless by the addition of modest amounts of the isotope Pu-240, or "denatured," as the phrase used to go—that these notions have been dangerously exaggerated. This observation is, of course, of no direct practical interest to the United States or the USSR, who have adequate supplies of weapon-grade plutonium, and have proved designs for weapons much better than could easily be made with plutonium from power reactors. To someone having no nuclear weapons at all, or no source of high-grade materials, however, the prospect of obtaining weapons—even of an "inferior" or "primitive" type—could present quite a different aspect.[45]

Not until the mid–1970s was this view recognized at the IAEA. What seems to have happened is that the United States informed the agency that all plutonium could be used for bombs, but did not provide supporting technical information that would make this convincing. Probably we did not want to encourage anyone to try it, or perhaps we were ambivalent about the consequences of that observation. In any case, as the top IAEA safeguards official told me in 1976, the IAEA safeguards system had, until shortly before then, been based on the notion that it was only necessary for it to observe the fueling of reactors to detect any move to produce weapons-grade plutonium by cycling the fuel more rapidly. As long as the reactors operated normally, the plutonium produced was not thought to be of particular concern. If there were a departure from the normal fuel cycle, there would still be warning well before weapons-grade plutonium was produced and separated.

The IAEA was not the only party to suffer confusion on this point. In the same year, the German official responsible for the West Germany–Brazil deal, which included a small reprocessing plant to extract plutonium from power reactor fuel, explained to me that there was nothing to worry about because his experts had informed him that the plutonium could not be used for weapons. Upon my return to Washington, I urged that a briefing be arranged for these and other officials to clarify the point. I happened to sit in on the briefing for the IAEA director-general, and I literally saw his jaw drop.

IAEA INSPECTIONS CANNOT PROTECT "PEACEFUL" PLUTONIUM STOCKS

If power reactor plutonium is an explosive, the safeguards problem is obviously very much harder. What we have to protect against is rapid appropriation of previously "peaceful" plutonium stocks, precisely the problem that worried Ambassador Wadsworth in 1956. A country interested in nuclear weapons now has every incentive to maintain the fiction of exclusively "peaceful" uses for as long as possible and then to traverse as quickly as it can the interval between the first clear sign of its weapons program and its possession of the weapons themselves.

In these circumstances, the shortest and cheapest way to a bomb is by appropriating plutonium, or highly enriched uranium, previously designated (perhaps with the best of intentions) as "peaceful." We should remember that, for beginners, getting the nuclear explosives in the requisite quantities is the most time-consuming and difficult aspect of nuclear bombmaking. That countries acquired nuclear explosives for weapons in the past by means of dedicated military production programs is no longer a useful guide to how countries might act in the future.

Ironically none of the countries we worry about—not even those outside the treaty—admit to the development of nuclear weapons, or even to an interest in acquiring them. India insists its nuclear explosion was peaceful. South Africa says its secret enrichment project is peaceful. So is Pakistan's. Iraq insists its research program is peaceful, as does Libya. And so on. There is in this a good measure of playing on the wishful thinking of the suppliers, and on their hypocrisy. But if, as the French say, hypocrisy is the homage that vice pays to virtue, then such protestations of innocence on all sides are something of a backhanded acknowledgment of the legitimacy of the norm established by the treaty, and of the risks—economic, political, and military—involved in an overt weapons program.

The basic illegitimacy of departing from the status established by the NPT makes the threat of sanctions plausible. Here the situation has changed over the past decade. Beyond expressing vague regrets, we hardly reacted to the 1974 Indian nuclear explosion (unlike the Canadians, who terminated their nuclear cooperation with India). The French actually sent a telegram of congratulations.[46] The next country to announce a nuclear bomb program cannot count on such a mild reaction from the world community.

Moreover, an overt nuclear weapons program that has not yet succeeded in manufacturing weapons is a tempting target for preemptive attack. Any doubt about this possibility was resolved by Israel's raid on the Iraqi research reactor in 1981. There is now speculation in the press over whether India might launch such an attack on Pakistani facilities, and what Pakistan might do in return. The sharp Soviet and U.S. reactions to what appeared to be preparations for a South African test explosion in the Kalahari desert demonstrated that the major states feel entitled to act not merely in response to treaty violations, but also in response to indigenous efforts. That is a new phenomenon, too.

Would-be bombmakers have in effect been forced to take cover. This limits their opportunities and increases their risks, which makes a decision to build weapons less likely. But it also means that those determined to obtain nuclear weapons will see the sudden appropriation of civilian plutonium or highly enriched uranium as the easiest way of obtaining a bomb. Inspections cannot sound a warning early enough to protect against this eventuality. It cannot be repeated too often that international inspections are a safeguard only if they can warn reliably of illicit activities in time for other countries to thwart the intended bombmaking. In other words, a burglar alarm is not much use if it takes longer for the police to arrive on the scene than it does for the burglars to make off with their loot. The relationship between the closeness of the nuclear activity to bombmaking and the extent to which it can be protected by inspections is such that most of the nuclear power reactors and their fuel are protectable, at least in principle. That is not, however, the case with highly enriched uranium and separated plutonium, the two fuels that are also nuclear explosives. They can be turned to bomb use too quickly—in a matter of days—for inspection to provide reliable protection. Even with a perfect inspection system, we could not count on there being enough time between diversion and bomb manufacture to stop the process. In reality, the response of the inspection system is sluggish and uncertain, and any potential diversion would likely be clouded in ambiguity, at least for a time. This means that the international alarm system must provide a healthy margin of safety. For this to be possible, nuclear materials have to be in a form that cannot be converted easily into explosives for bombs.

To sharpen the point, let us imagine a situation in which the IAEA, instead of inspecting fuel, was checking on actual nuclear weapons. What would be the value of such an inspection? If weapons existed in a particular country, its neighbors would likely want to know how many there were. At the same time, no one would confuse a periodic verification of the count, interesting as it may be, with protection against the use of such weapons. Counted or not, they can still be used rapidly. Yet, without the surrounding chemical explosives and firing circuits, we are left with the nuclear explosive material, which in another setting is widely considered to be adequately protected by IAEA "safeguards" (that is, inspections). In fact, there is no known way of safeguarding (that is, protecting) separated plutonium by inspection or other technical means now available.

SAFEGUARDS AND TECHNOLOGY CONTROL: YOU CAN'T HAVE ONE WITHOUT THE OTHER

In the end, we are left with the question, what shall we do now? There are two levels to the problem: First, how shall we deal with the hold-out countries, the ones that have not accepted IAEA inspection on all their nuclear activities? And, second, what shall we do to limit access to weapons-usable materials— the nuclear explosives, plutonium, and highly enriched uranium—even if it is covered by the IAEA inspection system? We have to deal with these questions in parallel. Nothing is gained if by extending the coverage of the inspection system the suppliers only legitimize wider national access to nuclear explosives.

In looking for answers, we would do well to return to some of the early Atoms for Peace proposals that were left on the cutting room floor. We have to return to the idea of uniformly requiring that all suppliers condition all exports on the customers' acceptance of comprehensive IAEA inspection.[47] Countries that are unwilling to accept such inspection should be clearly understood to be interested in obtaining nuclear weapons. We also need to find some way either to keep separated plutonium and highly enriched uranium out of commercial channels or to gain international control over them. In other words, we have to come to grips with the very problem Ambassador Wadsworth was talking about in 1956.[48]

This is a tall order, and we have failed so far, despite years of trying, even to achieve the first objective. But if we succeeded to the point where the countries with bombs on their minds are ashamed to admit it, I am convinced we can shame the major suppliers into accepting full-scope safeguards as an export requirement.

If there are important things for the IAEA to do, it is also true that it needs to do them better than it has. That everything is not right is clear from the Nuclear Regulatory Commission's 1981 letter to Congress in which the commission stated that it was "concerned that the IAEA safeguards system would not detect a diversion in at least some types of facilities" and that, in addition, it was "not confident that the member states would be notified of a diversion in a timely fashion."[49] The agency must tighten up its performance.

The safeguards system cannot be improved if its flaws are papered over, and there has been too much of a tendency in this direction. It is only natural that the IAEA, as an international institution and a creature of its member states, should be worried about offending any of its members. But this has been carried much too far in the direction of secrecy about the operation of the safeguards system and defensiveness about its performance. The IAEA, and also the countries that are heavily involved in nuclear trade, are extremely touchy about any criticism of the effectiveness of safeguards. The IAEA's annual Safeguards Implementation Reports (SIRs), which assess safeguards' effectiveness, are not made public even though they are carefully written to make it difficult to identify any of the countries discussed. In this country, the SIRs are actually classified on grounds of national security. Instead, the IAEA should make these general reports public and also make known the facts about the effectiveness of the safeguards that are in place at specific facilities. I would go even further: After the IAEA has conducted an inspection, a report of those results should also be made public.

The usual fears that opening the IAEA safeguards system to greater public scrutiny would "undermine" the system are misplaced. It is true that the IAEA's inspections of national facilities already involves an unprecedented surrender of national sovereignty in the interest of collective security, and that these inspections, even on current terms, are a vitally important international foot in the door. In the long run, however, the threat to the safeguards systems lies not in acknowledging its limitations and deficiencies, but in making inflated claims about its effectiveness.

The IAEA should be clearer with its members about the intrinsic limitations of its safeguards as they apply to weapons-usable materials. There has been an increase in candor on this point under the current director-general, Hans Blix, but much remains to be done. The IAEA should acknowledge that its inspections will not protect against the sudden diversion of plutonium or highly enriched uranium, and that this is the reason technology controls are needed.

Finally, the suppliers must use such controls to get a better handle on plutonium and highly enriched uranium. It is just not acceptable to drift toward a state of affairs in which many countries have stockpiles of "peaceful" nuclear explosive material or the capacity to produce them quickly. There has been more than a little reluctance to deal seriously with the plutonium question, as it appeared to threaten the legitimacy of plutonium-based programs in many countries.

In the end, it comes down to what has always been regarded as the central dilemma for the international nuclear enterprise: how to restrain the spread of nuclear weapons without crippling the development and use of commercial nuclear power. President Reagan was remarkably candid about this. When asked what he thought was our proper role in preventing the spread of nuclear weapons and nuclear weapons technology, he replied:

> Well, our position is and it is unqualified, that we are opposed to the proliferation of nuclear weapons and do everything in our power to prevent it. I don't believe, however, that that should carry over into the development of nuclear power for peaceful purposes and so it increases the difficulty, if you are going to encourage the one, because you have at least opened a crack in the door where someone can proceed to the development of weapons.[50]

The president was also direct about safeguards. Shortly after the Israeli attack on Iraq's reactor, he remarked, ". . . How many countries do we know that have signed [the NPT] that very possibly are going ahead with nuclear weapons? It's again, something that doesn't lend itself to verification."[51] The State Department hastened to "clarify" that he meant to say that safeguards were not foolproof, but no clarification was necessary—the president correctly perceived there is a serious problem with safeguards.

If the dangers of plutonium commerce (and of that in highly enriched uranium) were explained in the same simple and direct manner, we might begin to dispel the metaphysical subtleties that have clouded the efforts to prevent the spread of nuclear weapons. Once we admit we cannot protect nuclear explosives in national hands, we may find that the dilemma is not as great as everyone had assumed. As President Ford said in 1976, effective controls over dangerous materials will not threaten the use of commercial nuclear power; these materials are not necessary to the generation of electricity anywhere in the world.

The fact that countries are ashamed to admit they are even interested in bombs gives us something to work with. There is substantial untapped power in the technology controls of the suppliers' club. If the commercial prospects of plutonium have indeed sunk, it may be the moment for putting some muscle in the supplier operation. We have to make it more difficult to take cover in semantic ambiguities like "safeguards" and "peaceful uses." The key is to make clear why there is a need for supplier controls and to apply them openly.

The last opportunity for a new initiative came and went eight years ago. The time is right to try again.

NOTES

1. See, for example, AEC, "A Brief History of Safeguards," printed in U.S. Congress, Joint Committee on Atomic Energy, *Background Material for the Review of the International Atomic Policies and Programs of the United States*, 86th Cong., 2nd Sess., 1960, Vol. 3, p. 851. See also Statement of Secretary of State Dean Rusk, February 23, 1966, in U.S. Congress, Joint Committee on Atomic Energy, *Hearings on Nonproliferation of Nuclear Weapons*, 89th Cong., 2nd Sess., 1966, pp. 3–29 and statement of AEC Chairman Glenn T. Seaborg, February 23, 1966, before the same committee, pp. 51–72.

2. "The system is not foolproof. It is not an absolutely ideal system. It is just better than nothing." Testimony of Kenneth Adelman, Director, Arms Control and Disarmament Agency, September 30, 1983, *Transcript of Joint Hearing on Nuclear Non-Proliferation Act*, before U.S. Senate Committee on Foreign Relations and Subcommittee on Energy, Nuclear Proliferation and Government Processes of the Committee on Governmental Affairs, p. 70.

3. Atomic Energy Act of 1946, Section 19(a)(1), Public Law 585, 79th Cong., 60 Stat. 755–75, 42 U.S.C. 1801–19.

4. Dwight D. Eisenhower, "Atomic Power for Peace," December 8, 1953, reprinted in U.S. Congress, Senate, *Atoms for Peace Manual*, 84th Cong., 1st Sess., 1955, p. 6.

5. Ibid.

6. In his speech to the United Nations, President Eisenhower stated that his proposal that the nuclear states contribute normal uranium and fissionable materials to an International Atomic Energy Agency "has the great virtue that it can be undertaken without the irritations and mutual suspicions incident to any attempt to set up a completely acceptable system of world-wide inspection and control" (Ibid.).

    See also AEC 751/41, December 30, 1955, Department of Energy (DOE) Archives.

7. Compare the April 24, 1956, Draft Statute of the International Atomic Energy Agency, Article XII, printed in the *Department of State Bulletin*, May 21, 1956, pp. 852–59, with the August 22,

1955, Draft Statute of the International Atomic Energy Agency, Article XIII, printed in the *Department of State Bulletin*, October 24, 1955, pp. 666–72.

8. AEC 751/41, Dec. 30, 1955, DOE Archives; Aide Memoire handed to Secretary Dulles by Foreign Minister V. M. Molotov, Geneva, April 27, 1954, printed in *Atoms for Peace Manual*, pp. 269–74.

The following passage from the aide memoire is particularly interesting:

> It is well known that it is practically feasible to carry out on an industrial scale a process of obtaining electrical power for peaceful needs by utilizing atomic materials, in which the quantity of the fissionable atomic materials applied in the process not only fails to decrease but, on the contrary, increases. And the harmless atomic materials are converted into explosive and fissionable materials which are the basis for the production of atomic and hydrogen weapons. In other words, the fact that the peaceful application of atomic energy is connected with the possibility of simultaneous production of atomic materials utilized for the manufacture of the atomic weapon is indisputable and has been proved in practice. Such a situation not only fails to lead to a reduction of the stocks of atomic materials utilized for the manufacture of atomic weapons, but also leads to an increase of these stocks without any limitations being applied either to the constantly increasing production of these materials in individual states or to production by the International Agency itself. Consequently the proposal of the USA concerning the allocation of a certain portion of atomic materials to be utilized for peaceful purposes not only fails to stop the atomic armament race but leads to its further intensification (p. 271).

9. National Security Council (NSC) 5507/2, March 12, 1955, cited in AEC 655/40, Appendix "B", November 28, 1955, DOE Archives.

10. My views on this point have been influenced by discussions I have had with Dr. Jack M. Holl, DOE chief historian. See also Jack M. Holl, "Eisenhower's Peaceful Atomic Diplomacy: Atoms for Peace and the Western Alliance," *Materials and Society* 7, nos. 3/4 (1983): 365–78.

11. AEC 751/41, December 30, 1955, DOE Archives, Annex 1 to Appendix "B", "A Proposal for Averting Dangers in the Atoms-for-Peace Program":

> The Proposal
>
> 4. A way out of this difficulty suggests itself: *The danger could be averted if all the 'have' powers, i.e., all the countries able to supply the*

needed materials and technology, agreed among themselves to adhere to a code of fair competition in dealing with underdeveloped countries, providing that henceforth the signatories would give help toward atomic power programs only to countries making a pledge of no atomic weapons plus submission to full inspection by an international body to be established for this purpose [emphasis in original].

12. NSC 5507/2, March 12, 1955, cited in AEC 655/40, Appendix "B", November 28, 1955, DOE Archives.

13. The Twelve Nation Draft would have given the agency the right to

> approve the means to be used for chemical processing of irradiated materials and to specify disposition of any special fissionable materials recovered or produced as a byproduct, and to require that such special fissionable materials be deposited with the Agency except for quantities authorized by the Agency to be retained for specified non-military use under continuing Agency safeguards (Draft Statute of the International Atomic Energy Agency unanimously approved in Washington, D.C., on April 18, 1956, by the Twelve Nation Negotiating group and circulated to the governments and specialized agencies, Article XII(A)(5), printed in the *Department of State Bulletin*, May 21, 1956).

This draft was considerably stricter than the preceding August 22, 1955, Draft Statute of International Atomic Energy Agency, printed in the *Department of State Bulletin,* October 24, 1955.

14. AEC, "The International Atomic Energy Agency," printed in *Background Material*, Vol. 3, pp. 732–33. Bertrand Goldschmidt, *The Atomic Complex: A Worldwide Political History of Nuclear Energy* (LaGrange Park, Illinois: American Nuclear Society, 1982), pp. 281–83.

15. *Background Material*, p. 734. Goldschmidt, *The Atomic Complex*, pp. 282–83. It is interesting to note that a report prepared for the Atomic Energy Commission later took the view that the statute approved by the conference "was essentially the same as that of the Twelve Nation Draft" (*Background Material*, p. 734) and that the principal substantive change was a further increase in the size of the Board of Governors.

16. Whereas the Twelve Nation Draft (Article XII[A][5]) gave the agency the absolute authority "to approve the means for the chemical processing of irradiated materials," the statute provided that the agency was given this authority "solely to ensure that this chemical processing will not lend itself to diversion of

materials for military purposes and will comply with applicable health and safety standards."

17. Where the Article XII(A)(5) of the Twelve Nation Draft gave the agency authority "to specify disposition" of special fissionable materials recovered or produced, the same article of the statute gave the IAEA authority only to require that such materials "be used for peaceful purposes under continuing agency safeguards for research or in reactors, existing or under construction, specified by the member. . . ."

18. Article XII(A)(5) of the Twelve Nation Draft gave the IAEA the authority to "require that such special fissionable materials be deposited with the Agency except for quantities authorized by the Agency to be retained for specified non-military use under continuing Agency safeguards."

> Article XII(A)(5) of the statute gave the agency the authority to require deposit with the Agency of any excess of any special fissionable materials recovered or produced as a byproduct over what is needed for the above-stated uses in order to prevent stockpiling of these materials, *provided that thereafter at the request of the member or members concerned special fissionable materials so deposited with the Agency shall be returned promptly to the member or members concerned for use under the same provisions as stated above . . ."* [emphasis added].

19. *Department of State Bulletin*, November 19, 1956, reporting remarks made by Ambassador Wadsworth on October 15, 1956.

20. An IAEA group of experts has been working for over three years on an international plutonium storage (IPS) scheme, thus far without reaching a consensus. It is reported that the IAEA is unlikely to be involved in the construction or operation of a facility but that, instead, "it would probably have some voice in decisions to release plutonium from storage and possibly verifying that it is used for the purpose declared when it was released" (Charles N. Van Doren, *Nuclear Supply and Non-Proliferation: The IAEA Committee on Assurances of Supply*, Congressional Research Service, Washington, D.C., October 1983, p. 108).

21. Treaty on the Non-Proliferation of Nuclear Weapons, Article III(1), 1970, cited in U.S. Senate, Committee on Environment and Public Works, *Nuclear Regulatory Legislation Through the Ninety-Sixth Congress, Second Session*, 97th Cong., 1st Sess., August 1981, Serial No. 97–03, pp. 405, 406.

> On the NPT generally, see Mohamed Ibrahim Shaker, *The Treaty on the Non-Proliferation of Nuclear Weapons: A Study Based on the Five Principles of UN General Assembly Resolution*

2028 (XX) (Université de Genève, 1976), the most complete and scholarly work on the subject.

22. As a result, the preamble to the NPT expresses the parties' support for "... the principle of safeguarding effectively the flow of source and special fissionable materials by use of instruments and other techniques *at certain strategic points* ..." [emphasis added]. This thought reappears in Article III which provides that, "The safeguards required by this article shall be implemented in a manner designed to comply with Article IV of this Treaty, and to avoid hampering the economic or technological development of the Parties or international cooperation in the field of peaceful nuclear activities ... in accordance with ... the principle of safeguarding set forth in the Preamble of the Treaty."

23. Atomic Energy Act of 1954, Section 128, 42 USC 2157; Nuclear Non-Proliferation Act of 1978, Section 306, P.L. 95–242, 92 Stat. 120.

24. Shaker, *Treaty on the Non-Proliferation of Nuclear Weapons*, pp. 24-33, also pp. 3–24 on earlier Irish proposals. The text of the Irish resolution is reproduced as Appendix 1, p. 839.

25. Treaty on the Non-Proliferation of Nuclear Weapons, Article IV, 1970, cited in U.S. Senate, Committee on Environment and Public Works, *Nuclear Regulatory Legislation Through the Ninety-Sixth Congress, Second Session*, 97th Cong., 1st Sess., August 1981, Serial No. 97–03, pp. 405, 406. Shaker, *Treaty on the Non-Proliferation of Nuclear Weapons*, p. 273.

26. Quoted in *International Negotiations on the Treaty on the Non-Proliferation of Nuclear Weapons, United States Arms Control and Disarmament Agency*, January 1969, p. 125.

27. Just how sensitive countries can be to developments in neighboring states is demonstrated by an article that appeared in the Madras *Hindu* on June 26, 1983:

> After considerable vacillation, the Government of India disclosed today that the monitoring station of the Atomic Energy Department at Gaurlbidanur near Bangalore, had recorded on June 13 a major seismic disturbance in Baluchistan. But even 12 days after the event, it was not able to confirm or deny whether this indicated that Pakistan had carried out an underground nuclear explosion. . . .
>
> The Pakistan Government today vehemently denied that it had detonated a nuclear device, describing the sensational report published by a Delhi newspaper as a "mischievous canard" and a "total fabrication." But the Indian spokesman said "it could be, it may not be" when asked whether the magnitude and pattern of the seismic disturbance indicated an underground atomic explosion . . .

(Cited in *Worldwide Report, Nuclear Development and Proliferation,* Foreign Broadcast Information Service, August 9, 1983).

28. "A Report on the International Control of Atomic Energy," Chapter 5, Department of State, Washington, D.C., March 16, 1946 (Department of State Publication 2498), now known as the Acheson-Lilienthal Report.

29. The Indian government's announcement stated that the Indian Energy Commission had carried out "a peaceful nuclear explosion experiment" (*The New York Times,* May 19, 1974, p. 1). Subsequently, Defense Minister Ram explained that "we are doing this for peaceful purposes and not for military uses. The armed forces know this is not for their use. It is only for peaceful uses, for mining, for oil and gas prospecting, for finding underground water, and for river diversion. It is for scientific and technological knowledge" (*The New York Times,* May 23, 1974, p. 6).

Shortly thereafter it was reported that Prime Minister Indira Gandhi had written Prime Minister Zulfikar Ali Bhutto that "India had only peaceful intentions in conducting the nuclear test" and that his "apprehensions about India's acquiring nuclear weapons or threatening Pakistan were 'completely unfounded'" (*The New York Times,* May 24, 1974, p. 6).

It should be noted that India used heavy water obtained from the United States to produce the material that was used in the 1974 device. The agreement under which this heavy water was transferred to India specified that "the heavy water sold hereunder shall be for use only in India by the Government in connection with research into and the use of atomic energy for peaceful purposes..." (Agreement between the United States Atomic Energy Commission and the President of India, March 16, 1956, paragraph 9). The Indian government has consistently claimed that the 1974 explosion was "peaceful" (*The New York Times,* May 19, 1974, p. 1; May 23, 1974, p. 6; and May 24, 1974, p. 6).

30. "Building International Order," speech by Secretary of State Henry A. Kissinger before the 30th Session of the UN General Assembly, September 22, 1975, text released by Department of State, Bureau of Public Affairs, Office of Media Services.

31. Acting Assistant Secretary of State for Oceans and International Environmental and Scientific Affairs, Myron Kratzer, announced that South Korea had canceled its plans to purchase a reprocessing plant from France at a hearing before the Senate Committee on Government Operations on January 29, 1976 (*Hearings before the Committee on Government Operations,*

United States Senate, 94th Cong., 2nd Sess., on S. 1439 [Export Reorganization Act of 1976], p. 419). The sale of a second French reprocessing plant, to Pakistan, was subsequently also canceled.

32. International Atomic Energy Agency, "Communications Received from Certain Member States Regarding Guidelines for the Export of Nuclear Material, Equipment or Technology," INFCIRC/254, Appendix, "Guidelines for Nuclear Transfers," Sections 2 and 4, February 1978.

33. Ibid., Section 7.

34. Ibid., Section 14.

35. Ibid., Section 9.

36. Ibid.

37. "Statement by the President on Nuclear Policy," Office of the White House Press Secretary, October 28, 1976, p. 4.

38. Ibid.

39. Ibid., p. 2.

40. IAEA, "International Nuclear Fuel Cycle Evaluation," INFCE/ PC/2/1–9, Vienna, January 1980.

41. Nuclear Non-Proliferation Act of 1978, 90 stat. 120, Section 120, Section 303; Atomic Energy Act of 1954, Section 131(b)(2), 42 USC 2121, 2164.

42. See, for example, Testimony of Dwight Porter, Vice President, International Affairs, Westinghouse Electric Corporation, before a Joint Hearing on Legislation to Amend the Nuclear Non-Proliferation Act of 1978, held by the Subcommittee on International Security and Scientific Affairs and the Subcommittee on International Economic Policy and Trade, Committee on Foreign Affairs, House of Representatives, October 20, 1983, transcript pp. 18–19.

43. The Acheson-Lilienthal report stated:

> A further point which will prove important in establishing the criteria for the safety or danger of an operation is this: U–235 and plutonium can be denatured materials; such denatured materials do not readily lend themselves to the making of atomic explosives, but they can still be used with no essential loss of effectiveness for the peaceful application of atomic energy.... It is important to understand the sense in which denaturing renders material safer. In the first place, it will make the material unuseable by any methods we now know for effective atomic explosives unless steps are taken to remove the denaturants. In the second place, the development of more ingenious methods in the field of atomic explosives which might make this material effectively useable is not only dubious, but is certainly not possible without a very major scientific and technical effort.

44. Albert Wohlstetter et al., *Swords and Plowshares: The Military Potential of Civilian Nuclear Energy* (Chicago: University of Chicago Press, 1979), pp. 53, 49–58. This contains a thorough and well-informed discussion of the dangers posed by, and the doubtful commercial viability of, the plutonium fuel cycle. This is also an incisive and sensible book on the spread of nuclear weapons. See also earlier works by the same authors cited therein.

45. J. C. Mark, "Nuclear Weapons Technology," in B. T. Feld et al., eds., *Impact of New Technologies on the Arms Race* (Cambridge, Mass.: MIT Press, 1971), pp. 133, 137–38.

46. Hong Kong Agence France Press Report of May 25, 1974, reporting an editorial in the Hindu nationalist newspaper *Motherland* discussing the possible effect on India's new nuclear status on its foreign policy. ". . . The editorial was prompted by a telegram sent by the President of the French Atomic Energy Commission, Andre Giraud, to his Indian Counterpart, H. N. Sethna, congratulating Indian scientists on their successful first step towards the mastery of nuclear techniques . . ." (Foreign Broadcast Information Service 95).

47. In this regard, I would note President Reagan's March 31, 1983, statement that

> . . . our Allies, as important nuclear exporters, also have a very important responsibility to prevent the spread of nuclear arms. To advance this goal, we should all adopt comprehensive safeguards as a condition for nuclear supply commitments that we make in the future. In the days ahead, I will be talking to other world leaders about the need for urgent movement on this and other measures against nuclear proliferation . . . (Remarks of the President to the Los Angeles World Affairs Council, text released by the White House Office of the Press Secretary, March 31, 1983, p. 6).

48. See Note 13, above.

49. Letter of November 27, 1981, from NRC chairman Palladino to the Honorable Charles Percy, Chairman, Subcommittee on Energy, Nuclear Proliferation and Government Processes, Committee on Governmental Affairs, U.S. Senate.

50. Press Conference of the President of the United States, June 16, 1981, transcript released by the Office of the Press Secretary, the White House, p. 5.

51. Ibid. The Department of State "clarification" appeared in an article entitled "U.S. Says It Wasn't Sure Iraq Sought Atomic Arms," *The New York Times*, June 18, 1981.

10 NUCLEAR NONPROLIFERATION: A Defense In-Depth

Lewis A. Dunn

July 16, 1985, marks the fortieth anniversary of the testing of the first nuclear weapon. That test released explosive energy of unprecedented destructiveness. Since that time, the United States and other nations have wrestled with the problem of controlling the military applications of nuclear energy while harnessing the atom for peaceful purposes.

The United States has undertaken arms control negotiations with the Soviet Union, in an effort to achieve more stable deterrence at drastically reduced nuclear force levels. Beginning with President Dwight D. Eisenhower's Atoms for Peace program of 1953, the United States has fostered peaceful nuclear cooperation with other countries in areas from the use of the atom to generate electricity to nuclear medicine. In addition, the United States and other countries have initiated strong measures to prevent the spread of nuclear weapons to additional countries around the globe. In retrospect what stands out is the relative success of these efforts: Nuclear weapons have not been used since Nagasaki; nuclear energy has been utilized for productive and peaceful purposes by both developed and developing countries; and far fewer countries have acquired nuclear weapons than was once feared.

MORE IS NOT BETTER

The longstanding commitment of the United States to prevent the further spread of nuclear weapons rests on the belief that nuclear proliferation threatens the security of the United States and other countries. Of equal concern is the detrimental impact of nuclear proliferation on world order.

In recent years, however, these assumptions have been challenged.[1] Critics of the "conventional wisdom" argue that concern about local nuclear conflicts in newly nuclear regions is exaggerated. They contend that the introduction of nuclear weapons to South Asia and the Middle East would lead to restraint on the part of regional rivals. In their view, the risk of escalation would preclude severe clashes and foster stability—if not peace settlements—in previously conflict-prone regions. In the words of one analyst, "More may be better."

At the heart of these views is a simple extrapolation from the non-use of nuclear weapons in the U.S.-Soviet context to the future non-use of those weapons in regions to which they might spread. This analogy is not tenable because it overlooks the unique factors that have ensured nuclear peace over the past decades. The non-use of nuclear weapons rested upon particular geopolitical and technical factors: the presence of cautious leaders; that neither national survival nor ideological purity was immediately at stake; the lack of common borders, thereby lessening flash points for conflict and impeding escalation; and adequate technical means to prevent accidental detonation and the unauthorized seizure or use of nuclear weapons. Without these measures, mere fear of atomic destruction, though itself important, might not have sufficed.[2]

The spread of nuclear weapons to conflict-prone regions, rather than encouraging the peaceful settlement of traditional disputes, is far more likely to enhance longstanding suspicions and tensions among rivals. In a region where progress toward the acquisition of nuclear weapons is asymmetrical, the country in the lead may contemplate using preemptive military force—conventional, most likely, though not necessarily so—to prevent a rival from matching its capabilities. Furthermore, there are cases where limited conflict or border clashes could escalate to the use of nuclear weapons. And given the stakes of many Third World conflicts, often calling into question an opponent's legitimate claim to national survival or involving pursuit of overarching religious-ideological goals, a leader might conclude that use of nuclear weapons is warranted.

Thus, in evaluating the risks of nuclear proliferation, the lingering war between Iran and Iraq is a better model than the postwar political competition between East and West. In the Persian Gulf war, both sides have violated international norms: Iraq has used chemical weapons and Iran has relied on young boys for suicide attacks. Only the relative military weaknesses of these two countries have dampened this conflict. Few doubt that nuclear weapons would have been used in the war if either party had had such weapons.

Thus, the premise that has animated the policy of the Reagan administration, and every other administration since 1945, remains valid: The spread of nuclear weapons would lead to a more dangerous and disorderly world. If so, what can be done?

PUTTING IN PLACE A DEFENSE IN-DEPTH

At the heart of the Reagan administration's nonproliferation policy is the recognition that there is no single technical or political answer to the problem of nuclear proliferation. Technical measures, political security initiatives, and institution building are all needed as part of a defense in-depth.

Acquisition of nuclear weapons material—whether plutonium or highly enriched uranium—and the design and fabrication of the explosives themselves are the two major barriers to obtaining nuclear weapons. Measures that technically frustrate a country's ability to cross these barriers are among the most important lines of proliferation defense.

As part of this effort, the Reagan administration has carefully monitored nuclear-related exports from the United States. For example, Department of Energy regulations regarding the export of nuclear technology from the United States have been tightened. Such restrictions have reduced the risk that foreign subsidiaries of U.S. firms could circumvent U.S. nuclear export controls.

More important, the United States has worked closely with other countries to upgrade and strengthen international norms and procedures for nuclear exports. In particular, new guidelines have been adopted to control the export of sensitive centrifuge uranium-enrichment technology, which could be used to produce nuclear weapons material. Similarly international controls have been upgraded on reprocessing technology. These initiatives, designed to strengthen nuclear export control policies, were responses to both the changing character of nuclear technology and a better understanding of how countries could circumvent existing controls.

President Ronald Reagan, in July 1981, urged the other major nuclear suppliers to require acceptance of safeguards on all peaceful nuclear activities in nonnuclear weapons states as a condition of new significant nuclear supply. Acceptance of such comprehensive safeguards can lessen regional suspicions and promote the effectiveness of the International Atomic Energy Agency (IAEA). Diplomatic initiatives have been taken in pursuit of this goal, but many suppliers continue to argue against a blanket policy. So-called nuclear export alerts are another important defense against nuclear proliferation. The Reagan administration has monitored the activities of countries that appear to be seeking a nuclear explosives capability, and has taken steps to prevent the export to them of sensitive items. These nuclear export alerts have frequently involved the cooperation of other suppliers.

Nonetheless, the global processes of industrialization and technology expansion have made it easier for countries to produce nuclear weapons. As a result, nuclear export controls, export alerts, and other technical steps can only buy time. In some cases, of course, that time may be considerable, particularly when a country has a low level of economic and industrial capacity. In most cases, however, only limited time may be gained. One must then use this time to fortify the other parts of the defense in-depth: steps that may lessen the political incentives for acquiring nuclear explosives and steps to buttress the institutional barriers against that decision.

At the center of the Reagan administration's policy to check the growth of those political incentives is the preservation of strong and credible U.S. alliances abroad. Because of those alliances, virtually all of our allies in Western Europe, as well as Japan, have found it unnecessary to seek nuclear weapons. Their security was and continues to be guaranteed by participation in a common alliance. American security ties with South Korea and with Taiwan help provide that basic sense of confidence and stability that makes the acquisition of nuclear explosives unnecessary—and counterproductive. Further, selective conventional arms sales have helped to reinforce that sense of security, by helping countries maintain a defense capability.

Political measures to stabilize conflict-prone regions and resolve local disputes also can reduce incentives to acquire nuclear explosives. For instance, though not intended as such, the Camp David accords between Israel and Egypt had an important nonproliferation impact in the Middle East. Improved political relations among South Asian countries similarly could check pressures in Pakistan and India to acquire nuclear weapons. With these goals in mind the Reagan administration has continued to work for peace in the Middle East and better relations between India and Pakistan.

Over the long term, deep reductions of U.S. and Soviet stockpiles of nuclear weapons, such as those proposed by President Reagan, can strengthen the nonproliferation regime. Admittedly such reductions would have little direct impact on countries seeking nuclear weapons because of local insecurities or fears of a traditional rival. However, by deemphasizing gradually the role of nuclear weapons in world politics, the reduction of U.S. and Soviet nuclear arsenals could strengthen the broader political constraints against acquiring nuclear weapons. And even for those countries most influenced by regional calculations, domestic justification of their acquisition of nuclear explosives would be made more difficult in the face of U.S.-Soviet reductions.

A third and especially important component of the Reagan administration's defense in-depth has been to buttress and build on existing political institutions against the spread of nuclear weapons. One critical institution is the Treaty on the Non-Proliferation of Nuclear Weapons (NPT). Opened for signature in 1968, the NPT was designed to foster the security of all countries by preventing the further spread of nuclear weapons, to contribute to the peaceful uses of nuclear energy, and to encourage negotiations to slow the nuclear arms race. Though its relative success in achieving these goals is often debated, the NPT has been a vital contribution to ensuring international security.

By adhering to the Non-Proliferation Treaty more than 120 nations have renounced the right to acquire nuclear weapons, demonstrating the growing acceptance of nonproliferation aims. The international perception that the acquisition of nuclear explosives is illegitimate is itself an important deterrent. Without such an international consensus, pressures to acquire those weapons for prestige or competition with a neighboring rival would increase considerably. Similarly the pledge in the treaty by the existing nuclear weapons states not to assist any country in acquiring such weapons, as well as the broader nuclear supply obligations in the treaty, help buttress the technical barriers to proliferation. In addition, the treaty's safeguards articles provide the basis for international inspections which can demonstrate that equipment and nuclear materials provided for the peaceful uses of nuclear energy are not being misused. This assurance is a key confidence-building measure that lessens suspicions among nations regarding others' nuclear programs.

To strengthen the Non-Proliferation Treaty, the Reagan administration has encouraged additional countries to adhere to the treaty. Greater international coordination of diplomatic initiatives promoting the treaty has been achieved. Since 1980 thirteen more countries have joined the treaty. Still, as part of the overall defense in-depth, additional attempts are called for to convince some of the key hold-out nations—from Spain to South Africa—to adhere to the NPT. Even if these hold-out countries cannot be convinced to join the nonproliferation regime, it is important to maintain the momentum behind the treaty by adding to the overall number of adherents.

In 1985 the NPT parties will review the implementation of the treaty. This third review conference could have an important impact upon the future of the nonproliferation regime— and will set the stage for the ten years leading up to 1995 when the parties to the treaty will decide whether to renew the NPT indefinitely or for a fixed period of time. The ultimate vitality of the NPT will depend on a recognition by all countries of the vital security benefits provided by the treaty and that its erosion will have a terribly destabilizing impact.

America's preparations for this review conference are well underway and have involved consultations with its Western allies, the Eastern Bloc, the Soviet Union, and the Non-Aligned nations. In those consultations, the Reagan administration has emphasized not only the readiness of the United States for a full debate, but also the critical contribution the treaty makes to international peace and security.

The debate at the conference will focus largely upon cooperation in the peaceful uses of nuclear energy (as provided for in Article IV of the NPT) and on the state of efforts to slow the nuclear arms race (Article VI). America's policies for assisting the peaceful nuclear programs of other countries are strong and effective; the United States continues to look for ways to improve them. The United States also has worked strenuously to reach agreement on deep reductions of nuclear weapons at the tactical and strategic levels and welcomed the resumption of arms control talks with the Soviet Union last March. Since then, it has worked to make those talks a success.

In reaching a final overall evaluation of the pluses and minuses of the Non-Proliferation Treaty, it is critical never to lose sight of the treaty's vital contribution to all countries' security. In its absence, political constraints to the spread of nuclear explosives would be weakened; regional suspicion and tensions heightened; and technical barriers to acquiring nuclear weapons lowered. The prospects for conflict would be increased, and peace and stability made even more difficult to achieve. For these reasons, it would be shortsighted to denigrate the Non-Proliferation Treaty to make a point about arms control: for in the long run that would not serve arms control and all countries would be worse off without the treaty.

Support for a strong International Atomic Energy Agency is another part of U.S. institution building in the nonproliferation area. The agency's safeguards system is designed to detect the diversion of nuclear material from peaceful to military purposes and, by the threat of such detection, to deter misuse. Moreover, by accepting international safeguards, nonnuclear weapons states demonstrate their peaceful nuclear intentions. As such, a strong IAEA safeguards system is a key confidence-building measure that can lessen pressures to acquire nuclear explosives.

Questions have arisen about the effectiveness of IAEA safeguards, particularly in the wake of Israel's 1981 attack on the Iraqi Osirak nuclear research reactor. The effectiveness of safeguards clearly varies from facility to facility and from country to country. On balance, however, the agency's system was and continues to act as an effective deterrent.

Nonetheless, the agency's safeguards system still can be improved. This task has been an important priority for the Reagan administration. For example, the United States has voluntarily contributed funds to develop and procure new safeguards equipment. Similarly many U.S. technical experts have been loaned to the IAEA without charge to improve the effectiveness and efficiency of safeguards. Diplomatic pressure also has been applied to help the agency resolve safeguards issues with particular problem countries and to encourage broader international adherence to the IAEA safeguards system.

In recent years the United States has worked closely as well with other countries to minimize extraneous political controversy within the agency—in an attempt to prevent the IAEA from simply becoming another faction-ridden body, on the order of the United Nations. Only by concentrating on the basic technical purposes for which it was created—fostering the peaceful uses of nuclear energy under adequate safeguards—can the agency continue to meet its nonproliferation responsibilities.

A final institutional barrier is the Treaty of Tlatelolco, established by the countries of Latin America themselves. Twenty-three nations in Latin America are now bound by this treaty; once in force for all nations in the region, this treaty will create a nuclear-weapon-free zone throughout Latin America. The Treaty of Tlatelolco is another important confidence-building measure that could reduce the suspicion and competition underlying a possible regional nuclear arms race. In support of the treaty, the United States in 1982 ratified Protocol I of the treaty which applied certain nonproliferation provisions to U.S. territories in the zone.

At this time, however, several additional steps must be taken by other countries to bring Tlatelolco into effect: France must ratify Protocol I; Argentina must ratify the treaty; and Cuba must also sign and ratify the agreement. The United States has encouraged these actions and has urged other countries, such as the Soviet Union, to use their influence to foster the Latin American free zone. Although the prospects of Tlatelolco's full entry-into-force appear limited for now, the United States has reiterated the importance of removing any remaining obstacles.

CONTINUITY AND CHANGE

Preventing the further spread of nuclear weapons has been a longstanding goal of the United States. Unlike many issues, most U.S. nonproliferation policies have enjoyed substantial nonpartisan political support. For its part, the Reagan administration has built on previous measures to strengthen technical constraints, to reinvigorate political barriers such as U.S. alliances, and to buttress nonproliferation institutions. Nevertheless, there are some significant differences separating the current administration from the past policies of President Carter and from the ideas of outside critics.[3]

One such difference concerns the balance to be struck between technical and political nonproliferation measures. As noted, the Reagan administration has worked to reinforce technical constraints that can delay the acquisition of nuclear explosives. This administration has stressed, however, that nuclear export policy can at best only slow countries' efforts to acquire nuclear explosives over the long term. Success, the president has argued, depends most heavily on measures that address the underlying political dimensions of the problem. In contrast with the views of some critics, nonproliferation policy is more than nuclear export control policy.

Present U.S. policy also reflects a different assessment of the legitimacy of nuclear power. The development of nuclear power is not an energy source of last resort, nor should it be viewed as automatically increasing the risks of nuclear proliferation; nuclear power is a potentially valuable source of energy for both developed and developing countries. Although a combination of reduced energy demand and increased financial constraints and public concern has virtually halted nuclear power development, these conditions are likely to change. The need to reduce U.S. dependence on imported oil and concern about the environmental effects of coal are likely to revive interest in nuclear power. Moreover, the risk of proliferation is not decreased by policies that inhibit the nuclear power programs of countries in Western Europe and Japan with strong commitments to nonproliferation. Furthermore, while the development of peaceful nuclear energy provides a country with basic nuclear technology and technical capabilities, none of the existing nuclear weapons states has relied on diversion from a civilian nuclear power program to acquire nuclear weapons.

In addition, the Reagan administration has emphasized the nonproliferation payoffs of being an active and reliable participant in the international nuclear market. Because the United States in the 1950s and 1960s was the preeminent force in nuclear commerce, it was able to take the lead in establishing strong nonproliferation guidelines and export conditions. If the United States drives its nuclear customers away, it will be less listened to by other countries, and less able to affect the "rules of the game." America's actions also can help set important precedents in terms of strict safeguards procedures and rigorous nonproliferation assurances. And, as an active supplier, the United States can head off sales by countries that might be less concerned about proliferation risks.

Efforts also have been made to restore the reliability of the United States as a nuclear partner. In the late 1970s unilateral changes in U.S. nonproliferation policy and passage of the 1978 Nuclear Non-Proliferation Act (NNPA)—with its retroactive provisions—created confusion and discontent among traditionally close U.S. trading partners. Indeed, former Chancellor Helmut Schmidt of the Federal Republic of Germany noted with considerable bitterness that the only energy embargo on his country had been initiated by the United States. American nuclear relations have improved, particularly with Japan and Western European countries which have advanced nuclear programs and good nonproliferation credentials. This cooperative climate has made it easier for the United States to gain these countries' consent on important nonproliferation questions—whether to block sensitive exports that could help a country acquire nuclear explosives; how to strengthen the International Atomic Energy Agency and combat its politicization; or how to strengthen the Non-Proliferation Treaty.

The Reagan administration's approach to the use of plutonium as a civil nuclear fuel also differs from the policies of past administrations. Underlying this approach is the premise that because plutonium can be used in nuclear weapons, its use must be closely evaluated and controlled. The use of plutonium fuel poses a significant proliferation risk in countries or regions that are politically unstable or where motivations to acquire nuclear weapons are high. In such cases, the United States would utilize its political and legal influence to prevent the sale or use of plutonium fuel.

At the same time, prohibiting all civilian use of plutonium is neither feasible nor desirable. The previous debate between the Carter administration and various West European nations and Japan had little impact on the latter's programs to develop breeder reactors and use plutonium in ways deemed necessary for their energy security. Moreover, the perception that the United States was interfering with its allies' sovereign energy policies for purely ideological reasons consequently hindered nonproliferation cooperation. The present administration has argued that the use of plutonium by these countries poses no such proliferation risk.

To ensure the tightest physical security and safeguards conditions for plutonium usage, the United States has and should continue to work with other countries to strengthen international standards for the physical protection and international transportation of sensitive nuclear materials. Now that agreement has been reached on an international convention on the physical protection of nuclear material, countries should sign and ratify it and take the legal steps for implementation. In addition, an international consensus must be established regarding the problem of how to safeguard commercial reprocessing plants and facilities which handle large quantities of plutonium nuclear fuel. With that aim, the Reagan administration has begun discussions among the key technology holders. The next step is to secure IAEA involvement in order to assess the new demands that safeguarding advanced nuclear facilities will impose on the agency's resources.

Another distinguishing aspect of the Reagan administration's nonproliferation policies is the attempt to foster limited nuclear cooperation as part of a dialogue on nonproliferation issues even with countries that disagree with the United States. As noted, for reasons of policy as well as law, there have been no significant U.S. nuclear exports to nonnuclear weapons states refusing safeguards on all their peaceful nuclear activities. Moreover, in no cases have exports been approved to unsafeguarded nuclear facilities.

However, in cases where U.S. nonproliferation interests are served, the Reagan administration has been prepared to approve limited nuclear dealings with countries that do not have safeguards on all their peaceful nuclear activities. Consequently the administration has opposed legislative measures to remove the flexibility provided by the current law to engage in such activities. The United States has very limited influence in a number of proliferation-sensitive countries. A total ban on nuclear contacts with such countries would have no effect on the capability of those countries to develop nuclear weapons and, in fact, would strengthen the factions in such countries interested in pursuing such programs.

For example, sale of a process control computer for use in Argentina's safeguarded heavy water plant and of nuclear scientific equipment to Brazil have been approved. In Brazil's case, a way was found to end a dispute over a uranium-enrichment contract that had been made unfulfillable by the NNPA's new requirements. This willingness to engage in limited nuclear cooperation helped foster a climate in which constructive discussions were held on certain nonproliferation policies, such as Argentina's and Brazil's interest in ensuring that their own nuclear export activities do not help others acquire nuclear weapons.

Similarly there has been very restricted cooperation by U.S. firms with South Africa, and here, too, outstanding disputes over earlier nuclear supply contracts have been resolved. During 1984 South Africa initiated discussions with the IAEA for safeguards on its semicommercial enrichment plant and announced its willingness to abide by the London Nuclear Suppliers' guidelines. Though limited, such developments, fostered by the improved diplomatic climate, bring these countries closer to internationally accepted nonproliferation norms.

The discussions with the People's Republic of China (PRC) regarding peaceful nuclear cooperation also demonstrate the importance of dialogue in bringing countries outside the non-proliferation regime closer to it. Over the past several years, the United States, France, the Federal Republic of Germany, Japan, and the United Kingdom have all held talks with Chinese officials about China's interest in initiating a peaceful nuclear power program. As these discussions continued, the PRC joined the International Atomic Energy Agency on January 1, 1984. The PRC also made clear its intention to require IAEA safeguards on its new nuclear export commitments after that date. This commitment by China is a major nonproliferation gain because such safeguards are one of the most critical linchpins of nonproliferation. American talks with China on nuclear cooperation—as well as those of other countries—encouraged this shift, enhancing the overall defense in-depth. Finally, the Reagan administration has established more regular and extensive discussions with the Soviet Union on nonproliferation matters. Since 1982 there have been four rounds of talks, each lasting several days. At the last meeting in Moscow in November 1984 it was agreed to hold two such sessions per year.

During these talks, exchanges have taken place on, for example, how to strengthen IAEA safeguards; measures to enhance nuclear export controls; the need to convince emerging nuclear suppliers to adhere to existing international export norms; problem countries; and steps to strengthen the Non-Proliferation Treaty, including preparations for the 1985 NPT Review Conference. In several areas, the outcome has been parallel actions to serve strong mutual nonproliferation interests.

FUTURE CHALLENGES

Additional initiatives are needed and are underway to defuse the possible longer term threats to the nonproliferation defense in-depth from problems such as competitive pressures on the nuclear suppliers. Though the major nuclear suppliers thus far have acted with restraint, there is a danger that their competition for the few remaining export sales could result in the offer of sensitive nuclear technology or a lowering of nonproliferation and safeguards conditions as "sweeteners" for such sales.

To meet this threat, the Reagan administration has held continuing, bilateral meetings with other suppliers. These contacts have allowed both sides to discuss particular exports of concern and to reaffirm their commitment to strong nuclear export guidelines. By seeking agreement among the major nuclear suppliers to require comprehensive safeguards in nonnuclear weapons states as a condition of significant new supply, President Reagan focused attention on the need to tighten, not weaken, nonproliferation conditions. These sessions have been a useful forum to ensure a common supplier approach and to avoid damaging competition. Doubtless, these bilateral and multilateral exchanges must be continued with the other nuclear suppliers in the years ahead.

For the long term, efforts must be made to ensure that international nuclear export controls keep pace with changing technological developments. The recent upgrading of the trigger list for centrifuge enrichment technology was a case in point; future initiatives should examine enhanced controls on other enrichment and heavy water technologies. More broadly, nonproliferation initiatives must focus on delivery vehicles for nuclear weapons rather than simply on the technical steps to acquire those weapons. In particular, while most countries now own advanced aircraft capable of delivering nuclear weapons, nuclear-bearing missiles have not yet become an item of concern.

Another potential problem is the emergence of additional suppliers of peaceful nuclear technology, equipment, or materials. Among these emerging suppliers are Argentina, Brazil, India, Israel, South Africa, South Korea, Spain, Yugoslavia, and Romania. A diverse group, virtually none has accepted multilateral norms for nuclear supply.

Pursuit of hard currency, or the need to barter nuclear assistance for access to scarce resources (e.g., oil) or for political favors could encourage emerging suppliers to engage in activities outside accepted international nuclear export standards. But there are countervailing pressures. Concern about possible adverse political reactions and loss of access to economic and nuclear assistance from the major suppliers could lead to a more cautious approach by these potential suppliers. Still, while several of these countries can supply some sensitive nuclear items, very few are able to export major nuclear power components or reactors. A number of these emerging suppliers also are parties to the NPT and are thus bound by its obligations concerning nuclear supply. Finally, these nations' desire to avoid widespread proliferation would push them toward cautious nuclear supply policies.

Considerable nonproliferation damage would result, however, if one of these countries were to become a renegade nuclear supplier. For instance, the export of nuclear fuel without requiring the necessary safeguards and peaceful-use assurances would remove an important political constraint on the misuse of such exports. Widespread traffic in sensitive nuclear reprocessing or enrichment technology would greatly assist countries seeking nuclear explosives to achieve that goal, and could heighten regional suspicions that might trigger other countries to acquire nuclear weapons as well. Although the new suppliers could not compete directly with the existing suppliers for sales of nuclear power plants, their capability to supply other items could engender competition and increase pressures on the major nuclear suppliers to dilute their own safeguards and other requirements.

To meet this challenge, continued bilateral exchanges along the lines already begun by the Reagan administration will be critical. The United States and the other major nuclear suppliers should urge these emerging suppliers to accept the basic nuclear export guidelines that have been adopted over the past decades. These norms include requiring safeguards on exports, government-to-government peaceful-use assurances, and assurances of adequate physical security. A commitment not to sell sensitive technology or facilities must be encouraged as well. In addition, bilateral contacts provide a suitable forum to help the emerging suppliers strengthen their nuclear export control systems, and to identify the types of articles that could be of assistance to a country seeking nuclear explosives.

Over the long haul, continued and growing attention will also have to be paid to renewal of the Non-Proliferation Treaty in 1995, the date twenty-five years after its entry into force when a conference is to be convened to discuss whether the treaty shall continue in force indefinitely, or only for an additional fixed period or periods. Strengthened peaceful nuclear cooperation with NPT parties can contribute to a climate conducive to such renewal. Similarly the degree of success in achieving the type of deep reductions of strategic and tactical nuclear weapons sought by the Reagan administration will also affect the long-term health of the treaty. Adding new members is also important since it demonstrates that the norm of nonproliferation embodied by the treaty has increasingly more universal support. But most of all, the ultimate vitality of the treaty will depend on a recognition by all parties of the vital security benefits provided by the treaty and that its erosion would leave them worse off.

THE PRECEPTS OF NONPROLIFERATION POLICY

In the final analysis, undergirding many of the preceding specific policy initiatives that comprise the defense in-depth is a set of basic precepts or ideas about how best to prevent the spread of nuclear weapons around the globe.

There is an emphasis on the need to deal with the world as it is today, rather than as one would like it to be. There is a recognition that a sensible policy does not sacrifice the practical, if limited, nonproliferation gains that are possible in a vain pursuit of even more. There is an understanding that the United States has only limited leverage and that the day has passed when the United States can unilaterally define the rules of the nuclear game. There is an appreciation that all countries are not the same and that a sound policy must differentiate among countries in terms of proliferation risk.

Not least, there is a recognition of the importance of cooperation. Cooperation is necessary with countries with whom we disagree, as well as with America's allies, present and future nuclear suppliers, and with key countries such as the Soviet Union to strengthen the defense in-depth and to achieve common nonproliferation goals. At home, there is need for enhanced cooperation between the executive branch and Congress in pursuit of shared nonproliferation objectives.

For nearly four decades, the United States has led international efforts both to foster the peaceful uses of nuclear energy and to control the dangers of the atom. Over the course of those decades much has been learned and much has been accomplished. Institutions have been established, norms have emerged, and patterns of behavior have taken root. As a result, nuclear weapons have spread far less than once was feared. Predictions, from the late 1950s and early 1960s, of a world of dozens of nuclear powers by 1975 have proved wrong.[4]

In the years ahead, the United States must continue to build on this strong foundation to ensure that the spread of nuclear weapons remains checked. Following the precepts described, the United States can solidify a defense in-depth, whose ultimate impact will be considerably greater than the sum of its parts. As a result, the future should again prove the pessimists incorrect.

NOTES

1. See, for example, Kenneth Waltz, *The Spread of Nuclear Weapons: More May Be Better*, Adelphi Papers, no. 171 (Autumn 1981); and the contribution by Shai Feldman in this volume.
2. For brief discussion of the changing technical environment, see Lewis A. Dunn, *Controlling the Bomb: Nuclear Proliferation in the 1980s* (New Haven: Yale University Press, 1982), pp. 24–32.
3. For one outside perspective, see *Stopping the Spread of Nuclear Weapons: Assessment of Current Policy, Agenda for Action*, prepared by the Working Group on Nuclear Explosives Control Policy, Washington, D.C., July 1984.
4. See, for example, *1970 Without Arms Control*, National Planning Association, Washington, D.C., 1958.

11 MANAGING NUCLEAR PROLIFERATION

Shai Feldman

Nuclear proliferation should be considered an ongoing process. This is clear in the case of "vertical" proliferation—namely, the superpowers' efforts to increase and perfect their huge nuclear arsenals. These efforts are brought to one's attention daily, mostly because the nuclear powers actively advertise their "achievements," though not always to their advantage. "Horizontal" proliferation, the process of additional states joining the nuclear club, has taken a subtler form. Aware of the superpowers' opposition to horizontal proliferation, potential proliferators advance their designs cautiously, disguising them as "peaceful efforts" while surrounding their military nuclear activities with much secrecy. Such behavior has been successful in providing the superpowers, especially the United States, with appropriate "fig leaves" to avoid pursuing their non-proliferation policies to their logical end, and thus avoiding the political costs entailed.

If proliferation is defined properly—namely, not as acts of detonation or official declaration of the possession of nuclear armaments, but as activities *aimed* at developing nuclear weapons—then nuclear proliferation should be considered as a process continuously taking place. In the Middle East, suspicion that Israel either already possesses a minimal nuclear arsenal

301

or the capacity to assemble one quickly is widespread. There is also little doubt that Iraq was headed toward the acquisition of a military nuclear potential until the 1981 Israeli bombing of its French-built research reactor (Osirak), and until Iraq's current struggle with Iran seriously disrupted its nuclear program. In South Asia, most observers concur that Pakistan continues to advance, despite the many difficulties, toward a nuclear arsenal. Despite the latter's denials of any such intentions and its current plans to avoid detonation and to keep its arsenal covert, Pakistan is a case of contemporary proliferation.

In Latin America, Argentina provides a case somewhat similar to Pakistan's. With its uranium-enrichment plant finally completed, Argentina is expected to begin assembling a nuclear arsenal shortly.[1] Few believe that Brazil will be slow to follow suit. In Africa, there is widespread speculation concerning South Africa's progress in the nuclear field. Questions about the relevance of nuclear weapons to Pretoria's strategic imperatives are beside the point; the possibility of nuclear use in that fragile subcontinent cannot be ignored.

Thus, three different continents provide cases of current proliferation. To pretend otherwise would be both pointless and dangerous. How to minimize the risks entailed in the process of horizontal proliferation and how the superpowers can diminish these risks without precipitating greater dangers are the issues addressed in this chapter.[2]

An assessment of how to deal with a world in which proliferation is occurring should not be mistaken for an endorsement of this trend. A world of many additional nuclear states is not recommended here.[3] Neither should addressing the question of proliferation management be mistaken for despair with respect to the prospects for halting or slowing the pace of nuclear proliferation. In the past, the superpowers' efforts in this realm have met with considerable success. The odds are that they will bear some fruit in the future as well.

Indeed, the superpowers' past and present success in halting proliferation enables one to approach the task of proliferation management with a measure of optimism. The rate at which the number of nuclear weapons states has increased has indeed been slow: two in the 1940s, one in the 1950s, and two in the 1960s. In 1974 India joined the nuclear club but without full membership. The country is widely perceived as having stopped short of developing nuclear weapons. Even if India, Pakistan, Israel, Iraq, Argentina, Brazil, Taiwan, South Korea, and South Africa all acquired military nuclear capabilities (a highly unlikely prospect), there would be no more than fourteen nuclear states by the year 2000. The acquisition of nuclear weapons by a dozen or more states would occur over fifty-five years. Such a slow rate provides the international system with ample time for adjustment.

Before turning to the task of managing proliferation, the nature and purposes of such management should be defined. The methods the superpowers might employ to counter direct threats to their security from new nuclear states will not be addressed here. Rather, our focus will be on the means of preventing regional nuclear war. Since regional instabilities following proliferation may well lead to such wars, the focus of this chapter is on the methods of diminishing such instabilities. What the superpowers can do to contribute to this goal is the core of proliferation management.

The superpowers are faced with four dilemmas in their task of managing nuclear proliferation. First, should nuclear weapons developed covertly remain covert; or should an overt posture be adopted once a state has acquired a rudimentary nuclear force? Second, should the superpowers attempt to delay a nuclear program even after an initial nuclear force has been obtained; or, alternatively, should they expedite the transition from a primitive to a secure second-strike nuclear force? Third, should the superpowers become deeply involved in attempts to manage regional proliferation, or should they intervene selectively? Finally, should the superpowers amend their thinking and actions with respect to their own nuclear forces in ways that diminish the danger that new nuclear states will adopt destabilizing doctrines and force structures?

The superpowers' efforts to manage proliferation must be based on the following propositions and stipulations:

1. Overt nuclear postures are less dangerous than the covert acquisition of nuclear weapons. Therefore, through their declaratory and other policies, the superpowers should make covert or ambiguous nuclear postures overt.

2. The risks involved in nuclear programs develop in a non-progressive fashion. The risks are often fewer at the purely conventional level and once a relatively invulnerable retaliatory nuclear force is acquired. The risks are greatest during the transition stage. Therefore, once a state attains a rudimentary nuclear force, making its eventual transition into a nuclear power inevitable, the superpowers should work to expedite this transition by helping the state make its nuclear force safer and less vulnerable to preemptive and preventive attack.

3. The superpowers should be extremely selective in choosing their responses to proliferation in specific regions. They must attempt to isolate specific cases and avoid responses that may lead to the globalization of the problem.

4. The doctrines and force structures of new nuclear states will be influenced by what the superpowers say and do about their own nuclear forces. In their rhetoric and actions, the superpowers must therefore exercise great caution.

Making Covert Postures Overt

The proliferation of advanced but covert nuclear weapons programs entails the gravest dangers. Regions where nuclear weapons have been introduced secretly will be the least stable.[4] There are three reasons why this is the case. First, if the production of nuclear weapons is kept secret and constantly denied, only a select few can be made aware of the weapons' existence.[5] The effect of keeping the decisionmaking circle limited is that a doctrine for these weapons will be formulated, if at all, by a very small group of people. Extrabureaucratic groups would not be involved. Civilian strategists, politicians, journalists, independent technical experts, and others would not be able to provide informed critiques of official policies and doctrines. Chances are that mistakes would be made in formulating doctrine, and these would go undetected because of the secrecy involved.

Faulty doctrines would be translated into various forms of standard operating procedures (SOPs). During a crisis these

SOPs would influence whether and how nuclear weapons would be utilized. The pace of the crisis would not allow a reevaluation of the doctrine. Strict secrecy in normal times implies that only once a crisis or war forces the utilization of these weapons would the various civilian strata become aware of their existence. By that time, a correction of faulty doctrines and force structures would no longer be possible.

In addition, under conditions of secrecy, the task of formulating a doctrine for the new nuclear force will probably be given to the military. After all, in most countries the military is best suited to making sure that secrets remain so. The likely result of placing this task with the military is that the doctrine formulated will be offensive, emphasizing the preemptive and preventive actual use of nuclear weapons.[6] Covert nuclear postures would give the militaries near-monopoly in influencing the mode in which such weapons will be used, possibly with extremely dangerous consequences.

Second, where the existence of nuclear weapons is not admitted, a state is unable to transmit its intentions regarding the circumstances that might lead it to employ these weapons. Leaders are then constrained from signalling to each other and are unable to convey perceptions, intentions, and warnings. The result is that one state may overinterpret the actions of another state, or one state may underestimate the extent to which the other may view its actions as threatening. In both cases these misperceptions would lead to dangerous escalation which could have been avoided if the existence of nuclear weapons and their strategic consequences had been discussed openly.

The Iran-Iraq war is a case in point. As Iraq's invasion of Iran initially succeeded, and as both parties bombed each other's infrastructure, many observers questioned whether Ayatollah Khomeini would have refrained from using nuclear weapons had such weapons been at his disposal. Conversely once Iran began to pose a strategic threat to Iraq's interior, the same question was raised with respect to President Saddam Hussein.

These hypothetical scenarios are relevant only to cases where the nuclear element is kept covert and is introduced only *after* conventional hostilities are already underway. However, had Iran been equipped with an overt nuclear force prior to the Iraqi invasion and had it openly threatened its use if invaded, would

Iraq have dared attack Iran? President Hussein is not exempt from making mistakes, but he is unlikely to have risked attacking a nuclear-armed Iran. Even Khomeini, despite the strong element of martyrdom in Shi'ite religion and culture, is unlikely to have risked the destruction of Shi'ite religious centers and a large proportion of his population by invading a nuclear-armed Iraq. Again, the prerequisite for such self-restraint is Khomeini's complete awareness, well before their conflict flared up, that Iraq was equipped with nuclear weapons.

The situation would not have differed significantly had both parties been nuclear-armed. The point is that to avoid the escalation of conventional war to the actual employment of nuclear weapons, conventional war must itself be prevented. Prevention can only be achieved through effective deterrence—namely, by the threatened party conveying to the potential aggressor that it is equipped with nuclear weapons and will use them if attacked. The transmission of messages regarding capabilities and intentions must be an ongoing activity; if it is delayed until the actual occurrence of war, escalation may not be avoidable. Clearly the prerequisite for this is that the presence of nuclear weapons be admitted.

Third, if nuclear weapons are introduced covertly, the public and relevant elites cannot be sensitized either to the dangers of nuclear retaliation or to the extent to which states enjoying a retaliatory force are secure. Elites of states faced with undeclared nuclear adversaries may pressure their respective leaders to pursue aggressive policies, unaware of the possibility that in the end this may lead their adversaries to nuclear retaliation. Or unsocialized elites may push their leaders to take action aimed at attaining wide security margins, unaware that this is unnecessary given the credible deterrence that their nuclear weapons provide. For example, were Israel covertly equipped with nuclear weapons, Syrian elites could pressure their leadership to attack Israel, unaware that such an attack might escalate and lead to nuclear punishment. Conversely, identifying Syrian plans to attack, Israeli elites, unaware of their country's ability to deter such an attack by bringing the state's nuclear capability out of the basement, might pressure their government to launch a preemptive war against Syria.

The presence of weapons with enormous destructive capabilities, without the socialization of the relevant elites to these weapons' strategic implications, could lead either to conventional war or to nuclear catastrophe. But the prerequisite for such socialization is that the nuclear capabilities be openly introduced. If the existence of nuclear weapons is not admitted, socialization cannot take place.

To reduce the risks of faulty or offensive doctrines being adopted or of dangerous misperceptions occurring, and to make sure that unsocialized elites will not push their respective leaders in dangerous directions, covert nuclear weapons programs should be made overt. At which point this should be done would have to be determined on a case-by-case basis. The superpowers can and must assume a central role both in making covert nuclear programs overt and in helping regional parties exploit the possibilities opened up by the disclosure. First, given their capabilities to monitor nuclear programs worldwide, they may determine that an operational nuclear force has been acquired and merits publicity. Second, their capacity to distribute information enables them to advertise these nuclear capabilities effectively. Following the advertisement stage, and with varied means of worldwide communication at their disposal, the superpowers could also help regional adversaries to communicate perceptions and intentions, as well as to define mutually shared "rules of the game."

In the Syrian-Israeli context, the United States has played precisely this role between the early 1970s and the early 1980s. The Israeli-Syrian "understanding" on Lebanon, which lasted between 1976 and 1981, was a set of "rules of the game" adopted by the two governments with Washington's help.[7] Once nuclear weapons proliferate, the superpowers' ability to render such services—in the Middle East, between Brazil and Argentina, between India and Pakistan, and elsewhere—will be of critical importance. Finally, given their capacity to distribute knowledge worldwide, the superpowers should socialize elites as to the effects and implications of nuclear weapons. With the printed, audio, and audio-visual means at their disposal, they can illustrate realistically the horrors of nuclear war. By improving elites' perceptions of the possible catastrophic costs of attacking nuclear-armed rivals, nuclear deterrence will be rendered more effective. In addition, the superpowers could illustrate the difficulty of preempting nuclear forces successfully. This would reduce the odds that such preemption will be attempted. Distributing communications, ranging from movies such as "The Day After" to detailed explanations of the enormous uncertainties and risks of conducting counterforce attacks, may thus contribute to greater stability.

Expediting versus Prolonging the Transition

As noted earlier, in formulating their strategy for managing proliferation, the superpowers will need to determine whether they should continue their efforts to slow down a nuclear program even after a small nuclear force has been obtained or, alternatively, whether they should help expedite a transition from primitive to secure second-strike nuclear forces.

The answer to this dilemma depends on theories as to how the risks of proliferation are distributed. If the superpowers are under the impression that the risks entailed in nuclear programs increase in a progressive fashion—namely, with each stage of the program—they might attempt to stop such programs at every threshold, even after a small nuclear force had already been acquired. But the risks of nuclear proliferation are greatest during the transition stage, right after a primitive nuclear force is obtained. The forces are then small and vulnerable, presenting both appealing targets for preemption and incentives for early use. Clearly a region containing such forces would be extremely unstable.

Thus, the superpowers' interest in regional and global stability requires that once the creation of a new nuclear force becomes a foregone conclusion, the transition should be expedited as quickly as possible. Rather than delay the transition at various firebreaks, new nuclear states should be encouraged and assisted in developing a diversified, deliverable force, with adequate safety procedures and sophisticated command, control, and early-warning facilities.

This suggestion should not be interpreted to imply that the superpowers should now assist the nuclear programs of countries like Israel, Iraq, India, Pakistan, Brazil, and Argentina.

The proposition advanced here is that the superpowers should provide assistance to nuclear programs *only after* an initial nuclear force has been acquired. Once the primitive force is in place, making this force safer and more sophisticated will enhance stability.

What could the superpowers do to ensure the safety of new nuclear forces? They could help the states involved to diversify their delivery capabilities in order to complicate attempts at preemption. The adversaries of these states would then have to devise a specific antidote for each type of delivery vehicle. Also, the superpowers could suggest ways of dispersing the forces and providing them with mobility. This would make their precise locations more difficult to ascertain, thereby decreasing their vulnerability to a counterforce attack. In addition, the superpowers could provide the expertise and means for hardening a very small number of land-based delivery systems, still an effective method of defense against a preemptive attack by a local rival. They could also export early-warning facilities to help states reduce the dangers and anxieties of surprise attack. And the superpowers can help states exploit the advantages of concealment and secrecy, again in an attempt to complicate targeting their nuclear weapons. Finally, the superpowers could export command and control systems such as the American "permissive action links" (PALs) to help states reduce the dangers of unauthorized access and usage.

Obviously both prescriptions advanced here—making covert forces overt and transforming primitive systems to safe and invulnerable forces—involve some compromising of nonproliferation goals. By making a covert nuclear force overt the likelihood is increased that other states in the region will perceive an imperative to launch nuclear programs of their own; states previously not completely aware of their neighbor's nuclear activity might see a need to produce counterdeterrents. In some cases, the disclosure of other states' nuclear capabilities might create enormous domestic pressures to emulate, even if strategically such emulation would be senseless. In addition, by making covert nuclear capabilities overt the superpowers would accord such capabilities a measure of legitimacy. This, in turn, would affect potential proliferators' calculation of the political costs involved in going nuclear. A similar difficulty exists in applying proposals for superpower assistance to new nuclear forces. Even if the assistance is provided only after a nuclear force has already been obtained, prior knowledge that such assistance will be forthcoming may encourage proliferation. Leaders who may consider developing nuclear weapons but are also concerned over the safety and vulnerability of these weapons will be relieved by such expected aid.

Thus, the superpowers will be forced to decide whether measures for proliferation management should be taken even at the expense of nonproliferation goals. While the dangers of more rapid proliferation are long term, the risks of tolerating vulnerable and unsafe nuclear forces are immediate. The superpowers would be wise to respond to the more immediate and more terrifying threat at the expense of faster proliferation. Greater security for existing nuclear forces should be provided to reduce the likelihood of preemptive nuclear war, even at the risk that making new nuclear forces more secure will encourage further proliferation.

Heavy versus Selective Superpower Involvement

The third difficult choice for the superpowers is whether to be involved heavily in attempts to manage regional proliferation, or rather to be selective in trying to influence the process. Doubtless, the superpowers should exercise extreme caution in determining their responses to proliferation in specific regions. They must attempt to isolate specific cases and avoid responses that may lead to the globalization of the problem. Analysts have suggested that one method for mitigating the consequences of proliferation would be for the United States to provide various "carrots" to potential or future proliferators, in an attempt to induce them to reduce their reliance on nuclear weapons. These "carrots" may include sales of advanced conventional arms, diplomatic support, military assistance, and even enhanced U.S. security ties, in the form of formal treaties or otherwise. Lewis Dunn, for example, suggests using such "carrots" to dissuade a covert nuclear state from going overt, to dissuade an overt state from crossing proliferation firebreaks, and to enhance the security of countries that face regional nuclear opponents and help them deter both nuclear and conventional conflicts that might escalate to a nuclear confrontation. Dunn even advocates the deployment of American ground forces and naval units, the supply of high-performance conventional systems to defend against small-scale nuclear attacks, and even the announcement that "some U.S. strategic forces—say a limited number of ICBMs—were being readied to retaliate on behalf of any one of these countries."[8] And, as noted earlier, Dunn suggests providing assistance not only to the rivals of new nuclear states but also to the new nuclear states themselves, in order to increase the latter's nuclear threshold:

> Steps might also be taken to make it less likely that new nuclear states would adopt a virtually all-nuclear defense posture—one in which conventional forces are only the thinnest of tripwires to all-out nuclear conflict. At a minimum, the United States could urge such countries to maintain robust conventional forces, warning of the dangers of overreliance on nuclear weapons. Future requests from new nuclear powers with longstanding ties to the United States ... to purchase advanced conventional arms might be approved as well, lest they be forced to rely solely on nuclear weapons.[9]

However, heavy involvement both with new nuclear states and with their regional rivals would require global intervention even more extensive than that experienced at the height of "containment" and the cold war. The Soviet Union may well suspect that proliferation management is merely a pretext for new American involvement and counter it with similar actions. With competing attachments in various regions, proliferation management may prove a catalyst for more intense superpower competition, increasing the danger of global confrontation. The cure may thus prove more deadly than the disease.

The suggested assistance to the rivals of new nuclear states in order to provide them with a nonnuclear alternative has some practical deficiencies as well. Primarily, identifying which states might become recipients of such enhanced U.S. aid is difficult. All potential nuclear states are currently more closely associated with the United States than with the Soviet Union. Israel, Pakistan, South Korea, Taiwan, South Africa, Brazil, and Argentina are all in this category. Even if these countries were to become nuclear weapons states, the United States would not abandon its traditional interests and policies and move suddenly to enhance the security of Syria, India, North Korea, China, Angola, and Mozambique simply to help deter nuclear and conventional attacks.

If enhanced assistance is provided to the new nuclear states instead of to their regional rivals, in an effort to increase the former's nuclear threshold, other problems will emerge. Most of the regional rivals of the new nuclear states are more closely associated with the Soviet Union. Therefore, enhanced conventional aid to the new nuclear states, coupled with their recent acquisition of nuclear weapons, would be regarded by the Soviet Union as extremely threatening to its regional interests. The Soviets would therefore be led to provide greater support to their local clients, and both superpowers would thus find themselves heavily involved. A regional problem of proliferation would incur global dimensions with all the risks entailed.

Instead of heavy superpower involvement, which may result in increased U.S.-Soviet rivalry in regions that would then be nuclear, the superpowers would be wise to limit possible damage and cut their losses by isolating instances of regional proliferation. They should enter into a dialogue immediately after a case of regional proliferation occurs. The aim of such a dialogue would be to reach an agreement on methods of isolating the incident, by both superpowers avoiding any high-cost high-risk increased involvement in the postproliferation affairs of the region. Unilateral steps that increase superpower competition in the region would have to be avoided. So should activities that would merely fuel regional conventional arms races. In general, managing the process of proliferation requires that regional stability be enhanced at lower levels of superpower involvement. Regional instabilities caused by cases of proliferation, especially during the transition state, should not be permitted to affect the central balance or the prospects for global stability.

A few examples demonstrate the dimensions of the problem. The wisdom of arming Brazil and Argentina to the teeth after they have gone nuclear, in order to enhance their nonnuclear alternative, seems questionable. Given the enormous social, political, and economic problems that the two countries face, involvement in strengthening their respective militaries may well boomerang. Since both countries are closely allied with the United States, U.S. long-term interests would not be served by supplying them with massive quantities of conventional arms.

On the other hand, from a global perspective, heavy U.S. involvement in managing proliferation in South America would present the least risky case. In South America, much more so than in Central America, the Soviets have accepted the Monroe Doctrine *de facto*. Hence, there is little danger that U.S. involvement in managing proliferation there would elicit Soviet counterinvolvement.

On the other hand, suggestions for U.S. involvement in the Middle East, such as those previously described, seem both impractical and dangerous. Providing the adversaries of a nuclear-armed Israel, such as Egypt, Jordan, and Saudi Arabia, with U.S. security commitments, in the form of undertakings to counter Israeli nuclear threats, would encounter tremendous domestic opposition in the United States. The United States also would be unable to enhance greatly Israel's nonnuclear alternative, since the latter's capacity to absorb additional conventional arms is already close to exhaustion. Furthermore, massive additional aid to Israel would surely force the Syrians to accept similar Soviet involvement. In a region that would then be nuclear, the dangers and costs of a superpower collision would be much higher than today. The Syrian-Israeli rivalry is therefore one from which the superpowers would be wise to disengage themselves following proliferation.

For the United States to increase its involvement in the conflict between North and South Korea and in the India-Pakistan region would be similarly dangerous. Additional U.S. aid or commitments to Pakistan and South Korea is likely to be matched by Soviet counteraid and countercommitments to India and North Korea, leading to higher levels of risk. Following nuclearization, the superpowers should agree to refrain from increasing their involvement in these regions.

Southern Africa presents a simpler case. Both U.S. and Soviet interests are more limited there, especially in comparison with the Middle East. Since U.S.-South African ties are extensive but cool, the United States is unlikely to help counter South Africa's nuclear capability or enhance the latter's nonnuclear alternative. While the Soviets are more closely associated with South Africa's adversaries, their relationships with Angola and Mozambique are also far from intimate. The region is therefore well suited for a superpower agreement to refrain from involvement in postproliferation regional affairs.

Proliferation and America's Nuclear Debate

As suggested earlier, influencing the perceptions of new nuclear states about the effects and implications of nuclear weapons should be given top priority in any effort to manage proliferation. Spreading perceptions of these weapons' horrifying effects will improve the odds that nuclear-armed states will not be challenged, allowing the deterrent to be kept in the arsenals. Similarly stability would be enhanced by encouraging

> the perception that, because of their awesome destructiveness as well as the danger that even the limited use of nuclear weapons might escalate, these weapons are not simply more advanced conventional weapons to be used when military efficiency dictates but are primarily instruments of deterrence. Uncertainty about the performance of even sophisticated nuclear forces, possible failures of command and communication, the difficulties of ending a nuclear war, and a myriad of other complications also could be stressed to discourage the adoption of a nuclear warfighting posture.[10]

The main difficulty, of course, is that the effectiveness of such nuclear teaching will be limited if the present nuclear powers do not take a similar attitude with respect to their own nuclear forces. In formulating their doctrines and force structures, new nuclear states will pay less attention to what the superpowers tell them to think about nuclear weapons and more to what the superpowers say and do about their own nuclear weapons. New nuclear states may simply attempt to imitate the superpowers on a smaller scale.

Since most of the next-generation nuclear states are more closely associated with the United States, they are likely to pay more attention to what Washington has said, is saying, and will say about the strategic effects and implications of nuclear weapons. And if what has been transmitted from Washington during the past few years will be the only factor determining the thinking and actions of new nuclear states, there will be cause for much concern. To be sure, some of the perceptions conveyed by Moscow are equally worrisome.

What can new nuclear states learn from Washington today? They can learn that nuclear weapons can deter others' use of nuclear weapons but not full-scale conventional attacks; that the deterrent of a nation possessing thousands of warheads in a highly diversified nuclear force may still be deficient and in need of being reconstituted; that the balance of terror is extremely delicate and that conventional war can be fought in Europe without becoming nuclear; that nuclear war can be limited; that even a superpower strategic nuclear exchange could be less than a superholocaust; and that, as Deputy Under Secretary of Defense T. K. Jones argues, the United States could recover or "walk away" from its effects within a few years.[11]

The superpowers must do their best to ensure that new nuclear states avoid nuclear warfighting postures. Unfortunately most of what such states can learn from the rhetoric in Washington today from recent accounts of the history of postwar American nuclear force planning and targeting and from manuals of Soviet military doctrine is all about nuclear warfighting.[12]

The prerequisite for postproliferation regional stability is that new nuclear states believe that their nuclear forces will deter their adversaries from attacking, even with conventional forces. Otherwise, proliferators will be driven to use their conventional or nuclear forces preemptively. New nuclear states must believe that to launch a conventional attack in a nuclear environment is extremely dangerous and that the odds of limiting nuclear war are very low. In addition, they must recognize that the assured survival of just a few nuclear weapons is sufficient to deter, and that the balance of forces is far from delicate. They must also realize that nuclear war will be an unmitigated disaster from which they may never fully recover. And finally, they must understand that there is no defense against nuclear weapons.

Confidence in their deterrent forces and proper perceptions of how small are the forces needed to attain a survivable and effective deterrent would lead future proliferators to be less fearful of their opponents and less compelled to take preventive and preemptive action. Only then would regional stability be enhanced. The opponents of new nuclear states must understand that they cannot attack, even with conventional forces, without enormous risk of escalation. They must also realize that they cannot hope to limit nuclear war or to build effective defense against nuclear weapons. Only then will proliferators be deterred from challenging their new nuclear opponents and the interest of regional stability be served.

But new nuclear states and their opponents are likely to learn this only by emulating present nuclear powers. There is little chance that the states involved will adopt such notions if the United States itself does not adhere to them. Hence, to enhance the purpose of proliferation management—namely, enhanced postproliferation regional stability—the United States and the Soviet Union must tailor their nuclear debates and force planning and doctrines along the lines stipulated above. Otherwise, if emulated, the result may well be regional preemptive or preventive nuclear war.

Conclusion

The dangers of horizontal proliferation cannot be eliminated completely. A measure of risk is associated with proliferation regardless of the efforts made to manage the process. However, if covert nuclear forces are made overt; if the transition of states from the possession of primitive nuclear weapons to the acquisition of a relatively invulnerable force is expedited; if the superpowers are selective in intervening to manage the process and gradually amend their own nuclear thinking and buildup, then regional nuclear war will be avoidable and the goals of proliferation management achieved.

NOTES

1. *The Economist* (November 26, 1983); Milton R. Benjamin, "Argentina Could Produce A-Bomb by '85," *International Herald Tribune*, December 7, 1983, p. 3.

2. Earlier discussions of the problem include: Lewis A. Dunn, *Controlling the Bomb: Nuclear Proliferation in the 1980s* (New Haven: Yale University Press, 1982); Dunn, "Aspects of Military Strategy and Arms Control in a More Proliferated World," in John Kerry King, ed., *International Political Effects of the Spread of Nuclear Weapons* (Washington, D.C.: Government Printing Office, April 1979); Thomas A. Halsted, "Nuclear Proliferation: How to Retard It, Manage It, Live with It" (Workshop report, Aspen Institute for Humanistic Studies, Program in International Affairs, 1977); and John J. Weltman, "Managing Nuclear Multipolarity," *International Security* 6, no. 3 (Winter 1981-82): 182–94.

3. Shai Feldman, *Israeli Nuclear Deterrence: A Strategy for the 1980s* (New York: Columbia University Press, 1982), and Feldman, "Peacemaking in the Middle East: The Next Step," *Foreign Affairs* 59, no. 4 (Spring 1981): 756–80. These works have recommended that a strategy of overt nuclear deterrence be adopted by Israel, a country faced with very specific strategic, political, economic, social, and historic imperatives. The adoption of such a strategy would bring about a somewhat more rapid proliferation process in the Middle East.

4. For the opposite view, arguing that covert nuclear capabilities are less dangerous than overt postures and should therefore be left covert, see Dunn, *Controlling the Bomb*, pp. 135–38.

5. This limitation does not apply to the technical echelon—namely, to the many who labor for the production of these weapons. But the technical echelon will probably be divorced from decision-making over these weapons' use. The limitation applies mainly to political echelons that would not be able to affect decisions on utilization if denied the knowledge that these weapons exist.

6. For the tendency of military organizations to formulate offensive doctrines, see Stephan Van Evera, "The Causes of War" (Ph.D. dissertation, University of California, 1984); Van Evera, "The Cult of the Offensive and the Origins of the First World War," *International Security* 9, no. 1 (Summer 1984): 58–107; Barry R. Posen, *The Sources of Military Doctrine: France, Britain and Germany between the World Wars* (Ithaca: Cornell University Press, 1984); Jack Lewis Snyder, "Defending the Offensive: Biases in French, German and Russian War Planning, 1870–1914" (Ph.D. dissertation, Columbia University, 1981); and Snyder, "Civil Military Relations and the Cult of the Offensive, 1914 and 1984," *International Security* 9, no. 1 (Summer 1984): 108–46.

7. See Zvi Lanir, "Israel's Intervention in Lebanon: A Precedent for an 'Open Game' with Syria," Paper no. 10, Center for Strategic Studies, Tel Aviv University, September 1980.

8. Dunn, *Controlling the Bomb*, p. 154.

9. Ibid., p. 152.

10. Ibid.

11. Robert Scheer, *With Enough Shovels: Reagan, Bush and Nuclear War* (New York: Random House, 1982), pp. 18–26.

12. Ibid., p. 129. Scheer cites a statement presented by Secretary of Defense Caspar Weinberger at hearings before the Committee on the Budget, House of Representatives, September 10, 21, 23, 25, and October 1, 1982: "Turning to specific forces and programs, our top priority is on doing whatever is necessary to ensure nuclear force parity, *across the full range of plausible nuclear warfighting scenarios*, with the Soviet Union."

12 THE CASE FOR A COMPREHENSIVE U.S. NONPROLIFERATION POLICY

Lawrence Scheinman

Nonproliferation of nuclear weapons has occupied a central place in American foreign policy since the dawn of the atomic age. The spread of nuclear weapons has been viewed as incompatible with U.S. security interests and with the goal of maintaining a stable and peaceful world order. American nonproliferation policy, also, has enjoyed consistent bipartisan support. Only since the mid–1970s have differences arisen over preferred strategies for achieving a nonproliferation regime. Varying definitions of what constitutes proliferation have emerged, and in particular, distinctions between the acquisition of nuclear weapons and the undertaking of particular nuclear fuel cycle activities that could facilitate access to such weapons. In turn, these distinctions have led to efforts to conceptualize proliferation as a sequence of events representing different rungs on metaphorical ladders.[1]

Yet, for all the attention that nonproliferation issues have drawn, the wealth of executive pronouncements, legislative hearings, and enactments, nonproliferation has not been the focus of American foreign policy. There is no reason to anticipate that this reality will change in the years to come. Indeed, some analysts of U.S. policy toward Pakistan may question whether nonproliferation might not already be losing ground to

319

other policy values, with the risk of even greater erosion as time passes.

Despite the attention given to nuclear issues and the plethora of initiatives taken in support of a policy of nuclear cooperation, a comprehensive nuclear nonproliferation strategy has never been implemented fully. The components of such a strategy have all been identified and in most cases relevant policies have been formulated, but an integrated strategy has yet to be devised. This chapter will explore what are for the United States two fundamental issues of nuclear nonproliferation. First, what constitutes a comprehensive approach to U.S. nonproliferation policy? Second, what measures are needed to achieve comprehensiveness and to increase the importance of nonproliferation on the U.S. foreign policy agenda?

DEFINITIONS OF COMPREHENSIVE

As a point of departure one may recall that following the Indian nuclear test in 1974 the debate over nonproliferation policy centered on four elements: motivation, capability, denial, and control. In reality, motivation concerns ends and capability relates to means, with denial and control representing different means for restricting capability; and all four are complementary elements. All too often, however, analysts have treated these elements distinctively, at times almost in opposition, as though they were contradictory and mutually exclusive alternatives, when in fact they are interdependent.[2]

To focus heavily on capability and to imply that enhanced capability may motivate proliferation where it otherwise would not exist can lead to an analysis overly skewed toward denial of access to capabilities. This simple but misleading analysis undermines the formulation of rational and balanced policies that reinforce national security and international stability.[3] Similarly since none of the five acknowledged nuclear weapons states obtained the necessary material from the civilian nuclear fuel cycle, one might conclude, as some observers have, that the civilian nuclear fuel cycle should not be regarded seriously as a source of fissile material for nuclear explosives. One should not, however, lose sight of the reality that the peaceful fuel cycle offers *a*, if not *the* most attractive route to nuclear weapons.[4] India is a case in point. Its research and development program, which was allegedly related to civilian power, nevertheless served as a vehicle for acquiring plutonium for a nuclear explosive device.

There are at least four ways to define comprehensive in the context of nonproliferation. They are discussed here in terms of their historic content and their relevance to two important criteria for any nonproliferation regime—effectiveness and acceptability.

"Comprehensive" implies universality in the sense of applying to all countries regardless of their status as nonnuclear or nuclear weapons states. Equality was foreclosed by the Treaty on the Non-Proliferation of Nuclear Weapons (NPT). The NPT codified a discriminatory situation by establishing two classes of states and sought to establish universal acceptance of the principle that the further spread of nuclear weapons contravened an international norm.

States that are parties to the NPT explicitly accept this discriminatory situation. Those states that have remained outside the treaty nevertheless find their behavior constrained because they are confronted with a widely supported international norm which, though not binding on them, at a minimum substantially complicates a decision to transgress that norm. No state since 1968 has openly acknowledged proliferation on its part. The one state to have tested a nuclear device, India, has been at pains to characterize its 1974 nuclear explosion as a test of a peaceful nuclear device and has refused to be considered as an addition to the nuclear weapons "club." Indeed, upon being approached by parties to the 1967 Treaty for the Prohibition of Nuclear Weapons in Latin America (Treaty of Tlatelolco) to adopt Protocol II, whereby weapons states undertake not to use or threaten to use nuclear weapons against treaty adherents, India declined on the grounds that it was not a nuclear weapons state.

There is an international consensus that the differential status between weapons and nonweapons states does not entitle the former to discriminate at the latter's expense, either with regard to nuclear arms control and disarmament, or in the development of nuclear energy.

Article VI of the NPT obliges the nuclear weapons parties to "pursue negotiations in good faith on effective measures relating to the cessation of the nuclear arms race at an early date and to nuclear disarmament. . . ." In a sense this article provides an appropriate element of balance. It is the functional equivalent of nonnuclear weapons states abstaining from the acquisition of nuclear arms.

Progress toward achieving nuclear disarmament is a standard against which nuclear weapons state behavior may be increasingly judged if the 1980 NPT Review Conference is any indication. Failure of the weapons states to make sincere and demonstrable efforts toward nuclear arms control, involving a reduction of nuclear arsenals, a comprehensive test ban, and reinforcement of nuclear-weapon-free zones, could pose substantial problems for the NPT in the longer term.[5]

A second aspect of universalism relates to the scope of activities in which nonweapons and weapons states may participate. Article IV(2) of the NPT expresses the right of parties to "the fullest possible exchange of equipment, materials and scientific and technological information for the peaceful uses of nuclear energy"—a particular concern to the developing countries. Article IV(1) states, "[N]othing in this Treaty shall be interpreted as affecting the inalienable right of all the Parties to the Treaty to develop research, production and use of nuclear energy for peaceful purposes without discrimination. . . ." This provision underscored the concern of advanced industrialized nonnuclear weapons states that discrimination not extend beyond nuclear weapons and served notice that these states would resist any claim that weapons status entailed special privilege in peaceful fuel cycle development.[6]

Sensitivity to these issues dissuaded even the nonproliferation-minded administration of President Jimmy Carter from embracing a suggestion that sensitive nuclear facilities, in particular reprocessing plants, be located only on the territory of nuclear weapons states. Japan and the Federal Republic of Germany insisted that placing the nuclear fuel cycles of the nonnuclear weapons states under safeguards and not those of the weapons states was another example of discrimination beyond nuclear weapons. The United States and United Kingdom responded by making voluntary offers to place their peaceful nuclear activities under the same international safeguards that would be applied to the nonnuclear weapons states. The Soviet Union recently made a similar offer and is negotiating implementation arrangements with the International Atomic Energy Agency (IAEA). While these actions by the nuclear weapons states might be interpreted as largely symbolic gestures, they add important support to the concept and legitimacy of international verification safeguards.

The nonweapons states are reluctant to countenance discrimination beyond nuclear weapons limitations especially among NPT parties, and they view differential treatment as an erosion of what they understood the NPT bargain to include. To achieve acceptability, a comprehensive approach to nonproliferation must be attentive to expectations of equity and should incorporate such considerations.

"Comprehensive" can also be defined in terms of the benefits and obligations underlying international nuclear cooperation and commerce. The balance between opportunity and obligation is particularly important with regard to nuclear technology, which has substantial security and even survival implications. Although many countries clearly feel that a strong and effective nonproliferation regime serves their security interests, this understanding invariably is coupled with expectations of assistance and cooperation. For better or worse many states were nurtured on Atoms for Peace pronouncements about the opportunities for the peaceful atom. Many states regarded commitments not to develop or manufacture nuclear weapons in exchange for peaceful nuclear cooperation and assistance (including assured supply of nuclear fuels) as quite compatible with their sovereign status. They believed the Atoms for Peace program positively contributed to their national securities by reducing suspicions of others regarding their nuclear intent, and thereby reducing if not removing possible incentives of their neighbors to obtain nuclear weapons themselves.

The events of 1974 and following, which require no discussion here, shook the foundations of the consensual balance described above, and ushered in a period of uncertainty and reassessment of the conventional wisdom regarding civilian nuclear fuel cycle development and controlled international cooperation. That turbulent period also led to policy and statutory adjustments in the United States. American nonproliferation policy subsequently swung between postures and positions that failed to maintain the necessary balance of effectiveness and acceptability: on the one hand, nuclear ambiguity, universality, unilateralism, and restraint; on the other hand, commitment to nuclear power (at least rhetorically), liberalization, selectivity, and expeditious cooperation.

In reality the continuities in U.S. nonproliferation policy have been greater than this pendulum metaphor would allow. Nevertheless, during the past decade there has been considerable debate over equity and balance. Given the limited ability of the prevailing regime to prevent or deter misappropriation or abuse of sensitive materials and technology, some analysts have argued that too many risks were being taken in return for any possible benefits that might accrue. Others maintained that the suppliers were imposing too many constraints as measured against what the recipients were asked to forfeit in the way of their nuclear birthrights.

The concern here is not to evaluate the merits, strengths, and weaknesses of these different views but to illustrate the point that a nonproliferation policy cannot be predicated on an excess either of obligations or benefits: An effective and acceptable nonproliferation policy has to accommodate both sets of concerns.

A third definition of "comprehensive" is, like the previous one, related to scope but focuses on the question of what a comprehensive policy must involve rather than on the issue of balance between benefits and obligations.

In the first decades of the nuclear age, primary emphasis was given to establishing principles and institutions, and developing means of implementation. Two features, peaceful-use undertakings and safeguards verifying compliance with these undertakings, emerged as core elements of the nonproliferation system.

The efficacy of safeguards in achieving nonproliferation has become a controversial issue in the past several years in large measure because, as in the case of proliferation, confusion has arisen over how the term is being used and what it is intended to cover.[7]

The Acheson-Lilienthal Report of 1946, upon which the Baruch Plan was based, expressed doubt about the ability of safeguard procedures alone to prevent proliferation. In addition, the authority of the IAEA to prevent misuse of nuclear materials, equipment, and facilities was cast in terms of the more modest and politically realistic purpose of monitoring, rather than direct control. The first comprehensive agency safeguards system, INFCIRC/66/REV. 2, stated that the purpose of safeguards was "to verify compliance with safeguard agreements" (paragraph 46). The ensuing Non-Proliferation Treaty obligated parties to accept safeguards "for the exclusive purpose of verification of the fulfillment of obligations assumed under this treaty. . . ."

These enactments reflect a conclusion that proliferation is essentially a political act that cannot be controlled or resolved by technical measures such as safeguards alone. In fact, however, safeguards have been interpreted and judged by critics of the nonproliferation system as bearing broader responsibilities, including prohibiting and preventing proliferation.[8]

In part, this tendency reflects a certain conceptual imprecision, resulting from implementation of the safeguards definition found in IAEA document INFCIRC/153. That document states the objective of safeguards to be the "timely detection or diversion of significant quantities of nuclear material . . . and deterrence of such diversion by the risk of early detection" (paragraph 28). This definition led to the adoption of a statement of quantitative goals, intended as a guide for measuring the agency's progress. Critics of the system have tended to interpret the goals as criteria for judging current safeguard effectiveness. The argument, explicitly or implicitly, is that if the goals are not being met now, safeguards are ineffective.[9] The view that safeguards are more than technical verification measures and should be evaluated in terms of their ability to prevent proliferation leads to claims that the nonproliferation regime is fundamentally unsound, and, in the more extreme case, that society and nuclear energy are incompatible and that the latter must go.

No doubt the further one moves from the core nonproliferation regime components—undertakings and commitments, international verification safeguards, and the NPT—toward new institutional approaches and arrangements, the more difficult it becomes to achieve consensus. Efforts in this direction are nevertheless essential because even under the best of circumstances safeguards cannot alone bear the full burden of nonproliferation, but require the reinforcement and load sharing that functionally specific additive institutional arrangements can provide.[10]

The concern of nonnuclear weapons states about the possible erosion of benefits under an increasingly bounded regime underscores the need to establish reasonable and defensible objective criteria (primarily economic and technical) that can justify and generate support for a more evolutionary approach to enlarging nuclear cooperation—including access to the benefits of some of the more sensitive and higher risk materials and technology. Securing agreement on criteria that permit differentiation without provoking charges of discrimination is a major challenge.

More important, however, is the question of what happens in the event of a violation of nonproliferation undertakings or safeguard commitments as a result of abrogation.[11] Unrequited challenges to proclaimed international norms and agreed-upon rules invite further violations of and deviations from the nonproliferation regime.

Many response measures that would comprise sanctions policy already have been identified and codified. They exist in the statute of the IAEA, in the Nuclear Suppliers Guidelines, in U.S. agreements for cooperation, in the Nuclear Non-Proliferation Act of 1978, in legislative enactments such the Glenn and Symington amendments of 1976–1977 to the U.S. Foreign Assistance Act of 1961, and in policy statements and commitments of different American administrations. The problem is to translate awareness and concern into an effective, integrated policy. Unilateral sanctions in a nonmonopoly environment easily can fail unless there is supplier state cooperation and coordination. However, nonproliferation may not be accorded the same priority by all of the relevant states. States may interpret ambiguous information differently; and even when priority and interpretation are synchronized, the political and economic costs of imposing sanctions may vary, resulting in uncoordinated or even divergent responses. Even if the major supplier states develop and pursue integrated policies, there remains the problem of newer suppliers who are outside the nonproliferation regime and who may feel themselves to be targets of the regime.

The difficulties surrounding U.S. efforts to achieve supplier consensus in dealing with Pakistan illustrate the scope and complexity of the problem. Supplier states differ in their assessment of whether the Pakistani nuclear program is aimed at securing a weapons option, of whether disengagement from cooperation is a sensible strategy for deterring proliferation, and of whether any preventive or punitive actions are appropriate in the absence of a clear violation. The challenge remains to develop a realistic approach and set of principles around which a meaningful consensus can gather: an approach that is neither so formalistic and mandatory in binding participants to specific actions as to lack plausibility, nor so obviously weak that it fails to put potential delinquents on notice that nuclear adventurism will be costly. As difficult as this task may be, without it there cannot be comprehensive nonproliferation.

A final definition of "comprehensive" involves the relationship between nonproliferation and broader foreign policy and arms control interests.

As discussed earlier, nonproliferation policy is not foreign policy but only a part thereof. In any given instance it is in competition with other policy values for priority and attention, and even where it has high priority it must accommodate related policy objectives. Pakistan once again offers a case in point. Over the past several years Pakistan's behavior has been sufficiently inconsistent with U.S. criteria for continued military and economic assistance as to cause the invocation of legislative provisions (e.g., Symington amendment) requiring cessation of such assistance. However, Pakistan's security position, in light of the Soviet invasion of Afghanistan, has been regarded as sufficiently important by Presidents Jimmy Carter and Ronald Reagan as to have induced them to seek waivers of those statutory provisions and to reinstate economic and military assistance.

Waiver of the legislative provisions can be interpreted in different ways. For example, one could argue that the waiver enables the United States to weave more interdependent ties with Pakistan, thereby providing the United States with new leverage over the Pakistani nuclear program. In 1981 Congress, in approving waiver of the Glenn/Symington amendments through 1987, included in the waiver the assertion that "it is in the mutual interest of Pakistan and the United States to avoid the profoundly destabilizing effects of the proliferation of nuclear explosive devices or the capacity to manufacture or otherwise acquire nuclear devices."[12] Congress also warned that "any transfer of a nuclear explosive device to a non-nuclear weapon state or, in the case of a non-nuclear weapon state, any receipt or detonation of a nuclear explosive device would cause grave damage to bilateral relations between the United States and that country."[13] Arguably this form of legislation advances the U.S. nonproliferation cause by placing foreign policy at the service of nonproliferation.

One can also argue, however, that nonproliferation policy was subordinated to other foreign policy interests insofar as the reason for the original suspension of assistance to Pakistan (continued efforts to import components for an enrichment plant) was concerned. The language of the waiver (receipt or detonation of a nuclear explosive device would cause grave damage to bilateral relations; a "mutual interest" in avoiding spread of capacity to manufacture explosive devices) provides Pakistan more room for maneuver in a "preweapons" stage. Given the ambiguity and uncertainty surrounding the Pakistani nuclear program, whether overall nonproliferation objectives are enhanced is less clear.

All U.S. administrations have supported and sustained nonproliferation, though not necessarily with the same vigor. President Carter elevated nonproliferation issues higher than perhaps any other president. The Reagan administration is not as evidently concerned about nonproliferation as its predecessor. While the current administration's policy may be explained in terms of the perceived greater importance of certain other issues, particularly Soviet-American relations, this judgment on relative priorities stands. Ironically, as other students of nonproliferation have noted, nonproliferation is an area in which for the past twenty years there has been a strongly shared U.S.-Soviet interest which is not being as fully exploited as it might be precisely because of the overlay of East-West tensions.

In regard to arms control, the main challenge is one of integrating strategic and nonproliferation interests into coherent and mutually reinforcing policies. Several points deserve mention here. One is the dilemma that the class of weapons (i.e., nuclear) that underwrites the central strategic balance balance and the principle of deterrence constitutes the object of nonproliferation policy. This dilemma raises the problem of maintaining a constant balance between the credibility of deterrence and the role of nuclear weapons therein, and of devaluing the nuclear coin in terms of its logic or utility for others. This is another side of the problem that deterrence only really works if there is a possibility that nuclear weapons will be used, but at the same time one does not want to make them appear so usable that there will be a temptation to employ them. One way of dealing with this problem is to underscore that while in the Soviet-American context the weapons serve a deterrent function, it is not at all clear that they are good for us either and that it is not so much the weapon as the underlying command, control, communications, and intelligence system that permits them to function as they do; further, that in the long run they may not provide the assumed deterrence. The peculiar combination of circumstance and luck should not be underestimated or taken for granted.

A second point relates to measures taken in support of weapons state commitments to work toward nuclear arms control and disarmament measures. This matter was briefly treated earlier. A number of nonproliferation experts have argued persuasively for the negotiation of a comprehensive test ban (CTB).[14] In arms control terms a CTB affects modernization and confidence in systems reliability rather than the types and numbers of nuclear weapons. Many analysts outside the national laboratories would contend that there is relatively little left to learn about nuclear warheads. A CTB, therefore, would be a low-cost, potentially rewarding initiative on America's part. Aside from this argument or the counterpoint—that with a comprehensive test ban the United States would risk stockpile deterioration and the loss of the highly skilled scientific and technical personnel—one cannot overlook the potential benefits that would accrue from a CTB adhered to by the same countries that endorsed the 1963 Partial Test Ban Treaty (several of which are not parties to the NPT). Here again is a case of competing interests in which the nonproliferation value either has not yet been sufficiently well presented, or having been so, has had to yield to more forceful claims. Regardless, the related issues of arms control cannot be ignored in the establishment of effective and acceptable nonproliferation policy.

Finally, mention must be made of the mutually reinforcing U.S. interests of nonproliferation and global stability. Global stability is a precondition to American pursuit of a wide array of economic and political interests in all regions of the world and with respect to a variety of countries. Proliferation threatens global stability both by the impact of the actual use of nuclear weapons and by the emergence of regional nuclear arms races.

The temptation to develop a weapons option or to test and manufacture nuclear arms flows largely from the fears and suspicions states have of their neighbors. Pakistan is driven by its perceptions of India, Israel by the hostility of its neighbors, South Africa by its regional and international isolation. These realities underscore two factors: first, the importance of effective and preferably comprehensive international safeguards that can monitor and verify all national nuclear development activities; and second, the value of encouraging and facilitating regional security arrangements, such as the Treaty of Tlatelolco, that embrace the concept of nuclear-weapon-free zones. These types of agreements would reinforce the principle underlying the NPT and reduce the risk that regional conflict will emerge over nuclear issues or entail nuclear weapons.

What impact will the spread of nuclear weapons have on the structure of the international political system, on the quality and reliability of security commitments, and on the cohesiveness of alliances? These are the major issues facing regime members.

SOME PRACTICAL APPROACHES

The emphasis on comprehensiveness should not be interpreted to mean that a universally endorsed regime is readily feasible. Realistically, achievement of global or near-global agreement on all of the issues surrounding the proliferation question is virtually impossible. Differences in security concerns, national agendas, energy situations, and regional relations, among other things, militate against an early global consensus. Adoption of more comprehensive measures will not solve the proliferation problem, but it could advance the cause and strengthen the nonproliferation regime. At this stage of regime development, to stand still could well lead to regression, and so consideration of additive measures is entirely relevant.

In the first instance there is a need to reinforce state perceptions of the contribution that the nonproliferation regime makes to national security. The regime may enhance a state's security by reducing the risk of nuclear proliferation, and raise a state's socioeconomic status by promoting effective and acceptable use of an advanced energy technology. Regarding the issue of security, one should note that a significant number of states technologically capable of acquiring nuclear weapons have chosen not to do so because they have decided that such weapons do not enhance their position of security. That these states find their security reinforced by support for nonproliferation, abstention from weapons development, and acceptance of international safeguards on their nuclear programs is a message that needs to be advertised.

Several policy initiatives can be identified that could support and strengthen the nonproliferation regime. One is the *promotion of universal adherence to the NPT*. The more inclusive the participation in the treaty, the stronger the presumption against the legitimacy of proliferation and the higher the threshold over which the would-be proliferator must pass. Universal adherence could facilitate developments that could respond more directly to some of the developing countries' concerns.

A number of important countries have chosen not to accede to the NPT and, at the same time, have not openly pursued nuclear weapons development. Accommodation of these "special circumstances" within the nonproliferation regime could undermine longer term interests of nonproliferation. Nonetheless, the regime's integrity could be preserved if the objective of both the hold-out states and the NPT signatories is the establishment of political and security conditions that would ensure universal adherence to the nonproliferation ethic. A frequently mentioned approach in this regard is the regional nuclear-weapon-free zone.

A second initiative is *supplier state consensus on the requirement of full-scope safeguards* as a condition for international cooperation and nuclear assistance. The agreement of all suppliers to such a condition would bring an even greater proportion of the material that will enter the global peaceful nuclear fuel cycle under international surveillance than already is covered under NPT agreements. It would also contribute to nonproliferation objectives as well as to improved confidence in the international safeguards system.

Efforts were made to achieve such an agreement in the Nuclear Suppliers Group in the mid–1970s, but failed due to the opposition of some states, notably France, to the idea of placing an embargo on states that accepted safeguards on transferred materials but refused to submit their full fuel cycle to safeguards, including purely indigenous materials. Opposition to the principle of full-scope safeguards has modified somewhat in recent years as states have become increasingly aware of the risks associated with nuclear development. Now may be the time to seek supplier agreement in the context of a search for a more stable international nuclear market.

Neither of these two recommendations—promoting the NPT and full-scope safeguards—is free of difficulties. NPT parties have discovered over time that their adherence to the treaty has not necessarily meant full access to peaceful nuclear technology despite the provisions in Article IV. Indeed, there have been times when it appeared that nonparties to the treaty fared better than members in terms of the balance of costs and benefits in their relations with supplier states.

This discussion leads to a third possible policy initiative: *NPT supplier states could offer preferential treatment to NPT parties.* What appears to be a fairly straightforward proposition—rewards for regime participation—is complicated by two other considerations. The first is that the ultimate intentions or motives of some NPT parties may be suspect, a possibility that creates a problem of discriminating among treaty adherents on the ground of suspicion or mistrust. The difficulty of practicing such blunt discrimination is evident, but so is the need to deter any illicit behavior. The answer to this dilemma may lie in part in institutional arrangements such as multinational enterprises that dilute any sovereign control of a state over particularly sensitive nuclear facilities. This arrangement could extend to nuclear materials or in the establishment of sanctions that are sufficiently credible to deter violation or abrogation of nonproliferation undertakings.[15]

The second complication is that while all of the traditional nuclear suppliers might be persuaded to adopt full-scope safeguards as a common export criterion, other newer suppliers may emerge and not be prepared to acquiesce in such an agreement. Some of these potential suppliers, such as India or Argentina, may not only be nonparticipants in the regime but may in fact be targets of some of the regime's restrictive policies. There is of course always the possibility of a "French solution." France, although not a party to the NPT, asserted some time ago its intention to behave as if it were and not to contribute to nuclear proliferation. This apparently is also the stated policy of the People's Republic of China, the only other nuclear weapons state not a party to the NPT.

A fourth possible policy initiative, which has been adopted on several occasions, is *conventional arms assistance*. Such assistance, however, may generate a spiraling and destabilizing arms race, and even stimulate interest in nuclear weapons capable of being delivered by some of the sophisticated equipment provided under the rubric of conventional assistance.

Finally, something needs to be said about disincentives to proliferation—that costs would be incurred for violation of undertakings or defection from agreements. Namely, the United States should seek agreement on *sanctions becoming operative when nonproliferation undertakings are violated*. This particularly important and challenging problem cannot be resolved in a single stroke. Rather, an incremental approach is in order wherein agreement is achieved on what actions and behavior constitute unambiguous violations of nonproliferation undertakings and on what range of measures would serve as appropriate responses.

While by no means exhaustive or exclusive, the policy initiatives discussed here indicate a number of possible ways in which the cause of comprehensiveness might be advanced. To achieve U.S. nonproliferation objectives and to secure the endorsement of particular strategies and policies, the United States must accommodate the concerns of those whose support it seeks. A collective, multilateral approach, grounded in a broad-based consensus, means that unilateral definition of the principles, standards, and "rules of the game" is not possible. The Carter administration's policy toward reprocessing plutonium engendered resentment because it legislated rules in apparent indifference to disparate supplier/client interests, economic and energy situations, and very different levels of proliferation risk. No longer a hegemon in the nuclear field, the United States cannot easily impose its views, and the costs of trying to do so may spread to other policy arenas where U.S. flexibility is more restricted. Indeed, this reality is perhaps the most salient argument in defense of multilaterally based comprehensive nonproliferation. One quality that the United States appears to have lost and must recover is confidence in its ability to be successfully persuasive in such contexts. The International Fuel Cycle Evaluation experience demonstrated that despite differences over fuel cycle development strategies, the United States still had considerable influence among the members of the nonproliferation regime when it came to reconfirming the importance of avoiding proliferation. America's success in elevating international consciousness on nuclear proliferation should be seen not as a termination but a point of departure for renewed U.S. leadership in this field.

NOTES

1. See Joseph S. Nye, "Nonproliferation: A Long Term Strategy," *Foreign Affairs* 56, no. 3 (Spring 1978); Lewis A. Dunn, *Controlling the Bomb: Nuclear Proliferation in the 1980s* (New Haven: Yale University Press, 1982).
2. This insight derives from discussion and communication with James deMontmollin of Sandia Laboratories who first underscored the point.
3. See Albert Wohlstetter et. al., *Swords from Plowshares* (Chicago: University of Chicago Press, 1979).
4. A moderate statement of this perspective can be found in Carl Walske, "Nuclear Electric Power and the Proliferation of

Nuclear Weapon States," *International Security* 1, no. 3 (Winter 1977).

5. Charles Van Doren, "Strategic Planning on Legal and Institutional Barriers to Proliferation, 1980–2000" (Paper presented at a conference, "Strategic Response to Conflict in the 1980s," Georgetown Center for Strategic and International Studies, September 22–23, 1982):

> It bears emphasis that Article X(2) of the NPT provides for an initial duration of 25 years after entry into force (1970) at which time the parties by simple majority vote may decide whether to continue the Treaty indefinitely or to renew it for a fixed period or periods thus making 1995 a crucial year. If a significant number of parties conclude that the Treaty is not being equitably implemented and that global and national security interests aren't being effectively served by the Treaty there is a real risk that it will either not muster the necessary majority to be continued, or that its continuance will be made contingent on some important conditions being met by the nuclear weapon states. The two review conferences held thus far (1975, 1980) have revealed some sharp differences between the weapon and non-weapon states with respect to the degree to which the former are living up to their commitments. The 1980 Conference was unable to achieve sufficient consensus to even issue a final declaration. This does not bode well for the future unless more comprehensiveness is generated.

6. For the relevance of this issue, see Bertrand Goldschmidt and Myron B. Kratzer, "Peaceful Nuclear Relations: A Study of the Creation and the Erosion of Confidence" (Prepared for the International Consultative Group on Nuclear Energy and published by the Rockefeller Foundation and the Royal Institute of International Affairs [New York and London, 1978]).

7. A comprehensive and excellent review of the development of international safeguards is to be found in the testimony of Myron B. Kratzer before the Subcommittees on International Security and Scientific Affairs and International Economic Policy and Trade of the Committee on Foreign Affairs, House of Representatives, 97th Cong., 2d Sess., March 3, 1982.

8. This is brought out in much of the testimony presented in congressional hearings following the Israeli bombing of the Iraqi Osirak reactor in June 1981. See not only the hearings cited in note 7 above, but also hearings before the same two subcommittees and the Subcommittee on Europe and the Middle East, June 25, 1981, and before the Subcommittee on Energy, Nuclear

Proliferation and Government Processes of the United States Senate, June 24, 1981.

9. For a critical view, see Lawrence Scheinman, testimony before Subcommittees on International Security and Scientific Affairs and on International Economic Policy and Trade of the Committee on Foreign Affairs, House of Representatives, 97th Cong., 2d Sess., March 3, 1982; and Scheinman, "The International Atomic Energy Agency: Politicization and Safeguards," in *Proceedings of the Annual Meeting of the Institute of Nuclear Materials Management* (Vail, Colo., July 1983).

10. For an interesting overview of possible strategies, their strengths and weaknesses, see Warren Donnelly and Joseph Pilat, "Nuclear Export Strategies to Restrain Further Spread of Nuclear Weapons in the 1980s" (Paper presented at the Georgetown Center for Strategic and International Studies, September 22, 1981).

11. The author is grateful to Harold Bengelsdorf, a colleague both in government and at International Energy Associates Limited, for sharing his views and judgments on the general question of sanctions and punitive measures.

12. See *The Congressional Record* (97th Cong., 1st Sess., 1981), p. H9655, for the provisions signed into law by President Reagan regarding application and waiver of the Glenn and Symington Amendments through 1987.

13. Ibid., p. H9656.

14. See Van Doren, "Strategic Planning."

15. For an analysis of these aspects of the problem, see Lawrence Scheinman, "Multinational Alternatives and Nuclear Nonproliferation," in George Quester, ed., *Nuclear Proliferation: Breaking the Chain* (Madison: University of Wisconsin Press, 1981); and Myron Kratzer, *Multinational Institutions and Nonproliferation: A New Look*, Occasional Paper no. 20 (Muscatine, Iowa: Stanley Foundation, 1979).

CONCLUSION

Jed C. Snyder and
Samuel F. Wells, Jr.

Since the dawning of the nuclear age at Alamogordo in July 1945, the international community has wrestled with the premier public policy issue of the postwar period—preventing a nuclear apocalypse. That a nuclear weapon has not been exploded in anger since the United States destroyed Hiroshima and Nagasaki reflects an important success for U.S. foreign policy. It is also a notable achievement in terms of restrained conduct by the declared and covert nuclear weapons states and a tribute to the effectiveness of the system of constraints against new states acquiring nuclear weapons. But today there is reason to believe that the carefully crafted postwar consensus on nuclear nonproliferation is slowly coming unraveled.

Many of the reasons for this erosion are found in the preceding twelve chapters. Strong evidence suggests that the international nonproliferation regime will be challenged during the next decade in ways which are neither appreciated by many specialists today nor anticipated by those who so carefully constructed the regime three decades ago. Although the nuclear club has not grown significantly over the past forty years, it is also true that the preceding decades represented the steepest segments of the learning curve, and we should not have expected a major expansion of the nuclear "haves" until the present day when many of the technological and resource barriers are being overcome.

The international geopolitical environment has changed significantly from its rigid bipolar character in the early postwar period. Today there exists a multipolar world characterized by an increasing economic, political, and military interdependence among many states that view their national interests as divergent from those of the superpowers. We believe this helps explain the increased political estrangement between the nonnuclear and the nuclear weapons states.

Postwar arms control policy has generally not included sufficient attention to problems of nonsuperpower proliferation. Arms control measures have focused on altering the state of the U.S.-Soviet nuclear balance; vertical proliferation has dominated the international debate, while horizontal proliferation has often received insufficient attention among political elites to create a consensus on the importance of the problem and on what policies to pursue. When landmark arms control accords are referred to, the Non-Proliferation Treaty is rarely noted in a list which invariably includes the Partial Test Ban, the ABM Treaty, and the SALT I agreement, all efforts at curbing vertical proliferation. Yet within the constraints established by these accords, the size and qualitative capability of the superpower nuclear arsenals have increased dramatically to the point where some have suggested that strategic nuclear arms control has only served to mask an arms race. Although one can debate the efficacy of the nonproliferation regime, one can plausibly argue that it has had substantial retardant effect on the growth of the nuclear fraternity and has been more successful than efforts to restrict vertical proliferation. The question is whether this regime can be made adequate to meet the increased challenges of the coming decades.

The United States should recognize the serious nature and new dimensions of the proliferation problem for national security and global stability, and this should lead administration officials to raise the priority of nonproliferation within the foreign policy agenda. Ideally, such a step would require U.S. opposition to any expansion of nuclear weapons capability among the threshold states. Regrettably, the complexities of differing stages of individual nuclear programs and varied U.S.

relations with each threshold state prevent the development of such consistent nonproliferation policies.

The threshold states vary significantly in their vulnerability to sanctions. Among the seven states examined in our selected cases, an analysis of the range of future technological choices suggests that these nuclear programs are so advanced that sanctions based upon technology denial are unlikely to have any significant retarding effect on the pace of any weapons-related research. In some cases, states are on the verge of obtaining a weapons capability, and there is simply no hope of reversing the program. The only course open to the United States is through negotiation and persuasion to attempt to steer the goals of such a program in a direction to minimize regional disruption and instability. Among states less technologically advanced, there is a wide diversity of progress in nuclear research, but all of these states are to some degree susceptible to sanctions. The extensive differences among the nuclear programs of the less advanced states make it virtually impossible to develop a universal set of standards and sanctions.

U.S. relations with the threshold states also reflect different interests and degrees of friendship that seriously limit the application of common policies. Nonproliferation policy must be designed and implemented within the context of U.S. political and military strategy for each region of the world. Some states, such as Israel, are tied closely to the United States and provide vital support for American interests, and in such cases nonproliferation policy assumes a subordinate role in shaping overall U.S. policy. Most American officials assume that Israel has virtually all of the elements of a nuclear weapons capability, but they prefer that this capability not be demonstrated or officially declared. To pursue this goal by applying direct pressure through economic or security assistance sanctions would create domestic political difficulties in the United States and would almost certainly be counterproductive in relations with Israel. Washington's only policy option is to try through diplomacy to persuade Israel that it is not in its interests to become an overt nuclear weapons state.

Yet within the same region the balance of considerations is quite different for Iraq. The United States clearly wants better relations with Iraq and has tilted in favor of Baghdad in its war against Iran. But U.S. leaders do not want to see Iraq, which has never renounced its longstanding threat to destroy Israel, develop a nuclear weapon which could achieve its stated goal against the Jewish state. At the same, Washington does not want to see Iraqi actions in nuclear development provide any incentives for the revival of the suspended nuclear power and weapons research program in Iran. U.S. interests with regard to the India-Pakistan and Argentina-Brazil rivalries are different but similarly complex. The result is that the United States cannot pursue a common policy toward the threshold states regarding sanctions, incentives, or guarantees. The administration needs flexibility in the laws passed by Congress in order to develop the best combination of policies in pursuit of the goal that most Americans share of maximum regional stability and a mimimum expansion of the nuclear community.

The development of coordinated nuclear supply policies can become an important element in restraining proliferation. Even if common policies cannot be developed for the threshold states, it is essential for all suppliers to agree on the identity of the problem countries and coordinate closely their policies on the export of nuclear and sensitive technologies to each. Some of the problem states are still dependent on external technical and financial assistance in order to achieve their nuclear ambitions, and common policies of denial of technology or financing could be effective nonproliferation instruments. Where evidence of a weapons program is not clear and convincing, suppliers will have to determine whether the nuclear program is basically for peaceful power and research purposes or part of an undeclared weapons program. Reaching such agreement with our allies will require difficult negotiations among the primary nuclear suppliers such as the United States, France, West Germany, and Canada. Agreement on a trigger list, restriction of certain dual-use technologies, and monitoring techniques will be critical elements of an integrated policy of nuclear supply. In order to achieve a common front, the United States will be forced to compromise on certain technologies when the allies and new suppliers such as Brazil, China, and India feel they must be allowed some flexibility to exploit sectors of the nuclear market where they retain a competitive advantage. The problem of consensus building will be enormous if the international demand for nuclear power reactors and the opportunities for profit continue at a low level.

Implicit in this whole approach to the coordination of supply policy is the recognition among the exporting nations that a nuclear weapons program in a developing state is frequently viewed as a national security choice that would bring enhanced international prestige. This means that confidence-building measures and political incentives can play a more substantial role than they have in the past. But in the case of security guarantees in the form of conventional arms sales, a judgment must be made about whether additional armament would function as a disincentive to the threshold state against a nuclear weapons program or whether it would simply add additional tension to the rivalries that already have unsettled South Asia and the Middle East. To make such a judgment accurately the exporting states must develop monitoring mechanisms that will confirm whether conventional arms transfers or confidence-building measures are in fact retarding the pursuit of a nuclear weapon. Although Washington made clear threats about the consequences of a nuclear weapons test, such compliance mechanisms were not insisted upon in the case of the Reagan administration's decision to provide Pakistan with $3.2 billion in advanced conventional arms in return for modifications in its nuclear research program. While Pakistan's potential contribution to Western security is acknowledged, the reliability of President Zia's guarantees and continued insistence that Pakistan is not pursuing a nuclear weapon remain questionable.

East-West cooperation among nuclear weapons states on nonproliferation policies might provide a helpful retardant to the growth of the nuclear community and at the same time create a valuable dialogue with benefits in other areas. The Reagan administration has sought to consult on nonproliferation policies with both the Soviet Union and the People's Republic of China (PRC). During a trip to the PRC in April 1984, President Reagan agreed to an unprecedented accord on nuclear cooperation with the Chinese. Shortly after his return, the original enthusiasm for the agreement began to fade before congressional criticism of Chinese assistance to the Pakistani nuclear program, especially the development of a uranium-enrichment program at the Kahuta plant in northern Pakistan.[1] Further, the Chinese were reportedly reluctant to agree to safeguards on their previously acquired or developed nuclear materials and equipment, but they have imposed IAEA safeguards on nuclear export commitments made after they joined the IAEA in January 1984. The 1978 Nuclear Non-Proliferation Act requires safeguards on U.S.-supplied materials being transferred to non-nuclear weapons states, and members of Congress served notice that these provisions would have to apply to any agreement with China. In addition to the political incentives which propelled the administration effort, U.S. reactor manufacturers eagerly anticipated a power-generation program which promised sales of $6 billion in reactor-related technology and assistance if the agreement were approved by Congress.[2]

The disagreement between the two governments over safeguards and assistance to Pakistan threatened to unravel other cooperative efforts including an arms sales agreement (for the provision of antitank and antiaircraft missiles) signed by U.S. Defense Secretary Caspar Weinberger and Chinese Defense Minister Zhang Aiping less than two months after the President's visit to the People's Republic.[3] Suspicion over China's motives are fueled by Beijing's continued refusal to accede to the NPT, although in December 1984 U.S. officials suggested that the PRC was considering whether it might allow IAEA inspection of its nuclear facilities. This may be an important signal to Washington that the Chinese leadership is sensitive to congressional concerns over nuclear aid to Pakistan and the lack of safeguard provisions in the proposed U.S.-PRC nuclear accord.[4] At this writing, the U.S.-PRC nuclear cooperation agreement still has not been submitted to the Congress.

Recent discussions between the two superpowers appear more promising. In November 1984, a U.S. delegation headed by Ambassador Richard T. Kennedy traveled to Moscow for the fourth set of bilateral meetings on nonproliferation issues since 1981. At the conclusion of these sessions, it was announced that building upon the previously undisclosed meetings, regular U.S.-Soviet consultations on nonproliferation questions would be held in future years. This announcement came just one week after the Soviet Union and the United States agreed to meet in January 1985 to discuss the resumption of strategic arms control negotiations, and it provides an opportunity for the super-powers to cooperate in stemming the spread of nuclear weapons to other states. Another hopeful action was the Soviet decision in February 1985 to accept for the first time limited inspection of some of its civilian nuclear power plants by the IAEA.[5]

The United States and Soviet Union ought to concentrate on regional rivalries in which each supports an opposing state and local arms races threaten to destabilize the region. The India-Pakistan rivalry is a case in point. U.S.-Soviet cooperation in reining in the Indian and Pakistani nuclear efforts will be hampered by historic differences between Washington and Moscow over India's weapons program. While the United States led the international criticism of India's 1974 peaceful nuclear explosion, the Soviet Union was silent on the matter and in fact continued its nuclear assistance to India after the test. Rajiv Gandhi's recent accession to the Indian presidency may increase the opportunities for the superpowers to encourage discussions between New Delhi and Islamabad over the direction of their respective nuclear programs.

The Soviets and Americans have also disagreed in the past over the proliferation dangers of using plutonium as a reactor fuel. In contrast to the United States, the Soviet Union has no restrictions on plutonium and uses reactors which produce it both for military purposes and to generate electric power in order to reduce the cost of the plutonium. As Arnold Kramish notes, "the prevailing concept in the Soviet Union has been, and continues to be, that civilian power subsidizes plutonium and thus military power—in reverse of the American rationale."[6] Kramish estimates that the current Soviet production rate of weapons-grade plutonium is six times that of the United States.[7] The Soviet lack of interest in limiting the production of bomb-grade plutonium illustrates our earlier point that super-power arms control efforts have ignored the proliferation aspects of weapons reduction. Limiting the production of bomb-grade fuel (particularly plutonium which the Soviets have favored) offers a new approach for arms control.

An opportunity for expanded superpower cooperation will occur in September 1985, when the signatories to the 1970 Nuclear Non-Proliferation Treaty meet for the third five-year review of the agreement. The two previous reviews have produced some consensus on ways to improve the agreement, although the emphasis has differed in each review. In 1975 the conferees focused on ways to bolster the nonproliferation regime, whereas in 1980 they deadlocked over nuclear testing.[8]

While the preparatory meetings for the 1985 review have gone well, there are indications that the conference will concentrate on Article VI, which urges all parties to the treaty (particularly the nuclear superpowers) "to pursue negotiations in good faith on effective measures relating to the cessation of the nuclear arms race at an early date and to nuclear disarmament. . . ." While the article is regarded by most Western analysts as visionary, the nonweapons signatories to the Non-Proliferation Treaty will likely cite the inability of the United States and the Soviet Union to reach an arms control accord as evidence of superpower cynicism over proliferation. Some officials in Washington who are preparing for the September 1985 review hope that sufficient progress will have occurred in strategic arms negotiations by then to dampen support for resolutions condemning the lack of U.S.-Soviet agreement. This would allow the parties to concentrate on measures to reinforce the nonproliferation regime, including possible discussion of whether the NPT should be extended beyond 1995, when it is due to expire. Disagreement over Article IV (which guarantees the right of all parties to the treaty to "the fullest possible exchange of equipment, materials, and scientific and technological information for the peaceful uses of nuclear energy") will probably be muted due chiefly to the current soft condition of the international nuclear market.

While it is unlikely to dominate the discussions, the parties will also discuss the necessity to improve safeguards. Many nonweapons states concerned with maintaining full autonomy object to the unequal burden imposed by the Non-Proliferation Treaty, which demands a pledge not to manufacture nuclear weapons and also imposes inspections of nuclear facilities. As George Quester notes, the nonproliferation regime has produced "a certain dilution and diminution of sovereignty."[9] Some states feel strongly that the inspection requirements (which are at the very heart of the IAEA safeguard system) are intrusive and constitute a serious challenge to national sovereignty. An effective nonproliferation regime must persuade the leaders of such states that their interests are best served by rejecting nuclear weapons and accepting adequate safeguards.

Limiting further proliferation will be very difficult unless safeguards are strengthened for NPT signatories and unless threshold states that have not signed the treaty can be persuaded to accept full-scope safeguards. Even if these goals are achieved, the IAEA inspection task will be enormous. Currently the agency's 156 inspectors are responsible for monitoring the condition of 48,000 tons of nuclear material in more than 50 countries. The current IAEA budget allocates $37 million for maintaining the safeguards regime out of a total 1984 budget of $143 million. The current IAEA inspection system does not generate the confidence required by many, and Senator John Glenn asserts that "serious doubts exist as to whether the IAEA will ever have sufficient trained manpower to meet its own technical objectives for ensuring the early detection of a diversion of nuclear material."[10]

Four initiatives would greatly increase the credibility of the IAEA system of safeguards. These include: (1) the continuous presence of IAEA inspectors when nuclear materials are accessible at all reactors operated by those countries who have agreed to accept full-scope safeguards; (2) periodic surprise inspections particularly at those facilities regarded as potentially troublesome; (3) publication by the IAEA of inspection results where serious suspicion of violations remain after careful investigation; and (4) development of procedures for investigating the existence of clandestine plutonium stockpiles. Currently the reporting procedures for compliance violations act effectively to protect the violator rather than to disseminate details of the offense. In addition, the reporting of violations to the IAEA Board of Governors is so obscured from public scrutiny that the credibility of the inspection and the board's determination are undermined. The goal of the safeguards system should be to inform the appropriate people inside and outside the IAEA about what is going on with regard to compliance.

These proposals will certainly encounter significant opposition on grounds of high cost and the increased intrusiveness of frequent inspections and published reports of violations. But advocates of a stronger nonproliferation regime must be realistic in estimating what steps are required. The system as it currently operates encourages subversion and this can only undermine confidence in the entire regime. Ultimately, the ability of the community to monitor the compliance of parties to an agreement must be regarded as a key test of whether the agreement is serving the interests of its signatories. There is an obvious synergism between the effectiveness of IAEA safeguards and the value of the NPT to its members. We hope that the 1985 Review Conference will recognize this relationship and move to strengthen both.

Nonproliferation presents the United States and the international community with a number of policy dilemmas that have to date been postponed for political, economic, and technological reasons. This volume illustrates how further postponement will pose increasing dangers to global security and stability as barriers to nuclear weapons acquisition are removed. Unless the United States assumes a firm leadership role, serious reform is doubtful and continued erosion of confidence in the nonproliferation regime is certain.

NOTES

1. "China-U.S. Nuclear Deal Still a Puzzle," *Science*, July 6, 1984, p. 29.
2. Lena H. Sun, "U.S.-China Energy Pact Faces Delay," *The Washington Post*, July 29, 1984.
3. Leslie H. Gelb, "Pakistan Link Perils U.S.-China Nuclear Pact," *The New York Times*, June 22, 1984.
4. "China May Permit Atomic Inspection," *The New York Times*, December 12, 1984.
5. Celestine Bohlen, "U.S., Soviets to Consult on Nuclear Non-Proliferation," *The Washington Post*, December 1, 1984; Bill Keller, "U.S. Praises Soviet Decision on Atom Plants, *The New York Times*, February 23, 1985.
6. Arnold Kramish, "America's Plutonium Predicament," *Strategic Review* 10 (Summer 1982): 50.
7. Ibid., p. 52.
8. Lewis Dunn, "The Non-Proliferation Treaty: An Arms Control Success," *Disarmament* (Winter 1985) (United Nations Publication).

9. George H. Quester, "Preventing Proliferation: The Impact on International Politics" in George H. Quester, ed., *Nuclear Proliferation: Breaking the Chain* (Madison: University of Wisconsin Press, 1981), p. 214.

10. John H. Glenn, "Nuclear Proliferation: The Current and Future Threat," *Issues in Science and Technology* 1 (Winter 1985): 35.

INDEX

ABM Treaty, xxiv, 338
Acheson-Lilienthal Report, xxvii,
      184, 262, 266, 280, 324-325
Adam, Heribert, 157
Adelman, Kenneth, 171
Afghanistan, 72, 195, 327
African National Congress
      (ANC), 163-164
Ahmad, Nazir, 65
Aiping, Zhang, 342
Alberto, Alvaro, 119-120
Alfonsin, Raul, 94, 99, 106, 111,
      113
Allon, Yigal, 47-48
Angola, 157, 159, 162-163, 170
Argentina: and Brazil, 94, 97,
      107-108, 117-118, 123-124,
      125, 129, 130, 137, 139, 141;
      energy shortages in, 96; and
      Libya, 235; and the NPT,
      91, 93, 95, 106, 107, 109,
      110, 113, 261; nuclear

policy, 89, 91, 96, 111-113,
      290-291; as nuclear supplier,
      93, 113n, 201; security
      motivations, 93-95, 97, 112;
      and the U.S., 106-107, 110,
      294; war with Great Britain,
      89, 108, 110, 117, 139
Argentine nuclear program: and
      Canada, 98-99; electricity
      from, 96-97; and the IAEA,
      92-93, 104, 105, 109-110;
      investment in, 92, 97, 98,
      99, 114n.; military
      involvement, 106; National
      Atomic Energy Commission
      (CNEA), 89-90, 92-93, 102,
      103, 104, 105, 106-107, 109,
      110-111, 112, 113, 239-240;
      and the nuclear fuel cycle,
      100-102; and plutonium,
      100, 103, 104-105; reactors,
      92, 95-96, 98-100, 103-104,

ABOUT THE EDITORS

Jed C. Snyder is Deputy Director of National Security Studies at the Hudson Institute in Washington, D.C. He is also a Guest Scholar at the Foreign Policy Institute, School of Advanced International Studies, Johns Hopkins University where he served on the faculty in 1984. He was formerly a Research Associate with the International Security Studies Program at the Woodrow Wilson International Center for Scholars, and served as the Senior Special Assistant to the Director of Politico-Military Affairs at the Department of State. Mr. Snyder received his M.A. in political science from the University of Chicago. His articles have appeared in a number of leading publications including *The New York Times, The Middle East Journal*, and *Orbis*. He is a consultant to a number of national security research firms including the Rand Corporation and R & D Associates. He is also a consultant to the Los Alamos National Laboratory and the Chairman and Founder of the Washington Strategy Seminar.

Samuel F. Wells, Jr. directs the International Security Studies Program at The Woodrow Wilson International Center for Scholars in Washington, D.C. He was educated at the University of North Carolina at Chapel Hill and at Harvard University and has taught history and defense studies at the University of North Carolina at Chapel Hill, where he directed the Richardson Fellows Program (an experimental leadership program for undergraduates) and was a member of the directing committee for the Curriculum in Peace, War, and Defense.

During 1974–76 Mr. Wells participated in an extensive study of "The Soviet-American Strategic Arms Competition" sponsored by the Department of Defense. He had earlier served as an artillery officer in the United States Marines Corps, rising to the rank of captain. He has held fellowship appointments at the Hoover Institution, Woodrow Wilson International Center for Scholars, and the Institut Français des Relations Internationales, and was the recipient of a three-year Ford Foundation grant for research in international security.

ABOUT THE CONTRIBUTORS

Peter A. Clausen is Senior Arms Analyst with the Union of Concerned Scientists. During 1982–83 he was a Fellow of the Woodrow Wilson International Center for Scholars, conducting research on nuclear proliferation. He has held government positions dealing with international energy and nuclear issues at the Department of Energy and the Central Intelligence Agency and holds a Ph.D. in Political Science from UCLA. He has published several articles on nuclear weapons and arms control topics.

Richard P. Cronin is a Specialist in Asian Affairs with the Congressional Research Service, a nonpartisan information arm of the U.S. Congress. He received his Ph.D. in modern South Asian history from Syracuse University in 1974. Since joining CRS in 1975 he has written and published widely on security and foreign policy issues confronting the United States in South and Southwest Asia, including nuclear proliferation.

Lewis A. Dunn is Assistant Director for Nuclear and Weapons Control of the United States Arms Control and Disarmament Agency. He was educated at Cornell University and received his Ph.D. from the University of Chicago. Before joining the government he taught political science at Kenyon College and was on the professional staff of the Hudson Institute. He has also served as Counselor to Ambassador at Large Richard T. Kennedy in the Department of State. He is the author of *Controlling the Bomb: Nuclear Proliferation in the 1980s* and many articles on international security and arms control topics.

Shai Feldman is a Senior Research Associate at Tel Aviv University's Jaffee Center for Strategic Studies. He received his Ph.D. from the University of California, Berkeley in 1980 and is also a member of Stanford University's Center for International Security and Arms Control. His research topics include nuclear proliferation, Third World defense issues, and Israel's national security policy. He is the author of *Israeli Nuclear Deterrence: A Strategy for the 1980s*.

Victor Gilinsky was a Commissioner of the U.S. Nuclear Regulatory Commission from 1975 to 1984. Prior to this position, he served as the Head of the Physical Science Department and as the Director of the Applied Science and Technology Program at the Rand Corporation, Santa Monica. He received his Ph.D. in physics from the California Institute of Technology. Currently he resides in Washington, working as a consultant.

Robert Jaster writes and lectures on African politics and regional security. He has taught at the Naval Postgraduate School and was a Fellow of the Woodrow Wilson International Center for Scholars in 1983–84. Since 1979 he has been associated with London's International Institute for Strategic Studies, which published his two Adelphi Papers: *South Africa's Narrowing Security Options* and *A Regional Security Role for Africa's Frontline States*. The Center for International Affairs at Harvard has recently published his book, *South Africa in Namibia: The Botha Strategy*. Currently Mr. Jaster is completing a book analyzing the Rhodesian conflict and peace settlement.

David J. Myers is an Associate Professor of Political Science and Director of the Telecommunications Project for the Americas at The Pennsylvania State University. His articles have appeared in such journals as *Polity, Comparative Politics*, and *The Western Political Quarterly*. He is the author of *Democratic*

Campaigning in Venezuela and coeditor with John Martz of *Venezuela: The Democratic Experience.*

Daniel Poneman was educated at Harvard and Oxford Universities. He is the author of *Nuclear Power in the Developing World* and numerous related articles which have appeared in *The New York Times, The Times* of London, *International Affairs,* and *Orbis.* Mr. Poneman has worked on nuclear issues for Senator John Glenn, the State Department, and Harvard University's Center for Science and International Affairs. He is currently practicing law and writing in Buenos Aires, Argentina.

William C. Potter is Executive Director of the Center for International and Strategic Affairs at UCLA and is Program Coordinator for the Rand/UCLA Center for the Study of Soviet International Behavior. He is the author of *Nuclear Power and Nonproliferation: An Interdisciplinary Perspective,* the editor of *Verification and SALT: The Challenge of Strategic Deception,* and the coeditor of *Soviet Decisionmaking for National Security.* He also has contributed to numerous scholarly books and journals. His current research focuses on Soviet nuclear export policy and verification of arms control agreements.

George H. Quester teaches courses on defense policy and arms control, and American foreign policy at the University of Maryland. Previously, he taught at Cornell University and Harvard University, UCLA, and the National War College. Mr. Quester is the author of *The Politics of Nuclear Proliferation, Offense and Defense in the International System,* and *American Foreign Policy: The Lost Consensus.*

Lawrence Scheinman is Professor of International Relations at Cornell University, where he also has served as Director of the Peace Studies and of the Science, Technology and Society programs. His government service includes senior policymaking posts in the Department of State and the Energy Research and Development Administration. He has written extensively and testified frequently before the Congress on nonproliferation.